SOUTH CAROLINIANS IN THE REVOLUTION

With Service Records and Miscellaneous Data

Also

Abstracrts of Wills, Laurens County (Ninety-Six District)
1775-1855

D1602241

SARA SULLIVAN ERVIN

Reprinted with an Index
and an added chapter on the
Sullivan Family

CLEARFIELD

Originally published
1949

Reprinted with an Index
and an added chapter on the Sullivan family
Genealogical Publishing Co., Inc.
Baltimore, Maryland
1965, 1971, 1976

Copyright © 1965
Genealogical Publishing Co., Inc.
Baltimore, Maryland
All Rights Reserved

Library of Congress Catalogue Card Number 65-24109

Reprinted for
Clearfield Company by
Genealogical Publishing Company
Baltimore, Maryland
1991, 1997, 2000, 2001, 2003, 2005, 2006, 2008, 2011

ISBN 978-0-8063-0104-4

Made in the United States of America

DEDICATION

THIS VOLUME IS RESPECTFULLY AND GRATEFULLY
DEDICATED TO THE INTREPID PIONEERS OF LAURENS
COUNTY, SOUTH CAROLINE, (PART OF OLD NINETY-SIX
DISTRICT) WHO "SACRIFICED THEIR LIVES AND THEIR
FORTUNES" IN THE GREAT STRUGGLE FOR INDEPEND-
ENCE, AND WHO SERVED THEIR COUNTRY IN THE
FOUNDING AND BUILDING OF OUR AMERICAN NATION,
THE MILITARY RECORDS AND WILLS OF MANY OF WHOM
WILL BE FOUND WITHIN THESE PAGES.

LAURENS COUNTY COURT HOUSE, LAURENS, S. C.

Carolina

The State Song

Call on thy children of the hill,
Wake swamp and rive, coast and rill,
Rouse all thy strength and all thy skill,
   Carolina!

Cite wealth and science, trade and art,
Touch with thy fire the cautious mart,
And pour thee through the people's heart,
   Carolina!

Hold up the glories of thy dead,
Say how thy elder children bled,
And point to Eutaw's battle-bed,
   Carolina!

Tell how the patriot's soul was tried,
And what his dauntless breast defied,
How Rutledge ruled and Laurens died,
   Carolina!

Cry! till thy summons, heard at last,
Shall fall like Marion's bugle-blast,
Re-echoed from the haunted past,
   Carolina!

Thy skirts indeed the foe may part,
Thy robe be pierced with sword and dart,
They shall not touch thy noble heart,
   Carolina!

Throw thy bold banner to the breeze,
Front with thy ranks the threatening seas,
Like thine own proud armorial trees,
   Carolina!

Girt with such wills to do and bear,
Assured in right, and mailed in prayer,
Thou wilt not bow thee to despair,
   Carolina!
    —HENRY TIMROD.

State Flag

State Flower of South Carolina
The Yellow Jessamine

"As fair as Southern chivalry
As pure as truth, and shaped like stars."

State Tree
PALMETTO

FOREWORD

Students of the Revolutionary Period, historical and genealogical researchers and all patriotic souls, have for years suffered because of the meager records of South Carolina for this momentous era. Buried in books and places inaccessible to the public generally and in local and private sources, are names and evidence of service of thousands of soldiers of the American Revolution. To run down a Revolutionary ancestor in South Carolina, may mean a long trek beginning in our capital city and visiting there the State Historical Commission, Secretary of State's Office and the State Library, then journey on to the city of Charleston to read the early wills and finally to Washington, D.C. to search at The Library of Congress and the National Archives. Many have followed this procedure but not being entirely successful, they realize that after all the missing link must be back home. In many old South Carolina communities, there has been little migration and it is not unusual to find the present generation attending the same church in which nearby cemetery their Revolutionary ancestors are buried. So the searcher now visits local cemeteries, examines church and Bible records, visits the county Court House and County Library. If he is diligent and persevering, he may find here that vital "missing link." Probably the richest field of undiscovered records today lies in these old communities where the pioneers settled. The National Society, Daughters Of The American Revolution, is doing a great work in unearthing much of this unpublished data and filing all of it in one place, their library in Washington. To help fill that urgent need for more accessible information about the soldiers and patriots of South Carolina who rendered service in the American Revolution, and for the convenience of those persons whose county and state libraries do-not contain the necessary records, the compiler has collected from various sources much data on this subject and brought it all together into one volume. You will find in this book the names with proof of service of many persons who rendered Revolutionary service, both men and women.

Referring to the Table of Contents: "South Carolina Pension Roll" - These records were found in the office of the Clerk of Court in the Laurens County Court House. The original document is fifty-three, finely-printed, loose-leaf pages, size about 8 x 4 inches, yellowed and spotted by time. It was rolled and wrapped in a paper addressed "To the Clerk of The Court Laurens, South Carolina." A round hole in the wrapper suggests that the package was fastened with a seal. The compiler of this volume, contacted the State Historian, the National Archives and The Library of Congress in an effort to learn more about this Pension Roll. The information I get is that it was part of a report published by the United States Government, probably in 1835. The present incumbent of the office of Clerk of Court, Mr. V. R. Fleming, kindly gave exclusive permission to the compiler (as representative of the Sullivan-Dunklin chapter, South Carolina, State Society, Daughters of the American Revolution, it being the only group in the county composed of descendants of Revolutionary soldiers) to reproduce this document. The South Carolina Society, D.A.R., held their State Conference at Greenwood, on March 24-27, 1942. The above described, "S.C. Pension Roll," was awarded at that time, the state history prize.

Contents "Names of Officers of S.C. Regiments, Continental Establishment." was "published by order of the General Assembly 1886." It appeared in the Year Book of the City of Charleston, S.C. in 1893. Contents "Medical Men of S.C. Who Served in the Revolution" was ab - stracted from the "Army Medical Bulletin no. 25" and other sources. Contents "The Roll of General Sumter's Brigade" was published by the "57th Congress, 1st Session---Senate---Document 447. Date 1902." The compiler was able to get this paper (and other data) through the courtesy of Miss Helen M. McMackin, Librarian General, N.S. D.A.R. It was contributed by J. T. Gantt and was published in the 4th volume D.A.R. Report to the Smithsonian Institution. This roll has been checked by other records in South Carolina, corrections made in spelling of names and some data added in lists of regimental officers.

Contents "Some Revolutionary War Prisoners of S.C." was obtained by permission, of Mr. J. H. Easterby, V-Pres., S.C. Historical Society, and is taken from the S.C. Historical and Genealogical Magazine, published at Charleston, Vols: 33, 34, 10.

Contents "South Carolina Women of the Revolution" was compiled from many sources: Mr. A. S. Salley, State Historian, kindly gave permission for me to abstract names of women who received Revolutionary Indents, from the twelve books edited by him, which were issued by the South Carolina Historical Commission; other records are from the S.C. Historical and Genealogical Magazine; South Carolina D.A.R. chapters; Lineage Books of N.S. D.A.R.; Sequi-Centennial and Anniversary Editions of S.C. Newspapers; County Histories; Family Genealogies and private papers.

Contents "Ancestral Roll of South Carolina D.A.R.," was used by permission of the State Regent of the S.C. Daughters of the American Revolution, Mrs. Henry J. Munnerlyn, and also by permission of the State Registrar, Mrs. James R. Carson, who in addition, kindly checked the list for misspelled names. Contents 15----- "Some Revolutionary Soldiers Claimed by Missouri, Texas, Iowa, etc:" The list of Missouri soldiers was sent to the compiler by Mrs. John F. McKinney. The compiler also obtained written permission from Mr. Floyd C. Shoemaker, Secretary of the State Historical Society of Missouri, to use these names, which appeared in Vol. 2, no. 1, pp. 55-60, Oct. 1907, and p. 128 , Oct. 1940 of the Missouri Historical Review. Some of this information previously appeared as a report of the State Historian, Missouri D.A.R . in 1903, and other data appeared in the Sedalia Democrat of July 1, 1940 and the Huntsville Randolph County Times-Herald of May 16, 1940. For other data I am indebted to Mrs. Brenda R. Gieseker, Librarian of the Missouri Historical Society, who kindly gave permission to copy

"Death Notices of Some Soldiers of the American Revolution Published in Missouri Newspapers," which appeared in the "Missouri Historical Society Collections, Vol. 7, no. 2, in Feb. 1928. Mrs. Harriet Smither, State Archivist of Texas State Library, obligingly sent the list of Revolutionary Soldiers buried in Texas, the information being taken from newspaper clippings giving an account of a contest conducted among Texas school children by W. P. Webb, Prof. of History at the University of Texas. The Revolutionary Soldiers of Iowa was received in exchange for a similiar list of S.C. soldiers, from the Librarian of the Historical Library, Iowa State Department of History and Archives.

Contents "Miscellaneous Notes and Data," in addition to the sources named: By permission, from the D.A.R. Magazine, issues of March and August 1945, published at 1720 D. St. N. W., Washington, D. C., which can also be checked by: Memoirs of the Revolution by Drayton, Vol. 1, p. 226; S.C. Under The Royal Government 1719-1776 by Edw. McCrady, pp. 743-744; History of the Old Cheraws by Gregg, p. 221; Anecdotes Of The Revolutionary War in America by Alex. Garden, p. 165; Diary of Josiah Smith & S.C. Histl. & Geneal. Magazine.

Contents 17------ Abstracts of the wills 1775-1855, of my home county, Laurens: Many of these were collected over a period of years as needed in my work as a genealogist. Some two years ago, on discovering that I already had so many, the decision was taken to try to get the rest of the old wills and so have a more complete record. If written out in full, these wills would fill several large volumes. Therefore abstractions were made, they were arranged alphabetically, and eliminations used in order to prepare them in such a manner that they could easily be incorporated in one book. By using these devices, it is believed that the wills will be more accessible for quick reference and much less expensive to purchase. Proper or surnames are not repeated in listing children if the name is the same as that of the person who made the will, but if different, the name is written out in full. The first date used is when the will was made or written, and the second date, when proved. If dates and other data are not shown, it is because they were not available.

Advice and help in compiling this volume has been received from many persons and many sources. Among these were: Mr. A. S. Salley, State Historian; The South Carolina Historical Society; Miss Ellen Perry, Greenville, S.C. Public Library; Mrs. Phil Huff, Laurens County Library. The pictures in this book were used by permission of Everett Waddy Company of Richmond, Va., except that of Rebecca Moote which was obtained through the courtesy of Mrs. Mary Simms Oliphant, author of "The New Simms History of South Carolina, pub. 1940. by The State Co., Columbia, S.C.

Service records are available for the men and women of the Revolution, named in this book, but lack of space prevents including much of such data in this volume.

The matter of copyrighted material has been thoroughly examined. The Institute of American Genealogy searched some of the data used. The Hon. Jos. R. Bryson, Congress of U.S., advised us that "Title 17 of the U.S. Code states that government publications are not subject to copyright. It is my understanding that ... if you wish to copyright your work, your copyright would cover only the portions that were your own, and not the quotations." Miss Estellene P. Walker, Executive Secretary of the S.C. Library Board and Miss Lois Barbare, rendered valuable help and put us in touch with Miss Sarah Leverette, Librarian, University of S.C. School of Law. Finally a search was made at the Copyright Office, The Library of Congress, Washington, D.C. Letters and reports were received from Mr. Sam B. Warner, Register of Copyrights, Mr. Arthur Fisher, Associate Register of Copyrights, and Mr. Richard S. MacCarteney, Chief, Reference Division. The latter advised, "...no copyright can subsist in any publication of the U.S. Government. Such publications are deemed to be public property and free for... use and reproduction by anyone..." (a report on various items to be searched was included) In another letter the Copyright Office advised that "the first term of copyright is 28 years with a possibility of renewal for an additional 28 years if an application is properly made during the final year of the original term."

It is hoped that this book will make revolutionary service records more accessible to the descendants of South Carolina soldiers who are now scattered over the whole United States. Also that it will furnish information to patriotic persons who are interested in these Heroes who lived in the most crucial period of our country's history and who won the independence of our nation. Finally perhaps this volume will help perpetuate the cherished memories and the spirit of patriotism of that period so that descendants may find in these records the stimulus helpful in acquiring the faith, the courage, and the strength of their forbears and realize that they have an obligation to play well their part on the stage of life and so dedicate themselves to the betterment of mankind and the freedom of the world.

"ERVIN-DALE"   (Mrs.) Sara Sullivan Ervin
Ware Shoals, Route 1
Laurens County
South Carolina

HAND SPINNING WHEEL

KEY TO ABBREVIATIONS

A-acre
acct-account
adm-administration
aft-after
AMER-American
amt-amount
b-born
beq-bequest
bk-book
bwt-between
Bro-brother
bptz-baptized
bur-buried
bx-box
Bh-bachelor
b.l.-bro-in-law
c-circa (about)
cem-cemetery
ch-church
CHN-children
ck-creek
Cpt-captain
Col-colonel
cos-cousins
CO-company
Com-committee
Daus-daughters
dec'd-deceased
div-divided
Dist-district
?-doubtful
dur-during
d-died

dept-department
est-estate
EXR-executors
et al(& elsewhere)
educ-educate
fam-family
fem-female
fks-forks
f.l.-father-in-law
Gr.chn-grand chn.
GRD-guardian
grt-great
Hist'l-historical
hus-husband
ibid-ibidem(in same place)
IS-issue
Invt-inventory
M-mother
m.l.-mother-in-law
Md-married
min-minor
Maj-Major
mgr-manager
ment-mentioned
memb-member
No.-number
O.B.-order book
Ods-oldest
p-page
Par-parish
pkg-package
Pres-president
prop-property

pvd-proved
pt-part
pesn-pension
plant-plantation
Qt-quarterly
Rec-recorded
recv'd-received
Regt-regiment
rem-remainder
rept-report
rd--road
Rev-Reverend
Revo.S--RevolutionaryS
riv-river
sect'y-secretary
sm-small
sps-springs
Sgt-sergeant
sub-submit
s.l.-son-in-law
Treas-treasurer
unmd-unmarried
Viz-namely
wid-widow
Wit-witnesses
w-wife
yrs-years
yg-youngest
Surg-surgeon
phy-physician
Chap-chaplain

A FLINT-LOCK GUN

MATCHLOCK GUN

George Washington

*Commander-in-Chief of the Armies of the United States
of America in the War of the Revolution*

TABLE OF CONTENTS

SOUTH CAROLINA PENSION ROLL.

SOUTH CAROLINA PENSION ROLL

————

A statement showing the names, rank, &c., of Invalid Pensioners residing in the district of Abbeville, in the State of South Carolina.

NAMES.	Rank.	Annual allowance.	Sums received.	Description of service.	When placed on the pension roll.	Commencement of pension.	Ages.	Laws under which inscribed; and remarks.
James Armstrong	Private	60 00	266 64	—	—	Nov. 15, 1911	—	Act July 5, 1812.
Do	Do	96 00	946 89	—	—	April 24, 1916	—	Act April 24, 1816.
Lewis Howland	Do	96 00	1,660 75	U. S. rifle reg't	Sept. 5, 1816	Nov. 11, 1814	—	Act military establishment. Died February 26, 1882.
John Martin	Do	30 00	153 32	—	—	Nov. 15, 1811	—	Act July 5, 1812. Died February 5, 1822.
Do	Do	48 00	277 57	—	—	April 24, 1816	—	Act April 24, 1816.
			3,285 17					

A statement showing the names, rank, &c., of Invalid Pensioners residing in the district of Anderson, in the State of South Carolina.

NAMES.	Rank.	Annual allowance.	Sums received.	Description of service.	When placed on the pension roll.	Commencement of pension.	Ages.	Laws under which inscribed; and remarks
Sion Holly	Private	63 96	1,152 15	N. C. militia under General Martin	Mar. 27, 1818	Feb. 28, 1816	—	Act March 3, 1817.
John Looney	Do	21 42	173 78	—	—	March 1, 1808	—	Act April 25, 1808.
Do	Do	34 12	592 52	—	—	April 24, 1816	—	Act April 24, 1816.
			1,918 45					

2

A statement showing the names, rank, &c., of Invalid Pensioners residing in the district of Barnwell, in the State of South Carolina.

NAMES.	Rank.	Annual allowance.	Sums received.	Description of service.	When placed on the pension roll.	Commencement of pension.	Ages.	Laws under which inscribed; and remarks.
Daniel Odom*	Captain -	55 78	1,422 39	Mil. reg. commanded by Col. Hardin	- -	Sept. 4, 1789	-	Transferred from Georgia from March 4, 1815.
Do - -	Do	55 78	63 62	-	- -	March 4, 1815		
Do - -	Do	89 12	1,591 98	-	- -	April 24, 1816		
			3,077 99					

A statement showing the names, rank, &c., of Invalid Pensioners residing in the district of Chester, in the State of South Carolina.

NAMES.	Rank.	Annual allowance.	Sums received.	Description of service.	When placed on the pension roll.	Commencement of pension.	Ages.	Laws under which inscribed; and remarks.
Joseph Gaston	Private	95 00	113 03	U. S. rifle regt.	Oct. 1, 1833	Jan. 1, 1833	-	Act March 2, 1833.
John Halcomb	Do	72 00	1,051 97		Jan. 11, 1821	July 26, 1819	-	Act military establishment.
			1,165 00					

* The books do not show when this pensioner was placed on the invalid pension list: and the papers upon which his claim was established were burnt in 1814, when the War Office was destroyed by the British troops. Hence no information on this point can be furnished. For the same reason, information required in other cases, marked thus, (*) cannot be given. N. B. In all cases where the ages are not indicated in the appropriate column, they could not be ascertained.

3

A statement showing the names, rank, &c., of Invalid Pensioners residing in the district of Charleston, in the State of South Carolina.

NAMES.	Rank.	Annual allowance.	Sums received.	Description of service.	When placed on the pension roll.	Commencement of pension.	Ages.	Laws under which inscribed; and remarks.
Joseph Clark*	Private	48 00	340 26	1st regt. U. S. rifle	Feb. 24, 1817	Aug. 3, 1815	-	Acts ex. military establishment.
William Laval	Captain	240 00	369 80	3d U. S. regt.	March 3, 1830	Feb. 19, 1830	-	Act April 10, 1806. Dropped under act May 1, 1820.
George Petrie	2d lieut.	240 00	428 38	S. C. cont'l line	May 29, 1818	May 22, 1818	-	
Do - -	Do	180 00	1,144 93	Col. Pinkney's reg.	July 30, 1823	July 3, 1823	-	Act February 4, 1822. Died July 12, 1831.
			2,283 37					

A statement showing the names, rank, &c., of Invalid Pensioners residing in the district of Edgefield, in the State of South Carolina.

NAMES.	Rank.	Annual allowance.	Sums received.	Description of service.	When placed on the pension roll.	Commencement of pension.	Ages.	Laws under which inscribed; and remarks.
Turner Crooker	Captain	240 00	1,496 69	9th regt. U. S. inf.	Dec. 11, 1819	Dec. 10, 1819	-	Act mily establish't. Transferred from Georgia March 24, 1826.
Do - -	Do	240 00	1,738 06	Do	Do	Do	-	Died May 31, 1833.
			3,234 75					

A statement showing the names, rank, &c., of Invalid Pensioners residing in the district of *Fairfield*, in the State of South Carolina.

Names.	Rank.	Annual allowance.	Sums received.	Description of service.	When placed on the pension roll.	Commencement of pension.	Ages.	Laws under which inscribed; and remarks.
Joseph Kerr -	Private	60 00	1,470 00	-	-	March 4, 1789	-	Act Sept. 29, 1789. Transfer from North Carolina from Sept. 4, 1813. Dead.
Do - -	Do	60 00	158 45	-	-	Do	-	Do
Do - -	Do	96 00	370 89	-	-	April 24, 1816	-	Act April 24, 1816.
Joseph King -	Do	30 00	75 49	-	-	Oct. 19, 1813	-	Act April 18, 1814.
Do - -	Do	48 00	113 44	-	-	April 24, 1816	-	Act April 24, 1816.
			2,188 27					

A statement showing the names, rank, &c. of Invalid Pensioners residing in the district of *Greenville*, in the State of South Carolina.

Names.	Rank.	Annual allowance.	Sums received.	Description of service.	When placed on the pension roll.	Commencement of pension.	Ages.	Laws under which inscribed; and remarks.
Thomas Smith, 1st -	Private	60 00	1,568 45	Army of the rev.	Oct. 19, 1821	March 4, 1790	-	Act Sept. 29, 1789. Transferred from North Carolina from 4th March, 1826.
Do - -	Do	96 00	946 89	Do	Do	April 24, 1816	-	Act April 24, 1816.
Do - -	Do	96 00	768 00	Do	Do	March 4, 1826	-	Do.
			3,283 34					

5

A statement of the names, &c., of the Heirs of non-commissioned Officers, Privates, &c., who died in the United States' service; who obtained five years' half pay in lieu of bounty land, under the second section of the act of April 16, 1816, and who resided in Greenville district, in the State of South Carolina.

Names of the original claimants.	Rank.	Description of service.	Time of decease.	Names of the heirs.	Annual allowance.	Sums received.	When placed on the roll.	Commencement of pension.	Ending of pension.
Noah Coleman	Private	3d regt. inf.	Aug. 27, 1815	Eliza and Mahala Coleman	48 00	240 00	Aug. 20, 1817	Feb. 17, 1815	Feb. 17, 1820
John Duncan	Do	Do	Nov. 13, 1813	James and Rebecca Duncan	48 00	240 00	Mar. 23, 1818	Do	Do
Atha Saxton	Do	Do	Mar. or April, 1815	Luraney, Noah, Polly, John, and Atha Saxton	48 00	240 00	Mar. 5, 1818	Do	Do

A statement of the names, &c., of the Heirs of non-commissioned Officers, Privates, &c., who died in the United States' service; who obtained five years' half pay in lieu of bounty land under the second section of the act of April 16, 1816, and who resided in Marlborough district, in the State of South Carolina.

Names of the original claimants.	Rank.	Description of service.	Time of decease.	Names of the heirs.	Annual allowance.	Sums received.	When placed on the roll.	Commencement of pension.	Ending of pension.
Joseph Clark	Private	18th regt. inf.	Mar. 21, 1814	Obedience, Henrietta, and Jesse Clark	48 00	240 00	May 10, 1820	Feb. 10, 1820	Feb. 10, 1825

6

A statement of the names, &c., of the Heirs of non-commissioned Officers, Privates, &c.. who died in the United States' service; who obtained five years' half-pay in lieu of bounty land, under the second section of the act of April 16, 1816, and who resided in Pendleton district, in the State of South Carolina.

Names of the original claimants.	Rank.	Description of service.	Time of decease.	Names of the heirs.	Annual allowance.	Sums received.	When placed on the roll.	Commencement of pension.	Ending of pension.
Jno. Cunningham	Private	3d regt. inf.	March, 1815	Catharine, Elizabeth, Elias, Jno. B., and Sarah Cunningham	48 00	240 00	Dec. 17, 1817	Feb. 17, 1815	Feb. 17, 1820
Thomas Pointer -	Do	Do	Feb. 20, 1815	Katy, Leanna, Polly, Melinda Fleming, Elizabeth, Lucinda John, and Jackson Pointer -	48 00	240 00	Do	Do	Do

A statement of the names, &c., of the Heirs of non-commissioned Officers, Privates, &c., who died in the United States' service; who obtained five years' half-pay in lieu of bounty land, under the second section of the act of April 16, 1816, and who resided in Richland district, in the State of South Carolina.

Names of the original claimants.	Rank.	Description of service.	Time of decease.	Names of the heirs.	Annual allowance.	Sums received.	When placed on the roll.	Commencement of pension.	Ending of pension.
Henry Williams -	Corporal	18th regt. inf.	Sept. 18, 1812	Mary, George, and Henry Williams - - - -	48 00	240 00	June 6, 1818	Feb. 17, 1815	Feb. 17, 1820
Jesse Holder -	Private	Do	Jan. 21, 1814	Jesse Holder - - - -	48 00	240 00	Sept. 23, 1819	Do	Do.

A statement of the names, &c., of the Heirs of *non-commissioned Officers, Privates, &c., who died in the United States' service; who obtained five years' half-pay in lieu of bounty land, under the second section of the act of April 16, 1816, and who resided in Spartanburgh district, in the State of South Carolina.*

Names of the original claimants.	Rank.	Description of service.	Time of decease.	Names of the heirs.	Annual allowance.	Sums received.	When placed on the roll.	Commencement of pension.	Ending of pension.
Benjamin Wells -	Private	8th regt. inf.	Nov. 9, 1814	Priscilla, Nancy, and Alexander Wells - - - -	48 00	240 00	Sept. 23, 1819	Feb. 17, 1815	Feb. 17, 1820

A statement showing the names, rank, &c. of Invalid Pensioners residing in the district of Pickens, in the State of South Carolina.

Names.	Rank.	Description of service.	When placed on the pension roll.	Sums received.	Annual allowance.	Commencement of pension.	Ages.	Laws under which inscribed; and remarks.
Andrew McAllister* -	Private	- -	- -	121 88	21 42	Sept. 4, 1810		Act April 24, 1816.
Do -	Do	- -	- -	508 47	34 12	April 24, 1816		
				630 35				

8

A statement showing the names, rank, &c., of Invalid Pensioners residing in the district of Spartansburgh, in the State of South Carolina.

NAMES.	Rank.	Annual allowance.	Sums received.	Description of service.	When placed on the pension roll.	Commencement of pension.	Age	Laws under which inscribed; and remarks.
Jesse Vincent - -	Private	48 00	89 18	7th regt. U. S. inf.	Nov. 1, 1831	Oct. 27, 1831	-	Acts ex. military establishment.
			89 18					

A statement showing the names, rank, &c., of Invalid Pensioners residing in the district of Union, in the State of South Carolina.

NAMES.	Rank.	Annual allowance.	Sums received	Description of service.	When placed on the pension roll.	Commencement of pension.	Ages.	Laws under which inscribed; and remarks.
Joseph Davidson -	Private	30 00	127 58	-	-	Jan. 23, 1812	-	Act Aug. 2, 1813. Died October 12, 1832.
Do -	Do	48 00	769 44	-	-	April 24, 1816	-	Act April 24, 1816.
Joseph McJunkin -	Major	144 00	2,792 20	U. States army	Dec. 23, 1811	Oct. 18, 1808	-	Act March 3, 1809.
Do -	Do	200 00	786 07	Do	Do	March 7, 1828	-	Act April 24, 1816.
Jasper Tomiton -	Private	225 00	503 58	Do	Do	Feb 11, 1832	-	Do do.
Do -	Do	30 00	131 23	-	-	Dec. 10, 1811	-	Act July 5, 1812. Died December 31, 1828.
Thomas Young - -	Do	48 00	417 00	-	-	April 24, 1816	-	Act April 24, 1816.
Do -	Do	72 00	430 23	Army of revolution	April 18, 1828	March 12, 1828	-	Act February 4, 1822.
			5,957 33					

A statement showing the names, rank, &c. of Invalid Pensioners residing in the district of York, in the State of South Carolina.

NAMES.	Rank.	Annual allowance.	Sums received.	Description of service.	When placed on the pension roll.	Commencement of pension.	Ages.	Laws under which inscribed; and remarks.
Alexander Haynes*	Private	42 00	351 26	U. States army	Jan. 28, 1822	Sept. 4, 1808	-	Transferred from North Carolina, from Sept. 4, 1826. Died Feb. 2, 1828.
Do	Do	67 20	427 62	Do	Do	April 24, 1816	-	Act April 24, 1816.
Do	Do	48 00	192 00	Do	Do	Sept. 4, 1822	-	Act March 3, 1819.
Do	Do	48 00	67 74	Do	Do	Sept. 4, 1826	-	
James McClain	Do	96 00	155 61	Ballarde's co. 3d rifl.	Jan. 19, 1828	Jan. 19, 1828	-	Acts military establishment. Died August 31, 1829.
Samuel Rose	Do	20 00	14 04	3d regt. U. S. rifle	-	Aug. 6, 1815	-	Acts military establishment.
Do	Do	32 00	251 62	Do	-	April 24, 1816	-	Act April 24, 1816.
Isaiah Twitchall	Do	60 00	57 66	Howards' co. 25 inf.	-	May 14, 1815	-	Acts ex. military establishment. Transferred from Connecticut, from March 4, 1824.
Do	Do	96 00	754 92	Do	-	April 24, 1816	-	Acts April 24, 1826.
Do	Do	96 00	960 00	Do	-	-	-	
			3,232 47					

A list of Invalid Pensioners who have been in the receipt of pensions at the agency of Charleston, in the State of South Carolina, and whose residence cannot be ascertained in consequence of the destruction of the papers in the War Office in 1801 and 1814,

NAMES.	Rank.	Annual allowance.	Sums received.	Description of service.	When placed on the pension roll.	Commencement of pension.	Ages.	Laws under which inscribed; and remarks.
John Calhoun -	Private	21 42	-	-	-	-	-	Act April 25, 1808.
Do -	Do	34 12	-	-	-	April 24, 1816	-	Act April 24, 1816.
William Dunlap* -	Do	21 42	-	-	-	Do	-	Do do.
Do -	Do	34 12	213 31	-	-	Nov. 15, 1811	-	Act July 5, 1812 Died May 26, 1820.
Malcom Keys -	Do	48 00	-	-	-	-	-	
Do -	Do	76 80	314 23	-	-	April 24, 1816	-	Act April 24, 1816.
George Mason* -	Do	55 12	-	-	-	March 4, 1809	-	Dead.
David Witherspoon* -	Do	21 42	76 04	-	-	-	-	Dead.
Henry Weems* -	Do	60 00	108 28	-	-	Nov. 15, 1811	-	Act July 5, 1812. Dead.
			711 86					

A statement showing the names, rank, &c., of persons residing in the district of Abbeville, in the State of South Carolina, who have been inscribed on the pension list under the act of Congress passed the 18th March, 1818.

NAMES.	Rank.	Annual allowance.	Sums received.	Description of service.	When placed on the pension roll.	Commencement of pension.	Ages.	Laws under which they were formerly inscribed on the pension roll; and remarks.
William Ashley -	Corporal	96 00	360 56	Pulaski's legion	Sept. 24, 1818	Aug. 11, 1818	77	Dropped under act May 1, 1820. Restored, commencing Dec. 27, 1831.
James Devlin -	Private	96 00	674 60	S. C. cont'l line	March 5, 1819	Aug. 26, 1818	75	Died November 26, 1825.
Hugh Houston -	Do	96 00	1,149 82	N. C. do	Nov. 25, 1819	June 8, 1818	79	Dropped under act May 1, 1820. Restored, commencing June 10, 1823.
Benjamin Kennard -	Do	96 00	949 56	Penn. do	July 31, 1819	June 14, 1819	83	Dropped under act May 1, 1820. Restored, commencing September 4, 1821.
Edward Lyon -	Do	96 00	425 02	Virginia do	March 5, 1819	Aug. 9, 1818	71	Died January 12, 1823.
Andrew Mellog -	Do	96 00	-	S. C. do	March 5, 1821	Nov. 13, 1818	-	Dropped under act May 1, 1818.
Henry Magner -	Do	96 00	1,415 43	N. C. do	Aug. 19, 1819	June 7, 1819	68	
Joshua Pruett -	Do	96 00	1,511 16	N. C. do	Sept. 6, 1819	June 8, 1818	80	
James Russell -	Do	96 00	438 20	S. C. do	March 5, 1819	Aug. 12, 1818	90	Died December 4, 1823.
			6 924 35					

A statement showing the names, rank, &c., of persons residing in the district of Anderson, in the State of South Carolina, who have been inscribed on the pension list under the act of Congress passed the 18th March, 1818.

NAMES.	Rank.	Annual allowance.	Sums received.	Description of service.	When placed on the pension roll	Commencement of pension.	Ages.	Laws under which they were formerly inscribed on the pension roll; and remarks.
William Day -	Private	96 00	1,490 57	Virginia cont'l line	Jan. 18, 1819	Aug. 26, 1818	78	
Coodman Harris -	Do	96 00	1,506 06	N. C. do	March 5, 1819	July 1, 1818	76	

NAMES.	Rank.	Annual allowance.	Sums received.	Description of service.	When placed on the pension roll.	Commencement of pension.	Ages.	Laws under which they were formerly inscribed on the pension roll; and remarks.
John Lewis - -	Do	96 00	340 57	Virginia do	Feb. 5, 1829	Feb. 3, 1829	78	Act March 18, 1818. Transferred from Rutherford co., N. Carolina, from September 4, 1833.
Do	Do	96 00	48 00	N. C. do	Feb. 5, 1829	Feb. 3, 1829	78	
William Noble - -	Do	96 00	1,489 56	N. C. do	March 5, 1819	Sept. 2, 1818	90	
James Young - -	Do	96 90	1,509 83	Virginia do	March 5, 1819	June 13, 1818	80	
			6,384 59					

A statement showing the names, rank, &c., of persons residing in the Beaufort district, in the State of South Carolina, who have been inscribed on the pension list under the act of Congress passed the 18th March, 1818.

NAMES.	Rank.	Annual allowance.	Sums received.	Description of service.	When placed on the pension roll.	Commencement of pension.	Ages.	Laws under which they were formerly inscribed on the pension roll; and remarks.
Isam Carter - -	Private	96 00	1,511 96	S. C. cont'l line	Aug. 2, 1819	June 5, 1818	-	Dropped under act May 1, 1820.
John Cook, 2d - -	Do	96 00	323 92	Do	Sept. 10, 1819	Sept. 16, 1818	80	Restored, commencing April 9, 1824.
George Gosling -	Do	96 00	123 96	Do	Sept. 7, 1819	Nov. 20, 1818	-	Dropped under act May 1, 1820.
John Wickly - -	Captain	240 00	422 58	Do	Aug. 2, 1819	June 1, 1818	78	Dropped under act May 1, 1820.
Levi Weeks - -	Private	96 00	1,169 06	Maryland do	April 22, 1820	July 1, 1818	78	Dropped under act May 1, 1820.
			3,551 48					

A statement showing the names, rank, &c., of persons residing in the district of Barnwell, in the State of South Carolina, who have been inscribed on the pension list under the act of Congress passed the 18th March, 1818.

NAMES.	Rank.	Annual allowance.	Sums received.	Description of service.	When placed on the pension roll.	Commencement of pension.	Ages.	Laws under which they were formerly inscribed on the pension roll; and remarks.
Jesse Griffin - -	Private	96 00	1,377 56	Pulaski's corps	Jan. 22, 1819	Nov. 3, 1818	78	
Dennis Scott - -	Do	96 00	777 03	N. C. cont'l line	Feb. 23, 1826	Feb. 1, 1826	74	
			2,154 59					

A statement showing the names, rank, &c., of persons residing in the district of Chester, in the State of South Carolina, who have been inscribed on the pension list under the act of Congress passed the 18th March, 1818.

NAMES.	Rank.	Annual allowance.	Sums received.	Description of service.	When placed on the pension roll.	Commencement of pension.	Ages.	Laws under which they were formerly inscribed on the pension roll; and remarks.
James Alverson -	Private	96 00	695 73	Virginia cont'l line	Dec. 30, 1826	Dec. 5, 1826	75	
Joseph Brown -	Do	96 00	1,357 18	N. C. do	March 5, 1819	July 16, 1818	75	
Archibald Brown -	Do	96 00	673 03	S. C. do	Oct. 11, 1823	March 1, 1823	74	Died April 16, 1833.
James Black -	Do	96 00	607 69	Do	Nov. 19, 1827	Nov. 6, 1827	77	Died July 21, 1831.
William Cockrell -	Do	96 00	1,501 15	Do	March 5, 1819	July 16, 1818	77	
Robert Conley -	Do	96 00	128 00	Do	Sept. 23, 1819	Nov. 4, 1818	66	
Robert Cowley -	Do	96 00	695 73	Do	Dec. 30, 1826	Dec. 6, 1826	81	Dropped under act May 1, 1820.
John Dougherty -	Do	96 00	686 47	Penn. do	April 19, 1819	July 11, 1818	91	
Lewis Hardin -	Do	96 00	1,500 12	N. C. do	Feb. 16, 1820	July 20, 1818	63	
William Knox -	Do	96 00	1,164 15	S. C. do	March 5, 1819	Do	82	
Charles Kea -	Do	96 00	253 15	Virginia do	March 5, 1819	July 16, 1818	85	
James Kirkpatrick -	Do	96 00	115 35	S. C. do	May 17, 1819	Dec. 23, 1818	-	Dropped under act May 1, 1820

NAMES.	Rank.	Annual allowance.	Sums received.	Description of service.	When placed on the pension ro'l.	Commencement of pension.	Ages.	Laws under which they were formerly inscribed on the pension roll; and remarks
Hugh Knox -	Do	96 00	128 77	Do	Sept. 23, 1819	Nov. 2, 1818	-	Dropped under act May 1, 1820.
Spencer Kirkpatrick -	Do	96 00	845 86	Do	Sept. 23, 1819	Nov. 13, 1818	72	Dead. Reported December, 1828.
John Miller -	Do	96 00	147 69	Virginia do	March 5, 1819	July 20, 1818	-	Dropped under act May 1, 1820.
Benjamin Rowan	Do	96 00	1,165 18	S. C. do	March 5, 1819	July 16, 1818	78	Died December 3, 1830.
			11,665 25					

A statement showing the names, rank, &c., of persons residing in the district of Charleston, in the State of South Carolina, who have been inscribed on the pension list under the act of Congress passed the 18th March, 1818.

NAMES.	Rank.	Annual allowance.	Sums received.	Description of service.	When placed on the pension ro'l.	Commencement of pension.	Ages.	Laws under which they were formerly inscribed on the pension roll; and remarks
John Betsell or Bedsell	Private	96 00	201 06	Virginia cont'l line	Sept. 18, 1820	Aug. 1, 1820	73	
Nathaniel Cudworth -	Major	240 00	1,868 38	Mass. do	May 4, 1818	April 9, 1818	79	Died January 21, 1826.
Francis Francum -	Private	96 00	420 26	S. C. do	May 17, 1825	May 9, 1825	70	Died September 23, 1829.
Henry Gray -	Lieutenant	240 00	85 80	Do	June 12, 1824	March 10, 1824	75	Died July 20, 1824.
John McCune -	Private	96 00	243 91	Do	March 19, 1827	Feb. 19, 1827	75	
David Sardezas -	Lieutenant	240 00	3,590 96	Georgia do	Jan. 12, 1819	May 19, 1818	73	
James Stewart -	Private	96 00	122 09	Do	April 8, 1819	Nov. 27, 1818	-	Dropped under act May 1, 1820.
James Waddell -	Sergeant	96 00	381 15	S. C. do	Aug. 3, 1820	March 16, 1820	62	Dead. Reported June 1, 1823.
			6,913 61					

A statement showing the names, rank, &c., of persons residing in the district of Chesterfield, in the State of South Carolina, who have been inscribed on the pension list under the act of Congress passed the 18th March, 1818.

NAMES.	Rank.	Annual allowance.	Sums received.	Description of service.	When placed on the pension roll.	Commencement of pension.	Ages.	Laws under which they were formerly inscribed on the pension roll; and remarks.
John Brown - -	Private	96 00	1,368 54 1,368 54	S. C. cont'l line	March 5, 1819	Dec. 3, 1818	73	

A statement showing the names, rank, &c., of persons residing in the district of Darlington, in the State South Carolina, who have been inscribed on the pension list under the act of Congress passed the 18th March, 1818.

NAMES.	Rank.	Annual allowance.	Sums received.	Description of service.	When placed on the pension roll.	Commencement of pension.	Ages.	Laws under which they were formerly inscribed on the pension roll; and remarks.
James Neal - -	Private	96 00	485 88 485 88	S. C. cont'l line	Feb. 12, 1829	Feb. 12, 1829	79	

16

A statement showing the names, rank, &c., of persons residing in the district of Edgefield, in the State of South Carolina, who have been inscribed on the pension list under the act of Congress passed the 18th March, 1818.

Names.	Rank.	Annual allowance.	Sums received.	Description of service.	When placed on the pension roll.	Commencement of pension	Ages.	Laws under which they were formerly inscribed on the pension roll; and remarks.
Richard Burton	Private	96 00	1,513 83	Georgia cont'l line	Sept. 18, 1818	June 2, 1818	75	
William Blaikley	Do	96 00	-	S. C. do	Dec. 14, 1818	June 3, 1818	-	Dropped under act May 1, 1818.
William Bryant	Do	96 00	347 61	N. C. do	March 24, 1819	July 22, 1818	83	
Joseph Croes	Do	96 00	580 93	Virginia cavalry	Jan. 4, 18:9	Aug. 17, 1818	76	
Thomas Dean	Do	96 00	840 76	3d reg't rangers	Sept. 18, 1818	June 2, 1818	73	
Julius Dean	Do	96 00	359 16	Georgia cont'l line	July 7, 1819	June 8, 1819	80	
Batte Evans	Do	96 00	776 54	Virginia do	March 5, 1819	A. g. 3, 1818	74	Dead. Reported June, 1832.
Samuel Garner	Do	96 00	134 19	S. C. do	March 24, 1819	Oct. 16, 1818	73	Died March 27, 1821.
John Glover	Ensign	240 00	587 08	Do	Feb. 3, 1820	Oct. 17, 1818	70	
Robert Hastings	Private	96 00	1,513 83	Delaware do	Sept. 18, 1818	June 2, 1818	90	Dropped under act May 1, 1830. Restored, commencing Nov. 14, 1825. Died July 25, 1827.
John Huffinan	Do	96 00	314 71	Virginia do	Jan. 4, 1819	Aug. 4, 1818	71	
Stephen Hutchinson	Do	96 00	1,499 35	Do	April 15, 1819	July 23, 1818	79	
Joshua J. Jackson	Do	96 00	504 79	N. York do	Sept. 18, 1818	June 2, 1818	89	Dropped under act May 1, 1820.
Thomas Inlo	Do	96 00	84 46	Virginia do	Jan 4, 1819	Sept. 7, 1818	78	Do do
James King	Do	96 00	159 73	Do	March 24, 1819	July 6, 1818	59	Do do
Basil Lowe	Do	96 00	168 23	Armand's legion	Sept. 18, 1819	June 4, 1818	61	
Dennis Lowe	Do	96 00	1,240 28	Do	Jan. 18, 1821	Oct. 4, 1820	70	
Isham Melton	Do	96 00	1,223 96	Virginia cont'l line	March 24, 1819	June 5, 1818	74	
William Martin	Do	96 00	809 56	S. C. do	Nov. 10, 1819	Sept. 29, 1819	74	Dead. Reported Dec., 1828.
Joshua Reams	Do	96 00	793 80	N. C. do	Sept 18, 1818	June 2, 1818	74	
Simeon Smith	Do	96 00	1,368 79	Do	Do	Do	83	
Charles Simpkins	Do	96 00	1,509 83	Mtl. cont'l line	Dec. 14, 1818	June 13, 1818	84	Dropped under act May 1, 1820. Restored, commencing Feb. 14, 1827. Died June 2, 1829.
Moses Spivey	Do	96 00	357 06	S. C. do	Jan. 4, 1819	Oct. 4, 1818	73	Dropped under act May 1, 1820.
George Turner	Do	96 00	168 76	Geo gia do	Sept. 18, 1818	June 2, 1818	75	Do
Jonathan Taylor	Do	96 00	136 77	Virginia do	March 24, 1819	Oct. 2, 1818	60	do

3

Statement of Edgefield district—Continued.

NAMES.	Rank.	Annual allowance.	Sums received.	Description of service.	When placed on the pension roll.	Commencement of pension.	Ages.	Laws under which they were formerly inscribed on the pension roll; and remarks.
Thomas Wiseman	Private	96 00	696 79	Md. cont'l line	Jan. 4, 1819	June 2, 1818	84	
Henry Weaver	Do	96 00	168 76	S. C. do	March 24, 1819	Do	83	Dropped under act May 1, 1820. Restored, commencing Aug. 7, 1828.
			17,859 56					

A statement showing the names, rank, &c., of persons residing in the district of Fairfield, in the State of South Carolina, who have been inscribed on the pension list under the act of Congress passed March 18, 1818.

NAMES.	Rank.	Annual allowance.	Sums received.	Description of service.	When placed on the pension roll.	Commencement of pension.	Ages.	Laws under which they were formerly inscribed on the pension roll; and remarks.
John Smith	Private	96 00	1,081 01	S. C. cont'l line	March 5, 1819	July 16, 1818	-	Dropped under act May 1, 1820. Restored, commencing July 21, 1824.
			1,081 01					

18

A statement showing the names, rank, &c., of persons residing in the district of Georgetown, in the State of South Carolina, who have been inscribed on the pension list under the act of Congress passed March 18, 1818.

Names.	Rank.	Annual allowance.	Sums received.	Description of service.	When placed on the pension roll.	Commencement of pension.	Ages.	Laws under which they were formerly inscribed on the pension roll; and remarks.
Peter Bacot - -	Captain	240 00	767 71	N. C. cont'l line	Sept. 28, 1818	June 2, 1818	67	Died August 13, 1821.
			767 71					

A statement showing the names, rank, &c., of persons residing in the district of Greenville, in the State of South Carolina, who have been inscribed on the pension list under the act of Congress passed March 18, 1818.

Names.	Rank.	Annual allowance.	Sums received.	Descript on of service.	When placed on the pension roll.	Commencement of pension.	Ages.	Laws under which they were formerly inscribed on the pension roll; and remarks.
Charles Bryant - -	Private	96 00	655 99	Virginia cont'l line	Jan. 14, 1824	Nov. 5, 1823	73	Died January 10, 1831.
William Berry - -	Do	96 00	752 79	Do	May 10, 1826	Nov. 2, 1825	79	
William Duncan -	Do	96 00	930 36	N. C. do	July 30, 1824	June 26, 1824	85	
Isaac Gregory - -	Do	96 00	1,471 16	Do	April 3, 1819	June 8, 1818	76	Dropped under act May 1, 1820.
Blackman Ligan -	Do	96 00	125 56	Virginia do	March 5, 1819	June 14, 1818	63	
Nicholas Latner -	Do	96 00	501 41	S. C. do	Jan. 10, 1829	Dec. 15, 1828	72	
Thomas Masters -	Do	96 00	1,473 56	Virginia do	March 5, 1819	Nov. 3, 1818	79	
Gipson Southern -	Do	96 00	1,324 64	Georgia do	Feb. 9, 1819	May 18, 1818	81	
			7,235 47					

A statement showing the names, rank, &c., of persons residing in the district of Horry, in the State of South Carolina, who have been inscribed on the pension list under the act of Congress passed March 18, 1818.

NAMES.	Rank.	Annual allowance.	Sums received.	Description of service.	When placed on the pension roll.	Commencement of pension.	Ages.	Laws under which they were formerly inscribed on the pension roll; and remarks.
Henry Gunter -	Private	96 00	609 28	S. C. cont'l line	Dec. 13, 1821	Oct. 31, 1820	83	
William Hardee -	Do	96 00	611 84	N. C. do	Oct. 3, 1822	April 4, 1821	71	Died August 18, 1827.
Moses Milligan -	Do	96 00	787 73	S. C. do	Dec. 13, 1821	Do	73	Died June 17, 1829.
Thomas Wallace -	Do	96 00	808 26	N. C. do	May 18, 1822	Do	80	
			2,817 11					

A statement showing the names, rank, &c., of persons residing in the district of Kershaw, in the State of South Carolina, who have been inscribed on the pension list under the act of Congress passed March 18, 1818.

NAMES.	Rank.	Annual allowance.	Sums received.	Description of service.	When placed on the pension roll.	Commencement of pension.	Ages.	Laws under which they were formerly inscribed on the pension roll; and remarks.
John Artiss -	Private	96 00	82 09	S. C. cont'l line	Dec. 3, 1819	April 27, 1819	79	Dropped under act May 1, 1820.
Do	Do	96 00	1,296 00	Do			91	
Richard Britt -	Do	96 00	1,085 03	Do	Dec. 4, 1819	Nov. 16, 18:9	78	
Lewis Cook -	Do	96 00	1,507 86	Virginia do	March 5, 1819	June 20, 1818	78	
John Cook -	Do	96 00	548 76	S. C. do	Do	June 17, 1818	-	Do
Johnson Elkins -	Sergeant	96 00	163 96	Do	July 27, 1819	June 20, 1818		do.

20

NAMES.	Rank.	Annual allowance.	Sums received.	Description of service.	When placed on the pension roll.	Commencement of pension.	Ages.	Laws under which they were formerly inscribed on the pension roll; and remarks.
Abraham Kelly -	Private	96 00	875 58	Do	Nov. 10, 1819	Aug. 20, 1819	87	Dropped under act May 1, 1820. Restored, commencing Nov. 21, 1823. Died June 18, 1832.
Oliver McHaffey -	Do	96 00	755 49	Do	May 11, 1826	April 18, 1826	72	
			6,314 77					

A statement showing the names, rank, &c., of persons residing in the district of Lancaster, in the State of South Carolina, who have been inscribed on the pension list under the act of Congress passed March 18, 1818.

NAMES.	Rank.	Annual allowance.	Sums received.	Description of service.	When placed on the pension roll.	Commencement of pension.	Ages.	Laws under which they were formerly inscribed on the pension roll; and remarks.
Joseph Haile - -	Private	96 00	109 93	N. C. cont'l line	Jan. 14, 1831	Jan. 13, 1831	77	Died July 13, 1832.
			109 93					

A statement showing the names, rank, &c., of persons residing in the district of Lexington, in the State of South Carolina, who have been inscribed on the pension list under the act of Congress passed March 18, 1818.

NAMES.	Rank.	Annual allowance.	Sums received.	Description of service.	When placed on the pension roll.	Commencement of pension.	Ages.	Laws under which they were formerly inscribed on the pension roll; and remarks.
John Reizer - -	Private	96 00	593 03	N. C. cont'l line	July 14, 1830.	Jan. 1, 1828	83	Special act, passed May 20, 1830.
			593 03					

A statement showing the names, rank, &c., of persons residing in the district of Laurens, in the State of South Carolina, who have been inscribed on the pension list under the act of Congress passed the 18th March, 1818.

NAMES.	Rank.	Annual allowance.	Sums received.	Description of service.	When placed on the pension roll.	Commencement of pension.	Ages.	Laws under which they were formerly inscribed on the pension roll; and remarks.
John Alverson*	Private	40 00	480 00	Virginia cont'l line	- -	Sept. 4, 1802	70	Transferred from North Carolina from September 4, 1814.
Do	Do	40 00	65 63	Do	- -	Do	70	Act April 24, 1816. Increased to $64 per annum per act April 24, 1816.
Do	Do	64 00	278 26	Do	- -	April 24, 1816	70	
Do	Do	96 00	814 00	Do	April 7, 1820	Sept. 4, 1820	70	Act March 18, 1818. Relinquished his invalid pension for the benefit of the act of March 18, 1818. Died February 25, 1829.
John Butler	Do	96 00	96 00	Do	Jan. 19, 1819	Sept. 25, 1818	58	Dropped under act May 1, 1820.
Richard Butler	Do	96 00	236 72	Maryland do	April 21, 1830	April 21, 1830	82	Died October 8, 1832.
William Canady	Do	96 00	1,465 83	Virginia do	May 9, 1820	Nov. 28, 1818	83	Dropped under act May 1, 1820. Restored, commencing July 4, 1827.
Thomas Gains	Do	96 00	762 86	Do	March 28, 1820	Do	80	
James Howerton	Do	96 00	204 93	Do do	April 24, 1820	June 21, 1819	67	Died August 9, 1821.
James Saxon	Do	96 00	1,429 53	S. C.	Feb. 16, 1820	April 13, 1819	80	
Flanders Thompson	Do	96 00	848 50	Virginia do	June 19, 1820	March 30, 1819	73	Dropped under act May 1, 1820. Restored, commencing March 1, 1823. Died January 27, 1831.
Thomas Turner	Do	96 00	484 26	Do	Sept. 5, 1820	June 15, 1818	66	
Thomas Word	Do	96 00	382 70	Do	March 10, 1830	March 10, 1830	78	Died September 19, 1823.
			7,549 57					

A statement showing the names, rank, &c., of persons residing in the district of Marion, in the State of South Carolina, who have been inscribed on the pension list under the act of Congress passed the 18th March, 1818.

NAMES.	Rank.	Annual allowance.	Sums received.	Description of service.	When placed on the pension roll.	Commencement of pension.	Ages.	Laws under which they were formerly inscribed on the pension roll; and remarks.
James Gassaway	Private	96 00	588 37	Virginia cont'l line	May 17, 1819	March 16, 1819	74	Dropped under act May 1, 1820. Restored, commencing January 8, 1829.
William Rozier	Do	96 00	282 06	do	July 14, 1819	Oct. 27, 1818	72	Died October 3, 1821.
			870 43					

A statement showing the names, rank, &c., of persons residing in the district of Newberry, in the State of South Carolina, who have been inscribed on the pension list under the act of Congress passed the 18th March, 1818.

NAMES.	Rank.	Annual allowance.	Sums received.	Description of service.	When placed on the pension roll.	Commencement of pension.	Ages.	Laws under which they were formerly inscribed on the pension roll; and remarks.
Charles Charity	Private	96 00	641 80	Virginia cont'l line	Aug. 9, 1827	July 2, 1827	77	
John Ellis	Do	96 00	379 86	N. C. do	May 29, 1826	March 21, 1826	76	
John Inlow	Do	96 00	1,063 76	S. C. do	Jan. 30, 1819	Aug. 6, 1818	-	Died. Reported June, 1830.
William Plantt, sen.	Do	96 00	22 96	Virginia do	May 25, 1820	Dec. 9, 1819	63	Dropped under act May 1, 1820.
John Smith, 2d	Do	96 00	66 89	S. C. do	April 27, 1820	June 24, 1819	73	Do do.
James Motes	Do	96 00	982 70	Do	March 28, 1820	Dec. 14, 1819	82	Do do. Restored, commencing September 1, 1823.
			3,157 97					

A statement showing the names, rank, &c. of persons residing in the district of Pickens, in the State of South Carolina, who have been inscribed on the pension list under the act of Congress passed the 18th March, 1818.

NAMES.	Rank.	Annual allowance.	Sums received.	Description of service.	When placed on the pension roll.	Commencement of pension.	Ages.	Laws under which they were formerly inscribed on the pension roll; and remarks.
Robert Farr	Private	96 00	588 90	Penn. cont'l line	Jan. 17, 1828	Jan. 17, 1828	82	
Stephen Fuller	Sergeant	96 00	545 06	Georgia do	Aug. 27, 1830	Jan. 1, 1828	81	Special act, passed May 20, 1830.
Levi Philips	Private	96 00	768 76	Virginia do	Nov. 26, 1819	May 15, 1818	84	
Edmund Singleton	Do	96 00	1,378 06	Do	June 2, 1820	Oct. 18, 1819	80	
John Wilson	Do	96 00	1,282 83	Do	Nov. 19, 1821	Oct. 25, 1820	79	
			4,563 61					

A statement showing the names, rank, &c. of persons residing in the district of Pendleton, in the State of South Carolina, who have been inscribed on the pension list under the act of Congress passed the 18th March, 1818.

NAMES.	Rank.	Annual allowance.	Sums received.	Description of service.	When placed on the pension roll	Commencement of pension.	Ages.	Laws under which they were formerly inscribed on the pension roll; and remarks.
Robert Clannahan	Private	96 00	1,115 61	Maryland cont'l line	March 5, 1819	May 17, 1818	74	Died December 2, 1829.
Thomas Cooper	Do	96 00	32 05	Virginia do	Nov. 25, 1819	Oct 28, 1819	-	Dropped under act May 1, 1820.
Pendleton Isbell	Do	96 00	172 12	Do	April 6, 1820	May 20, 1818	77	Do do.
Robert Miller	Do	96 00	274 35	Do	July 16, 1821	Oct. 27, 1818	85	
John Powell	Do	96 00	537 31	do	May 7, 1821	Jan. 31, 1820	80	
Peter Rowland	Do	96 00	332 15	S. C.	April 6, 1820	March 20, 1819		
John Swords	Do	96 00	87 43	Do	June 2, 1820	April 7, 1819	-	Do do
John Winn	Do	96 00	886 18	Virginia do	Oct. 16, 1822	May 16, 1818	84	Died August 8, 1827
			3,437 21					

A statement showing the names, rank, &c. of persons residing in the district of Richland, in the State of South Carolina, who have been inscribed on the pension list under the act of Congress passed the 18th March, 1818.

NAMES.	Rank.	Annual allowance.	Sums received.	Description of service.	When placed on the pension roll.	Commencement of pension	Ages.	Laws under which they were formerly inscribed on the pension roll; and remarks.
James Brown	Private	96 00	1,465 03	S. C. cont'l line	March 5, 1819	Dec. 1, 1818	77	
John Barry, or Berry	Do	96 00	81 83	Georgia do	June 17, 1820	April 28, 1819	81	Transferred from Georgia from March 4, 1820.
Do	Do	-	816 00	Do	Do	Do	91	
Thomas Cole	Do	96 00	1,182 22	N. C. do	Oct. 5, 1819	May 12, 1819	-	
Deason Enlow	Do	96 00	162 89	S. C. do	March 5, 1819	June 24, 1818	66	
Philip Martin Frey	Drummer	96 00	115 61	Do do	Do	Dec. 22, 1818	79	Dropped under act May 1, 1820.
Meshac Fuller	Private	96 00	1,034 57	Georgia do	Feb. 17, 1821	May 26, 1818	80	Do do.
James Strange	Matross	96 00	1,522 36	S. C. artillery	Oct. 14, 1818	April 26, 1818	61	
Edward Sims	Private	96 00	125 56	Virginia cont'l line	Sept. 7, 1820	Nov. 14, 1818	-	Do do.
Stephen Truhitt	Do	96 00	130 35	N. C. do	Nov. 29, 1819	Oct. 26, 1818		Do do.
William Taylor	Sergeant	96 00	666 57	S. C. do	May 18, 1822	March 26, 1821	71	Died June 10, 1828.
William Ware	Private	96 00	954 32	Virginia do	May 12, 1823	March 27, 1823	74	

4

A statement showing the names, rank, &c. of persons residing in the district of Spartanburgh, in the State of South Carolina, who have been inscribed on the pension list under the act of Congress passed the 18th March, 1818.

NAMES.	Rank.	Annual allowance.	Sums received.	Description of service.	When placed on the pension roll.	Commencement of pension.	Ages.	Laws under which they were formerly inscribed on the pension roll; and remarks.
Robert Belcher	Private	96 00	1,279 69	Virginia cont'l line	Dec. 28, 1821	Nov. 6, 1820		Dropped under act May 1, 1820. Restored, commencing December 4, 1828.
Henry Cole	Do	96 00	508 74	N. C. do	June 4, 1819	Feb. 15, 1819	81	
Martin Cole	Do	96 00	1,349 03	Do	Do	Do	76	Died March 20, 1833.
Ellis Cannon	Do	96 00	251 89	Virginia do	Feb. 18, 1830	Jan. 21, 1830	86	Died June 12, 1830.
James Flemming	Do	96 00	759 16	N. C. do	Feb. 3, 1823	April 8, 1822	76	Died March 4, 1832.
James Fisher	Do	96 00	425 11	Maryland do	Oct. 15, 1827	Sept. 28, 1827	81	Died April 13, 1828.
John Gunter	Do	96 00	305 74	Virginia do	Feb. 25, 1825	Feb. 7, 1825	87	Died April 13, 1828.
Joshua Hawkins*	Do	36 00	185 07	Do		March 4, 1811	80	Act March 3, 1809. } Increased to $57 60 per annum, per act April 24, 1816.
Do	Do	57 60	251 33	Do		April 24, 1816	80	Act April 24, 1816 }
Do	Do	96 00	1,299 09	Do	Feb. 9, 1819	Aug. 24, 1818	80	Relinquished his invalid pension for the benefit of the act of March 18, 1818.
James Halks	Do	96 00	-	S. C. do	Sept. 23, 1819	Dec. 28, 1818	-	Dropped under act May 1, 1818.
Clairbourn Holt	Do	96 00	563 43	Virginia do	May 17, 1828	April 22, 1828	83	
Robert Kimble	Do	96 00	854 36	Do	Sept. 30, 1822	April 11, 1822	77	
John Low	Lieutenant	240 00	1,722 66	N. C. do	June 21, 1820	April 5, 1819	80	Died June 8, 1826.
James Lett	Private	96 00	1,143 16	Do	Feb. 12, 1823	April 8, 1822	85	
Martin Martin	Do	96 00	1,441 03	S. C. do	June 9, 1820	March 1, 1819	78	
Archibald McCrery	Serg't maj.	96 00	534 19	N. C. do	Aug. 27, 1828	Aug. 12, 1828	89	
John Peace	Do	96 00	566 36	Maryland do	Jan. 5, 1821	April 11, 1820	79	
Thomas Pope	Private	96 00	43 43	Virginia do	April 10, 1822	Nov. 7, 1820	66	
William West	Do	96 00	1,339 87	S. C. do	April 13, 1821	March 17, 1820	71	
George Walker	Do	96 00	842 83	Virginia do	June 17, 1825	May 25, 1825	73	Dead. Reported June 30, 1825.

A statement showing the names, rank, &c., of persons residing in the district of Sumpter, in the State of South Carolina, who have been inscribed on the pension list under the act of Congress passed the 18th March, 1818.

NAMES.	Rank.	Annual allowance.	Sums received.	Description of service.	When placed on the pension roll.	Commencement of pension.	Ages.	Laws under which they were formerly inscribed on the pension roll; and remarks.
William Brown -	Private	96 00	1,510 09	S. C. cont'l line	May 17, 1819	June 12, 1818	83	
Peter David -	Do	96 00	1,445 88	Do	Do	Feb. 12, 1819	80	
Samuel Francis -	Do	96 00	821 63	Do	Nov. 20, 1819	Feb. 13, 1819	99	
Adam Gibhart -	Do	96 00	1,301 63	Maryland do	Do	Do	81	
Thomas Garrett -	Do	96 00	804 38	S. C. do	Dec. 13, 1825	Oct. 19, 1825	83	
David Garrett -	Do	96 00	321 32	Do	April 30, 1830	April 30, 1830	78	
Thomas Kolb -	Sergeant	96 00	-	Do	May 17, 1819	Feb. 13, 1819	-	
George St. George -	Private	96 00	166 09	Conn. do	Do	June 12, 1818	82	Dropped under act May 1, 1820.
James Scott -	Do	96 00	790 12	S. C. do	Do	Do	81	Do do
John Thompson -	Do	96 00	419 35	Do	Nov. 10, 1819	Oct. 22, 1819	79	

A statement showing the names, rank, &c., of persons residing in the district of Union, in the State of South Carolina, who have been inscribed on the pension list under the act of Congress passed the 18th March, 1818.

NAMES.	Rank.	Annual allowance.	Sums received.	Description of service.	When placed on the pension roll.	Commencement of pension.	Ages.	Laws under which they were formerly inscribed on the pension roll; and remarks.
John Bird - -	Lieut.	240 00	3,758 70	S. C. cont'l line	Jan. 8, 1819	July 7, 1818	77	
John Crawford - -	Private	96 00	584 57	Do	Sept. 23, 1819	Feb. 3, 1819	82	

Statement of the district of *Union*—Continued.

NAMES.	Rank.	Annual allowance.	Sums received.	Description of service.	When placed on the pension roll.	Commencement of pension	Ages.	Laws under which they were formerly inscribed on the pension roll; and remarks.
Charles Dick - -	Private	96 00	283 39	S. C. cont'l line	March 5, 1819	Oct. 15, 1818	88	Dropped under act May 1, 1820. Restored, commencing October 15, 1825. Died June 7, 1827.
Perry Evans - -	Do	96 00	152 21	Maryland do	July 20, 1819	Aug. 3, 1818	60	Dropped under act May 1, 1820.
Joshua Foster - -	Do	96 00	148 64	Virginia do	April 6, 1820	Aug. 18, 1818	67	Do do.
Thomas Owens - -	Do	96 00	-	Penn. do	March 5, 1819	Sept. 16, 1818	-	Do do.
Nicholas Rochester -	Do	96 00	148 64	N. C. do	Do	Aug. 18, 1818	68	Do do.
William Townsend -	Do	96 00	92 90	Virginia do	May 17, 1819	March 16, 1819	-	Do do.

A statement showing the names, rank, &c., of persons residing in the district of Williamsburgh, in the State of South Carolina, who have been inscribed on the pension list under the act of Congress passed March 18, 1818.

NAMES.	Rank.	Annual allowance.	Sums received.	Description of service.	When placed on the pension roll.	Commencement of pension.	Ages.	Laws under which they were formerly inscribed on the pension roll; and remarks.
Ludford Berry - -	Private	96 00	372 15	Virginia cont'l line	March 5, 1819	Oct. 20, 1818	79	Dropped under act May 1, 1820.
Samuel Bratcher -	Do	96 00	-	N. C. do	Do	Do	35	Do do.
Grant Knowlton -	Do	96 00	131 61	S. C. do	Do	Oct. 22, 1818	66	Do do.
Aaron Odam - -	Do	96 00	131 61	N. C. do	Do	Oct. 20, 1818	-	Do do.
Needham Perrit -	Do	96 00	83 89	Do do	Do	Do	72	Do do.
William Smith - -	Do	96 00	110 18	S. C. do	Sept. 22, 1819	Do	-	Died December 12, 1819.

A statement showing the names, rank, &c., of persons residing in the district of York, in the State of South Carolina, who have been inscribed on the pension list under the act of Congress passed March 18, 1818.

NAMES.	Rank.	Annual allowance.	Sums received.	Description of service.	When placed on the pension roll.	Commencement of pension.	Ages.	Laws under which they were formerly inscribed on the pension roll; and remarks.
Jesse Boswell - -	Private	96 00	967 42	Md. cont'l line	March 18, 1819	Oct. 27, 1818	73	Died November 23, 1828.
Peter Cherry - -	Sergeant	96 00	1,098 51	Penn. do	Jan. 31, 1820	March 23, 1819	81	Dropped under act May 1, 1820. Restored, com'g Sept. 8, 1823.
Daniel Gilmore - -	Private	96 00	1,474 32	Virginia do	March 5, 1819	Oct. 27, 1818	79	
Richard M. Head -	Cornet	240 00	2,174 33	Armand's legion	April 24, 1818	April 24, 1818	82	Died May 15, 1827.
Robert Marsh - -	Private	96 00	1,430 07	Virginia cont'l line	March 5, 1819	April 17, 1818	76	

A statement showing the names, rank, &c., of persons residing in the State of South Carolina,* who have been inscribed on the pension list under the act of Congress passed March 18, 1818.

NAMES.	Rank.	Annual allowance.	Sums received.	Description of service.	When placed on the pension roll.	Commencement of pension.	Ages.	Laws under which they were formerly inscribed on the pension roll; and remarks.
Isaac Smith - -	Sergeant	96 00	-	Virginia cont'l line	March 10, 1820	Feb. 8, 1820	-	Dropped under act May 1, 1820.

* District unknown.

A statement showing the names, rank, &c., of persons residing in the district of Anderson, in the State of South Carolina, who have been inscribed on the pension list under the act of Congress passed June 7, 1832.

NAMES.	Rank.	Annual allowance.	Sums received.	Description of service.	When placed on the pension roll.	Commencement of pension.	Ages.	Laws under which they were formerly inscribed on the pension roll; and remarks.
Jehu Atkinson	Private	20 00	50 00	Virginia line	July 19, 1833	March 4, 1831	74	
William Armstrong	Do	80 00	240 00	do	April 30, 1834	Do	69	
Reuben Broch	Pri. of cav.	25 00	75 00	S. C. militia	Feb. 14, 1833	Do	80	
William Brewster	Private	33 33	99 99	Do	May 16, 1833	Do	77	
Thomas Banister	Do	30 00	90 00	Do		Do	71	
Charles Bennett	Pri. & ser.	30 00	90 00	N. C. do	Aug. 17, 1833	Do	71	
Benjam'n Bowen	Private	46 66	139 98	N. C. troops	Dec. 7, 1833	Do	78	
James Brown	Do	75 10	225 30	S. C. do	April 19, 1834	Do	75	
Joshua Betterton	Do	50 00	150 00	Do	Do	Do	-	
John Bagwell	Do	26 66	-	N. C. line	May 14, 1834	Do	72	
Abraham Campbell	Do	45 00	-	S. C. do	May 16, 1833	Do	72	
Harmen Comins	Do	96 00	138 86	Virginia cont'l line	Nov. 26, 1819	March 25, 1819	-	
Do	Do	80 00	240 00	-	Nov. 5, 1833	March 4, 1831	75	Act March 18, 1818. Dropped under act May 1, 1820.
William Dodd	Do	22 31	66 93	S. C. troops	April 19, 1834	Do		
David Galtry	Bo	20 00	60 00	Virginia line	May 17, 1833	Do	70	
Aaron Guyton	Do	31 66	94 98	S. C. do	Oct. 24, 1833	Do	70	
John Harris	Do	54 43	163 29	Do	Dec. 9, 1833	Do	71	
Andrew Hood	Do	20 00		N. C. cont'l line	June 5, 1834	Do	90	
John Looney	Do	80 00	240 00	S. C. troops	April 8, 1834	Do	80	
William McIntosh	Do	80 00	240 00	Virginia cont'l line	Feb. 14, 1833	Do		
James Merret	Pri. of inf. & cav'y.	20 00	60 00	S. C. line	May 16, 1833	Do	71	
William Milwee	Pri. & cap.	36 97	92 42	N. C. do	Aug. 27, 1833	Do	79	
John Milford	Private	373 32	1,119 96	S. C. do	Oct. 21, 1833	Do	80	
Peter McMahon	Do	40 00	120 00	Do	Do	Do	74	
		80 00	200 00	N. C. do	Nov. 21, 1833	Do	78	
George Oldham	Ensign & captain.	120 00	360 00	Do	Aug. 7, 1833	Do	84	

Frederick Owen	Private	80 00	240 00	S. C. do	Oct. 21, 1833	Do	81
David Pressley	Do	48 33	144 99	Do	May 29, 1833	Do	70
Richard Reid	Do	33 33	99 99	Do	May 16, 1833	Do	71
George Reese	Do	27 54	68 85	N. C. do	Aug. 27, 1833	Do	81
John Scott	Do	23 33	69 99	S. C. do	May 17, 1833	Do	92
David Sadler	Do	76 66	229 98	Do	April 8, 1834	Do	72
John Wilson	Pri. of inf. & cav'y	58 33	174 99	N. C. do	May 17, 1833	Do	78
William Williamson	Private	21 55	64 65	Virginia cont'l line	Aug. 7, 1833	Do	69
John Wornoch	Do	80 00	-	S. C. do	June 16, 1834	Do	76

A statement showing the names, rank, &c., of persons residing in the district of Abbeville, in the State of South Carolina, who have been inscribed on the pension list under the act of Congress passed June 7, 1832.

NAMES.	Rank.	Annual allowance.	Sums received.	Description of service.	When placed on the pension roll.	Commencement of pension.	Ages.	Laws under which they were formerly inscribed on the pension roll; and remarks.
Thomas Anderson	Private	20 00	60 00	Virginia troops	Dec. 7, 1833	March 4, 1831	72	
John Black, 1st	Pri. of art.	50 88	152 64	S. Carolina militia	Feb. 16, 1833	Do	71	
Pollard Brown	Private	20 00	50 00	Virginia line	June 28, 1833	Do	71	
William Buckhanan	Do	52 11	130 27	S. C. do	Do	Do	72	
Joseph Black	Do	55 33	165 99	N. C. do	Jan. 9, 1834	Do	71	
Zachariah Carvil	Do	80 00	240 00	Virginia cont'l line	Dec. 28, 1832	Do	84	
James Conner	Do	30 00	75 00	N. C. do	Aug. 7, 1833	Do	72	
James Frazier	Do	43 33	107 32	S. C. do	May 29, 1833	Do	67	
John Finley	Do	60 00	180 00	Do	July 8, 1833	Do	74	
Frederick Gray	Pri, lieut, & captain	260 01	780 03	S. Carolina troops	Dec. 7, 1833	Do	76	
George Green	Private	53 33	159 99	S. Carolina line	April 19, 1834	Do	71	

Statement of the district of Abberville, South Carolina—Continued.

NAMES.	Rank.	Annual allowance.	Sums received.	Description of service.	When placed on the pension roll.	Commencement of pension.	Ages.	Laws under which they were formerly inscribed on the pension roll; and remarks.
John Hodges - -	Private	70 00	210 00	S. Carolina line	April 20, 1833	March 4, 1831	79	
Solomon Hall, sen. -	Do	52 78	158 34	N. C. cont'l line	Aug. 7, 1833	Do	77	
Andrew Logan - -	Do	27 21	68 02	S. Carolina line	April 20, 1833	Do	69	
Henry Livingston -	Do	24 66	73 98	S. Carolina troops	Dec. 7, 1833	Do	73	
Thomas Moore - -	Pri. of inf. & cavalry							
Joseph Moseley, sen.	Private	55 00	165 00	S. Carolina line	May 29, 1833	Do	70	
John McAdam - -	Do	20 00	50 00	Virginia do	July 19, 1833	Do	70	
George McFarlin -	Do	80 00	240 00	S. Carolina do	Aug. 7, 1833	Do	75	
Thomas Norwood -	Do	26 66	79 98	Do	Feb. 5, 1834	Do	70	
Samuel Pruett - -	Do	30 00	75 00	Do	May 29, 1833	Do	73	
Samuel Porter - -	Do	33 44	100 32	N. Carolina do	July 8, 1833	Do	84	
Alex. Patterson, sen.	Do	23 33	69 99	Do	Aug. 7, 1833	Do	71	
William Reeve - -	Do	71 88	-	S. Carolina do	April 8, 1834	Do	83	
Willis Scoggins -	Do	23 22	58 05	Virginia militia	May 29, 1833	Do	78	
Austin Smith - -	Do	41 10	123 30	N. C. cont'l line	April 20, 1833	Do	73	
Newell Walton - -	Do	28 88	86 64	S. Carolina line	Aug. 7, 1833	Do	71	
Simpson Warren -	Do	25 99	64 97	Virginia do	July 20, 1833	Do	71	
	Do	20 00	60 00	S. Carolina do	Feb. 5, 1834	Do	72	

32

A statement showing the names, rank, &c., of persons residing in the district of Barnwell, in the State of South Carolina, who have been inscribed on the pension list under the act of Congress passed June 7, 1832.

NAMES.	Rank.	Annual allowance.	Sums received.	Description of service.	When placed on the pension roll.	Commencement of pension.	Ages.	Laws under which they were formerly inscribed on the pension roll; and remarks.
Tarlton Brown	Lt. & cap. of inf.	356 00	1,068 00	S. C. cont'l line	June 10, 1833	March 4, 1831	77	

5

A statement showing the names, rank, &c., of persons residing in the district of Chesterfield, in the State of South Carolina, who have been inscribed on the pension list under the act of Congress passed June 7, 1832.

NAMES.	Rank.	Annual allowance.	Sums received.	Description of service.	When placed on the pension roll.	Commencement of pension.	Ages.	Laws under which they were formerly inscribed on the pension roll; and remarks.
Abraham Blackwell -	Private	80 00	240 00	S. Carolina militia	Feb. 17, 1834	March 4, 1831	81	
James James -	Do	80 00	-	N. Carolina do	April 17, 1834	Do	86	
James McMillan -	Pri. of cav.	100 00	-	S. C. cont'l line	May 8, 1834	Do	81	
William Roberts -	Private	20 00	60 00	S. C. militia	Oct. 21, 1833	Do	72	

33

A statement showing the names, rank, &c., of persons residing in the district of Colleton, in the State of South Carolina, who have been inscribed on the pension list under the act of Congress passed June 7, 1832.

NAMES.	Rank.	Annual allowance.	Sums received.	Description of service.	When placed on the pension roll.	Commencement of pension.	Ages.	Laws under which they were formerly inscribed on the pension roll; and remarks.
John Hiott, sen. -	Musician	88 00	264 00	S. C. cont'l line	Dec. 30, 1833	March 4, 1831	78	
Albert Strobel -	Private	46 66	139 98	S. Carolina militia	Dec. 18, 1833	Do	74	

A statement showing the names, rank, &c., of persons residing in the district of Chester, in the State of South Carolina, who have been inscribed on the pension list under the act of Congress passed June 7, 1832.

NAMES.	Rank.	Annual allowance.	Sums received.	Description of service.	When placed on the pension roll.	Commencement of pension.	Ages.	Laws under which they were formerly inscribed on the pension roll; and remarks.
James Adair -	Private	26 66	79 98	S. Carolina militia	April 20, 1833	March 4, 1831	82	
John Allen -	Pri. & ens.	40 00	120 00	N. Carolina do	April 8, 1834	Do	82	
James Anderson -	Pri. & lt.	190 00	570 00	S. Carolina do	Do	Do	76	
William Bobbit -	Pri. inf. and cav.	34 99	104 97	N. Carolina do	May 16, 1833	Do	73	
William Boyd -	Private	23 33	69 99	S. Carolina do	July 19, 1833	Do	68	
John Bishop -	Do	56 66	169 98	S. C. cont'l line	April 8, 1834	Do	69	
Stephen Crain -	Do	40 00	100 00	N. Carolina militia	Sept. 3, 1833	Do	74	
John Conn -	Do	66 66	199 98	N. C. cont'l line	March 8, 1834	Do	79	
John Caldwell -	Do	50 00	150 00	S. Carolina militia	April 8, 1834	Do	72	
Moses Grisham -	Do	80 00	240 00	Do	May 29, 1853	Do	75	
George Gill -	Pri. cav. and inf.	90 35	271 05	Do	June 28, 1833	Do	73	

Names.	Rank.	Annual allowance.	Sums received.	Description of service.	When placed on the pension roll.	Commencement of pension.	Ages.	Laws under which they were formerly inscribed on the pension roll; and remarks.
James Graham	Private	55 88	167 64	Do	Aug. 7, 1833	Do	73	
Joseph Gaston	Do	39 66	118 98	Do	April 4, 1834	Do	71	
James Harbison	Do	62 78	188 34	S. C. cont'l line	Aug. 31, 1833	Do	72	
Benjamin Jackson	Do	52 92	105 84	N. Carolina militia	May 16, 1833	Do	76	
James Jamieson	Pri., lt., & capt.	383 31	1,149 93	N. Carolina do	June 12, 1833	Do	71	
Joseph Morrow	Private	39 00	117 00	S. Carolina do	July 19, 1833	Do	74	
Thomas McClurken	Do	55 00	137 50	Do	Aug. 7, 1833	Do	78	
John McDill	Do,	29 00	72 50	Do	Do	Do	72	
Daniel McMillan	Do	41 55	124 65	Do	Oct. 18, 1833	Do	82	
James McCaw	Do	80 00	240 00	Do	April 8, 1834	Do	72	
Micajah Proctor	Do	32 33	80 82	Virginia do	May 16, 1833	Do	74	
Edward Steedman	Do	80 00	240 00	S. Carolina do	April 8, 1834	Do	74	
William White	Do	80 00	216 39	Do	Do	Do	80	
George Wier	Do	60 00	180 00	Do	Do	Do	82	Died November 18, 1833.

A statement showing the names, rank, &c., of persons residing in the district of Charleston, in the State of South Carolina, who have been inscribed on the pension list under the act of Congress passed June 7, 1832.

Names.	Rank.	Annual allowance.	Sums received.	Description of service.	When placed on the pension roll.	Commencement of pension.	Ages.	Laws under which they were formerly inscribed on the pension roll; and remarks.
Jeremiah Bunch	Private	55 33	159 99	S. Carolina militia	March 22, 1834	March 4, 1831	72	
Thomas Burbage	Do	80 00	240 00	Do cont'l	April 4, 1834	Do	74	
David N. Cardozo	Sergeant	60 00	180 00	Do militia	Aug. 3, 1833	Do	80	
John Cart	Pri. inf. & cav.	29 66	88 98	Do do	Oct. 16, 1833	Do	73	
William Hasell Gibbes	Lt art.	400 00	1,176 52	Do do	Dec. 26, 1832	Do	80	Died February 13, 1834.
John Girardeau	Private	80 00	240 00	Georgia do	March 25, 1834	Do	78	
Marks Lazarus	Pri. & ser.	28 33	84 99	S. Carolina do	Oct. 16, 1833	Do	77	
Solomon Legare	Private	68 00	204 00	Do cont'l	Do	Do	80	
Job Palmer	Do	22 33	66 99	Do militia	Do	Do	87	
	Do	50 00	150 00	do	Do	Do	73	

Statement of the district of Charleston, South Carolina—Continued.

NAMES.	Rank.	Annual allowance.	Sums received.	Description of service.	When placed on the pension roll.	Commencement of pension.	Ages.	Laws under which they were formerly inscribed on the pension roll; and remarks.
Samuel Rivers -	Private	80 00	240 00	S. Carolina militia	Jan. 6, 1834	March 4, 1831	83	
Joseph Righton	Sergeant	120 00	360 00	Do	June 20, 1834	Do		
Daniel Stevens -	Ser. & lt. art.							
Jacob Sass -	Lieut.	376 66	1,129 98	Do	March 31, 1834	Do	88	
		198 25	594 75	N. Carolina do	Oct. 16, 1833	Do	84	
James Wallace -	Private	80 00	240 00	Virginia do	June 28, 1833	Do	82	
Richard Wall -	Midship'n	144 00	432 00	Frigate Rd. P. Jones	Oct. 26, 1833	Do	80	

A statement showing the names, rank, &c., of persons residing in the district of Darlington, in the State of South Carolina, who have been inscribed on the pension list under the act of Congress passed June 7, 1832.

NAMES.	Rank.	Annual allowance.	Sums received.	Description of service.	When placed on the pension roll.	Commencement of pension	Ages.	Laws under which they were formerly inscribed on the pension roll; and remarks.
Thomas Goodson -	Private	80 00	240 00	S. C. cont'l line	March 22, 1833	March 4, 1831	72	
Ephraim Gaudy -	Do	60 00	-	S. Carolina militia	March 6, 1834	Do	82	
Jesse Hicks -	Do	20 00	-	N. Carolina do	April 19, 1834	Do	72	
Jehu Kolb -	Do	47 88	-	S. Carolina do	March 14, 1833	Do	76	
Nicholas Powers -	Pri. & ser.	103 04	309 12	S. C. cont'l line	Feb. 5, 1834	Do	78	
John Stewart -	Private	46 66	-	S. Carolina militia	May 15, 1834	Do	72	
Zachariah Winn -	Do	40 00	-	N. C. cont'l line	March 31, 1834	Do	73	
Henry Wilson -	Do	20 00	60 00	S. Carolina militia	April 10, 1834	Do	73	
Albert Fort -	Do	26 66	-	Do	April 28, 1834	Do	76	

A statement showing the names, rank, &c., of persons residing in the district of Edgefield, in the State of South Carolina, who have been inscribed on the pension list under the act of Congress passed June 7, 1832.

NAMES.	Rank.	Annual allowance.	Sums received.	Description of service.	When placed on the pension roll.	Commencement of pension.	Ages.	Laws under which they were formerly inscribed on the pension roll; and remarks.
Zachariah S. Brooks -	Private	40 00	120 00	S. Carolina militia	Feb. 14, 1833	March 4, 1831	69	
William Cooke -	Pri. cav.	100 00	300 00	Virginia cont'l line	July 8, 1833	Do	80	
Richard Christmas -	Private	20 00	-	N. Carolina militia	Dec. 14, 1833	Do	70	
Abner Corley -	Pri. inf. & cav.	55 00	165 00	S. Carolina do	Do	Do	76	
Robert Cochran -	Pri. & lt.	93 33	279 99	Do	March 8, 1834	Do	79	
William Flinn -	Private	47 00	141 00	Virginia do	Jan. 6, 1834	Do	74	
Drury Hearn -	Do	80 00	240 00	N. C. cont'l line	Jan. 24, 1833	Do	79	
William Howl, sen. -	Do	80 00	240 00	Georgia militia	July 8, 1833	Do	80	
Samuel Hammond -	Maj. & col.	600 00	1,800 00	Virginia do	July 11, 1833	Do	77	
Peter Hilyard -	Private	50 44	151 32	S. C. do	Jan. 20, 1834	Do	78	
Samuel Price -	Do	80 00	200 00	S. C. cont'l line	July 8, 1833	Do	82	
Daniel Rogers -	Do	73 33	219 99	S. Carolina militia	March 8, 1834	Do	73	
William S. Stubblefield -	Pri. & ser.	67 66	169 15	Virginia do	Sept. 20, 1833	Do	70	
William Wash -	Sergeant	120 00	360 00	Geo. & Va. do	Jan. 24, 1833	Do	81	

A statement showing the names, rank, &c., of persons residing in Fairfield district, in the State of South Carolina, who have been inscribed on the pension list under the act of Congress passed June 7, 1832.

NAMES.	Rank.	Annual allowance.	Sums received.	Description of service.	When placed on the pension roll.	Commencement of pension.	Ages.	Laws under which they were formerly inscribed on the pension roll; and remarks.
William Aiken -	Private	20 00	40 00	S. Carolina militia	May 21, 1833	March 4, 1833	74	
John Broom -	Do	27 77	83 31	Do	Sept. 18, 1833	Do	71	

Statement of the district of *Fairfield, South Carolina*—Continued.

NAMES.	Rank.	Annual allowance.	Sums received.	Description of service.	When placed on the pension roll.	Commencement of pension.	Ages.	Laws under which they were formerly inscribed on the pension roll; and remarks.
Cannon Cason - -	Private	40 00	120 00	S. Carolina militia	May 21, 1833	March 4, 1833	80	
Charnel Durham -	Pri. & cap.	263 33	789 99	do	May 21, 1833	Do	81	
William Hogan -	Private	35 33	-	do	Do	Do	74	
David Hamilton -	Pri. & q. m.	144 16	432 48	do	July 20, 1833	Do	75	
John Hollis -	Private	110 00	330 00	do	Sept. 20, 1833	Do	77	
Robert Kilpatrick -	Pri. & Lt.	102 50	307 50	do	April 8, 1834	Do	95	
John Lee -	Private	80 00	200 00	cont'l	April 18, 1833	Do	75	
Robert McCreight	Pri. & Lt.	151 88	455 64	militia	July 20, 1833	Do	73	
James Nelson, sen.	Private	29 66	88 98	do	Nov. 29, 1833	Do	86	
William Robertson -	Do	30 00	75 00	do	July 20, 1833	Do	74	
John Sullivan -	Pri. & ser.	94 83	284 49	do	Sept. 17, 1833	Do	74	
John Sloan -	Private	80 00	240 00	do	April 8, 1834	Do	73	
Jacob Stone -	Do	33 33	99 99	do	April 17, 1834	Do	76	
Meredith Taylor -	Do	46 66	116 65	do	May 21, 1833	Do	70	
Jeremiah Taylor -	Do	43 33	108 32	do	Do	Do	72	
Dixsey Ward -	Do	80 00	240 00	do	July 20, 1833	Do	74	
Bolling Wright -	Do	36 66	-	Virginia	May 31, 1834	Do	75	

A statement showing the names, rank, &c., of persons residing in Greenville district, in the State of South Carolina, who have been inscribed on the pension list under the act of Congress passed June 7, 1832.

NAMES.	Rank.	Annual allowance.	Sums received.	Description of service.	When placed on the pension roll.	Commencement of pension.	Ages	Laws under which they were formerly inscribed on the pension roll; and remarks.
James Altorn	Private	40 00	84 53	N. Carolina militia	April 18, 1833	March 4, 1831	81	Died April 15, 1833.
David Burn	Do	80 00	240 00	Do do	Dec. 3, 1832	Do	77	
John Brookshire	Do	55 00	165 00	Do do	April 17, 1834	Do	75	
Joel Callahan	Do	40 22	120 66	S. Carolina do	June 26, 1833	Do	80	
William Crane	Do	20 00	60 00	Do do	Nov. 21, 1833	Do	68	
Henry Cannon	Do	33 33	99 99	Virginia do	April 17, 1834	Do	83	
Benjamin Dispair	Do	26 66	79 98	N. Carolina do	April 20, 1833	Do	77	
Nathaniel Dacus	Do	20 00	50 00	S. Carolina do	May 17, 1833	Do	85	
Jonathan Davis	Do	32 44	-	N. Carolina do	April 8, 1834	Do	75	
David Dickey	Pri. & ser.	37 50	112 50	Do do	April 20, 1834	Do	87	
Philip Evans	Private	50 00	150 00	N. Carolina do	March 6, 1834	Do	75	
Shadrach Farmer	Do	33 33	99 99	S. Carolina do	July 8, 1833	Do	79	
John Farmer	Do	40 00	120 00	Do do	Do	Do	78	
John Goodlett	Do	24 88	74 64	Do do	April 17, 1834	Do	78	
Abraham Hester	Do	22 88	68 64	N. Carolina do	Nov. 21, 1833	Do	84	
Stephen Huff	Do	46 66	139 98	S. Carolina do	Feb. 5, 1834	Do	78	
Esle Hunt	Do	38 66	115 98	N. Carolina do	April 17, 1834	Do	76	
Ezekiel Henderson	Do	57 50	172 50	Do do	Do	Do	71	
Jacob Kytle	Pri. cor. & sergeant	90 66	271 98	Do cont'l	May 24, 1833	Do	74	
Lewis Land	Private	80 00	240 00	Virginia do	April 18, 1833	Do	72	
George Mitchell	Do	36 66	109 98	S. Carolina militia	Sept. 18, 1833	Do	82	
Samuel Melson	Do	80 00	240 00	N. Carolina do	March 6, 1834	Do	98	
Thomas Pander	Do	60 00	180 00	Do cont'l	July 8, 1833	Do	69	
Henry Prince	Do	40 00	120 00	S. Carolina line	April 8, 1834	Do	86	
John Waldrop	Do	33 33	66 66	N. Carolina do	April 20, 1833	Do	81	
Asa Wright	Do	80 00	-	Do cont'l	April 8, 1834	Do	75	
William Ward	Do	30 00	90 00	Do line	Do	Do	82	
John Young	Do	80 00	240 00	S. Carolina do	Sept. 18, 1833	Do	72	

A statement showing the names, rank, &c., of persons residing in the district of Horry, in the State of South Carolina, who have been inscribed on the pension list under the act of Congress passed the 7th June, 1832.

NAMES.	Rank.	Annual allowance.	Sums received.	Description of service.	When placed on the pension roll.	Commencement of pension.	Ages.	Laws under which they were formerly inscibed on the pension roll; and remarks.
Nicholas Prince	Pri. & gun'r	102 00	306 00	S. Carolina militia	Nov. 25, 1833	March 4, 1831	76	

A statement showing the names, rank, &c., of persons residing in the district of Kershaw, in the State of South Carolina, who have been inscribed on the pension list under the act of Congress passed June 7, 1832.

NAMES.	Rank.	Annual allowance.	Sums received.	Description of service.	When placed on the pension roll.	Commencement of pension.	Ages.	Laws under which they were formerly inscibed on the pension roll; and remarks.
John Brockington	Pri. cav.	46 80	140 40	S. C. militia	Feb. 9, 1833	March 4, 1831	70	
Nathaniel Jones	Pri. inf. cav.	56 83	142 07	Do	Feb. 5, 1834	Do	81	
Samuel Jones	Private	80 00	240 00	Virginia cont'l line	Jan. 10, 1834.	Do	71	
Kenneth McKaskell	Do	20 00	-	N. C. troops	March 12, 1834	Do	74	
William Nettles	Captain	480 00	1,200 00	S. C. militia	Aug. 29, 1832	Do	92	
David Scott	Private	96 00	166 09	N. C. cont'l line	May 17, 1819	June 12, 1818	-	
Do	Do	80 00	240 00	Do	July 14, 1832	March 4, 1831		Dropped under act May 1, 1820.

A statement showing the names, rank, &c., of persons residing in the district of Lancaster, in the State of South Carolina, who have been inscribed on the pension list under the act of Congress passed June 7, 1832.

NAMES.	Rank.	Annual allowance.	Sums received.	Description of service.	When placed on the pension roll.	Commencement of pension.	Ages.	Laws under which they were formerly inscribed on the pension roll; and remarks.
James Cunningham -	Private	21 33	-	S. Carolina militia	Dec. 18, 1833	March 4, 1831	72	
Do	Do	30 00	-	S. C. cont'l line	May 20, 1834	Do	72	
Robert Gault -	Do	40 00	100 00	S. Carolina militia	Aug. 27, 1833	Do	69	
Philip Gruber -	Do	80 00	240 00	Do	Nov. 21, 1833	Do	77	
James Holliman -	Do	20 00	50 00	N. Carolina do	Nov. 18, 1833	Do	84	
Samuel Love -	Do	80 00	240 00	S. Carolina do	Jan. 31, 1833	Do	-	
Thomas McDow -	Do	20 00	60 00	Do	Do	Do	90	
Thomas Mackey -	Do	33 33	99 99	Do	May 29, 1833	Do	72	
John McMurry -	Do	43 33	129 99	Do	Aug. 7, 1833	Do	83	
Henry Massey -	Pri.inf.& cavalry	63 33	189 99	Do	Feb. 5, 1834	Do	72	
William Owens -	Private	30 00	90 00	Do	Jan. 31, 1833	Do	-	
Wm. Valandingham -	Do	30 00	90 00	N. Carolina do	Jan. 30, 1833	Do	81	

A statement showing the names, rank, &c., of persons residing in the district of Laurens, in the State of South Carolina, who have been inscribed on the pension list under the act of Congress passed June 7, 1832.

NAMES.	Rank.	Annual allowance.	Sums received.	Description of service.	When placed on the pension roll.	Commencement of pension.	Ages.	Laws under which they were formerly inscribed on the pension roll; and remarks.
George Adams	Pri. inf. & cavalry	67 50	202 50	N. Carolina militia	Feb. 20, 1833	March 4, 1831	92	
David Anderson	Private	80 00	-	S. Carolina do	April 17, 1834	Do	69	
Abraham Bolt, sen.	Do	30 00	90 00	Do	Feb. 20, 1833	Do	71	
Andrew Burnsides	Do	23 33	69 99	Do	Do	Do	71	
Leonard Beasley	Pri. inf. & cavalry	22 50	45 00	Virginia militia		Do	67	
William Blakely	Private	21 10	52 75	S. Carolina do	Sept. 17, 1833	Do	74	
Thomas Blakely	Do	30 00	75 00	Do	Do	Do	79	
John Burns	Do	43 33	-	S. Carolina do	July 24, 1834	Do	74	
Robert Culbertson	Do	30 00	75 00	N. Carolina do	Nov. 9, 1833	Do	83	
John Colhoun	Do	40 00	120 00	N. C. cont'l line	Dec. 14, 1833	Do	77	
Ellis Check	Do	53 33	159 99	S. Carolina militia	April 17, 1834	Do	74	
William Dunlap	Do	80 00	240 00	S. Carolina do	Feb. 20, 1835	Do	79	
James Dillard	Pri. lieut. & capt.	160 00	480 00	S. Carolina do	June 12, 1834	Do	-	
Samuel Freeman	Private	20 00	50 00	S. Carolina do	Feb. 20, 1833	Do	69	
Paul Finley	Do	80 00	240 00	S. Carolina do	Dec. 2, 1833	Do	72	
Samuel Franks	Do	40 00	120 00	S. Carolina do	April 19, 1834	Do	70	
Arthur Fuller	Do	20 00	40 00	N. C. cont'l line	Dec. 16, 1832	Do	78	Transf. from Granville co. N. C.
Reuben Golding	Pri. & lt.	51 79	155 37	S. Carolina militia	Dec. 14, 1833	Do	91	
Robert Long	Private	40 00	-	S. Carolina do	July 24, 1834	Do	71	
Henry Meredith	Pri. inf. & cavalry	47 50	118 75	N. C. cont'l line	Dec. 28, 1832	Do	77	
John McMahan	Private	80 00	240 00	Virginia cont'l line	March 25, 1834	Do	79	
John Osborn	Do	26 66	79 98	Virginia militia	Feb. 20, 1833	Do	72	
Richard Owings	Do	40 00	100 00	S. Carolina militia	Do	Do	87	
James Pool, sen.	Do	40 00	120 00	Virginia militia	Do	Do	87	
Henry Pitts	Do	33 33	-	S. Carolina do	June 26, 1834	Do	75	

NAMES.	Rank.	Annual allowance.	Sums received.	Description of service.	When placed on the pension roll.	Commencement of pension	Ages.	Laws under which they were formerly inscribed on the pension roll; and remarks.
John Ridgeway	Do	60 00	180 00	S. Carolina militia	Nov. 29, 1833	Do	74	
Amos Strange	Pri. inf. & cavalry	27 27	68 17	N. Carolina do	Feb. 20, 1833	Do	75	
George F. Sloane	Ser. & mar.	56 66	169 98	Navy	March 15, 1834	Do	77	
Thomas Wilkes, sen.	Private	30 00	90 00	Virginia militia	Feb. 20, 1833	Do	75	
John Wait	Do	80 00	240 00	Virginia cont'l line	April 17, 1834	Do	77	
Calvin Williamson	Do	31 10	93 30	S. Carolina militia	April 19, 1834	Do	76	

A statement showing the names, rank, &c., of persons residing in Lexington district in the State of South Carolina, who have been inscribed on the pension list under the act of Congress, passed the 7th June, 1832.

NAMES.	Rank.	Annual allowance.	Sums received.	Description of service.	When placed on the pension roll.	Commencement of pension	Ages.	Laws under which they were formerly inscribed on the pension roll; and remarks.
Nedom Busby	Private	43 33	129 99	S. Carolina militia	April 19, 1834	March 4, 1831	82	
Jacob Fulmer	Do	40 00	120 00	Do	Do	Do	72	
John Lohner	Do	20 00	60 00	Do	Oct. 16, 1833	Do	70	
George Summer	Do	51 66	154 98	Do	Do	Do	75	

A statement showing the names, rank, &c., of persons residing in the district of Marlborough, in the State of South Carolina, who have been inscribed on the pension list under the act of Congress passed the 7th June 1832.

NAMES.	Rank.	Annual allowance.	Sums received.	Description of service.	When placed on the pension roll.	Commencement of pension.	Ages.	Laws under which they were formerly inscribed on the pension roll; and remarks.
Joshua Ammons	Private	80 00	168 19	S. C. cont'l line	May 16, 1833	March 4, 1831	77	Died April 11, 1833.
William Cox	Do	56 66	169 98	Do, militia	Oct. 26, 1833	Do	71	
Samuel Cox	Do	50 00	150 00	Do do	Dec. 7, 1833	Do	75	

Statement of the district of Marlborough, South Carolina—Continued.

NAMES.	Rank.	Annual allowance.	Sums received.	Description of service.	When placed on the pension roll.	Commencement of pension.	Ages.	Laws under which they were formerly inscribed on the pension roll; and remarks.
John Haskew	Private	26 66	79 98	S. Carolina militia	March 11,1833	March 4, 1831	81	
William Hodges	Do	26 66	79 98	Do do	July 20, 1833	Do	72	
William Johnson	Do	29 00	87 00	N. Carolina do	May 8, 1834	Do	75	
William Lister	Do	20 00	50 00	S. Carolina do	Aug. 7, 1833	Do	74	
John Morris	Pri. cav.	100 00	300 00	Virginia cont'l line	April 17, 1833	Do	75	Died August 31, 1833.
Jesse Miles	Private	50 00	124 52	S. Carolina do	Oct. 16, 1833	Do	72	
Sion Odom	Do	80 00	240 00	Do cont'l line	May 16, 1833	Do	79	
Lewis Stubbs	Do	40 00	100 00	Do militia	Aug. 27, 1833	Do		
William Stubbs	Do	56 66	169 98	Do	April 9, 1834	Do	86	

A statement showing the names, rank, &c., of persons residing in the district of Marion, in the State of South Carolina, who have been inscribed on the pension list under the act of Congress passed the 7th June, 1832.

NAMES.	Rank.	Annual allowance.	Sums received.	Description of service.	When placed on the pension roll.	Commencement of pension	Ages.	Laws under which they were formerly inscribed on the pension roll; and remarks.
John Booth	Private	80 00	240 00	S. Caroline militia	May 17, 1933	March 4, 1831	74	
Henry Braswell	Do	26 66	79 98	Do	Feb. 5, 1834	Do	68	
Ezekiel Daniel	Do	20 00	60 00	Do	Aug. 7, 1833	Do	69	
Archibald Kirby	Do	22 22	66 66	Do	Nov. 9, 1835	Do	70	
Levi Odom	Do	36 66	103 32	N. Caroline militia	April 17, 1833	Do	75	
Drura Pilkington	Do	80 00	200 00	Virginia do	May 2, 1833	Do	72	
Nathan Wittington	Do	21 10	63 30	S. Carolina do	April 3, 1833	Do	72	

A statement showing the names, rank, &c., of persons residing in the district of Newberry, in the State of South Carolina, who have been inscribed on the pension list under the act of Congress passed the 7th June, 1832.

NAMES.	Rank.	Annual allowance.	Sums received.	Description of service.	When placed on the pension roll.	Commencement of pension.	Ages.	Laws under which they were formerly inscribed on the pension roll; and remarks.
William Calmes	Pri. & lt.	130 00	390 00	Virginia militia	Feb. 20, 1833	March 4, 1831	72	
James Caldwell	Private	26 66	-	S. Carolina do	May 12, 1834	Do	76	
Henry Dominick	Do	26 66	53 32	Do do	Feb. 20, 1853	Do	77	
John Davis	Do	20 00	-	N. Carolina do	Jan. 9, 1833	Do	78	Died June 26, 1833.
John Floyd	Do	22 22	-	Pennsylvania do	May 20, 1834	Do	75	
Donald McDonald	Do	33 33	99 99	S. Carolina do	Feb. 20, 1833	De	77	
William Morrow	Do	21 55	-	N. Carolina do	Feb. 5, 1834	Do	67	
Thomas Perkins	Do	40 00	120 00	S. C. cont'l line	Feb. 20, 1833	Do	77	
John Ritchie	Do	80 00	240 00	S. Carolina militia	Do	Do	76	
Christopher Stockman	Do	20 00	-	N. Carolina do	May 20, 1834	Do	79	
Edward Thiveatt	Do	20 00	60 00	S. Carolina do	Feb. 20, 1833	Do	70	
Peter Weedman	Do	37 21	111 63	Do do	May 16, 1833	Do	78	
Peter Wilhelm	Do	20 22	40 44	Do do		Do	80	
David Watts	Do	80 00	240 00	Do do	March 12,1834	Do	78	

A statement showing the names, rank, &c., of persons residing in the district of Orangeburgh, in the State of South Carolina, who have been inscribed on the pension list under the act of Congress passed the 7th June, 1832.

NAMES.	Rank.	Annual allowance.	Sums received.	Description of service.	When placed on the pension roll.	Commencement of pension.	Ages.	Laws under which they were formerly inscribed on the pension roll; and remarks.
John Amaker	Private	26 66	53 32	S. Carolina militia	Feb. 12, 1833	March 4, 1831	77	
Leven Argor	Do	53 33	159 99	N. C. cont'l do	Feb. 5, 1834	Do	80	

Statement of the district of Orangeburgh, South Carolina—Continued.

NAMES.	Rank.	Annual allowance.	Sums received.	Description of service.	When placed on the pension roll.	Commencement of pension.	Ages.	Laws under which they were formerly inscribed on the pension roll; and remarks.
Lazarus Chaves	Private	46 66	139 98	S. Carolina militia	Feb. 6, 1833	March 4, 1831	77	
Daniel Carn	Pri. art'y	70 83	177 07	N. Carolina do	Sept. 5, 1833	Do	71	
Lewis Carn	Pri. cav.	70 83	177 07	Do	Dec. 14, 1833	Do	73	
George Fisher	Steward	120 00	360 00	S. Carolina do	Do	Do	76	
Erasmus Gibson	Private	30 00	90 00	Virginia do	Do	Do	74	
Jacob Haigler	Do	43 33	129 99	S. Carolina do	Do	Do	76	
Andrew Houser	Do	80 00	240 00	Do	Do	Do	79	
Jeremiah Jones	Do	35 83	107 49	N. Carolina do	March 8, 1834	Do	75	
Peter Oliver, sen.	Do	80 00	-	S. Carolina do	Dec. 24, 1833	Do	82	Died October 27, 1832.
William Paulling	Pri. cav.	41 66		Do	May 16, 1833	Do	67	
Hugh Philip	Private	60 00	180 00	New Jersey do	Dec. 14, 1833	Do	74	
Joseph Winningham	Do	33 33	99 99	S. Carolina do	Feb. 8, 1833	Do	71	

A statement showing the names, rank, &c., of persons residing in Pickens district, in the State of South Carolina, who have been inscribed on the pension list under the act of Congress, passed June 7, 1832.

NAMES.	Rank.	Annual allowance.	Sums received.	Description of service.	When placed on the pension roll.	Commencement of pension.	Ages.	Laws under which they were formerly inscribed on the pension roll; and remarks.
Jeoffrey Beck	Pri. inf. & cav.	42 50	127 50	N. Carolina militia	May 16, 1833	March 4, 1831	82	
Francis Bradley	Private	80 00	240 00	N. C. cont'l line	April 19, 1834	Do	82	
Richard Carver	Do	20 00	60 00	Virginia militia	May 16, 1833	Do	70	
James Carter	Do	30 00	90 00	S. Carolina do	May 18, 1833	Do	75	

Name	Rank	Sum 1	Sum 2	State / Line	Date	Date	Age	Remarks
Joseph Chapman	Pri. inf. & cav.	42 28	243 75	Do militia	Oct. 26, 1833	Do	88	
William Copeland	Pri. & cap.	81 25	125 00	· Do	March 5, 1834	Do	81	
Stafford Graham	Private	50 00	240 00	N. Carolina do	Feb. 14, 1833	Do	77	
John Gray	Do	80 00	80 31	Georgia do	June 28, 1833	Do	76	
John Gresham	Do	26 77	240 00	Virginia do	July 20, 1833	Do	75	
Benjamin Grist	Do	80 00	240 00	S. Carolina do	Sept. 18, 1833	Do	75	
William Guest	Do	80 00	720 00	N. Carolina do	April 19, 1834	Do	71	
David Humphreys, sr.	Captain	240 00	720 00	Do do	Feb. 14, 1833	Do	81	
William Hubbard	Private	41 55	124 65	S. Carolina do	May 17, 1833	Do	78	Died April 25, 1833.
Jesse Hall	Corporal	44 00	-	N. C. cont'l line	June 24, 1833	Do	74	
Ezekiel Howard	Private	20 00	60 00	Do militia	Oct. 23, 1833	Do	84	
David Hamilton	Do	80 00	240 00	Do cont'l line	April 8, 1834	Do	72	
Thomas Henderson	Lieuten't	520 00	960 00	S. Carolina militia	April 17, 1834	Do	81	
Jacob Jones	Private	96 00	173 41	N. C. cont'l line	April 3, 1819	May 15, 1818	81	Act March 18, 1818. Dropped under act May 1, 1820.
Do	Do	80 00	240 00	Maryland militia	May 16, 1833	March 4, 1831	77	
Elisha Jarvis	Do	20 00	60 00	Virginia cont'l line	Oct. 23, 1833	Do	77	
John Mason	Do	80 00	240 00	N. Carolina militia	April 20, 1833	Do	71	
Archibald McMahan	Do	50 00	150 00	Do	May 17, 1833	Do	75	
Jesse Nevelle	Do	80 00	240 00	S. Carolina do	July 20, 1833	Do	79	
Tilson Oliver	Do	30 00	90 00	N. Carolina do	May 18, 1833	Do	75	
John Peterson	Do	24 16	60 40	Do do	Feb. 14, 1835	Do	75	
John Richey	Do	56 66	169 98	Do do	April 19, 1834	Do	70	
James Southerland	Do	20 00	60 00	Do cont'l line	May 16, 1833	Do	75	
Buckner Smith	Do	80 00	240 00	Do militia	July 20, 1833	Do	79	
James Standridge	Do	20 00	60 00	Do	Oct. 24, 1833	Do	75	
John Thrift	Do	20 00	60 00	S. Carolina militia	July 20, 1833	Do	70	
Charles Taylor	Do	20 00	60 00	Virginia do	Sept. 20, 1833	Do	70	
George Vandever	Do	36 66	109 98	do	Feb. 14, 1834	Do	71	
John Verner	Do	48 32	-	S. C.	July 24, 1834	Do	70	
Levi Young	Do	31 55	94 65	Do	Oct. 26, 1833	Do	75	

47

A statement showing the names, rank, &c., of persons residing in the district of Richland, in the State of South Carolina, who have been inscribed on the pension list under the act of Congress passed June 7, 1832.

NAMES.	Rank.	Annual allowance.	Sums received.	Description of service.	When placed on the pension roll.	Commencement of pension.	Ages.	Laws under which they were formerly inscribed on the pension roll; and remarks.
Hicks Chappell -	Lt. & cap.	400 00	1,200 00	S. C. cont'l line	Jan. 9, 1834	March 4, 1831	77	
Benjamin Hodge -	Private	70 00	210 00	Do	May 4, 1833	Do	82	
Andrew Hamilton, sen. -	Captain	404 66	-	S. Carolina militia	March 31, 1834	Do		
Allen Jeffers -	Private	80 00	240 00	N. C. cont'l line	May 21, 1833	Do	80	
Thomas Parrott -	Do	80 00	240 00	S. Carolina militia	Oct. 16, 1833	Do	74	
Adam Team -	Do	53 33	159 99	Do	May 16, 1833	Do	74	

A statement showing the names, rank, &c., of persons residing in the district of Sumpter, in the State of South Carolina, who have been inscribed on the pension list under the act of Congress passed June 7, 1832.

NAMES.	Rank.	Annual allowance.	Sums received.	Description of service.	When placed on the pension roll.	Commencement of pension.	Ages.	Laws under which they were formerly inscribed on the pension roll; and remarks.
Ripley Copeland -	Private	96 00	48 00	N. C. cont'l line	Nov. 26, 1819	Oct. 10, 1819	73	Act March 18, 1818. Dropped under act May 1, 1820.
Do	Do	80 00	240 00	Do	Dec. 28, 1832	March 4, 1831	73	
John China, sen. -	Do	53 33	159 99	S. Carolina militia	Sept. 17, 1833	Do	69	
Staughan Conyers -	Do	30 00	90 00	Do	April 8, 1834	Do	70	
Peter Dubose -	Ens., lie't. & cap.	410 00	1,230 00	Do	June 21, 1833	Do	75	
Elijah Johnson, sen. -	Private	20 00	60 00	N. C. cont'l line	March 6, 1834	Do	80	
James Jenkins -	Do	40 00	120 00	S. Carolina militia	Mar. 12, 1834	Do	69	

Names	Rank	Annual allowance	Sums received	Description of service	When placed on the pension roll	Commencement of pension	Ages	Remarks
John Mayrant, sen.	Lt. navy	360 00	1,080 00	S. Carolina navy	April 17, 1833	Do	72	
William McIntosh	Pri. inf. & cav.	83 33	208 32	S. Carolina militia	May 4, 1833	Do		
William McElveen, sr.	Private	48 00	120 00	Do	August 7, 1833	Do	77	
John McDonald	Do	80 00	240 00	Do	Mar. 12, 1834	Do	75	
Redden McCoy	Ser. cav.	180 00	540 00	Do	June 7, 1834	Do	71	Died January 2, 1833.
Robert Roberts	Private	63 33	110 70	Do	Feb. 9, 1833	Do	85	
Richard Rawlins	Do	51 11	127 77	S. Carolina do	Oct. 21, 1833	Do	75	
James Spann	Do	80 00	222 14	S. Carolina do	March 1, 1833	Do	81	Died January 29, 1833.
Charles Spann	Do	33 33	99 99	N. Carolina do	May 16, 1833	Do	79	
Obadiah Spears	Do	65 11	195 33	N. Carolina do	April 19, 1834	Do	80	
William Vaughan	Pri. cav.	83 33	249 99	S. Carolina do	Jan. 24, 1834	Do	78	
Richard Williford	Pri. & ser.	40 00	-	N. Carolina do	Sept. 25, 1833	Do	79	
Joseph West	Private	80 00	240 00	S. Carolina do	Feb. 5, 1834	Io		Died January 18, 1834.
Thomas Wilson	Do	43 33	124 42	S. Carolina do	Mar. 12, 1834	Do	70	

A statement showing the names, rank, &c., of persons residing in the district of Spartansburgh, State of South Carolina, who have been inscribed on the pension list under the act of Congress, passed June 7, 1832.

Names	Rank	Annual allowance	Sums received	Description of service	When placed on the pension roll	Commencement of pension	Ages	Laws under which they were formerly inscribed on the pension roll; and remarks
James Byers	Private	23 33	69 99	S. Carolina militia	Sep. 25, 1833	March 4, 1831	73	
William Bishop	Do	33 33	99 99	Do	Oct. 18, 1833	Do	74	
Abraham Crow	Do	26 00	52 00	North Carolina do	April 17, 1833	Do	71	
Solomon Crocker	Do	26 66	79 98	South Carolina do	May 4, 1833	Do	77	
Anthony Crocker	Do	26 66	79 98	Do	Do	Do	76	
Paul Castlebury	Do	63 33	189 99	Georgia do	June 27, 1833	Io	73	
Edmund Clement	Do	80 00	240 00	Virginia do	Aug. 27, 1833	Do	75	
John Collins	Captain	480 00	1,440 00	South Carolina do	May 15, 1834	Do	80	
William Caldwell	Private	26 66	79 98	Georgia do	June 10, 1834	Do	70	
Henry Emerson	Do	30 00	75 00	N. C. cont'l line	Aug. 27, 1833	Do	71	

Statement of the district of Spartansburgh, South Carolina—Continued.

Names.	Rank.	Annual allowance.	Sums received.	Description of service.	When placed on the pension roll.	Commencement of pension.	Ages.	Laws under which they were formerly inscribed on the pension roll; and remarks.
Thomas Farrow	Pri. & lt.	293 99	881 97	N. Carolina militia	Jan. 24, 1834	March 4, 1831	79	
Isaac Gordin	Private	31 11	93 33	Virginia cont'l line	April 17, 1833	Do	80	
William Goode	Do	80 00	240 00	Maryland do	April 17, 1834	Do	72	
Absalom Hastin	Do	43 00	107 50	Virginia militia	Aug. 27, 1833	Do	73	
Drury Hutchinson	Do	40 00	120 00	Do	May 8, 1834	Do	89	
Thomas Hanna	Lt. & cap.	320 00	960 00	S. C. do	July 8, 1834	Do	75	
Howell Johnson	Private	20 00	60 00	Virginia do	Aug. 27, 1833	Do	72	
Rowland Johnson	Do	21 66	64 98	Do	Sept. 25, 1833	Do	76	
Ellis Johnson	Do	50 22	150 66	S. C. do	April 28, 1834	Do	74	
John King	Do	96 00	96 51	Virginia cont'l line	May 17, 1819	March 3, 1819	76	Act March 18, 1818. Dropped der act May 1, 1820.
Do	Do	80 00	240 00	Do	Nov. 2, 1832	March 4, 1831		
James Lawrence	Do	53 33	159 99	Virginia militia	Oct. 18, 1833	Do	74	
Samuel Morrow	Pri. & cor.	81 32	243 96	S. C.	Mar. 28, 1834	Do	75	
John Meadows	Private	43 33		do	April 28, 1834	Do	72	
Reuben Newman	Do	80 00	240 00	N. C. cont'l line	June 6, 1833	Do	77	
Samuel Noblit	Do	30 00	90 00	Pennsylv'a militia	April 12, 1833	Do	90	
John Osheals	Do	80 00	240 00	S. Carolina do	Mar. 12, 1834	Do	73	
Drury Parham	Do	63 33	189 99	S. Carolina do	March 2, 1833	Do	77	
William Pollard	Do	34 66	103 98	Virginia do	April 17, 1834	Do	75	
George Roebuck	Do	95 00	101 03	N. C. cont'l line	June 4, 1819	Feb. 15, 1819	77	Act March 18, 1818. Dropped under act May 1, 1820.
Do	Do	80 00	240 00	Do	Mar. 27, 1833	March 4, 1831		
Joshua Richards	Pri. inf. & cav.	42 50	127 50	N. Carolina militia	Oct. 22, 1833	Do	74	
William Smith	Captain	480 00	1,200 00	N. Carolina do	March 2, 1833	Do	83	
James Seay	Private	96 00	126 09	Virginia cont'l line	Feb. 9, 1819	Nov. 13, 1818	79	Act March 18, 1818. Dropped under act May 1, 1820.
Do	Do	80 00	240 00	Do	April 18, 1833	March 4, 1831		
Ephraim Sizemore	Private	30 00	90 00	Virginia militia	Aug. 27, 1833	March 4, 1831	86	

Names	Rank	Annual allowance	Sums received	Description of service	When placed on the pension roll	Commencement of pension	Age
James Tinsley	Do	80 00	200 00	S. Carolina militia	Feb. 28, 1833	March 4, 1831	74
John Thomas	Do	40 00	120 00	Virginia cont'l line	July 8, 1833	Do	81
Golding Tinsley	Do	68 33	-	N. Carolina do	March 6, 1834	Do	76
Thomas Vaughan	Do	80 00	240 00	Virginia militia	Oct. 26, 1833	Do	73
John Vaughan	Do	21 10	63 30	Virginia do	April 17, 1834	Do	74
John Wood	Do	20 00	60 00	Virginia do	Aug. 27, 1833	Do	76
Daniel White	Do	34 88	87 20	N. C. do	Do	Do	73
Newman Wilson	Do	40 00	100 00	Do	Aug. 31, 1833	Do	78
William Wingo	Do	80 00	-	Virginia do	June 5, 1834	Do	74

A statement showing the names, rank, &c., of persons residing in the district of Union, in the State of South Carolina, who have been inscribed on the pension list, under the act of Congress passed June 7, 1832.

Names	Rank	Annual allowance	Sums received	Description of service	When placed on the pension roll	Commencement of pension	Age	Laws under which they were formerly inscribed on the pension roll; and remarks.
Richard Addis	Private	$60 00	180 00	S. Carolina militia	July 19, 1833	March 4, 1831	86	
Christopher Brandon	Do	80 00	240 00	Do do	March 2, 1833	Do	70	
William Bailey	Do	80 00	240 00	Virginia do	April 17, 1833	Do	74	
Henry Cogburn	Do	33 77	84 42	N. Carolina do	July 19, 1833	Do	85	
Mordecai Chandler	Do	80 00	240 00	Do do	Jan. 20, 1834	Do	72	
Daniel Crownover	Do	20 00	-	S. Carolina do	Do	Do	71	
John Gibson	Do	20 00	50 00	Virginia do	April 20, 1833	Do	86	
James Guthery	Do	40 44	121 32	N. C. cont'l line	Sept. 25, 1833	Do	78	
Daniel Holder	Do	46 66	139 98	S. Carolina militia	March 2, 1833	Do	76	
James Hollis	Do	66 00	198 00	N. C. cont'l line	June 6, 1833	Do	77	
John Hodge	Private	23 33	57 32	N. Carolina militia	Aug. 31, 1833	Do	72	
Drury Harrington	Pri. & Lt.	116 66	349 98	Do do	April 17, 1834	Do	81	
James Jeter	Private	43 66	109 15	S. Carolina do	Sept. 20, 1833	Do	75	
William McBride	Sergeant	35 00	105 00	N. Jersey do	April 20, 1833	Do	78	
William Mitchell	Private	20 00	60 00	Virginia cont'l line	July 8, 1833	Do	75	
James Mosely, sen.	Do	27 44	68 60	S. Carolina militia	Aug. 7, 1833	Do	77	
James McDonald	Do	43 33	129 99	Do do	Jan. 20, 1834	Do	77	

Statement of *Union district, South Carolina*—Continued.

NAMES.	Rank.	Annual allowance.	Sums received.	Description of service.	When placed on the pension roll.	Commencement of pension.	Ages.	Laws under which they were formerly inscribed on the pension roll; and remarks.
James McWhiter	Private	32 33	-	S. Carolina militia	July 1, 1834	March 4, 1831	74	
Sherwood Nance	Do	33 33	99 99	N. C. cont'l line	July 8, 1833	Do	80	
Stephen Neal	Do	40 00	120 00	N. Carolina militia	Jan. 20, 1834	Do	72	
Hancock Porter	Do	45 33	129 99	S. Carolina de	July 8, 1833	Do	79	
Joshua Palmer	Pri. & cap.	280 00	700 00	Do do	Aug. 7, 1833	Do	84	
Matthew Patton	Captain	260 00	780 00	Do do	Mar. 14, 1834	Do	77	
Daniel Palmer	Private	44 66	133 98	Virginia do	May 8, 1834	Do	78	
Nathaniel Rogers	Do	46 66	139 98	S. Carolina do	Sept. 17, 1833	Do	73	
James Smith	Do	30 00	90 00	Do do	July 8, 1833	Do	83	
Thomas Sanders	Do	37 21	111 63	Do do	Do	Do	76	
Edmond Simpson	Do	43 33	86 66	N. Carolina do	July 19, 1833	Do	69	
Samuel Smith	Do	30 00	90 00	S. Carolina do	Sept. 31, 1833	Do	79	
James Tracy, sen.	Do	53 33	159 99	Do do	July 19, 1833	Do	74	
John Van Lew	Do	36 66	109 98	N. Jersey do	April 20, 1833	Do	79	

A statement showing the names, rank, &c. of persons residing in the district of York, in the State of South Carolina, who have been inscribed on the pension list under the act of Congress passed the 7th June, 1832.

NAMES.	Rank.	Annual allowance.	Sums received.	Description of service.	When placed on the pension roll.	Commencement of pension.	Ages.	Laws under which they were formerly inscribed on the pension roll; and remarks.
Jeremiah Blalock	Private	$20 00	$50 00	S. Carolina militia	Feb. 10, 1833	March 4, 1831	80	
Jacob Black	Do	72 33	216 99	Do	Feb. 16, 1833	Do	76	
John Black, 2d	Do	35 67	107 01	Do	Do	Do	80	

Name	Rank	Amount		State / Line	Date		Age
Joseph Bingham	Do	35 55	106 65	Do	Do	Do	74
Thomas Baily	Artificer	144 00	432 00	Do	May 17, 1833	Do	78
Samuel Burns	Private	30 00	75 00	Pennsylvania militia	July 8, 1833	Do	78
James Campbell	Do	28 21	70 52	N. Carolina do	April 22, 1833	Do	79
John Clark	Pri. & adj.	169 99	424 97	S. Carolina do	June 27, 1833	Do	87
William Clark	Private	26 99	80 97	N. Carolina do	Dec. 24, 1833	Do	74
George Davis	Do	26 66	79 98	S. Carolina do	July 8, 1833	Do	70
Andrew Floyd	Pri. & adj.	120 22	360 66	Maryland cont'l line	Jan. 9, 1834	Do	85
James B. Fulton	Private	22 00	66 00	N. Carolina militia	March 14, 1834	Do	69
James Glenn	Do	50 00	150 00	S. Carolina do	Sept. 24, 1833	Do	75
Samuel Henderson	Do	43 33	108 32	N. Carolina do	Feb. 2, 1833	Do	79
Richard Horseley	Do	33 33	99 99	S. C. cont'l line	April 3, 1833	Do	79
Robert Hanna	Pri. & lt.	186 66	559 98	S. Carolina militia	June 12, 1833	Do	73
Samuel Hutchison	Private	94 66	236 65	Do	Oct. 16, 1833	Do	80
Joseph Jamieson	Do	24 10	72 30	Do	Feb. 4, 1833	Do	70
Andrew Kerr	Do	28 21	70 52	Do	May 17, 1833	Do	78
John Kenmoure	Do	50 00	125 00	N. C. cont'l line	July 19, 1833	Do	74
Joseph Moss	Do	80 00	240 00	S. Carolina militia	Feb. 23, 1833	Do	83
Thomas Martin	Pri. cav.	25 00	62 50	Do	April 22, 1833	Do	78
James Martin	Captain	480 00	1,440 00	N. Carolina do	May 4, 1833	Do	79
John Moore	Private	20 00	60 00	S. Carolina do	Feb. 5, 1834	Do	79
Daniel Quinn	Do	76 66	229 98	S. Carolina do	June 28, 1833	Do	74
John Rooker	Do	43 33	108 32	Do	Feb. 2, 1833	Do	79
Henry Rea	Do	80 00	240 00	Do	June 12, 1833	Do	75
William Summerford	Do	40 00	120 00	s. C. cont'l line	May 29, 1833	Do	72
Robert Wilson	Do	80 00	240 00	S. Carolina militia	Jan. 16, 1833	Do	76
Aaron Wood	Do	63 33	158 32		Feb. 2, 1833	Do	77

The "Best Friend of Charleston" was the first locomotive entirely built in this   country:

THE NAMES,

AS FAR AS CAN BE ASCERTAINED OF THE

OFFICERS

WHO SERVED IN THE

SOUTH CAROLINA REGIMENTS

ON THE CÓNTINENTAL ESTABLISHMENT

PREPARED BY

WILMOT G. DeSAUSSURE.

PUBLISHED BY ORDER OF THE GENERAL ASSEMBLY, 1886.

This list is made from the Journals of the Provincial Congress, so far as the same have been accessible; from the Journals of the Council of Safety, so far as the same have been accessible; from Moultrie Revolution, from Ramsay Revolution, from such orderly books of General William Moultrie and General Francis Marion as are accessible, from various books relating to the Revolution, from extracts from the revolutionary muster-rolls, &c., on file in the Department of State at Washington, and from whatever other sources information on this subject could be gathered.

The list is doubtless imperfect, but so many names as are here gathered, are by this list preserved from oblivion.

Adair, William	Lieutenant 6th Regiment	
Alexander Charles	" " "	
Alexander, Nathaniel	Surgeon's mate	
Anderson, David	Captain 5th Regiment	
Armstrong, John	" " "	Died 3d October, 1778.
Armstrong, Robert.	Lieutenant 1st Regiment	
Armstrong, William	Major " "	
Ashby, Anthony	Lieutenant 2d Regiment	Resigned Feb. 16, 1778.
Axson, Samuel J	Surgeon's mate	
Airs, ——	Surgeon	Died ——, 1777.
Bailey, ——	Lieutenant 3rd Regiment	Killed Savannah, 9th October. 1779.
Baker, Jesse	Captain " "	
Baker, Richard Bohun	" 2nd "	
Barnwell, John	" 1st "	Resigned, Dec. 11, 1775.
Beekman, Barnard	Colonel 4th Regiment Art'y	
Beekman, Samuel	Lieutenant — Regiment	
Belin, Allard	" 1st "	" 1777.

GATEWAY TO FORTUNE WOODS PARK. CAPTAIN JOHN BUCHANAN, A SOLDIER OF THE REVOLUTION, GAVE THIS TRACT OF LAND TO HIS SLAVE, FORTUNE, WHEN HE GAVE HIM HIS FREEDOM. FORTUNE ACTED AS BODY-SERVANT TO LAFAYETTE WHEN THE LATTER WAS IN CAMP WITH CAPTAIN BUCHANAN AT GEORGE-TOWN DURING THE REVOLUTION.

OLD HIBBEN HOUSE, MT. PLEASANT, S. C., NEAR CHARLESTON. HERE STAYED GEN. WILLIAM MOULTRIE, GENERAL PINCKNEY AND OTHER CONTINENTAL OFFICERS ON PAROLE WHEN THE BRITISH OCCUPIED CHARLES-TON IN 1781. WASHINGTON VISITED HERE IN 1791.

Blake, John	Lieutenant 2d Regiment	Resigned April 25, 1778.
Blameyer, William	Captain 5th "	" Nov. 1778.
Bowie, John	" " "	[tober 1779.
Boyce, Alexander	" 6th "	Killed Savannah, 9th Oc-
Boykin, Francis	Lieutenant 3d Regiment	
Bradwell, Nathaniel	" 1st "	
Bremar, Francis	Dep. Must. Mast.	
Brown, Charles	Lieutenant 1st Regiment	
Brown, John	Captain 5th "	
Brown, Richard	" 3d "	
Brown, William	" 6th "	Resigned Dec, 1778
Brownfield, Robert	Surgeon's mate	
Brownson, Nathaniel	Dep. Sun. Med. Dep't	
Buchanan, John	Captain 3d Regiment	
Budd, John Shivers	Surgeon 4th Reg't Artillery	
Burke, Ædanus	Lieutenant 2d Regiment	Resigned 22d Feb., 1778.
Bush, John	" " "	Killed Savannah, 9th Oc-
Buchanan, ——	" " "	[tober, 1779.
Brown, Benjamin	" 6th '.	
Baker, S	" " "	
Caddett, ——	Lieutenant — Regiment	
Caldwell, John	Captain 3d "	
Caldwell, William	" " "	
Cameron, Allan	Lieutenant " "	
Capers, William	" 2d "	
Carne, John	Ass't Dep't Apothecary	
*Caltell, Benjamin	Captain 1st Regiment	
*Caltell, William	" " "	
Charnock, William	" 2d "	Resigned Nov. 25, 1778.
Chesnut, John	Paymaster 3d Regiment	
Cleiland. John	Surgeon's mate 3d Reg't	
Cogdell, George	Captain 5th Reg't	
Coit, ——	" 6th "	Resigned Sept. 3, 1778.
Conyers, Clement	" 5th "	
Cooper, Leonard	" " "	
Crowther, Isaac	Lieutenant 3d Regiment	
Corterier, John	Capt. — Reg't Lt, Drag.	
Cole, ——	Ensign 2d "	
Daniel, John	Lieutenant — Regiment	
Dark, John Sandford	Paymaster 1st "	
Davis, Harman	Captain — "	
Davis, John	Lieutenant 3d "	
Davis, William Ransom	Captain 5th "	
DeBraham, ——	Major Engineers	
D'Ellient, Andrew	Brigade Major	[tober, 1779.
DeSaussure, Louis	Lieutenant 3d Regiment	Killed Savannah, 9th Oc-
DeTreville, John LaB	Captain 4th Reg't Art'y	
Deveaux, ——	"	
Dickenson, Benjamin	Lieutenant 1st Regiment	
Dixon, Henry	Brigade Inspector	[1779.
Doggatt. ——	Captain 6th Regiment	Killed, Stono, June 20,
Donaldson, James	Captain 3rd Regiment	[tober, 1779.
Donnom, William	" 4th Reg't Art'y	Killed, Savannah, 9th Oc-
Downes, William	Adjutant 2nd Regiment	Resigned 6th October,
D'Oyley, Daniel	Captain 1st Regiment	[1878.
Drayton, Charles	" 4th Reg't Ar'y	
Drayton, Glen	Lieutenant 2nd Regiment	Resigned August, 1779.
Drayton, Stephen	Dep. Quartermaster Gen'l	
Dubose, Isaac	Lieutenant 2nd Regiment	[tober, 1779.
Dubois, David	Captain — Reg't Drag.	Killed, Savannah, 9th Oc-
Duff, James	" 6th Regiment	
Dunbar, Thomas	Lieutenant 2d Regiment	
Dunham, ——	Captain 4th Reg't Art'y	
Dutarque, Louis	Lieutenant 3d Regiment	Resigned Jan. 30, 1776.
Doggatt, Joel	" 6th "	
Earle, Samuel	Captain 5th Regiment	
Edmunds, David	Lieutenant — Regiment	
Elliott, Barnard	Lieut. Col. 4th "	Died 5th October, 1778.
Elliott, Joseph	Lieutenant 1st "	Died.
Elliot, Thomas	" 2d "	
Esom, John	Adjutant 3d "	
Evance, Thomas	Paymaster 2d "	Died 18th Dec., 1777.
Evans, George	Lieutenant " "	
Eveleigh, George	" " "	Died ——, 1777.
Eveleigh, Michael	Captain — "	Probably a mistake for
Eveleigh, Nicolas	Dep. Adjutant General	[Nicholas Eveleigh.

* So in printed pamphlet, but believed to be misprint for *Cattell.*

15

Edmunds, David	Lieutenant — Regiment	Died ——, 1778.
Farr, John	Lieutenant 2d Regiment	
Farrar, Field	Captain 3d "	
Farrar, Thomas	Lieutenant — "	
Fayssoux, Peter	Paymaster and Surgeon	
Ferguson, ——	Major 3d Regiment	
Field, James	Lieut. 4th Reg't Art'y	
Fildloath, ——	" " "	
Fisby, ——	Lieut 2d Bat. Lt. Inf'y	
Fishburne, William	Lieutenant 1st Regiment	
Fitzpatrick, William	" 3d "	Resigned Aug. 24, 1778.
Flagg, Henry C.	Surgeon — "	
Foissin, Peter	Lieutenant 2d Regiment	[15th March, 1781.
Forbes, John	Captain — "	Killed, Guilford C. H.,
Ford, Tobias	Lieutenant — Regiment	
Fraser, Alexander	" 1st "	
Frierson, John	" 2d "	
Fuller, Richard	" 1st "	Died.
Gadsden, Christopher	Brigadier General	Resigned ——. 1777.
Gadsden, Thomas	Captain 1st Regiment	
Galvan, William	Lieutenant 2d Regiment	Resigned 5th July, 1778.
Garden, Alexander	Cornet Lee's Legion	[tober, 1779.
Gaston, Robert	Lieutenant 3d Regiment	Killed, Savannah, 9th Oc-
Gervais, John Lewis	Dep. Paym'r Gen., S. Dep.	
Giles, Thomas	Capt. — Reg't Lt. Drag.	
Glover, Wilson	Lieutenant 1st Regiment	
Goodwyn, John	Captain " "	
Goodwyn, John	" 4th Reg't Art'y	
Goodwyn, Richard	Capt. — Reg't Lt. Drag.	
Goodwyn, Robert	Captain 3d Regiment	Resigned May 30, 1778.
Goodwyn, Uriah	" 2d "	
Goodwyn, William	Lieutenant 3d Regiment	Resigned May 30, 1778.
Gray, George	" 1st "	Lost on schr Randolph.
Gray, Henry	" 2d "	Resigned Dec. 15, 1777.
Gray, James	" 2d "	Killed, Savannah, 9th Oc-
Gray, Peter	Captain 2d "	[tober, 1779.
Grayson, John	Lieut. 4th Reg't Art'y	
Grimke, John F	Lieut. Col. Dep. Adj. Gen.	
Guerry, Samuel	Lieutenant 2d Regiment	Died 12th July, 1779.
Guerry, Stephen	Captain 5th "	Resigned August, 1779,
Gould, ——	Surgeon 1st Regiment	
Gordon, ——	Lieutenant 5th Regiment	
Hall, John	Quartermaster 2d Reg't	
Hall, Thomas	Captain " "	
Hambleton, ——	Lieutenant — "	
Hamilton, John	" 1st "	
Hampton, John	Capt. — Reg't Lt. Drag.	
Hampton, Richard	Lt. Col. — Reg't Lt. Drag.	
Hampton Wade	" " " "	
Hardaway, Joel	Lieutenant 1st Regiment	
Harleston, Isaac	Major 6th "	
Harthorn, Joseph	Captain 6th "	Resigned Aug. 9, 1778.
Hart, John	" 2d "	
Hart, Oliver	Surgeon	
Hazzard, William	Lieutenant 1st Regiment	
Healtey, Charles	" 3d "	Resigned Jan. 30, 1776.
Heard, John	Lt. Fireworker 4th Reg't	
Henderson, William	Lieut Col. 6th Regiment	
Hennenton, John	Lieutenant " "	
Hext, William	Captain 1st "	
Hodges, Benjamin	Lieutenant 3d "	
Hogan, ——	Captain 5th "	
Hopkins, David	" 1st "	
Horry, Daniel,	" " "	
Horry, Peter	Lieut. Col. 2d "	
Hourston, James	Surgeon	[May, 1779.
Huger, Benjamin	Major 5th Regiment	Killed, Charlestown, 11th
Huger, Francis	Captain 1st Regiment	
Huger, Isaac	Brigadier General	[tober, 1779.
Hughes, Henry	Lieutenant 1st Regiment	Killed, Savannah, 9th Oc-
Hume, Alexander	" 2d "	
Hyrne, Edmund	Lieut. Col. Dep. Adj. Gen.	
Heyward, William	Lieutenant 1st Regiment	Resigned 22d Oct., 1777.

Hampton, Henry	Captain 6th Regiment	
Imhoff, John L. S.	Lieutenant 3d Regiment	
Joor, Joseph	Lieutenant 2d Regiment.	
Jackson, Bazil	" — "	Lost on schr. Randolph
Jackson, William	Captain 1st "	
Jenkins, Joseph	Lieutenant 1st "	
Jewey, Thomas	Capt. Dep. Must. Mast.	
Johnson, Robert	Hospital Physician	Resigned Nov. 1778.
Jones, John	Lieutenant 3d Regiment	
Jones Richard	" " "	
Jervey, ——	Captain 5th "	
Jones, ——	Lieutenant 5th "	
*Kaltiesen, Michel	Capt. Wagonmaster Gen'l	
Knap, John	Lieutenant 1st Regiment	
Keith, Alexander	Capt. 3d "	
Kennedy, James	Lieutenant 1st "	
Kershaw, Ely	Captain 3d "	Resigned October, 1777.
Kirkland, Moses	" " "	
Kobb, Josiah	Lieutenant 2d "	
Lacy, James	Lieutenant 6th Regiment	Died December 20, 1778.
Ladson, James	" 2d "	
Langford, Daniel	" " "	
Laurens, John	Lieut. Col. of D. C	Killed, Combahee, Aug.
Legare, James	Lieutenant 2d Regiment	[27, 1781.
Lesesne, Thomas	Captain " "	Resigned 6th Aug. 1779.
Levacher, St. Marie	" 1st "	
Liddell, George	Lieutenant 3d "	
Lining, Charles	Captain 1st "	
Leston, Thomas	Lieutenant — Regiment	
Lisle, John	" 3d "	Resigned August, 1779.
Lloyd, Benjamin	" — "	
Lloyd Edward	' " "	
Lochman, John	Surgeon	
Lyell, Robert	Captain 3d Regiment	
Lynch, Thomas, Jr	" 1st "	
La Marzell, ——	Lieutenant 4th Regiment	Resigned ——, 1777.
Love, William	" 3d "	
Maham, Hezekiah	Capt. 5th Reg't Lt. Col. Regiment Light Drag.	
Marion, Francis	Lieut. Col. 2d Regiment	
Marion, Gabriel, Jr	Lieutenant " "	Killed ——, 1781.
Martin, James	Surgeon	
Martin, John	Captain 2d Regiment	
Mason, Luke	Lieutenant 3d Regiment	
Mason, Richard	Captain 2d "	
Mason, William	" 1st "	
Massey, William	Adjutant 1st "	
Mayson, James	Lieut. Col. 3d "	
Mazyck, Daniel	Captain 2d "	
Mazyck, Stephen	Lieutenant 2d "	
McDonald, Adam	Captain 1st "	Died ——, 1778.
McDonald, James	" " "	
McGinnis, Charles	Lieutenant — Regiment	
McGuire, Merry	" 2d "	
McIntosh, Alexander	Major " "	
McQueen, Alexander	Lieutenant 1st "	
Middleton, Hugh	" 3d "	
Middleton, John	Cornet Lee's Legion	
Milling, Hugh	Capt. Lieut. 6th Regiment	
Mitchell, Ephraim	Major — Regiment	
Mitchell, James	Captain 4th Reg't Art'y	
Mitchell, William	Lt. Fireworker 4th Reg't	
Monaghan, David	Lieutenant 3d Regiment	Resigned 24th, ——, 1775.
Moore, Francis	Major	[October, 1779.
Moore, Henry	Lieut. 4th Reg't Art'y	Killed, Savannah, 9th
Motte, Charles	Captain 2d Regiment	Resigned Sept. 23, 1778.
Motte, Isaac	Lieut. Col. 2d Regiment	Resigned ——, 1777.
Moualt, William	Captain 1st "	Killed, Charlestown,
Moultrie, Thomas	" 2d "	[May, 1780.
Moultrie, Wiliam	Major General	
Moultrie, William	Lieutenant 2d Regiment	

*So in printed pamphlet, but should be " Michael Kalteissen."

Mowatt, John	Lieutenant 1st "	
Marshall, ——	Captain 2d "	
Monterip, Richard	Lieutenant 5th "	
McNeill, Daniel	Surg. mate 2d "	
Marshall, Thomas	Captain 3d Regiment	
McKinney, James	Lieutenant 5th "	
Nelson, John	Major	
Neufville, William	Regimental Surgeon	
Newson, Benjamin	Lieutenant 2d Regiment	[May, 1780.
Neyle, Philip	" 1st "	Killed, Charlestown,
Nixon, George	Adjutant 4th Reg't Art'y	
Ogier, George	Lieutenant 2d Regiment	
Oliphant, David	Medical Director	
Oliphant, William	Lieutenant 2d Regiment	Resigned Oct. 20, 1777.
Ousby, Thomas	" — "	
Paggett, ——	Captain — Regiment	
Parham, ——	Lieutenant 1st Regiment	
Parsons, ——	" 5th "	
Partridge, William	" 1st "	
Peronneau, Henry	" 2d "	Resigned July 15, 1778.
Peronneau, James	" 1st "	
Petrie, Alexander	Captain 5th "	Resigned 8th Oct. 1778.
Petrie, George [worth	Lieutenant 2d "	
Pinckney, Chas. Cotes-	Colonel 1st "	
Pinckney, Thomas	Major "	
Platen, Frederick Von	Lieut. 4th Reg't Art'y	
Pledger, Joseph	Lieutenant 3d Regiment	Resigned Jan. 30, 1776.
Polk, Ezekiel	Captain " "	
Pollard, Richard		
Postell, Benjamin	Lieutenant 1st "	
Potts, Thomas	Captain 5th "	
Poyas, John E	Hospital mate	
Prescott, Joseph	Surgeon	
Prince, Francis	Captain 5th Regiment	
Provaux, Adrian	" 2d "	
Purcell, Henry, Rev	Brigade Chaplain	
Purvis, John	Captain 3d Regiment	
Peronneau, John	Lieutenant 2d Regiment	Resigned Dec. 12, 1777,
Ramsay, Henry	Lieutenant —— Regiment	
Ramsay, Joseph H	Surgeon	
Rasche, John Henry	Surgeon's mate 2d Reg't	
Rayford, ——	Captain —— Regiment	
Read, William	Physician and Surgeon	
Redmond, ——	Lieutenant 6th Regiment	
Richardson, Edward	Captain 3d "	Resigned Jan 30, 1776,
Richardson, Richard, Jr	" 6th "	
Richardson, William	" 5th "	[1779.
Roberts, Owen	Colonel 4th Reg't Artillery	Killed, Stono, 20th June,
Roberts, Richard Brooks	Captain " " "	
Roberson, James	Lieutenant 3d Regiment	
Rodgers, Alexander	Surgeon 3d "	
Rogers, Christopher, Jr	Lieutenant 2d "	
Rose, Hugh	Surgeon " "	
Rothmaler, Erasmus	Lieutenant — "	
Roux, Albert	Captain 2d "	
Russell, Thos. Com'ndr	Lieutenant 1st "	
Raphel, ——	Lieut 4th Reg't Art'y	Died October, 1777.
Rolando, ——	" 5th "	Resigned ——. 1777.
Rutledge, Andrew	Dep. Wagonmaster Gen'l	
Sanders, Roger Parker	Captain 1st Regiment	Resigned 8th Oct. 1778.
Schreiber, Jacob	" Engineers	
Scott, William	Lieut Col —— Regiment	
Screven, Benjamin	Capt —— Reg't Lt Drag	
Senf, Christian	Captain Engineers	
Shubrick, Jacob	Lieutenant 2d Regiment	Died 27th April, 1778.
Shubrick, Richard	" " "	Died 8th Nov, 1777,
Shubrick, Thomas	Captain " "	
Simons, James	Cornet Lee's Legion	
Singleton, Richard	Lieutenant 1st Regiment	

GENERAL CHRISTOPHER GADSDEN

1724-1805

AMERICAN PATRIOT AND REVOLUTIONARY GENERAL. HE RECEIVED HIS EDUCATION IN ENGLAND. HE WAS A DELEGATE TO THE FIRST COLONIAL CONGRESS IN 1765, AND MEMBER OF THE FIRST CONTINENTAL CONGRESS 1774-1776; AN OFFICER IN THE CONTINENTAL ARMY IN THE DEFENSE OF CHARLESTON 1776-1780. AT THE BEGINNING OF THE REVOLUTION HE ENTERED THE ARMY AS A COLONEL. IN 1776 HE WAS PROMOTED TO THE RANK OF BRIGADIER-GENERAL. HE WAS LIEUTENANT-GOVERNOR OF SOUTH CAROLINA 1778-1780. IN 1782 HE WAS ELECTED GOVERNOR.

FLAG BORNE BY AMERICAN TROOPS AT THE SOUTH AT THE BEGINNING OF THE REVOLUTION.

The battle of King's Mountain was the beginning of that great return wave which broke the British power, and swept it, not only from South Carolina, but from all the States which had declared for independence.

Skirving, Charles	Lieutenant 1st "	
Smith, Aaron	" 2d "	
Smith, Daniel	Dep Med Surveyor	
Smith, John Caraway	Captain 2d Regiment	
Smith, Press	Lieutenant 1st Regiment	
Smith, Robert, Rt Rev	Hospital Chaplain	
Smith, Samuel	Lieutenant 1st Regiment	Resigned August 1779.
Springer, Sylvester	Surgeon's mate, 2d Regiment	
Stevens, Wm S	Junior Surgeon	
Sumter, Thomas	Lieut Col 6th Regiment	Resigned Sept. 23, 1778.
Sunn, Frederick	Reg't Surgeon. —— Reg't	
Shackelford, ——	Captain 5th "	Resigned 7th Dec. 1777.
Spencer, ——		
Simons, ——	Lieutenant —— Regiment	Lost on schr. Randolph.
Simpson, Robert	Adjutant 5th "	Resigned Nov. 1778.
Taggart, William	Lieutenant 3d Regiment	
Tate, Wm	Capt Lieut 5th "	Resigned 22d Dec. 1777
Taylor, Samuel	Major 6th "	
Theus, Jeremiah	Surgeon 2d "	
Theus, Simeon	Captain 1st "	
Thompson, William	Colonel 3d "	
Thompson, ——	Lieutenant 3d "	
Towles, Oliver	Captain " "	
Townsend, Paul	Paymaster 4th Reg't Artil'ry	
Tucker, Thomas Tudor	Physician and Surgeon	
Turner, George	Captain 1st Regiment	
Tutt, Benjamin	" 5th "	
Tutt, Richard	" " "	
Taylor, Thomas	" 3d "	Resigned October, 1777.
Valentine, Wm	Lieutenant 1st Regiment	
Vanderhorst, James	—— —— "	
Vanderhorst, John	Major 2d "	
Vaughan, ——	Surgeon	[October, 1779.
Vlieland, Cornelius Van	Lieutenant 2d "	Killed, Savannah, 9th
Vickars, Samuel	Hospital Physician	
Wage, George	Captain 6th Regiment	
Wallace, John	Surgeon	
Walter, John Allen	Lieutenant 2d "	
Ward, John Peter	" 1st "	
Ward, Wm	" " "	
Warley, Felix	Captain " "	
Warley, George	" 2d "	
Warley, Joseph	" " "	
Warley, Paul	Lieutenant " "	Resigned —— 1777.
Warren, Samuel	Captain 5th "	
Watson, Samuel	Lieutenant 3d "	
West, Cato	" " "	Resigned Sept. 14, 1778.
White, Sims	Captain 4th Reg't Art'ly	Resigned ——, 1777.
Wickley, John	" — Regiment	[October, 1779.
Wickom, John	Ensign 2d "	Killed, Savannah, 9th
Williamson, John	Captain 1st "	
Wilson, ——	Capt. Lt 4th Reg't Art'ly	
Wilson, ——	Lieutenant " "	
Winn, Richard	Lieutenant 3d Regiment	[October, 1779.
Wise, Samuel	Major " "	Killed, Savannah, 9th
Withers, William R	Ensign — " "	
Woodward, Thomas	Captain 3d "	Resigned Jan. 30, 1779.

AMERICAN ARTILLERY DRAWN BY OXEN.

MORGAN.

Soldier of the Continental
Army.

General Lincoln.

The following are the names of various different Military militia organizations which existed at and during the Revlutionary War. These names are taken from the various authorities cited, as the authorities from whom the names of the Militia officers hereinafter given are taken, to wit :

Charles Town Battalion of Artillery. Charles Town. 2 companies.

Charles Town Volunteers.　　Charles Town.
Charles Town Light Infantry.　　　"　　　"
Charles Town Fusileers, German.　"　　　"
True Blue Company.　　　　　　 "　　　"
Grenadier Company.　　　　　　 "　　　"
Cannon's Company of Volunteers.　"　　　"
Charles Town Rangers.　　　　　"　　　"
Beaufort Light Infantry. Beaufort.
Beaufort Artillery.　　　　　　 "
Beaufort Company of Volunteers. Beaufort.
St. Helena Volunteers.
Euhaw Volunteers.
Huspa Volunteers.
Foot Rangers or Rovers, Raccoon Company.
James Island Company.
Salt Catcher Company.

Horry's Light Dragoons, — Regiment. State troops enlisted.

63

William Moultrie, commander of the
little fort on Sullivan's Island,
afterwards named in his honor.

MORGAN'S ESCAPE FROM THE INDIANS

Maham's Light Dragoons,—Regiment. State troops, enlisted.
Wade Hampton's Light Dragoons,—Reg't. " "   "
Richard Hampton's "   " " " " "   "
Boykin's Company of Catawba Indians.
Round O Volunteers.
Pon Pon Company.
Dozier's Company of Volunteers.
Indian Field Company.
Postell's Company of Volunteers.
Edisto Island Volunteers,
John's Island Company.
Kingstree Company.
Stono Company.
Militia Rangers Volunteers.
Wando Company, Christ Church.
Port's Company of Volunteers.
St. George's Company.
Georgetown Artillery. Georgetown.
Light Horse, or Pocotaligo Hunters.
Oakely Creek Company.
St. Peter's Company.
Black Swamp Company.
Pipe Creek Company.
Boggy Gut Company.
New Windsor Company.
Upper Three Runs Company.

Brig. Gen. Francis Marion's Brigade consisted of–
Lieut. Col. McDonald's Regiment.
Col. Richardson's   "
Col. Irwin's   "
Col. Benbow's   "
Col. Maybank's   "

In Gen. Marion's Brigade, Jacob Brawler, who lived in
the present Marion County, and his 23 sons served ; he and
22 of his sons were killed or died in service, and the one
son who survived came out of the war a cripple, and imbe-
cile from exposure and hardships.
16

LIST OF OFFICERS.

Of the Militia of South Carolina who took part in the War of the Revolution 1775–1783.

The sources from whence these names are obtained are set opposite to their respective names. Very often several of these authorities mention the same officer, and in this list where double authorities are cited, it is because the rank of the officer or the term of service has been of a different grade or different period.

In the citation of the Journal of the Council of Safety as authority, these citations should very frequently have been Journal of the Provincial Congress. When the Congress was in session, the officers were appointed by it; when it was not in session, the Council of Safety appointed; and hence the Journal of the Council is cited merely for uniformity of citation.

This list is doubtless very imperfect, but so many names as are here gathered are by this list preserved from oblivion.

LA FAYETTE.

Governor Rutledge.

Charles Pinckney,

Count Pulaski.

Henry Laurens

Name	Rank	Remarks	Command	Authority
Abney, Nathaniel	Captain.	Expedition under Major Williamson.	Marion Brigade,	Gibbes's Documentary History, 19 Nov., 1775.
Alexander, James	"		"	Johnson's Traditions of Revolution, 1781.
Allen, Jeremiah	Lieutenant.			Gregg's History of Old Cheraws, 1782.
Allison, Robert	Captain.		Marion Brigade	Gibbes's Documentary History, 1781.
Allston, John	"	Col. Peter Horry's Reg't Dragoons.		Jour. Coun. Safety, 30 Dec. 1775 Moul. Rev. 1778.
Allston, William	Major.	Wounded.		Gibbes's Documentary History, 1781.
Ancrum, —	Captain.	Expedition under Major Williamson.		Moultrie's Revoluion 1778.
Anderson, John	"	"		Gibbes's Documentary History, 19 Nov., 1775.
Anderson, Robert	Adjutant,			"
Anderson, —	Lieut. Colonel.			
Andrews, John	Captain.			Ramsay's Revolution, 1780.
Adams, —	"		Col. George Hick's Regiment.	Gregg's History of Old Cheraws, 1780.
All, Jacob	Lieutenant.		South Carolina State Troops.	Johnson's Traditions of Revolution, 1781.
Bacot. Peter	Captain.	Light Infantry Company.	Marion Brigade,	Gregg's History of Old Cheraws, 1782.
Bacot. Samuel	Colonel.		Charles Town Militia.	Jour. of Coun. of Safety, 22 Dec., 1775. Moultrie's
Baddeley, John	Brig. General.			Gibbes's Doc. His., 1780, [Rev., 1778.
Baker, —	Captain.	Beaufort Company.		Garden's Anecdotes, 1781.
Barnwell, John	"			Moultrie's Revolution, 1779.
Barnwell, Robert	Major.			Johnson's Traditions of Revolution, 1780.
Barry, John	Lieutenant.	Wounded Quinby Bridge, 1782.	Col. William Harden's Command.	Gibbes's Documentary History, 1781.
Baxter, —	Captain.			Moultrie's Revolution, 1781.
Beal, —	"			Gibbes's Documentary History, 1781.
Beaty, —	"			Lossing's Field Book of Revolution, 1780.
Bennett, —	Lieutenant.			Gibbes's Doc. His., 1781. [His., 1780.
Benson, —	Colonel.			Lossing's Field Book of Rev., 1781. Gibbes's Doc.
Bentham, James	"	Wounded near Nelson's Ferry.	Marion Brigade.	Journal of Council of Safety. 22 Dec., 1775.
Benton, Sam	"		Charles Town Militia.	Gibbes's Documentary History, 19 Nov., 1775.
Berand, Matthew	Lieutenant.		Marion Brigade.	
Beresford, —	Colonel.	Expedition under Major Williamson.		Johnson's Traditions of Revolution, 1780.
Black, —	Captain.	Prisoner at St. Augustine.	Aide to Gen. William Moultrie.	Gibbes's Documentary History, 1781.
Bleakney, John	"	St. David's Parish.	Marion Brigade.	Journal of Council of Safety, 30 November, 1775.
Bleauford, —	"			Gibbes's Documentary History, 1781.
Bocquet, —	Major.			"
Boroneau, —	Captain.			"
Boroneau, —	"			
Boon, —	Lieutenant.	Wounded Savannah, 9 October, 1779. " Eutaw, 8 September, 1781.	Marion Brigade.	Ramsay's Revolution, 1779. 1781.
Bossard, —	Captain.			Gibbes's Documentary History, 1780.
Bonnetheau, Peter	Lieutenant.	Battalion of Artillery.		Garden's Anecdotes, 1780.
Bowman, —	Captain.		Charles Town Militia.	Ramsay's Revolution, 1780.
Boykin, Samuel	"	Company of Catawba Indians Dragoons.		Journal of Council of Safety, 14 Jan...1776.
Boykin, —	"			Johnson's Tradition of Revolution, 1780.
Brandon, T	Colonel.			
Bratton, William	Lieutenant.	Capt. Port's Co. Vols. St. David's Parish. Company of Volunteers.		Lossing's Field Book of Revolution, 1781. Journal of Council of Safety, 30 Nov., 1775. 21 Feb., 1776.
Britton, Daniel	"	Light Infantry Company.	Charles Town Militia.	Johnson's Traditions of Revolution, 1776.
Britton, Henry	Captain.			Gibbes's Documentary History, 1781.
Brown, Archibald	"			Moultrie's Revolution, 1779. Ramsay's Revolution.
Brown, —	"			Johnson's Traditions Revolution, 1781.
Brown, —	Lieutenant.	Wounded Stono, 1779.	Col. William Harden's Command.	
Brown, Tarleton	Captain.			

Name	Rank	Company / Notes	Regiment	Reference
Buckhold, Abraham	Major.		Craven County Regiment.	Col. Isaac Hayne's, Register, 1779.
Buckholdt, Peter	Captain.		Granville County Regiment.	Gregg's History of Old Cheraws, 1775.
Bull, Stephen	Colonel.			Capt. Lining's Order Book, 1776.
Bull, —	Captain.			Journal of Council of Safety, 6 Dec. 1775.
Burton, Sam	Lieutenant.			" 25 Jan., 1776.
Butler, James	Captain.	Capt. Port's Co. Vols. St. David's Parish.		" 30 Nov., 1775.
Butler, John	"		Col. Benton's Reg't, Marion Brigade.	Johnson's Traditions of Revolution, 1776.
Butler, Pierce	Major.			Gregg's History of Old Cheraws, 1781.
Butler, William	Captain, Colonel.			Johnson's Traditions of Revolution, 1780.
Butler, William	Lieutenant.			Gibbes's Documentary history, 1781.
Butler, —	Major.			Johnson's Traditions of Revolution, 1780.
Burnett, Jacob	"			Moultrie's Revolution, 1778.
Basquin, William	Lieutenant.	Col. Maham's Reg't Light Dragoons.		1782.
Bryan, John	Cornet.	"		"
Barnett, William	Adjutant.			"
Bachelor, Garner	Captain.			1781.
Benton, —	Lieutenant.			
Baxter, —	"			
Cannon, Daniel	Captain.	Wounded Quinby Bridge. Cannon's Volunteers.	Charles Town Militia.	Journal of Council of Safety, 1 Dec., 1775.
Cantey, —	Lieutenant.			" 9 " "
Capers, William	Captain.	Volunteer Company, Beaufort. [Rovers.	Marion Brigade.	Johnson's Traditions of Revolution, 1783.
Cater, Thomas	Lieutenant.			Journal of Council of Safety, 26 Feb. 1776.
Clark, —	Captain.	Capt. John Allen's Foot Rangers, or Pon Pon Company.	Colleton County Regiment.	Gibbes's Documentary History, 1781.
Clegg, —	Lieutenant.	Capt. John Allen's Foot Rangers, or [Rovers.		Journal of Council of Safety, 11 Feb., 1776.
Clefford, Charles	"			" 30 Jan., "
Coachman, James	Captain.			" 16 Dec., 1775.
Coachman, —	"			" 15 " "
Cochran, Robert	Adjutant.	Ordnance Storekeeper. Expedition under Major Williamson.		" 2 " "
Colson, Jacob	Captain.		Col. Benton's Reg't, Marion Brigade.	Gibbes's Documentary History, 19 Nov. 1775.
Conn, Thomas	Lieutenant.			Gregg's History of Old Cheraws, 1781.
Conyers, Daniel	Major.			Gibbes's Documentary History, 1781.
Conyers, James	Captain.			Wallace's History of Williamsburg Church, 1780.
Cook, Wilsor (with- [drawn])	"	Round O Volunteers.	Colleton County Regiment.	Journal of Council of Safety, 11 Jan., 1776.
Cooper, S [drawn]	"		Marion Brigade.	Gibbes's Documentary History, 1781.
Corfey, John	Lieutenant.	Capt. William Butler's Company.		Journal of Council of Revolution, 1780.
Council, —	Major.			Gregg's History of Old Cheraws,
Couturier, John	Captain.	Wounded Eutaw, 8 September, 1781.	South Carolina State Troops.	Journal of Council of Safety, 28 Dec., 1775.
Cowan, —	"			Gibbes's Documentary History, 1781.
Crangthead, —	"			Johnson's Traditions of Revolution, 1780.
Crawford, Robert	Major.	Killed Fort Motte, 1781.		Lossing's Field Book of Revolution, 1780.
Crawford, —	Lieutenant.			Lossing's Field Book of Revolution, 1781.
Cruger, —	"			" 1781.
Culpeper, —	"	Wounded at Eutaw, 8 September, 1781	South Carolina State troops.	Gibbes's Documentary History, 1781.
Cunningham, Arthur	"	Capt Edward Plowden's Company.		Journal of Council of Safety, 18 Jan., 1776.
Campbell, Robert (mis)	"	Col. Maham's Reg't Light Dragoons.		1782.
Capers, William	"		Col. Richardson's Regiment.	1778.
Dabbs, Joseph	Captain.			Gregg's History of Old Cheraws, 1781.
Daniel, Aaron	Ensign.	St. David's Parish.	Col. G. G. Powell's Regiment.	Journal of Council of Safety, 21 Feb., 1776.
Daniell, Joseph	Captain.			" 13 Jan., "

Name	Rank	Company / Command	Reference
Danell, John	Captain.		Moultrie's Revolution, 1778.
David, David	Lieutenant.	Volunteer Company, St. David's Parish.	Gregg's History of Old Cheraws, 1780.
Davis, Henry	"	"	Journal of Council of Safety, 21 Feb., 1776.
Davis, Ransom	Captain.	Marion Brigade.	" "
Davrs, William	"	Col. G. G. Powell's Regiment.	
Deal, —	Lieutenant.		Gibbes's Documentary History, 1781.
DeSaussure, Daniel	Captain.	Marion Brigade.	Journal of Council of Safety, 21 Feb., 1776.
Dewitt, Charles	Lieutenant.	Col. G. G. Powell's Regiment.	Ramsay's Revolution, 1779.
Dillard, —	Captain.		Harper's Memoir, 1778.
Doharty, James	"	Volunteer Company, St. David's Parish.	Gregg's History of Old Cheraws, 1781.
Dozier, John	"	Wounded Stono, 1779.	Johnson's Traditions of Revolution, 1781.
Dubois, —	"	Volunteer Company, Beaufort.	Moultrie's Revolution, 1778.
Dubose, Andrew	"		Journal of Council of Safety, 21 Feb., 1776.
Dubose, Elias	Lieutenant.	Killed near Beaufort.	Moultrie's Revolution, 1778.
Dupont, —	Captain.	Volunteer Company, St. David's Parish.	Gregg's History of Old Cheraws, 1781.
Durham, Chamel	Lieutenant.	Col. G. G. Powell's Regiment.	"
Daver, B,	Cadet.		
Drayton, Thomas	Quartermaster.	Marion Brigade.	Siegling's Centennial Oration, 1776.
Ederington, Francis	Captain.	"	Ederington's Recollections, 1780.
Ellerbee, Thomas	"	Charles Town Militia.	
Elliott, Benjamin	Lieutenant Colonel.		Ederington's Recollections, 1780.
Elliott, Samuel	Major.	German Fusileers.	Gregg's History of Old Cheraws, 1781.
Ellison, —	Colonel.		Journal of Council of Safety, 28 Dec., 1775.
Erskine, —	Lieutenant.		" " 17 17
Ervin, John	Ensigt.	Marion Brigade.	Moultrie's Revolution, 1778.
Erwin, James	Captain.		Gibbes's Documentary History, 1781.
Eubank, John	Lieutenant.	Colleton County Regiment.	Wallace's His. of W'msb'g Ch. Gibbes's Doc. His.
Evans, Charles	"	Wounded Eutaw, 8 September, 1781.	Journal of Council of Safety, 18 Jan., 1776.
Evans, Enoch		South Carolina State Troops.	" " 30 Nov., 1775.
Evans, George	A. D., C., Gen. Marion.	Col. Rothmaler's Regiment.	" " 21 Feb., 1776.
Elliott, Thomas	"	Volunteer Company, St. David's Parish.	Gregg's History of Old Cheraws, 1781.
Edwards, John	Judge Advocate.	Col. G. G. Powell's Regiment,	" 1780.
Elliott, —	Captain.	Col. Hick's Reg't, Marion Brigade.	1781.
Falls, —	"	Capt. Irby's Company.	
Farr, Thomas, Jr.	Lieutenant.	"	Garden's Anecdotes.
Farrow, Thomas	"	Killed Ransom's Mills.	Journal of Council of Safety, 14 Jan., 1776.
Fenwick, Thomas	Major.	Commissary General and Paymaster.	Johnson's Traditions of Revolution, 1780.
Fitzgerald, John	Lieutenant.		Journal of Council of Safety, 1 Dec., 1775.
Ford, George	"	Charles Town Rangers.	Capt. Lining's Order Book, 1776.
Fletcher, —	Captain.	Capt. Archibald McDaniel's Company.	Journal of Council of Safety, 16 Dec., 1775.
Ford, James	"		Lossing's Field Book of Revolution, 1780.
Fogartie, James	Lieutenant.	St. David's Parish.	Journal of Council of Safety, 21 Feb., 1776.
Fogartie, Joseph	Captain.	Capt. Benjamin Marion's Company.	Capt. Lining's Order Book, 1776.
Freer, Charles	Lieutenant.	Capt. Wigfall's Company.	Journal of Council of Safety, 1 Dec., 1775.
Fuller, Nathaniel	Captain.	Capt. Lining's Company.	Garden's Anecdotes.
Fullerton, John	Lieutenant.	Indian Field Company.	Journal of Council of Safety, 1 Dec., 1775.
Futhy, William	Captain.	Capt. Postell's Company.	" 18 Jan., 1776.
Fox, —	Lieutenant.	Wounded Quinby Bridge, 1781.	
Galliway, James	"	St. David's Parish.	Journal of Council of Safety, 21 Feb., 1776.

Name	Rank	Command	Brigade/Regiment	References
Gamble, John	Major.	Williamsburg County. Capt. Wigfall's Company.	Marion Brigade. Berkeley County Regiment.	Wallace's History of Williamsburg Church, 1780. Journal of Council of Safety, 1 Dec., 1775.
Garden, John	Lieutenant.		Marion Brigade.	Moultrie's Revolution, 1775.
Garden, —	Colonel.		"	Gregg's History of Old Cheraws, 1781.
Gay, —	Lieutenant.			Ramsay's History, 1781.
Gee, —	Captain.	Wounded Eutaw, 8 Sept., 1781.	Charles Town Militia.	Garden's Anecdotes, 1776.
Gibbes, William Hasell	Capt., Lieutenant.	Battalion Artillery.	South Carolina State Troops.	Gibbes's Documentary History, 1781.
Giles, —	Captain.	Wounded Eutaw, 8 Sept., 1781.		Gregg's History of Old Cheraws.
Gillespie, —				Siegling's Centennial Oration, 1776.
Gillon, Alexander	Captain.	German Fusileers.	Charles Town Militia.	Journal of Council of Safety, 9 Dec., 1776.
Glover, Joseph	Colonel.		Colleton County Regiment.	Resolutions of General Assembly.
Goodman, Joseph	Quartermaster.			Capt. Linng's Order Book, 1776.
Godbolt, James	Lieutenant.		Craven County Regiment.	Wallace's History of Williamsburg Church. 1781.
Gordon, Roger			Marion Brigade.	Capt Lining's Order Book, 1776.
Gough, John	Captain.	Capt. Peter Buckholt's Company.	Berkeley County Regiment.	Garden's Anecdotes.
Gough, Richard				Gibbes's Documentary History, 1781.
Gough, —	Lieutenant.	Capt. James Skirving's Company.		Journal of Council of Safety, 21 Feb., 1776.
Graves, Joseph	Captain.		Marion Brigade.	Gregg's History of Old Cheraws, 1780.
Gregg, James		Volunteer Company, St. David's Parish. Britton's Neck.	Col. G. G. Powell's Regiment. Col. Erviu's Regiment.	Jour. of Coun. of Safety, 26 Feb., 1776. Moultrie's [Rev., 1718. 1781.
Griffith, Joseph				
Grimball, Thomas	Major.	Battalion of Artillery.	Charles Town Militia.	
Grahan	Captain.	Capt. Postell's Company.		
Grist, —	Lieutenant.			Garden's Anecdotes.
Greer, —	Colonel.			Jour. Coun. Saiety, 23 Dec., '75. Gibbes's Doc. His.
Grisset, —	Major.			Gibbes's Locumentary History, 19 Nov., 1775.
Green, I.		Expedition under Major Williamson	Artillery.	Johnson's Traditions of the Revolution.
Hall, George Abbott	Captain.			Jour, of Coun. of Safety, 24 Jan., 1776.
Hamilton, Andrew	"			Jour. of Coun. of Safety, 23 Jan., '76. Gibbes's Doc. [His. 1781.
Hamilton, Joseph	"			
Hammond, George	"			Lossing's Field Book, of Rev., 1780.
Hammond, John	"	Wounded Eutaw, 8 September, 1781.	State Troops, South Carolina.	Gibbes's Documentary History, 1781.
Hammond, LeKoy	Colonel.			Johnson's Traditions of Revolution.
Hammond, Samuel	"			1775,
Hammond, —	Lieutenant.	Expedition under Major Williamson.		Jour. of Coun. of Safety, 26 Feb., '76, Gibbes's Doc.
Hampton, Edward	Captain.	Artillery Company, Beaufort.		Gibbes's Doc. His., 1781. [His., 1781.
Hampton, Henry	"	Col. William Harden's Regiment.		Journal of Council of Safety, 21 Feb., 1776.
Harden, William	Colonel.	St. David's Parish.		"
Harden, —	Ensign.			
Hardyman, Joseph	Captain.			Moultrie's Revolution, 1778.
Hardyman, Thomas	Colonel.			Journal of Council of Safety, 9 Jan., 1776.
Harleston, John	Colonel.			" 21 Feb. "
Hargrave, Robert	Captain.	St. David's Parish. Pee Dee.		Gregg's History of Old Cheraws, 1780.
Hargrave, Samuel	Lieutenant.			Moultrie's Revolution, 1778.
Harlow, Benjamin	"			O'Neall's Annals of Newberry.
Harrington, Wm. Henry	Colonel.	Col. Richard Hampton's Regiment.		Gibbes's Documentary History, 1781.
Harris —	Lieutenant.			Mills's Statistics South Carolina.
Harriss, Micajah	Major.			Lossing's Field Book of Revolution, 1780.
Hart, Derrill	Captain.			Moultrie's Revolution, 1781.
Harvey, Thomas	"			
Hawhorne, —	Colonel.			
Hayes, —	"			

Name	Rank	Company / Command	Regiment / Brigade	Authority
Hayne, Isaac	Colonel.	Pon Pon Company.		Jour. of Coun. of Safety, 15 Jan., '76. Gibbes's Doc. [His., 1781.
Hendricks, William	Captain.		Marion Brigade.	Gregg's His. Old Cheraws, 1782.
Heron, —	Lieutenant.	Capt. Peter Buckholt's Company.	Craven County Regiment.	Capt. Lining's Order Book, 1776.
Heyward, Daniel, Jr.	Captain.	Volunteer Company, Beaufort.		Journal of Council of Sa ety, 26 Feb., 1776.
Heyward, John	Ensign.	"		
Heyward, Thomas, Jr.	Captain.	Battalion of Artillery.		
Hicks, George	Major.		Charles Town Militia.	Moultrie's Revolution, 1776. [Old Cheraws, 1781.
Hill, William	Colonel.			Jour. Coun. of Safety, 18 Feb., '76. regg's His.
Hinds, —	Lieutenant.			Lossing's Field Book of Revolution, 1780.
Hird, John		Round O Company.		Gregg's History of Old Cheraw, 1780.
Hogg, —	Major.		Marion Brigade.	
Holding, Matthew	Lieutenant.			Moultrie's Revolution, 1778.
Hollis, Moses	"			Journal of Council of Safety, 21 Feb., 1776.
Holmes, —				Gregg's History of Old Cheraws, 1783.
Horry, Hugh	Colonel.	Capt. Robert Lide's Company.	Col. G. G. Powell's Regiment.	Ramsay's Revoluti n, 1781.
Huger, John	Captain.	Killed Eutaw, 8 September, 1781.	Col. Benson's Regiment.	Lossing's Field Book of Revolution, 1781.
Huggins, John	Lieut. and Adjutant.	Charles Town Volunteers.		Gibbes's Documentary History, 1776.
Huggins, Benjamin	Lieutenant.		Marion Brigade.	Gregg's History of Old Cheraws, 1779.
Hughes, Thomas	Colonel.	Artillery Company, Beaufort.		Gibbes's Documentary History, 1781.
Hughes, —	Captain.	Expedition under Major Williamson.		Journal of Council of Safety, 21 Nov., 1775.
Hunter, David			Col. Hugh Giles's Regiment.	Johnson's Traditions of Revolution, 1780.
Hyrne, Henry	Lieutenant.		Col. Peter Horry's Reg't Dragoons	Gibbes's Documentary History, 19 Nov., 1775.
Huss, —	Captain.			Journal of Council of Safety, 23 Dec., 1775.
Inman, S.		Killed Musgrove Mills.	Col. George Hick's Regiment.	
Irby, Edmund	Colonel.			Johnson's Traditions of Revolution, 1780.
Irvine, —			Marion Brigade.	Gregg's History of Old Cheraws, 1780.
Irwin, —	Lieutenant.		Col. Geo. Hick's Reg't, Marion Brig-	Lossing's Field Look of Revolution, 1780.
Jackson, John	Captain.		Col. Kolb's " "	Moultrie's Revolution, 1781.
Jackson, Stephen	Lieutenant.			Gregg's History of Old Cheraws, 1780.
James, Alexander	"			
James, John [Lake.				
James, John, Jr., of the	Major.			Wallace's History of Williamsburg Church, 1776. 1780.
Jamieson, —	Captain.			
Jeneret, Jacob	Ensign.	Edisto Island Volunteer Company.	Colleton County Regiment.	Gibbes's Documentary History, 1779.
Jenkins, Benjamin	Captain.	St. Helena Island Volunteers.		Captain Lining's Order Book, 1716.
Jenkins, John	"	Edisto Island Volunteers.		Journal of Council of Safety, 11 Feb., 1776.
Jen ins, Joseph			Col. Rothmaler's Regiment.	" 7 Dec., 1775.
Jenkins, Joseph	Lieutenant.		Coleton County Regiment.	" 9 Jan, 1776.
Jenkins, Reuben			Col. Kolb's Reg't, Marion Brigade.	" 11 Feb., 1776.
Jenkins, Thomas	Captain.		Col. Rothmaler's Regiment.	Gregg's History of Old Cheraws, 1782.
Jinkins, James	Lieutenant.		Col. Benton's Reg't, Marion Brigade.	Journal of Council of Safety, 9 Jan., 1776.
Johnson, Richard	Captain.	Col. William Harden's Command.		Gregg's History of Old Cheraws, 1782.
Johnson, William	Ensign.		Col.G.G. Powell's Reg't,Marion Brig	Johnson's Tra. Rev., '80. [Book Rev. 1781.
Joiner, John	Major.			Jour. Coun. Safety, 21 Feb., 1776. Lossing's Field
Jolley, —	Captain.			Journal of Council of Safety, 27 Jan., 1776.
Jones, Adam C.		Artillery Company, Beaufort.		Johnson's Traditions of Revolution, 1780.
Jones, Edward		Expedition under Major Williamson.		Gibbes's Documentary History, 19 Nov.., 1775.
Jordon, Jonathan	Lieutenant.		Marion Brigade.	Gregg's History of Old Cheraws, 1780.
Kalteisen, Michael	Captain.	Wagon Master General.	Col. Rothmaler's Regiment.	" 9 Jan., 1776.
Karwon, Thomas	Ensign.	Capt. Benjamin Marion's Company.	Col. Singleton's Regiment.	" 2 Dec., 1775.
				" 23 Dec., 1775.

Name	Rank	Remarks	Command	Authority
Kee, Thomas	Captain.		Berkeley County Regiment.	Johnson's Traditions of Revolution, 1781.
Kelly, Daniel	Lieutenant,	Capt. Daniel Linder's Company.		Captain Lining's Order Book, 1778.
Kelly, James	"			O'Neall's Annals of Newberry.
Kershaw, Joseph	Colonel.			Moultrie's Revolution, 1775.
Kimbrough, John	Captain.	Com'y of Volunteers, St. David's Parish Cavalry.	Col. G. G. Powell's Regiment.	Journal of Council of Safety, 30 Nov, 1775. Mill's Statistics South Carolina.
Kincaid, James	"		Col. G. G. Powell's Regiment.	Journal of Council of Safety, 21 Feb, 1776. Gibbes's Documentary History, 1781.
King, George	"			Journal of Council of Safety, 30 Nov, 1775.
Kirkburn, —	Lieutenant.	Com'y of Volunteers, St. David's Parish Round O Volunteers.	Col. G. G. Powell's Regiment. Colleton County Regiment.	Gibbes' Doc. [His. 1781
Knight, James, Sr.				Jour. Coun. Safety, 21 Feb, 1776. 11 Jan, 1776 1781.
Koger, Jos. (withdrawn)				Siegling's Cent. Oration, 1779.
Kobb, Abel	Captain.	Killed Savannah, 9 October, 1779.	German Fusileers, Charles Town Mil. Col. Postell's Regiment.	
Kinnill, Joseph	Lieutenant.			Lossing's Field Book of Revolution, 1780.
Kimbell, Frederick	Lieut. Colonel.	King's Mountain.		Captain Lining's Order Book, 1776.
Jacy, Edward	Colonel.	Capt. Benjamin Marion's Company. John's Island Company.	Colleton County Regiment. Marion Brigade.	Journal of Council of Safety, 2 December, 1775.
Ladson, Abraham	Lieutenant.			Gibbes's Documentary History, 1781
Ladson, Thomas	Captain.			Garden's Anecdotes.
Ladson, —	Major.			Gibbes's Documentary History, 19 November, 1775.
Land, —	Captain.	Expedition under Major Williamson. Prisoner St. Augustine.	Charles Town Militia.	Johnson's Traditions of Revolution, 1780. Journal of Council of Safety, 31 Jan, 1776. "
Langdon, Thomas		Light Infantry Company.		
Lee, William	Lieutenant.		Marion Brigade.	Gibbes's Documentary History, 1781.
Legare, Benjamin	Captain.		"	
Legare, Samuel	"			
Leuud, —	"			
Lesesne, —	"			
Liddle, Moses	"		Col. G. G. Powell's Regiment.	Johnson's Traditions of Revolution, 1780.
Lide, Thomas	"	St. David's Parish.	Craven County Reg't, Marion Brig.	Journal of Council of Safety, 21 Feb, 1776.
Lide, Robert	"		Berkeley County Regiment.	Capt Lining's Order Book, 1776. Gregg's His. Old "76. (Cheraws, 82
Linder, Daniel	Major.			Gregg's His. Old Cheraws, 1775.
Lining, —	"	96 District.		Journal of Council of Safety, 1 December, 1775.
Lindsey, John	Colonel.			O'Neall's Annals of Newberry. Moultrie's Revolution, 1778.
Liste, —		German Fusileers.	Charles Town Militia.	Mill's Statistics South Carolina.
Lethgow, R.	Lieutenant,	Capt. James Skirving's Company.	Berkeley County Regiment.	Siegling's Centennial Oration, 1781.
Livingston, William	Captain.	Expedition under Major Williamson.		Captain Lining's Order Book, 1778.
Lloyd, Martin	Lieutenant.			Gibbes's Documentary History, 19 November, 1775.
Logan, Francis	Captain.			Mill's Statistics South Carolina.
Logan, George	"			Johnson's Traditions of Revolution, 1780.
Love, —				Gibbes's Doc. His., 1781. [Rev. 1784
Lush, —	Adjutant.	Killed Eutaw, 8 September, 1781.	South Carolina State Troops. Charles Town Militia.	Jour. Coun. Safety, 22 Dec, 1775. Johnson's Tra.
Lushington, Richard	Lieut,			Edrington's Recollections.
Lyles, Arramans	Colonel,			O'Neall's Annals of Newberry.
Lyles, James	"			
Lyles, John	Captain.		Col. Benton's Reg't, Marion Brigade	Gregg's History o: Old Cheraws, 1781.
Lyons, Guthridge	Lieutenant.		Sumter Brigade.	Gibbes's Documentary History, 1781. 1781
Lyons, —	"			
Lynes, William	Captain.			
Lewis, W.,	Major.	Wounded Eutaw, 8 September, 1781. Artillery, killed siege of Augusta.	Berkeley County Regiment. South Carolina State Troops.	Wallace's History of Williamsburg Church, 1780.
Macauly, John	Captain.			Jour. Coun. of Safety, 22 Dec, '75. Capt Linne's
Marion, Benjamin	"			Gibbes's Doc. His., '81. [Order Book, 21 April, '76
Martin, N.				Lossing's Field Book of Revolution, 1781.
Martin, William				

Name	Rank	Company / Regiment	Authority
Mathewes, Benjamin	Lieutenant.	John's Island Company	Journal of Council of Safety, 2 December, 1775. Johnson's Traditions of Revolution, 1779.
Mathewes, John Raven	"	"	Garden's Anecdotes.
Maxwell, —	Major.		Journal of Council of Safety, 30 January, 1776.
Maybank, Joseph	Lieutenant.	Colleton County Regiment.	" 1 December, 1775
Mazyck, Stephen	"	Berkeley County Regiment.	" 21 February, 1770. " 1 December, 1775.
Megee, or Magee, Elisha	Lieut. Colonel.	Col. G. G. Powell's Regiment.	
Middleton, Thomas, Jr	Lieutenant.	Berkeley County Parish.	Gibbes's Documentary History, 1781.
Middleton, —	Lieutenant.	Captain Ravenel's Company. St. David's Parish.	Gregg's History of Old Cheraws, 1781.
Nikell, John	Lieut. Colonel.	Captain Smith's Company. Wounded Eutaw, 1 September 1781.	Garden's Anecdotes 1781
Miller, John D	Lieut. Colonel.	South Carolina State Troops.	Journal of Council of Safety, 30 January, 1776.
Miller, Stephen	Captain.	Marion Brigade.	Gibbes's Documentary History, 1781.
Mitchell, —	Lieutenant.	Battalion of Artillery.	Gibbes's Documentary History, 1781.
Moffit, —	"	Berkeley County Regiment.	Lossing's Field Book of Revolution, 1780.
Morgan, William	Captain.	Marion Brigade.	Garden's Anecdotes.
Moody, Charles	Lieutenant.	Battalion of Artillery. St. David's Parish.	Journal of Council of Safety, 21 February, 1776.
Mone, —	Captain.		Gibbes's Documentary History, 1781.
Mouzon, Henry	Lieutenant.	Charles Town Militia.	Wallace's History of Williamsburg Church, 1780.
Munnerlyn, James	Captain.	Co. G. G. Powell's Regim't. Kingstree Company.	Gregg's History of Old Cheraws, 1781. [Brig.
Murphy Maurice	Lieut. Colonel.	South Carolina State Troops.	Journal of Council of Safety, 21 Feb., 1776. Gregg's History of Old Cheraws, 1781. Gibbes's Documentary History, 1781.
Murrell, —	Lieutenant.	Christ Church Company.	Journal of Council of Safety, January 22, 1776. 1778.
May, Benjamin	Captain.		1781.
Moultrie, Alexander	Lieutenant	Marion Brigade.	
Martin, John	Brigade Major.	Musketeers.	Gibbes's Documentary History, 19 November, 1775.
Milton, —	Captain.	Killed Strawbery.	Gregg's History of Old Cheraws, 1781.
Maurice, —	Lieutenant.	Charles Town Militia.	Carrington's Bat. Rev., '80, Johnson's Tra. Rev., '80.
Muller, Albert A.	Major. Colonel.	Col. Richardson's Regiment.	Lossing's Field Book of Revolution, 1780.
McCall, James	Captain.	Expedition under Major Williamson.	Wallace's History of Williamsburg Church, 1780.
McCall, John	Ensign.	Marion Brigade.	Gibbes's Documentary History, 19 November, 1775.
McCall, Hugh	Captain.	South Carolina State Troops.	Gregg's History of Old Cheraws, 1782.
McClure, John	"	Ramsay says "Col McCall of the Lt. [Horse.	Captain Lining's Order Book, 1776.
McClure, —		Killed Hanging Rock, ——, 1780.	Gibbes's Documentary History, 1781.
McColtrey, William		Expedition under Major Williamson.	Carrington's, Battle's of Revolution, 1780.
McCreery, Robert			Gregg's History of Old Cheraws, 1781.
McCullough George			Johnson's Traditions of Revolution, 1780.
McDaniel, Archibald	Lieut. Colonel.	Marion Brigade.	Gibbes's Documentary History, 1781.
McDonald, —	Major.		Lee's Memoirs, 1781.
McDowell, —	Captain.	Marion Brigade.	Johnson's Traditions of Revolution, 1780.
McIntosh, Alexander	"	Col. Benton's Reg't, Marion Brigade.	Journal of Council of Safety, 31 November, 1775. Gregg's History of Old Cheraws, 1782.
McJunkin, Joseph	Lieut. Colonel.	Col. William Hardin's Command.	Journal of Council of Safety, 1 December, 1775. " 21 February, 1776.
McKoy, —	Captain.	Company of Volunt'rs, St. David's Parish.	1781.
McLachlin, —	Lientenant.	Marion Brigade.	
McLelle, —		Charles Town Militia.	
McManess, Thomas	Captain	The Rangers. St. David's Parish.	
McMuldrough, —	Lieutenant.	Col. G. G. Powell's Regiment.	
McQueen, John	Captain.		
McRae, Duncan			
McCauley, —			
McCleeland William		St. David's Parish.	
Neavil, Isaac	Lieuteuant.	Col. G. G. Powell's Regiment.	Journal of Council of Safety, 21 Feb, 1776.

Name	Rank	Service / Notes	Regiment / Brigade	References
Neil, Thomas	Colonel.	Killed Rocky Mount, ——, 1780	Charles Town Militia.	Journal of Council of Safety, 7 Nov., 1775, 1780. Wallace's History of Williamsburg Church. Garden's Anecdotes. Moultrie's Revolution, 1778.
Nelson, John	Captain.	Battalion of Artillery.		
Neufville, Edward	Lieutenant.			
Newman, ——	Captain.	Stono Company.	Colleton County Regiment.	Journal of Council of Safety, 23 Jan., 1776. Johnson's Traditions of Revolution, 1780. Gibbes's Documentary History, 19 Nov., 1775. Johnson's Traditions of Revolution, 1780.
Nichols, Henry	Ensign.			
Nixon, John	Lieut. Colonel.	Expedition under Major Williamson. Prisoner at St. Augustine.		
Noble, Alexander	Captain.		Marion Brigade.	Gregg's History of Old Cheraws, 1782. Gibbes's Documentary History, 1781. " 1779.
North, Edward	"			
Norwood, John				
Odingsell, ——	Captain.			
O'Neill, ——	"			
Oswald, William	Lieutenant.	Round O Company. Capt. Daniel Linder's Company.	Colleton County Regiment. Berkeley County Regiment.	Journal of Council of Safety, 17 Jan., 1776. Captain Lining's Order Book, 1776. Mills's Statistics South Carolina. Ramsay's Revolution, 1779. Gregg's History of Old Cheraws, 1782. " 1781
Olt, Abraham	"			
Ottersen, Samuel	Captain.	Wounded Savannah, 9 October, 1779. Of Horse.	Marion Brigade. "	
Parker, ——	Lieutenant.			
Parrott, Thomas	Captain.	Wounded Eutaw, 8 September, 1781. St. David's Parish.	Col. Benton's Reg't Marion Brigade.	Mills's Statistics South Carolina. Gregg's History of Old Cheraws, 1781. Ramsay's Revolution, 1781
Pasley, Robert				
Pearson, John	Major	Killed Siege of Ninety-Six, ——, 1781.	Col. G. G. Powell's Regiment.	Journal of Council of Safety, 21 Feb., 1776. Lossing's Field Book of Revolution, 1780. National Portrait Gallery, 1781. Gibbes's Documentary History, 1781. Gregg's History of Old Cheraws, 1781. Journal of Council of Safety, 18 Jan., 1776.
Pearson, Moses	Captain.			
Pegee, or Pegue, Claudi- [us]	Ensign.			
Perkins, David	Brig. General.			
Pickens, Andrew				
Pickens, Joseph	Captain.	Militia Rangers, Volunteers. Killed Eutaw, 8 September, 1781.	Col. Hicks's Reg't Marion Brigade. Col. Rothmaler's Regiment. 10th Regiment, new acquisition. " Marion Brigade.	Jour. Coun Safety, 4 Nov. '75. Gibbes's Doc. Hist. 1781. 4 Nov. 1775. Moultrie's Rev. Lossing's Field Book Rev., 1781.
Pinckney, ——	"			
Pledger, John	Lieutenant.			
Plowder, Edward	Captain.			
Polk, Ezekiel	Colonel.			
Polk, William	Lieutenant.			
Postell, James	Major. Colonel.			
Postell, John	Captain.			
Powell, Gabriel G	Colonel.	Wounded Stono, ——, 1779. Light Infantry Company, Volunteer Company, St. David's Parish.	Charles Town Militia. Col. G. G. Powell's Regiment. Col. Hicks's Reg't, Marion Brigade.	Journal of Council of Safety, 16 Feb., 1776. Ramsay's Revolution, 1779. Journal of Council of Safety, 31 Jan., 1776. " 21 Feb., 1776. Gregg's History of Old Cheraws, 1790. 1781.
Prince. ——	Lieutenant			
Prioleau, Hext	"			
Prior, Luke	Captain.			
Purvis, John	Lieut. Colonel.	Killed Quinby Bridge. Wando Company.	Berkeley County Regiment,	Journal of Council of Safety, 10 December, 1775. " 1 December, 1775.
Parker, John	Lieutenant.			
Price, ——				
Post, John	Captain.	Prisoner at St. Augustine.		Johnson's Traditions of Revolution, 1780. Captain Lining's Order Book, 1876. Gibbes's Documentary History, 19 November, 1775. Journal of Council of Safety, 30 November, 1775.
Perry, ——	Lieutenant.			
Quelch, Andrew	Captain.	Expedition under Major Williamson. Volunteer Company, St. David's Parish. Captain Post's Company.		
Ravenel, ——				
Read, Jacob	"			
Redmund, John	"			
Reed, George				
Reynolds, John	Lieutenant.			
Reynolds, Richard				
Rhodes, ——				
Richardson, Richard	Colonel. General.		Marion Brigade.	Garden's Anecdotes. [1780, Jour. Coun. Safety, 2 Dec. '75. Johnson's Tra. Rev. 26 December, 1775. Gibbes's Documentary History, 1781.
Richardson, Richard, Jr	Captain. Colonel.			
Richardson, William	"			

Name	Rank	Remarks	Regiment	Authority
Richardson, —	Lieut. Colonel.			Gibbes's Documentary History, 1781.
Robinson, George	Captain.			Journal of Council of Safety, 25 February, 1776. 22 December, 1775.
Roche, Patrick	Ensign.	Expedition under Major Williamson.	Charles Town Militia.	Gibbes's Documentary History, 19 November, 1775.
Rodgers, John	Captain.			Johnson's Traditions of Revolution, 1780.
Roebuck, Benjamin	Colonel.			Journal of Council of Safety, 2 December, 1775.
Rothmaler, Job	Co onel.			Captain Lining's Order Book, 1776.
Rowe, Henry	Captain.	St. Mark's Parish.	St. Mark's Parish.	Gregg's History of Old Cheraws, 1782.
Rushing, John	Lieutenant.			Gibbes's Documentary History, 1781.
Rutherford, —	Major.	Discharged 12 April, 1776.	Col. Benton's Reg't, Marion Brigade	Johnson's Traditions of Revolution, 1776.
Rutledge, Edward	Captain.		South Carolina State Troops.	Journal of Council of Safety, 15 February, 1776.
Rutledge, Thomas	Adjutant.	Killed Eutaw, 8 September, 1781.	Charles Town Militia.	Johnson's Traditions of Revolution, 1780.
Ryan, James	Captain.	Battalion of Artillery, 2d Company.	Granville County Regiment.	1777
Rouse, Albert	Lieutenant.		Colonel Richardson's Regiment.	1781
Rogers, —				Journal of Council of Safety, 16 December, 1775.
St. John, Andeon	Ensign.	Pon Pon Company.	Colleton County Regiment.	Jour. Coun. Safety, 27 Jan, 1776. Gibbes's Doc
Sanders, William	Captain.	Round O Company.	Col. Benton's Reg't, Marion Brigade	Gregg's His. Old Cheraws, 1781. [His, 1781.
Saunders, Nathaniel	Lieutenant.			Journal of Council of Safety, 7 December, 1775.
Savage, John	Colonel.			Moultrie's Revolution, 1778.
Sawyer, —	Lieutenant.			Wallace's History of Williamsburg Church.
Scott, Joseph	Colonel.	The Rangers.	Charles Town Militia.	Gibbes's Documentary History, 1781.
Scriven, —	Lieutenant.	Killed Savannah, 9 October, 1779.	German Fusil's, Charles Town Milit'a	Moultrie's Revolution, 1779.
Sharp, James	Captain.	Light Infantry Company.	Charles Town Militia.	Journal of Council of Safety, 31 Jan, 1776.
Shepherd, —	Ensign.	Killed Eutaw, 8 September, 1781.		Ramsay's Revoution, 1781.
Shibrick, Thomas, Jr	Lieutenant.			Garden's Anecdotes, 1781.
Simons, —	Brig. Major.		Marion Brigade.	Moultrie's Revolution, 1778.
Simons, Keating	Colonel.			Mills's Statistics South Carolina.
Simons, Maurice	Captain.			Moultrie's Revolution, 1778
Simpkins, Ar.hur	"		Marion Brigade.	Johnson's Traditions of Revolution, 1780.
Sinclair, —	"			Journal of Council of Safety, 28 Dec, 1775 1 Dec, 1775
"	"			
Singleton, John	Colonel.	Expedition under Major Williamson.	Berkeley County Regiment.	Gibbes's Documentary History,19 Nov, 1775
Singleton, Matthew	Captain.			Captain Lining's Order Book, 1776.
Singleton, —	"			Moultrie's Revolution, 1778
Singlefield, Francis	Colonel.	Expedition under Major Williamson.	Berkeley County Regiment.	O'Neall', Annals of Newberry.
Skirving, James	Captain.			Gibbes's Documentary History, 19 Nov, 1775.
Skirving, —	"			Journal of Council of Safety, 1 Dec, 1775 21 Feb, 1776 1 Dec, 1775
Sloan, John	"	Volunteer Company. St. David's Parish.	Berkeley County Regiment.	
Smith, Aaron	"	St. George Company.	Col. G. G. Powell's Regiment.	
Smith, Benjamin	Lieutenant.			Gibbes's Documentary His, 1781. [His, 1781.
Smith, Samuel	"		Marion Brigade. Sumter Brigade.	Jour. Coun. Safety, 27 Jan, 1776. Gibbes's Doc
Smith, Thomas	"		Marion Brigade.	Gibbes's Documentary History, 1781. 1776.
Smizer, —	Captain.	Wounded Eutaw, 8 September, 1781.	Col. Benton's Reg't, Marion Brigade	Gregg's History of Old Cheraws, 1781.
Snipes, William Clay	"		Colonel G. G. Powell's Regiment.	Gibbes's Documentary History, 1781.
Snow, William		St David's Parish.		Journal of Council of Safety, 21 Feb, 1776. [Cheraws, 1781
Spraggins, —	Lieutenant.	Wounded Parker's Ferry, 31 Aug, 1781.	Col Benton's Reg't, Marion Brigade	Gibbes's Doc. His, 1781.
Sparks, Daniel	Captain.	Volunteer Company, St. David's Parish.		Jour. Coun. Safety, 30 Nov, '75. Gregg's His. Old
Spivey, George	Lieutenant.			Johnson's Traditions of Revolution.
Stafford, —	Colonel.		Marion Brigade.	Gibbes's Documentary History, 1781.
Standard, William	Ensign.			
Starke, John	Captain.			
Stephens, —	Lieutenant.			

Name	Rank	Company / Notes	Regiment	Reference
Stevens, Daniel	Lieutenant.	Battalion of Artillery.	Charles Town Militia.	Johnson's Traditions of Revolution.
Stevens, Jervis Henry	"		Col. H. Maham's Regiment.	Garden's Anecdotes.
Stone, Benjamin	Captain.			Journal of Council of Safety, 21 December, 1775
Steward, Chas. Augustus	Lieut. Colonel.			Gregg's History of Old Cheraws, 1775.
Strobel, Daniel	Lieutenant.	German Fusileers.	Charles Town Militia.	Siegling's ent Oranton, 1779
Strother, George	"		Marion Brigade.	Gregg's History of Old Cheraws, 1781
Sutton, John	Ensign.	Capt Robt Lide's Co, St. David's Parish	Colonel G. G. Powell's Regiment.	Journal of Council of Safety, 21 Feb, 1776
Sutton, Robert	Captain.		Colonel Rothmaler's Regiment.	9 Jan, 1776
Swinton, James	Major.	Wounded Quinby Bridge, —, 1782.		Moultrie's Revolution, 1781
Simons, James	Captain.	Col Maham's Reg't Light Dragoons.		1782.
Smith, James	Lieutenant.	"		
Syders, —	"			Johnson's Traditions of Revolution, 1775
Sinkler, —	"			Lossing's Field Book Rev., '80, Moultrie's Rev., '81
Screven, — T.	Colonel.			Journal of Council of Safety, 21 Nov, 1775
Taylor, James	Captain.	Artillery Company, Beaufort.		Mill's Statistics South Carolina.
Taylor, Thomas	Colonel.		Col. Benton's Reg't, Marion Brigade	Gregg's History of Old Cheraws, 1782.
Tebout, Tunis	Lieutenant.			1781.
Templeman, —	Captain.	Capt Benj. Marion's Company.	Colonel Singleton's Regiment.	Journal of Council of Safety, 22 Dec, 1775.
Terrell, James	Lieutenant.			7 Nov, 1775.
Terrell, Samuel	"			Johnson's Tra. Rev., '80, Carrington's Bat Rev, '80
Thomas, Edward	Colonel.			Johnson's Traditions of Revolution, 1780.
Thomas, John	"		Col Benton's Reg't, Marion Brigade	Gregg's History of Old Cheraws, 1781.
Thomas, John, Jr.	Captain.	Round O Company.	Colleton County Regiment.	Journal of Council of Safety 11 Jan, 1776
Thomas, Robert	Major.			Gregg's History of Old Cheraws, 1780
Thomas, Tresham.	Captain.			Mill's Statistics South Carolina.
Thompson, Jas, (with-) [drawn]	Major.			Johnson's Traditions of Revolution, 1775
Thornby, —	"			Moultrie's Revolution, 1781
Timmons, John	Captain.	Battalion of Artillery,	Charles Town Militia.	Journal of Council of Safety, 26 Feb, 1776.
Toomer, Anthony	Lieutenant.			Moultrie's Revolution, 1781
Toomer, Joshua	Captain.	Artillery Company, Georgetown.		Moultrie's Revolution, 1781
Trapier, Paul	"			Johnson's Traditions of Revolution, 1780.
Turner, —	"	Col Maham's Regiment Light Dragoons		1782
Turner, Sterling	"	"		
Theus, Perrin	"			1776
Taylor, Samuel	"			1777
Tinincase, Henry	Lieutenant.		Colonel Richardson's Regiment.	1781
Theus, Perrin	Surgeon.			1781
Thompson, Thomas	Major.			1781
Thompson, J.	"			
Thompson, —	Lieutenant.	Captain — Ravenel's Company.	Berkeley County Regiment.	Journal of Council of Safety, 25 Dec, 1775
Tate, —	Colonel.	Wounded, Savannah, 9 October, 1779		"
Tenhimen, James	Lieutenant.	John's Island Company.		Ramsay's Revolution, 1779
Vanderhorst, Arnoldus	Lieutenant.	Prisoner at St. Augustine.	Colleton County Regiment.	Journal of Council of Safety, 1 Dec, 1775
Videau, Peter	Lieutenant.	Wounded Savannah, 9 October, 1779		Johnson's Traditions of Revolution, 1780.
Wade, —	Ensign.			Ramsay's Revolution, 1779
Waiht, Abraham	"	St. David's Parish.	Col G. G. Powell's Regiment.	Journal of Council of Safety, 21 Feb, 1776.
Wakefield, John	Lieutenant.	Battalion Art'y, killed Charles Town '80.	Charles Town Militia.	Ramsay's Revolution, 1780.
Walker, —	"			
Wall, Wright	Lieutenant.			
Warham, Charles	Adjutant.			

Name	Rank	Company / Notes	Reference
Waring, B	Captain.	St. George's Company	Gibbes's Documentary History, 1781,
Waring, Morton	Lieutenant.		Journal of Council of Safety, 1 Dec,.. 1775.
Waring, Richard	Captain.		
Waters, Philemon	"	South Carolina State Troops.	O'Neall's Annals of Newberry,
Watson, Michael			Johnson's Traditions of Revolution, 1780.
Weyman, Edward	Lieutenant.	Battalion of Artillery.	Garden's Anecdotes, 1776,
Weyman, —	Captain.	Artillery.	Gibbes's Documentary History, 1781.
White, Henry	Colonel.		Johnson's Traditions of Revolution, 1780.
White, Sims	Lieutenant.	Battalion of Artillery	Garden's Anecdotes, 1776,
Whitefield, Luke	Lieutenant.	St. David's Parish.	Journal of Council of Safety, 21 Feb, 1776.
Whittington, Ephraim	Captain.	Charles Town Militia.	Gregg's History of Old Cheraws, 1781.
Wigg, —	Lieutenant.	Col. G. G. Powell's Regiment	Garden's Anecdotes, 1779.
Wilds, Jesse	Captain.	Col. Benton's Reg't, Marion Bri-[gade.	Gregg's History of Old Cheraws, 1782.
Wilds, John	Lieutenant.	Col. Benton's Reg't, Marion Bri-[gade.	Gibbes's Documentary History, 1771
Wilkie, —	Captain.	"	Ramsay's Revolution, 1780.
Wilkins, Benjamin	Lieutenant.	Charles Town Militia.	Moultrie's Revolution, 1778.
Wilkinson, —	Colonel.		Gibbes's Documentary History, 1781.
Williams, Charles	Captain.		" 19 Nov., 1775.
Williams, Daniel	Colonel.	Col. Benton's Reg't Marion Bri-[gade.	Gregg's History of Old Cheraws, 1782
Williams, James	Major,		Carrington's Battles of the Revolution, 1780.
Williamson, Andrew	Lieutenant.	Killed King's Mountain, ——, 1780.	Journal of Council of Safety, 30 Nov., 1775.
Williamson, Shadrack	Captain.	Snow Campaign 1775, Commander.	Gregg's History of Old Cheraws, 1782
Williamson, Thomas	Lieut.	Col. Benton's Reg't, Marion	Journal of Council of Safety, 21 Feb., 1776.
Windham, Amos	Major,	Col. G. G. Powell's Regiment.	
Winn, Richard	Captain.	St. David's Parish.	Gregg's History of Old Cheraws, 1782.
Wishes, John	Lieut. Captain	Col. Koll's Reg't, Marion Brngade;	Lossing's Field Book of the Revolution, 1780.
Witherspoon, Gavin	Captain.	Indian Co. of Foot Rangers or Rovers.	Jour Coun. Safety, 21 Feb. '76. Gibbes's Doc. His.
Witherspoon, John	Lieutenant.	Marion Brigade-	Wallace's His. Williamsburg Church, 1781. [1781.
Witherspoon, Robert	"	Capt. Thos. Port's Co., St. David's Par.	Journal of Council of Safety, 30 Nov., 1775.
Wright, Isaac			18 Jan., 1776.
Wilson, William	Captain.		2 Dec., 1775.
Warden, —	Major.	John's Island Company.	Gibbes's Documentary History, 19 Nov., 1775.
Witherspoon, Joseph	Lieutenant.	Expedition under Major Williamson.	
Young, Thomas	Captain.		Johnson's Traditions of Revolution, 1780.
			Mills Statistics South Carolina.

FROM GENERAL WASHINGTON'S ORDERS, AS GIVEN IN MOULTRIE'S REVOLUTION, VOL. II, p. 361:

"The Major Generals to wear a blue coat with buff facings and linings, yellow buttons, with white or buff underclothes, two epaulets with two stars upon each, and a black and white feather in the hat..Brig. Generals..one star..and a white feather..Aide-de Camps..of Maj. Generals and Brig. Generals..a green feather in their hats; those of the Commander-in-Chief, a white and green..All officers as well warranted as commissioned, to wear side arms, either swords or genteel bayonets.."

—Photo by Kosiner-Palmetto, Beaufort, S. C.

RIBAUT MONUMENT

Now standing on the original site of Charlesfort built in 1562 by Ribaut. Unsung and unheralded this monument in this day and age stands on what is to become one of the most hallowed spots in America. Jean Ribaut came to America to escape religious persecution in France. Charlesfort represents the first foothold of protestantism in America.

WAGONS AND CARRIAGES OF THAT TIME.

MEDICAL MEN IN THE
AMERICAN REVOLUTION
SOUTH CAROLINA

Airs-Surg.d.1777..Alexander, Nathl.Surg.M.Axon,Saml.
Surg.M . .Brown, James . .Budd, Jno. Surg. 4th Artil.
Rgt . .Brownfield, Robt.S.M . .Carnes, Pat'k, Surg. M.
1st Cont. Drag. Aug 1777-1781 . .Carnes, Jno. Asst. D
Apoth. . .Chalmers, Lionel. Attend. Pris. . .Clieland,
Jno. Surg. M. 3rd Rgt. . .Crane, Jno. Apothecary. . .
Dayton, Johnthan Attend Pris..DeLa Horne-At.Wounded..
Elliott, Benj. Surg.M . .Farrar, Field-Prov. Cong. . .
Fayssoux, Peter-1st. Lt. SC Rgt. 1778 . .Ferguson, Saml-
S.M. . .Flagg, Henry C.-Surg. 1st Rgt. 1775. Apoth.
Genl. 1779. . .Garden, Alex-Surg. to Pris. . .Gillett,
Abram-Surg . .Gould--Surg 1st Rgt. 1775-76. . .Haig--
Assemb . .Haley, Jno-M. Mil. . .Hart, Oliver, Surg. . .
Harris, Tucker-Surg. Mil. . .Houston, James-Phy. &
Surg . .Irvine, Wm-Surg . .Johnson, Robt-Hosp. Phy . .
Johnson, Thos . .Lockman, Chas-S.M. .Lochman, Jno -
Surg. . .Martin, Jas-Surg. . .McNeil, Danl-Surg. 2nd
Rgt. 1775-6 . .Milligan, George, Mil . .Motette, Lewis-
Surg. . .Neufville, Wm-Rgt. Surg. . .Oliphant, David-
Surg. Med. Directr, S. Div. . .Perry, Benj-Surg. . .
Poinsette, E-Surg.M . . Poyas, Jno. E-S.M. . Prescott,
James-Surg. . .Prescott, Joseph-Surg. . .Ramsay, Jos-
Surg. . .Ramsay, David-Surg. & Statesman. . .Ramsey,
Jesse-Surg. M. . . .Rasche, Isaac-Surg. M. 2nd Rgt.
1775-6. . .Rasche, Jon. H-Surg.M. . .Read, Wm-Hos.
Phy. & Surg. . .Reed, Wm-Hosp. Phy. 1780. . .Rogers,
Alex-Surg. 3rd Rgt. 1775-6. . .Rose, Hugh-Surg. . .
Smith, Robt-M. & Chap. .Smith, Danl-Dup. Md. Surv. . .
Springer, Sylvester-M. 2nd Rgt. . .Stevens, Wm-Jr.
Surg. . . .Sunn, Fredk-Rgt.
Surg. . .Toomer, Anthony-
Surg. . .Tucker, Thos. T-
Hosp. Phy. & Surg. Turnbill ,
Andrw-Surg. Theus,Jeremh-
Surg. . Taliaferro, Dr. Jno. .
Vaughan-Hosp. Surg. . . . .
Vickers, Joseph-Hosp. Phy. .
Vickers, Saml-Surg. . .Vidian
Saml-Hosp. Surg. .Wallace,
John-Surg. . .Weatherspoon,
J-Surg. . . .Wharry, Robt-
Surg.M. . . .Wilson, Saml-
Und. Marion. . Witherspoon,
Jno-Surg.

GENERAL NATHANAEL GREENE

MEN OF GENERAL SUMTER'S BRIGADE, S.C.

Ramsay in his history of South Carolina says that a party of exiles who had fled into N.C., as the British advanced. .made choice of Col. Sumter to be their leader. .and that he took the field against the victorious British at a time when the inhabitants had generally abandoned the idea of supporting their independence. The British had burned Sumter's home and turned his family out of doors. They also burned the home and library of the local clergyman, Rev.

General Sumter.

Mr. Simpson and all Bibles which contained the Scots translations of the Psalms. . "The people. .arranged themselves under Sumter. .with the enthusiasm of men called upon to defend not only their civil liberties but their Holy Religion.". . These men were woodsmen of the frontier up-country living mostly in the north eastern part of the state. South Carolina was no longer in a condition to pay, clothe or feed troops, therefore Sumter's men furnished their own horses and brought along their muskets and rifles. Often "iron tools of neighboring farms were worked up by blacksmiths into rude weapons. .bullets were made by melting pewter. .furnished by housekeepers. (In battles) some kept at a   distance till by the fall of others, they were supplied with arms. When victorious, they rifled the dead. .of weapons." General Sumter was so daring and fearless he was called "The Gamecock."

-- -- -- -- -- -- --

LIEUT-COL. WADE HAMPTON-1st REGT. STATE TROOPS--GEN. SUMTERS
BRIGADE

Rutherford, James Majr. . .Snoddy, Andrw. Adjt. . .Withers, E. Adjt. . . Harris, John Qt. Mas. . .Linton, Saml. Qt. Mas. . .Allison, Thos. Pay Mas. . . TROOP COMMANDERS: Cpts-Alexander, R. W. . .Alexander, B. Wm. . .Burns, Peter. . .Reid, John.

CAPT. WM. ALEXANDER

Alexander, Andrw. 1st Lt. . .Gaylord, Saml. 2nd Lt. . .Hays, David Sergt. . . Wallis, Matt. Sergt. . .Alexander, David, Sergt. . .Alexander, Saml. . .Alexander, George. . .Brown, Alex. . .Barnett, Robt. . .Bruidson, Jno. . .Baker, Wm. . .Clark, James. . Cadner, Jno. . Clark, Jos. . Carothers, Wm. . Cowen, Isham. . Crawford, George. . Elliott, Wm. . .Ferguson, Moses. . .Hogshead, Saml. . .Hunter, Thos. . . Hemphill, Wm. . .Holland, Matthew. . .Johnston, David. . .Johnston, Thos. . .King, Hugh. . .Kennady, Alex. . .Linton, Saml. . .Meeks, Moses. . .McCleary, Saml. . . Millin, Jno. . .Mitchell, John. . .Ross, John. . .Robertson, Jno. . .Shelbie, Evan. . . Shealor, Wm. . .Shealor, Ino. . .Stewart, Danl. . .Williams, Jno. . .

CAPT. ALEXANDER

Alexander, Wm. . .Albright, Simon. . .Ballings, Fredk. . .Bonds, Morris. . .Boney, Jacob. . Cammich, David. . .Chapman, Wm. . .Culpepper, Jos. . .Dobbins, David. . . Earnwood, Wm. . .Forrister, Jno. . .Forister, Wm. . .Foust, Jno. . .Foust, Wm. . . Glass, Fredk. . .Gosard, Isaac. . .Hayes, David. . .Hewet, Jno. . .Hook, Martin . . Hyde, Martin. . .Hylie, Jacob. . .Jackson, Jno. . .Jacob, Shadrack. . .James, Benj. . .

Johannes, Peter. . .Jon, Henry. . .Joyner, Wm. . .Knight, Jno. . .Legran, Oliver,
. . .Loch Alex. . Lyons,Wm., & Robt. . .Mashburn,James. . .McCloud,Donald. . .
Minich, Adam. . .Osman, George. . .Pellam, Wm. . . .Robertson, Jas. . .Rodgers ,
Majr. . .Sallers, Jno. . Tomlinson, Thos(2). . Trull, Jos. . Watson, Jno. . .Watson ,
Robt. . .Wells, Edward.

CAPT. PETER BURNS (Pay Roll A & D)

Alexander, Abram. . .Alexander, Nathl. . .Alexander, Wm. . .Burns, Peter. . .
Black, Jos. . .Beaver, Mathias. . .Culpepper, Benj. . .Campbell, Jno. . .Campbell,
Robt. . .Caruthers, Hugh. . .Crawford, Jas. . .Cochran, Wm. . .Giles, Nathl. . .
Greer, Thos. . .Harris, Jno. . .Hayes, Jno. . .Holloway, Taylor. . .Harris, Drury. . .
Jones Jno. . . .Jackson, Ambrose. . . .Kesler, Jno. . .Lucust, Matthew. . .Miller ,
Adam. . .Maafield, Jno. . .Newell, David. . .Purvine, Jas. . .Purvine, Jno. . .Rass,
Gustavus. . .Roberts, Jno. . .Sell, Phillip. . .Smith, David. . .Smith, Jno. . .Slown
or Sloan, Jno. . Shenpecker, Lawr. . .Team, Adam. . .Wilson, Humphrey. . .White,
David. . .Young, Adnrw. . .Young, Jacob.

CAPT. JOHN REID

Archibald, Saml. . Brotherton, Wm. . .Bone, Jno. . .Bone, Wm. . .Bowman, Jas. . .
Baker, Barnabas. . .Carter, Danl 1st Lt. . .Corson, Linsey. . .Corson, Robt. . .
Campbell, Danl. . .Dickey, David. . .Gracy, Robt. . .Hill, Abram. . .Harris, Edw. . .
Love, Alex. . .Limerick, Patk. . Lawrence, Michael. . .Landsder, Robt. . .McMullen
Jno. Serg. Maj. . .McWherter, Alexr. Q. M. Serg. . .McCaferty, Jno. . .McGachy,
Jno. . .Neel, Wm. . .Nichols, Joseph. . .Potts, Wm. . .Robinson, Jno. . .Rutledge,
James. . .Rodgers, Joseph. . .Snoddy, Fergus 2nd. Lt. . .Scott, Joshua. . .Ware,
James. . .Worsley, Zacharia. . .Webb, John.

COL. HENRY HAMPTON'S REGT. OF LIGHT DRAGOONS

Welsh, Patrick Majr. . .Foster, Jno. Cpt. . .Barnett, Jacob Cpt. . .Mills, Jno. Cpt. . .
Tate, Robt Cpt. . .Fathern, Benj. Lt. . .Rogers, Wm. Lt. . .Porter, Robt. Lt. . . .
Barnett, Wm. Lt. . .Gill, Archd. Lt. . .Hamilton, James Fog. Mr. . .Andrew, Jno.
Qr. Mr. . .Wood, Thos. St. Mjr. . .Caroll, Joseph Qr. Mr. St.

CAPT. JACOB BARNETT

Baxter, Andrw. Lt. . .Barnett, Saml. Sergt. . . .Barnett, Wm. . .Bassett, Fran
Sergt. . . .Bourk, Robt. . .Brewster, Hugh, Jno. & Sheriff. . .Broom, Thos. . .
Caldwell, Robt. . . .Carter, Jno. . .Clark, Gideon. . .Colly, Mainyard. . .Craig,
Alex. . .Chapell, Wm. . .Bourk, Jno. . .Dennis, Isaiah. . .Flanagan, James Lt. . .
Forbes, Thos. . .Franklin, Jno. . .Gilham, Jacob. . .Gray, Jacob. . .Givens, Saml. . .
Grisham, Mjr. . .Gribble, Thos. . .Hand, Jno. . .Hargett, Jno. . .Harris, James
Sgt. . .Haws, Jno. . .Hazleton, Wm. . .Hodge, Wm. . .Howard, Wm. . .Huff, Benj.
Sgt. . . .Humphreys, Absolom. . .Jenkins, Arthur. . .Kelly, Jno. . .Karr, Wm. . .
King, Fran. . .McCamon, Jno. . .McCurdy, Jno. . .McKinzie, Alex. . .McWherter,
Jesse Sgt. . .McWherter, Aaron & George. . .Moore, David. . .Parker, Danl. . .
Peoples, Jno. . .Porter, Hugh. . .Poston, Thos. . .Pristly, Chas. . .Rightly, Jno. . .
Roberts, Jesse. . .Shaddyn, David. . .Smith, Chas. & Ralph. . .Stewart, Jno. . .
Stinson, David. . .Tracey, James Sgt. . .Walker, Saml. . .Wallace, Levy. . .Watta ,
George. . .Wharton, Aaron. . .White, Stephen. . .Williams, Jno.

CAPT. JOHN MILLS

Brown, Alex. . .Brown, Saml. . .Bishop, Jas. . .Bunch, Huck. . .Byrd, Jonas. . .
Cameron, Jno. . .Cougaler, Fran. . .Crosley, Saml. . .Cummins, Jno. . .Curtiss,
James. . .Dearmon, Wm. . .Deshasser, Jno. . .Duffie, Jno. . .Fibger, Lawr. . .Gill,

81

George. . Griffin, Gideon. . Parson, James. . Paull, James. . .Proudlove, Wm. . .
Singleton, Rich. . Taylor, Jno. . Walker, Phil. . Wallace, David. . .White, Rich. . .
Wier, Wm. . . .Wylie, James. . .Wylie, Jno. . .Hamilton, Wm. . .Hart, Jacob. . .
Hugh, Chas. . Hyatt, Jacob. . Kelson, Saml. . Kirk, Thos. . Lott, Wm. . McCammon,
Matt. . McClary, Robt. . McClure, James. . McClure, Saml. . .McFadden, Isaac. . .
Miller, Jno. . .Mills, Jno. . .Morrow, Jno. . .Off, Isaac.

LT. COL. JOHN THOMAS REGT. LIGHT DRAGOONS--GEN. SUMTER'S BRIGADE

Moore, John Majr. . .Smith, Wm. Cpt. . .Waters, Philip Cpt. . .Lusk, James ADJT. . .
Martin, Peter Q. M. . .Johnson, Levi Cpt. . .Vanzant, Garrott, Lt. . .Glynn, David
Cpt. . .Lusk, Robt. Cpt. . .Boyer, John Lt. . .Thomson, Wm. Lt. . .Hayes, Nathl
Lt. . .Newberry, Thos. Lt. . .

CAPT. PHILEMON WATERS

Armstrong, Jno. . .Bates, Dennis. . .Briges, Jno. Sgt. . .Calk, James. . .Calk, Wm.
Sgt. . .Chitwood, Danl & James. . .Childers, Jacob. . .Clark, James. . .Collends,
Jno. . .Crane, Wm. . .Crane, Mafeald. . .Downs, Wm. . .French Joseph. . .Jackson ,
Saml. Lt. . .Jacobs, Joshua Sgt. . .Johnston, David. . .Magruer, Elijah. . .Makentier,
Jno. . .Mode, James. . .More, Saml. . .Morrison, Patrick & John. . .Murphy, Wm.
S:M. .Noland, Shadrack. .Presnoll, Jacob. . .Pruit, Abraham. . .Rife, Cunrod. . .
Roberts, Benj. . . .Thomson, Charles. . .Tramell, Samson. . .Turner, James &
Thos. .Vaughan, Joell. .Veach, Eliza. . .Waldrop, Jno. . .Waters, West & Philip. . .
Webb, Jerry. . .Walles, Lazerus. . .Wilson, Wm. Lt. . .White, Jerry & Stephen.

CAPT. WILLIAM SMITH

Antly; George. . . .Bearden, Richard, John & Wm. . .Bird, Nathan. . .Coldwell,
Wm. . .Chandler, Jesse. . .Dawkins, James. . .Day, Saml. . .Eliott, Chas. . .Flinn,
James. . . . Gaston, James. . . .Griffis, Thos. . .Glasgo, Robt. . .Harris, Jno. . .
Houlditch, Wm. .Herrin, Wm. .Toney, Abram & Drewry. . .Wolliston, Joseph. . .
White, Archb. . .Young, Wm. . .Jones, Jonathan. . .Lancaster, Saml. Sgt. . .Lusk.
Robt. Jr. 2nd Lt. . .Motlow, Jno. 1st Lt. . .Neal, James. . .Neighbours, Benj. . .
Pettitt, Henry. . . .Rest, Jno. . .Seagler, Wm. . .Smith, Wm. & Zopher. . .Smith,
Nathan. . . .Scott, Robt. . .Steel, Jno. . .Strother, Jas. . .Swords, Wm. . .Hughes,
Geo. . .Jeffris, Geo. & Lt. Berry & Allen. . .Jackson, Wm.

LT. COL. WILLIAM POLK'S REGT. Light Dragoons-Gen. Sumter's Brigade.

Snipes, Wm. C. Maj. . . .Martin, Saml. Cpt. . .Martin, Nat. M. Cpt. . .Shelby,
Thos. Cpt. . .Polk, Chas. Lt. . .Long, Jno. Lt. . .McCurby, Archd. Lt. . .Clarke,
Jno. Adjt. . .Conner, James Q. Mas.

CAPT. NATHL. M. MARTIN

Adams, Thos. . .Beryhia, Alexr. . .Black, Wm. . .Bryan, Henry. . .Clarke, Jonas
1st. Lt. . .Clarke, Jesse Sgt. . .Cooke, Nathl. . .Dunn, Andrw. . .Davis, James. . .
Dickson, James. . .Evance, James. . .Farson, Jno. Sgt. . .Frizell, Jno. . .Forden,
Jno. . . .Freeman, Michl. . . .Grimes, Wm. . .Hayes, Adam, Hugh, John, Moses,
Wm. .Haynes, Barthw. .Harris, Wm. .Hughes, Saml. . .Irwin, Robt. . .McGwigin,
Danl. . . .McDowell, Thos. . .Mitchell, Wm. . .Miller, David. . .Jenny, James. . .
Rhodes, Jacob. . .Ried, Jno. . .Rogers, Seth. . .Rodgers, Nathl. . .Russell, Jno. . .
Robineff, Jesse. .Smith, Thos. .Sandford, Saml. .Short, Abram. . .Smith, Wm. . .
Stuart, Thos. .Smith, Saml. .Saxton, James. . .Simons, Ishml. . .Sample, Wm. . .
Shelby, Moses. . .Thomson, Wm. . .Walker, Robt. 2nd Lt. . .Witherspoon, Wm.
Sgt. . .White, Benj. Sgt. . .Walker, Robt. . .Woods, Wm. . .Wyatt, James.

CAPT. SAMUEL MARTIN

Adams, Joseph Sgt. . .Allen, Wm. . .Alexander, Joel. . .Baker, Peter. . .Benson,
Thos. . .Barr, Will. . .Bonner, Will. . .Barron, James. . .Carruth, Alex. Sgt. . .
Carson, Jno. . . .Cumpton, Thos. . .Crayton, Chas. . .Cazza, Henry. ; .Coleman,
Chas. . . .Clendening, Mattw. . .Clendening, Wm. . .Cress, Phil. . .Cunningham,
Robt. . . .Deepnest, Wm. . . .Dupriest, John. . .Eliott, Jno. Sgt. . .Furman, Benj.
Sergt.M. .Frazer, San. . .Fitten, Isaiah. . .Huffman, Jno. . .Gray, Jno. . .Gillaspi,
James Sgt. .Garrison, Isaac. .Hemphill, Sam 2nd Lt. .Hager, Cymon. . .Houston,
Geo. . . .Irwin, Jno. . .Jack, James 2nd Lt. . .Johnston, Matt. . .Kline, Michl. . .
Knowls, Abram. . .Logan, Hugh. . .Lessonbury, Reuben. . .Linn, Alex. . .Lisse,
Leonard. .McCain, Hans & Hugh. .Merneal, Jno. . .McCallaster, Jno. . .McFalls,
Jno. .Mitchell, James. .McCracken, James. . .McEntire, Robt. . .Moyer, Elias. . .
McDonald, Pat. . .McCracken, Hugh. . .McCoy, Mechd. . .Nelson, Robt. Sgt. . .
Nelson, James. . . .Oliphant, Robt. . .Osborn, Robt. . .Pendleton, Jno. . .Philips,
Wm. . . .Polk, Thos. 1st Lt. . .Rogers, Alex. Q. M. S. . .Rea, Robt. . .Russell,
Thos. John. . .Robinson, Wm. . .Scot, Wm. Sgt. . .Sloan, Robt. . .Shield, Thos. . .
Shield, Robt. .Stoner, Peter. . .Sadler, Jno. . .Sullivan, Dan. . .Savage, Henry. . .
Walker, James. . .Wells, Wm. . .Wilson, Joseph. . .Williams, Thomas.

COL. WILLIAM HILL'S REGT. Of State Troops

Buford, Wm. Majr. . .Giles, James Cpt. . .McGay, Wm. Cpt. . .McKenzey, Will.
Cpt. . .Neely, Sam Cpt. . .Reese, Chas. Lt. . .Camil. Jno. Lt. . .McDowl, James
Lt. . .Reed, John Lt.

CAPT. JAMES GILES

Brian, Matt. . . .Calhoon, Davd. . .Clark, James. . .Cohorn, Hugh. . .Cummens,
Jon. . . .Cunngham, Miles. . .Curry, Robt. . .Davies, Joseph, Lt. . .Davies, Jon.
Sgt. . .Dowall, Jno. . .Denny, Jas. . .Graham, George Lt. . .Gerret, Wm. . Green,
Wm. . .Hains, Davd. . .Hall, Sam. . .Hill, Wm. . .Hutchison, Sam Q. Mst. Sgt. . .
Inis, Martin & Wil. . .Knox, Sam. . .Liveston, Henry & Abram. . .Liddy, Jno. Q.
Mst. .McCall, Jon & David. .McGibenay, Hugh. . .Moor, Jno. . .Nicleson, Jon. . .
Nicles, Thos. . .Reed, Geo. & Thos. . .Smith, Wil & Jon. . .Waker, Jon Sgt. . .
Wilson, James Sgt. .Wilson, Wm. . .Wilson, Jon. . .Williams, Thos... .Ward, Wil.

CAPT. WM. McKINZEY

Adams, Jno. Carrol Arm. . . .Alexander, Abram. . .Armstrong, Nathen. . .Baty,
Simon. . .Bowell, Thos. .Bryan, James. . .Cobb, Abrous. . .Collins, Jo. . Con,
Wm. .Davis, Sneed. .Dowell, Geo. Elkins Jno. . .Fortinberg, Jno. . .Green, Isaac
& Thos. . .Gules or Jiles, Wm. . .Hodgiss, Saml. . .Humberger, Josua. . .Hunt,
Jo. . . .Hunter, Edw. . . .Hunter, Jno. . .Hutson, Drury. . .James, Rollen. . .Jiles,
Wm. . .Lequeare, Jno. . .Mattock, Wm. . .McCain, Jos. . .McCracken, Wm. . .
McGuinis, Andrw. . . .McMichea, Davd. . . .McGlane, Jno. . .McKenzie, Wm. . .
Mullinax, Mathea. . .Rackley, Francis & Parson. . .Rackley, Jos. . .Rhinehardt,
Prunen. .Rhinehardt, Coonrad. . .Robertson, Israel. . .Robertson, Jas. . .Sallins,
Jas. .Shope, Peter. .Smith, Thos. . .Starnes, Jno. . .Templeman, Aron. . .Twitty,
Wm. . .Whitehead, Geo. . .Withers, Valentine.

COL. CHARLES MYDDLETON'S REGT - 2nd Regt. State Dragoons

Boykin, Francis Mjr. .Reid, Wm. Cpt. .Adams, Godfrey, Cpt. . .Moore, Francis
Cpt. .Ross, Isaac Cpt. . .Willson, Jno. Lt. . .Lloyd, Joseph Adj. . .Hayes, Andrw
Qm. . .Sharp, James QM. . .Gosling, Geo. Sgt. Mjr.

CAPT. FRANCIS MOORE

Abshaw, Jacob. .Anthony, Jno. .Baker, Demion. . .Baker, Jehu. . .Barns, James. . .
Brown, Richard & Geo. . .Brandon, Matt. . .Brazeel, Richard. . .Croft, Jno. 2nd.
Lt. . .Deal, Michl. . .Evance, Jno. . .Forbes, Jno. & Robt. . .Harison, Constn. . .
Hart, Jos. Sgt. . . .Hart, Jas. Sgt. . . .Huston, Jno. . .Hood, Jno. . .Kerr, Jos. . .
Mathews, Rowld. . .Miller, Robt. . .Murray, Davd & Josh. . .McNeely, Davd. . .
McWaters, Jno. .McDowell, Thos. .McCree, Wm. . .McGoch, Jno. . .McCormick,
Robt. . . .McCamon, James. . .Neele, Wm. . .Owens, Jno. . .Reed, Wm. . .Roney,
Maurice Sgt. . . .Richards, Jno. . .Saylor, Michl. . .Sloan, Jas. . .Steele, Jas. . .
Suthmyer, Jacob. .Spencer, Benj. .Scott, Rich. .Smith, Phil. .Thomson, Moses. . .
Wadle, Robt. .Wilson, Jno. .Wenkler, Conrad. .Wilson, Ezekel. . .West, Leond. . .
Campbell, Miss Robt. 1st Lt.

CAPT. ISAAC ROSS

Akins, Wm. .Bell, Jas. . .Boyce, Wm. Sgt. . .Bowders, Jno. Sgt. . .Brannan, Danl
Sgt. . .Boyd, Ed. . .Carick, Adam. . .Carter, Jno. Sgt. . .Campbell, Geo. Sgt. . .
Cooke, Burrill Sgt. . .Disto, Jesse Sgt. . .Duggin, Leo Sgt. . .Dash, Jno. . .Ezell,
Jno. Sgt. . . .Flint, Jno. Sgt. . .Graham, Alexr. . .Gatam, Jno. . .Gregory, Thos.
Sgt. . .Griffin, Jno. Sgt. . .Hayes, Jas. Sgt. . .Hill, Lodwk. Sgt. . .Hatfield, Saml.
Sgt. .Hardgrove, Jno. Sgt. .Harris, Mason Sgt. . .Harris, Griffin Sgt. . .Howser,
Andrw. .Henson, Jesse. .Irish, Martin. . .Jackson, Thos. 2nd Lt. . .Jones, Britton
Sgt. . .Jenkins, Shadk. . .Jackson, Jno. . .James, Henry. . .Keer, Hance. . .Kitts,
Martin. . .Laws, Matt. . .Miller, Abram. . .Martin, Martin. . .McGrew, Wm. . .
Murchey, Wm. .Outson, Jonth. . .Pullam, Wm. Sgt. . .Pennington, Kinchin Sgt. . .
Pone, Davd. Sgt. . .Pawling, Wm. . .Swetman, Stephen Sgt. . .Sellers, Jacob. . .
Smith, Henry. . .Tayley, Jno. Sgt. . .Whitaker, Jno. 2nd Lt. . .White, Jon. Sgt. . .
Wilkinson, Wm. Sgt. .Wilkinson, Jno. Sgt. .Wilkinson, Thos. Sgt. . .Watts, Thos.
Sgt. . .Ware, Wm. . .Winingham, Jas. . .Kelly, Miss Jas. . .Yates,Thos.

STAFF OFFICERS AND ARTIFICERS OF STATE TROOPS

Alexander, Chas. . . .Dysert, Corn. . .Dickson, Will. . .Jinkens, Jno. . .Lipham,
Fred. .Mee, Geo. . .Murrell, Wm. . .Miller, Chas. . .McClerath, Wm. . .Provoe,
Mr. . . .Price, Isaac. . .Shields, Mr. . .Simpson, Wm. . .Tenell, Wm. . .Taylor,
Saml. . .Withers, Enoch. . .White, Jno. . .White, Henry. . . White, Hugh. . .White
Jno. . .

THOS. SUMTER

A list of "Sundry Persons who received pay for cloathing-who are not included in Sumters List," and Special Bounty:

Adams, Richard. .Bordin, Richard & Wm. .Bryant, Henry. .Cardock, George. . .
Crawford, Saml. .Chitwood, Jno. . .Curweethus, Wm. . .Caruthers, Wm. . .Clark,
Joseph. .Edmaston, Jno. .Gardner, Wm. & Jno. .Gill, Jno. . .Gilbraith, Joseph. . .
Heran, Jno. . .Harris, Drury. . .Hunter, Saml. . .Jeffers, Littlebury. . .McClery,
Saml. . .McDaniel, Wm. . .Sadler, Jno. . .Shield, Wm. & Jno. . .Elliott, Wm. . .
Ziegler, William.

Charleston GATES

In Charleston we find the outstanding work of artists who designed in iron. Some of the wrought-iron gates certainly antedate the Revolution, as those before the Brewton Houses. The Gates of Saint Michael's Churchyard are believed by many to be the lovliest of their kind in America. Among others are: Simonton's, known as the "Sword Gates" (house prior to 1776); The Pineapple Gates at Geo. Edward's House (1770); Sass Gates; John Rutledge House; Lesne Gate.

GATES OF ST. PHILIP'S

Sword Gates

The Leseane Gate.

SMYTHE HOUSE—14 Legare. Built 1770.

ST. MICHAEL'S CHURCHYARD GATES.

HARRIETTA PLANTATION

The Waring Gateway

MEMORIAL To The Four South Carolina Signers Of The Constitution of The United States (Courtesy of D.A.R. Mag.).

— — — — — — — — — — — — — —

THE FOUR FUNDAMENTAL DOCUMENTS OF THE U. S. GOVERNMENT ARE: The Articles of Association 1774; The Declaration of Independence 1776; The Articles of Confederation 1778; The Federal Constitution 1787. South Carolina Signers of the Declaration of Independence were: Thomas Lynch Jr., Thomas Heyward Jr., Edward Rutledge, Arthur Middleton...Signers of The Constitution were: John Rutledge, Charles Cotesworth Pinckney, Charles Pinckney, Pierce Butler.

SOME REVOLUTIONARY WAR PRISONERS OF SOUTH CAROLINA

The Historian Ramsay says that some of the first prisoners were confined in vaults with the dead, and later, crowded on prison ships in such numbers there was only standing room. In thirteen months of captivity about a third had perished. The following data is taken from the South Carolina Historical and Genealogical Magazine, and checked with Ramsay and other sources.

On Sunday 27 Aug. 1780, following persons, prisoners on parole in Charleston, were suddenly taken from their homes by armed British Troops and conveyed to the ship, SANDWICH, moored near Ft. Johnson, and in a few days transported to St. Augustine:
Budd, Dr. John. . .Blake, Edward. . .Cochran, Robert. . .Edwards, John. . .Flagg, George. .Fayssoux, Dr. Peter. . .Gadsden, Christopher, Lt. Gov. . .Gibbs, Wm. Hasel. . .Hall, Wm. & Thos. . .Heyward, Thos. Jr. . .Holmes, Isaac. . .Hutson, Richard. . . .Johnson, Wm. . . . .Lewis, Rev. John. . .Livingston, Wm. . . .Loveday, Jno. . .Lushington, Cpt. Richard. . .Moultrie, Alex. . .McCrady, Edw. . .Mouatt, Jno. . . .Neufville, Jno. . . .North, Cpt. Edw. . .Parker, Maj. Jos: . . .Poyas, Jno. Earnest. .Ramsey, Dav. .Read, Cpt. Jacob. . .Rutledge, Hugh & Edw. . .Sansum, Jno. . . .Savage, Thos. . .Singleton, Thos. . .Smith, Josiah Jr. . .Thompson, Jas. Hamden. . . .Timothy, Peter. . .Todd, Jno. . .Toomer, Anthony. . .Massey, Col. William.

On Nov. 15, 1780 the following persons joined the above group:
Bee, Joseph. .Beresford, Rich. . .Berwick, Jno. . .Bordeaux, Daniel. . .Cudworth, Benj. . . .Crouch, Henry. . .Cripps, Jno. Splatt. . .Darrell, Edw. . .DeSaussure, Daniel. . .Hall, Geo. Abbott. . .Grimball, Thos. . .Jones, N. W. . .Lee, Wm. . . Logan, Wm. . .Middleton, Arthur. . ,Peters, Chris. . .Postell, Benj. . .Prioleau, Saml. . . .Smith, Philip. . . .Waller, Benj. . . .Wakefield, Jno. or Jas. . .Weyman, Edw. . .Morton, Wilkinson. . .Masters, Vendue. . .Savage, Thos. . .Isaacs, Col. Elijah. .Rutherford, Gen. Griffith, N. C. Mil., Rich. H. Thomson. .Mrs. Moultrie & daus. . .Jno. Morrell.

On 17 May 1781, the following persons were sent on board the prison ship TORBAY and the schooner PACKHORSE:
Arthur, Geo. . .Atmore, Ralph. . .Axson, Wm. . .Ash, Saml. . .Anthony, Jno. . . Blake, Jno. .Baddely, Jno. .Barnwell, Jno., Edw., Robt. . .Bounetheau, Peter. . . Bambridge, Henry. .Branford, Wm. . .Blundel, Nathan. . .Baskins, Wm. . .Bayle, Jos. .Bricken, Jas. .Bellamy, David. .Bonniot, Jno. . .Cummins, Rich. . .Cochran, Thos. .Clarke, Jonathan. . .Cray, Jos. . .Conyers, Norwood. . .Cox, Jas. . .Cooke, Thomas. . .Cohen, Jacob. . .Calhoun, Jno. . .DeSaussure, Wm. . .DeWar, Robt. . . Dunlap, Jos. .Dorsius, Jno. .Edmonds, Rev. Jas. . . .Elliott, Thos. O. . .Edwards, Warren Jr. & Jno. Jr. . . .Eberly, Jno. . .Eveleigh, Thos. . .Evans, Jno. . .Egan, Jno. . .Elliott, Wm. & Thos. Jr. & Jos. . .Gadsden, Philip. . .Girraud, Peter. . . Graves, Jno. & Wm. .Grayson, Thos. .Glover, Jos. . .Gibbons, Jno. . .Guerrard, Benj. . . .Gaskie, Michael. . .Grott, Francis. . .Geer, Christian. . .Holmes, Bee Jno. & Wm. .Hughes, Thos. .Hews, Thos. .Hamilton, David. . .Heyward, Jas. . . . Harris, Thos. .Henry, Jacob. .Harvey, Wm. H. .Hornby, Wm. . .Jacobs, Danl. . . Jones, Geo. . . .Keowin, Thos. . .Kent, Chas. . .Kennon, Henry. . .Kean, Jno. . . Lebby, Nathl. .Lesene, Jno. .Lever, Abram. . .Legare, Thos. . .Liston, Thos. . . .

Lee, Stephen. .Lybert, Henry. .Lockhardt, Saml. .Layle, Wm. .Legare, Benj. . .
Michael, Jno. . .Meyer, Philip. . .Minot, Jno. Sr. & Jr. & Abram. . .McDonald,
Chas. .Moss, Geo. . .Moncrief, Jno. . .Milner, Solomon. . .Monk, Geo. . .Morgan,
Jonathan. . . .Miller, Saml. . .Moore, Stephen. . .Murphy, Wm. . .Neufville, Jno.
Jr. & Wm. .Owen, Jno. . .Prioleau, Saml. Sr. & Philip. . .Poyas, Jas. . .Palmer,
Job. . . .Pinckney, Chas. Jr. . . .Robertson, Jos. . .Rhodes, Danl. . .Reid, Geo. .
Singleton, Ripley. . .Skottowe, Saml. . .Shrewsberry, Stephen. . .Snyder, Paul. . .
Smith, Saml. . .Sanders, Jno. . .Stephenson, Jno. Jr. . .Scott, Jno. Sr. . .Snelling,
Wm. .Troussiger, Jas. . .Taylor, Paul. . .Waring, Thos Jr. . .Waties, Jno. Jr. . .
Wigg, Wim. . .Wilkins, Jas. . .White, Sims. . .Waring, Rich. . .Warham, Chas.&
David. . .White, Isaac. . .Wrighton, Jos. . .Wilkie, Wm. . .Welch, Geo. & Jno. . .
Wheeler, Benj. . .Wilcox, Wm. . .Yeadon, Rich. . .You, Thomas.

The following were sent on the PACKHORSE:
Baird, Jonas. .Boquet, Peter. .Bordeaux, Nathl. . .Durham, Charnell. . .Fowles ,
Oliver. . .Hancock, Clement. . .Kilgore, Benj. . .Sarrazin, Jon'a. . .Ryan, Jno. . .
Turpin, Jos. . .Sudre, Peter. . .Wyatt, William.

On 31 Dec. 1781, the Edict of Col. Balfour Commandant of Charleston,
BANISHED all who would not take protection from the British. The heads of
families of these persons are hereby given. (Except the women who are given
in a separate list)
Arthur Geo. . . .Atmar Ralph. . .Axson Wm. . .Anthony Jno. . .Anderson Rich. . .
Butler Pierce. .Baldwin Saml. . .Blake, Edw. . .Budd Jno. Dr. . .Bouequet Peter
Jr. .Bremar Francis. .Berwick Jno. . .Bricken Jas. . .Berrisford Rich. . .Bonnist
Jno. .Bee Jos. . .Ball Jos. . .Bourdeaux Danl. . .Bourdeaux Nathl. . .Blake Jno. . .
Burke Adinus. .Cudworth Benj. .Conyers Norwood. .Cox Jas. . .Crouch Henry. . .
Costeng Jno. . .Cochran Robt. . .Cochran Thos. . .Cripps Wm. . .Cripps Splatt
Jno. .Crawley Chas. . .Crawford Bellamy. . .Dewar Robt. . .DeSaussure Danl. . .
Darrell Edw. .Eveleigh Thos. .Edwards Jno. .Edwards Jno. Jr. . .Elliott Thos. . .
Elliot O. Thos. .Edmonds Jas. Rev. . .Ford Benj. . .Fisher Jas. . .Fuller Wm. . .
Ferguson Thos. . .Flagg Geo. . .Garkey Michael. . .Gross Francis. . .Grimball
Thos. Jr. .Graves Jno. . .Graves Wm. . .Gadsden Christopher. . .Guillaud Jas. . .
Gibbons Jno. .Gibbes Hazel Wm. .Guerrard Benj. . .Gaze Noel. . .Harvey Henry
Wm. .Hall Abbott Geo. . .Harris Thos. . .Hart Oliver Rev. . .Hart Oliver Jr. . .
Hutson Rich. .Hall Thos. Jr. .Holmes Wm. . .Hamilton David. . .Hughs Thos. . .
Holmes Isaac. .Heyward Thos. . .Heyward Jas. . .Holroy Turpin. . .Hall Wm. . .
Johnson Wm. . . .Kean Jno. . .Kennan Henry. . .Legare Benj. . .Lee Stephen. . .
Lesesne Jno. .Logan Wm. . .Lee Wm. . .Lybert Henry. . .Lebby Nathl. . .Loveday
Jno. . .Livingston Wm. . .Lewis Jno. Rev. . .Legare Thos. . .Lushington Rich. . .
Lochman Jno D. . .McBride Jas. . .Mey Florian Chas. . .Mercer Rich. . .Mayret
Abram. . .Massey Wm. . .Miller Saml. . .McDonald Chas. . .Monk Geo. . .Minot
Jon. Jr. . .McLean Jane. . .Michael Jno. . .Moultrie Alex. . .Mouat Jno. . .Moore
Thankful. .Moultrie Wm. Cpt. . .McCall Hext. . .McCrady Edw. . .Moultrie Wm.
Genl. .Neufville Wm. . .Neufville Jno. . .Neufville Jno. Jr. . .North Edw. . .Nones
Benj. . .Owen Jno. . .Pinckney Cotes. Chas. . .Pinckney Thos. . .Poyas Ernest
Jno. .Prioleau Saml Jr. . .Peters Christopher. . .Postell Benj. . .Parker Jos. . .
Palmer Job. .Prioleau Philip. .Pillans Robt. . .Parker Wm. . .Pickering Wm. . .
Pinckney Chas. Jr. .Righton Jos. . .Rooks Wm. . .Read Jacob. . .Robinson Jno. . .
Rutledge Thos. .Rutledge Hugh. . .Rutledge Edw. . .Ramsay Dav. Dr. . .Robinson
Jos. . .Shrewsberry Stephen. . .Singleton Thos. . .Stone Chas. . .Stiles Edw. . .
Stone Wm-Pilot. .Starnes Danl Jr. . .Smith Thos-Pilot. . .Sansum Jno. . .Stafford
Arthur. . . .Stevens Danl. . . .Smith Josiah Rev. . .Smith Josiah Jr. . .Sararazin
Jonathan. . . .Stinson Jas. . .Synder Paul. .Smith Robt. Rev. . .Smith Saml. . .
Threaderaft Bethel. . .Todd Jno. . .Tousiger James&c. . .Tufts Simon. . .Toomer
Anthony. .Thomson H. Jas &c. .Taylor Paul. . .Turpin Jos. Jr. . .Timothy Peter

Peter &c. . . .Thomson Andrw. . .Welch Geo. . .Wilkie Wm. . .Waller Benj. . ..
Warham Dav. . .Wilkinson Morton. . .Way Robt. . .Welch Jno. . .Wilkins Jas. . .
Wheeler Benj. .Wakefield Jas. .Weyman Edw. . .Waring Rich. . .Waring Thos. . .
White Isaac. .Wil Philip. . .Yeaden Rich. . .Cattell Benj. . .Henry Jacob. . .Jones
W. Noble Dr. . . .Savage Thos. . .Oliphant Dav. Dr. . .Brown Dennis. . .Dunlap
Jos. . .Gadsden Thos. Cpt. . .Kirk Jno. . .Cooke Thos. . .Dacosta Isaac Sr.

"Besides the Persons mentioned...a number of Men, both Officers in the
Continental Line, and Militia Men of S. Carolina, were landed from Cartel
Vessels at Jamestown in Virginia..." This data and above list of names was
copied from the Josiah Smith Diary as published in the S. C. Histl. & Geneal.
Magazine of April 1933.

LIST OF MILITARY PRISONERS AT PLYMOUTH

Ashton, Lt. Jno. .Ball, Thos. .Duff, Andrw. . .Kennedy, Jas. . .Markham, Jas. . .
M'llahany, Wm. .Pitts, Wm. . .Russel, Danl. . .Ripley, Paul. . .Singleterry, Jos.
& Jno. . . .Steele, Wm. . . .Stobo, Lt. Jacob. . .Vestals Jas. . .Wells, Andrw. . ..
Wilkes, Hardy (From S. C. Histl. Mag. Vol. 10)

PRISONERS BUTCHERED AT HAY'S STATION, LAURENS COUNTY, S. C.

Cook, Jno. . . .Feris, Jas. . .Goodman, Benj. . .Hays, Col. Joseph. . .Hardy, Lt.
Christopher. . .Hancock, Clement. . .Irby, Joseph Sr. & Jr. & Greaf. . .Milvern,
Jno. . .Neel, Lt. John. . .Williams, Cpt. Daniel & Joseph. . .Saxon, Yancy. . .Hays,
Danl. . .Leonard, Lock.

Ramsey says that in the summer of 1780...20 or 30 citizens of most re-
spectable character...were shut up in prison...and loaded with irons, among them
were: Alexander, Col. . .Bradley, Jas. . .Boykin, Cpt. . .Chesnut, Cpt. Jno. . .
Few, Col. .Kershaw, Mr. .Hunter, Col. .Irwin, Mr. . .Strother, Mr. . .Winn, Col.

"Near Camden (the following with others whose names are unknown) were
taken out of goal and hung without ceremony: Andrews, Saml. .Gayle, Josiah. .
Miles, Jno. . .Smith, Eleazer. . .Tucker, Richard."

CAYCE HOUSE, OVERLOOKING CONGAREE RIVER, NEAR WHERE "LIGHT HORSE HARRY" LEE AND HIS REVOLU-
TIONARY TROOPS CAPTURED FORT GRANBY FROM THE BRITISH MAY 15, 1781.

87

Original church
built in 1684

Only Huguenot church
in America adhering
exactly to the liturgy
of the French
Protestant Church.

FRENCH PROTESTANT (HUGUENOT) CHURCH, CHARLESTON, S. C.

Commemorative services of the two hundred and fifty-fifth Anniversary of the Revocation of the Edict of Nantes were held on October 20th, 1940, in the Huguenot Church in Charleston.

Medway, built in 1687, home of one of the landgraves, the
oldest house standing in South Carolina.

SOME SOUTH CAROLINA HEROINES
OF THE REVOLUTION

(These names were abstracted from D.A.R. records, newspapers, family records including Bible and cemetery data and county histories.)
Adair, Mary. . .Arnett, Hannah White. . .Arnold, Mrs. Anne Hendrick. . .Arnold, Temp. .Allen, Judith. . .Beale, Unice. . .Barry, Marg. C. Moore. . .Bradley, Mrs. Elizabeth. . .Bratton, Martha. . .Butler, Behethland Foote. . .Dillard, Mrs. Mary W. of Cpt. Jas. .Dunklin, Mary. .Ervin, Mrs. Elizabeth James. .Ervin, Elizabeth Ellison. . .Ervin, Jane Witherspoon. . .Elliott, Susanna. . .Elliott, Jane. . .Elliott, Anne. .Farrow, Rosannah Waters. . .Gaunt, Hannah (Mooney). . .Geiger, Emily. . . Gibbes, Sarah, R. . .Gilliam, Elizabeth C. . .Gordon, Margaret Gregg. . .Hay, Ann Hawks. .Heyward, Mrs. Thomas. .Holtzclaw, Catherine R. . .Hopton, Mrs. Sarah & Daus. . . .Jackson, Mrs. Elizabeth. . .James, Mrs. Sarah. . .Kennedy, Anne. . . Lee, Nancy. . . .Leonard, Mrs. Mary G. . . .Leitner, Maria Beard. . .Langston, Laodicea. .Lindley, Elizabeth Hall. .Motte, Rebecca. .Musgrove, Mary. . .Morris, Anne E. . . .Mclean, Jane. . .Moore, Thankful. . .Noot, Mrs. Angelen. . .Pickens, Rebecca C. .Philips, Mourning. . .Moultrie, Mrs. & Daus. . .McDowell, Margaret O'Neal. . .Otterson, Mrs. Saml. . .Scott, Joyce Callahan. . .Steele, Elizabeth. . . Sullivan, Mrs. Mary Charlton. . . .Thomas, Jane Black. . . .Richardson, Dorcas Nelson. . .Waring, Elizabeth Grace. . . .Watson, Martha. . .Walker, Esther. . . . Wilkerson, Eliza Younge. . . .Listed on the roll of Cpt. Jno. Irving's Co., Col. Williamson, are: The widows-Thomas, Forbes, Brown, Parker. .On roll of Cpt. Francis Moore, Myddleton's Regt is-Miss Robt. Campbell. On the roll of Cpt. Ross, Myddleton's Rgt. is-Miss Jas. Kelly. On the roll of Cpt. Phil. Waters, Col. Thomas, Sumter's Brigade is Eliza Veach. At Hist'l Commission, Lib. U, is Mary Richie, N. 342.

The names listed next are taken from the S.C. Historical & Genealogical Magazine of April 1933. "Dec. 31, 1781. The Cruel Edict of Lieut. Col.Balfour Commandant of Charleston, for BANISHING from thence the Wives, Children & others dependent on those Virtuous Citizens, that wou'd not Sully their honour by taking protection...hereunto inserted their Names..." (I give only the women in this list who were heads of families):
Moore Thankful. . .McLean Jane. . .Anderson, Rebecca. . .Baker, Mary. . .Beale, Unice. . . .Brewton, Mary. . .Campble, Elizabeth. . .Dubertas, Widow. . .Dewees, Sarah. . . .Eldsworth, Susannah. . . .Glaze, Ann. . .Guerraud, Elizabeth. . .Gillon, Mary. . .Gleadow, Mary. . .Maltby, Elizabeth. . .Main, Rachel. .Noles, Mary. . . Owen, Elizabeth. .Springer, Margaret. . .Tobias, Elizabeth. . .Melvin, Martha. . . Dickerson, Sarah. .Sheed, Eleanor. There were 186 men, 120 women (including wives of heads of families) and 264 children.
"The distressed Situation of the familys that were ordered to leave Charleston by the first of August...occasion'd...in Congress...a Loan of $30,000 for the support of such citizens...as have been driven from their Country...(&) relief of said Sufferers."

SOUTH CAROLINA WOMEN WHO RECEIVED REVOLUTIONARY INDENTS

This list has been compiled from the records in the nine volumes of STUB ENTRIES TO INDENTS and the three volumes of ACCOUNTS AUDITED of Revolutionary Claims against South Carolina, issued by the Historical Commission of South Carolina. Some of these women loaned money to the state, some furnished supplies or rendered other services.

A ********************** A

Indents Bk. I: Annas Mrs. Elizbth p.65. . . .Bk. B: Anderson Mrs. Ann 68. . . . Atchison Mary 62. .Axson Elizbth 3,42. .Accts. Aud. Vol. 1: Abney Martha 34. .. Aberlay Mrs. Ann 13. .Adams Mrs. Mary 66. . .Addison Mrs. Mary 103,105. . . Akin Mrs. Ann 120. . .Alcorn Mrs. Catherine 128. . .Allen Mrs. Agnes 175. . . Accts. Aud. Vol 2: Anderson Mrs. Rebecca 72. .Anderson Ruth 66,67. .Anderson Mrs. Margt wid. of Cpt. Geo. 64,65. . . .Anderson Mrs. Margt wid. of Thos. of Camden 112. .Allison Dorothy 4,5. .Allison Mrs. Sarah 10. .Allison Rachel 7,9.. Allston Elizbth 32. . . .Allston Mrs. Rachel 34. . .Altman Mrs. Sarah 35,37. . .. Andrews Mrs. Jane 127. . .Accts. Aud. Vol 3: Ayer Mrs. Frances 13. . .Ayers Mrs. Margt 15. .Bk. L-N:Altman Mrs. Sarah 3. . .Bk. R-T Adair Mrs. Elizbt h 101. . .Adair Mrs. Sarah 162. .Andrews Mrs. Jane 57. . .Arnett Mrs. Jane 56. . . Bk. U-W: Adams Mrs. Sarah 25. . .Arnst Mrs. Maria 203. . .Atkins Mrs. Elisha 205. . . .Austin Mrs. Elizbth 204. . . .Bk. Y-Z: Aberly Mrs. Ann 161. . .Alcorn Catherine 161. . . .Allison Rachel 319. . .Anderson Mrs. Ann 104. . .Attoy Mrs. Mary 111. . .Bk. O-Q: Altman Mrs. Sarah 273. Anderson Sara 89.from Bk. B

B ********************** B

Indents Bk. I: Bails Mrs. Elizbth 66. . .Bair Mrs. Barbara 66. . .Barber Mrs. Mary 66. . .Barron Mrs. Rebecca 66. . .Beard Mrs. Mary 104. . .Bk. U-W: Box Mrs. Margt 248. . .Boyls Mrs. Martha 152. . .Bk. Y-Z: Baxter Mary 313. . .. Baynard Eliza 210. . .Berwick Mrs. Ann 217. . .Bolton Agnes 12. . .Brice Mrs. Margt (Lockhardt) 206. .Budd Susannah 62. . .Bugg Elizbth 126. . .Burke Elizbth 217. . .Bk. X. Pt. 1: Bayley Mrs. Lucy 145. . .Brandon Mrs. Agnew 142,196. . . Breed Mrs. Briscilla 142. . .Brown Mrs. Grizell 143. . .Bk. O-Q: Benbow Mrs. Martha 114. .Beverly Mrs. 309. . .Booth Mrs. May 179. . .Bowers Mrs. Sylvana 273. . .Bradley Mrs. Margt 46. . . .Brumfield Mrs. Elizbth 48. . .Bk. X. Pt. 2: Buzzard Elizbth 27. .Bk. L-N: Bagwell Mrs. Jane. .Brazell Hannah 6. . .Bridges Mrs. Mary 265. . .Brown Mrs. Sarah 264. . .Bryant Mrs. Sarah 264. . .Bk. R-T: Babb Mrs. Mary 164. . . .Babilitman Mrs. Zaba 9. . .Bonneau Mrs. Ann 106. . . Bowman Mrs. Sarah 165. .Box Mrs. Mary 163. .Boyd Mrs. Martha 9. . .Brazzel Mrs. Hannah 8. .Burns Mrs. Mary 166. . .Accts. Aud. Vol. 3: Babb Mrs. Mary 17. . .Bacot Mary 32. . .Ball Mrs. Elizbth 96. . .Bails Mrs. Elizbth 50-2. . .Bair Mrs. Barbara 52. . . .Baird Mrs. Winifred 55. . .Baker Charlotte Bohun 71. . . Bampfield Mrs. Rebecca 127-30. . .Barber Mrs. Mary 142. . . .Bare Mrs. John Christopher 143. .Bk. B: Bacot Mrs. Mary 27. . .Baker Charlotte B.59. . .Baker Elizbth E. 137. . .Ball Elizbth 44. . .Bampfield Mrs. Rebecca 162,208. . .Barron Mrs. Sarah 127. . . .Batchelor Mrs. Mary 22. . .Bancart Mary 137. . .Beresford Dorothy 34. .Beresford Sarah 18,105,110. .Berwick Mrs. Ann 90. . .Boobe Sarah 56. . .Bounetheau Mrs. Mary 220. . .Bower Mrs. Katherine 139. . .Boyd Elizbth 153. . .Broughton Ann 20. . .Burrington Elizbth 127. . . .Butler Sarah 36. .Butler Jane 87.

C ✲✲✲✲✲✲✲✲✲✲✲✲✲✲✲✲✲✲✲✲✲✲✲✲ C

Bk. B: Caesar Mrs. Hannah 116. . . .Campbell Lady Sarah Izard 152. . .Camon (Cannon) Mrs. Mary 102. . . .Cardin Judith 161. . .Cardy Mrs. Ann 40. . .Cattell Mrs. Sabina 159. .Chalmers Ann 130. .Chalmers Elizbth 80. . .Chalmers Martha 130. .Cockfield Mrs. Mary 140. . .Cook Margt 67. . .Cook Rebecca 67. . .Cooper Mrs. Mary 95. . .Cordes Mrs. Ann 80. . .Cowen Jane 190. . .Accts. Aud. Vol. 3: Colleton Mrs. Margt Swainton 162. . . .Bk. U-W: Caldwell Mary 65. . .Cottheen Mrs. Charoty 226. . .Bk. Y-Z: Campbell Elizbth 13. . .Carr Mrs. Jane 172. . . Carroll Mrs. Mary 173. . . .Clyatt Hannah 173. . .Corben Elizbth 212. . .Creech Ann 12. . .Creighington Mrs. Elizbth 253. . .Crouch Mary 126. . .Bk. O-Q: Caw Mrs. Rachel 178. . . .Clyatt Mrs. Hannah 172. . .Cottheen Mrs. Charity 223. . . Crosby Mrs. Hannah 278. . .Bk. L-N: Connell Mrs. Mary 268. . .Cooper Mrs. Elizbth 269. .Concil Mrs. Elizbth 271. . .Conturier Martha 9. . .Bk. R-T: Cason Mrs. Rosey 12. .Castellaw Mrs. Ann 70. . .Cobb Mrs. Judith 106. . .Collins Mrs. Mary 106. . .Craig Mrs. Eleanor 170.

D ✲✲✲✲✲✲✲✲✲✲✲✲✲✲✲✲✲✲✲✲✲✲✲ D

Indents Bk. I: Davis Mrs. Agnes 38. . .Bk. B: Dart Mrs. Amelia 117. . .Darrell Mrs. Frances 17. .Dawney Mrs. Sarah 81. . .Daws Margt 239. . .Delaney Elizbth 18. .DeWar Mrs. Elizbth 11. .Donnom Mrs. Susan 183. . .Doughty Elizbth 78. . . Doughty Mrs. Mary 78. . . .Dunlap Mrs. Margt 17. . .Accts. Aud. Vol 3: Darby Elizbth 28. . .Dawkins Mrs. Elizbth wid. 57. . .Bk. L-N: Daughtery Mrs. Mary 275. . .Bk. R-T: Davis Mrs. Mary 70. . .Bk. U-W: Durn Elizbth 261. . .Bk. Y-Z Davis Mrs. Mary 15,215. . .DeSaussure Mrs. Jane 130. . .Dick Mary 76. . .Droze Mrs. Mary 114. . . .Bk. X. Pt. 1: Davidson Mrs. Sarah 65,152. . .Dawkins Mrs. Chloe 151. .Bk. O-Q: Davis Mrs. Jane 106. .DeSaussure Mrs. Jane 310. . .Dobin Mrs. Elizbth 173. . .Bk. X. Pt. 2: Darling Mary 56. . .Dawkins Elizbth 127. . . DePre Mrs. Mary Elizbth 128.

E ✲✲✲✲✲✲✲✲✲✲✲✲✲✲✲✲✲✲✲✲✲✲✲ E

Bk.L-N: Elliott Mrs. Sabina 288. . .Evans Mrs. Elizbth 12. . .Bk. R-T: Edwards Mrs. Elizbth 189. . .Bk. U-W: Ellison Elizbth 67. . .Bk. O-Q: Elkins Mrs. Ann 280. . . .Ellis Mrs. Elizbth 310. . .Bk. B: Edwards Margt 185. . .Edwards Mary 185. . .Edwards Rebecca 100. . .Edwards Sarah 52. . .Ellington Amarinthia 85. . . Elliott Mrs. Mary 35. . .Elliott Mrs. Sarah 117. . .Ellis Mary 30. . .Ellis Mrs. Mary 45. . .Entelwein Martha 23. . .Eikester, Mrs. Mary 71.

F ✲✲✲✲✲✲✲✲✲✲✲✲✲✲✲✲✲✲✲✲✲✲✲ F

Bk. I: Ferguson Mrs. Mary 45. .Ferguson Mrs. Elizbth 45. .Fogle Mrs. Barbara 72. .Bk. B: Frazer Elizbth 92. . .Freer Mrs. Ann 224. . .Frierson Mary 156. . . Fripp Mrs. Elizbth 30. .Fuller Mrs. Judith 127. .Bk. L-N: Flanagan Mrs. 279. . Bk. R-T: Fisher Mrs. Sarah 22. . .Bk. Y-Z: Frashers Ann 52. . .Bk. O-Q:Faust Mrs. 311. . .Felder Mrs. Sarah 228. . .Fonches Mrs. Catherine 281. . .Fox Mrs. Mary 71.

G ✲✲✲✲✲✲✲✲✲✲✲✲✲✲✲✲✲✲✲✲✲✲✲ G

Bk. B: Gardner Lucy 243. .Gignilliat Mrs. Mary Magdalen 11. . .Gignilliat Susan 12. .Gillon Mrs. Mary 150. .Griffis Mrs. Barbara 6. . .Bk. U-W: Gardiner Lucy 268. . . .Bk. Y-Z: Gaddis Mrs. Christana 175. . .Gest Sarah 52. . .Gordon Mrs. Margt 150. . . .Gore Margt 41. . .Graham Mrs. Sarah. . .Bk. O-Q: Griffin Mrs. Mary. . .Greenwell Mrs. Mary 233. . .Grimball Mrs. Sarah 284. . .Gupbell Mrs. Elizbth 283. . .Bk. L-N: Gore Mrs. Rachel 14. . .Gray Mrs. Mary 253. . .Accts. Aud Vol. 1: Gloster Margt 141.

H-✲✲✲✲✲✲✲✲✲✲✲✲✲✲✲✲✲✲✲✲✲✲✲✲-H

Bk. I: Hartzog Mrs. Catherine 74 (Hartsuck). . .Hoffman Mrs. Catherine 76. . . Hutto Mrs. Ann 76. .Bk. B: Haley Mary 18. .Hall Mary 217. . .Hall Susan 43. . . Hall Mrs. Susana T. 84. .Hart Mrs. Ann 112. .Hill Mrs. Hannah 221. . .Hodsden Mrs. Mary 97. .Hoyland Mrs. Anna M. 102. . .Huger Mrs. Martha 193. . .Huger Mary E 11. .Huntingdon Lady Selina Countess 11. . .Hyrne Mary 37. . .Bk. U-W: Heath Ethel 168,174. . . .Hill Mrs. Mary 153. . . .Howe Mrs. Jane 153. . .Howell Martha 69. . .Bk. Y-Z: Hadden Mary 128. . .Hall Mary Ann 42. . .Hamilton Mrs.

Rachel 122. . .Harden Mrs. Elizbth 177. . .Harleston Mrs. Ann (Ashby) 121. . .
Hilton Amey 164. .Howell Mrs. Martha Eppes 177. .Hyrne Sarah Ann 53,168. . .
Bk. X. Pt. 1: Holcomb Mrs. Lucy 159. . .Bk. O-Q: Hadden Mrs. Jennett 78. . .
Heyward Mrs. Elizbth 288. . . .Hopkins Mrs. Sarah 285. . .Howell Mrs. Martha
288. . .Huggins Mrs. Mary 106. . .Accts. Aud. Vol. 2: Haddick Sarah 82. . .Bk.
L-N: Hayne Mrs. Susan 255. . . .Hicks Mrs. Jane 325. . .Hodges Mrs. Rebecca
324. . .Hubbard Mrs. Manoah 322. . .Bk. R-T: Haddock Mrs. Sarah 108. . .Hanby
Mrs. Jeremiah 220. . . .Hanby Mrs. Susannah 220. . .Heap or Heays Mrs. Sarah
29. . .Hill Mrs. Milly 202. . .Hubbard Mrs. Abigail 200.

I **************ʃ************* K

Bk. B: Izard Mrs. Charlotte 108. .Bk. R-T: Inabinet Margt 211. . .Bk. B: James
Eliz Ann Mrs. 103. . .Bk. L-N: James Mrs. Sarah 328. . .Johnson Mrs. Grissett
330. . .James Mrs. America. .Bk. Y-Z: Johnston Mrs. Martha 122. .Bk. X. Pt. 1:
Johnston Mrs. Sarah 162. .Jones Elizbth 73. .Bk. O-Q: Jenkins Mrs. Phoebe 3. .
Bk. X. Pt. 2: Jackson Amey 134. . .Bk. L-N: Keith Mrs. Margt 331. . .Bk. R-T:
Kelley Mrs. Margt 224. .Kessel Mrs. 212. .Bk. U-W: Keith Margt 115. . .Knight
Catherine 71. . . .Knox Sarah 70. . .Bk. O-Q: Kettle Mrs. Elizbth 290. . . Bk. I:
Kennelley Mrs. Elizbth 78. .Kibler (Keebler) Mrs. Lucretia 79. . .Kirkland Mrs.
Susannah 79. .Bk. B, Kelsal Mary Elizbth 137. .Kennan Mary Ann 101. . .Kinloch
Mrs. Ann 11. . .Knap Mrs. Mary 35. . .Knox Elizbth 4.

L ********************** L

Bk. B: LaRoche Mrs. Elizbth 71. .LaTour Mrs. Susan 126. .Ladson Eliz 217. .
Lance Mrs. Ann M. 116. . .Lane Mrs. Catherine 139. .Lesesne, Mary 54. . .Lind
Agnes 138. .Lining Mrs. Sarah 15. . .Liston Martha 44. . .Logan Elizbth 147. . .
Logan Martha 4. . . .Bk. R-T: Lesesne Mrs. Mary 148. . .Lewis Mrs. Eleanor
225. .Bk. U-W: Lance Ann 184. .Lowry Mrs. Jane 155. .Bk. Y-Z: Lenud Elizbth
5. .Little Mary 264. . .Lipton Mary. . .Bk. X. Pt. 1: Lesesne Mrs. Mary 225. . .
Bk. O-Q: Linn Mrs. Mary 5. . .Lootholts Mrs. Sarah 176. . .Accts. Aud. 1: Lee
Sarah 66.

M ************************ M

Bk. B: Marion Catherine 69. .Mazyck Mrs. Mary 155. .McWharter Mrs. Elizbth
221. . .Melvile Mrs. Jane 91. . .Mercer Mrs. Grace 133. . .Bk. 1 Maid Mrs Ann
65. .Moorer (Morreau) Mrs. Mary 83. .Myers Mrs. Mary 82. . .Bk. L-N: Mason
Mrs. Martha 341. . .McClwur Mrs. Mary 40. . .Morgan Mrs. Elizbth 337. . .Bk.
R-T: Mallard Mrs. Susan 45. . .Martin Mrs. Mary 213. . .McElveen Mrs. Mary
151. .Miller Mrs. 213. .Miller Mrs. Mary 158. . .Miller Jane 90. . .Minter Mrs.
282. .Minnich Mrs. Rebecca 213. .Bk. U-W: Magdalen Mrs. Mary 210. .Maxwell
Mrs. Sarah 284. . . .Marshall Sarah 72. . . .Mason Eleanor 286. . .McCord Mrs.
Sophianisba 283. .McKelveen Mrs. Mary 146. . .Miads Mrs. Sarah 224. . .Moore
Sarah 73. . . .Bk. Y-Z: Marr Elizbth 169. . .Marshall Mrs. Mary 134. . .McKay
Mrs. Cabton 135. . .McPherson Sarah 192. . .Melvill Mrs. Jane 82. . .Mucklewain
Mrs. Mary 132. . .Bk. X. Pt. 1: McKendrick Mrs. Catherine 173. . .McInSmith
Mrs. Catherine 173. .Mixon Mrs. Frances 14. .Bk. O-Q: McDonald Mrs. Rachel
11. . .Mann Mrs. Susanna 183. . .Marshall Mrs. Mary 3. . .Martin Mrs. Susanna
261. .McGill Hannah 184. .McIlveen Mrs. Mary 183. . .Moore Mrs. Dolley 41. . .
Bk. X. Pt. 2: McCarty Martha 158. . .Murphy Sarah 136.

N ************************ O

Bk. R-T: Newton Mrs. Jane 46. .Bk. U-W: Nieley Sarah 187. .Bk. Y-Z:Novelton
Mrs. 207. . .Bk. O-Q: Nance Mrs. Elizbth 294. . .Bk. R-ᵀ: Odom Margt 289. . .
Bk. Y-Z: O'Bannon Mrs. Abigail 176. .Olephant Catherine 315. .Bk. L-N: Oswald
Margt 26. . .

p.************************ P

Bk. L-N: Pagan Mrs. Jennett 53. . .Parsons Mrs. Susan 26. . .Patton Mrs. Jane
304. . . .Pitman Mrs. Priscilla 27. . .Powell Elizbth 304. . .Bk. R-T: Pon Mrs.
Elizbth 51,214. .Printer Mrs. Margt 294. .Bk. U-W: Pelot Mrs. Frances 150. . .
Pelot Mrs. Mary 150. .Penney Ann 77. .Petty Elizbth 189. . .Potts Mrs. Eleanor

132. .Pratt Mary 79. .Prescott Mrs. Esther 131,149. .Priggs Mrs. Eliza 155. . .
Bk. Y-Z: Patton Mrs. Sarah 158. .Pearson Tabitha 200. .Pendarvis Sarah 44. . .
Powell Mrs. Sarah. .Punch Mary 192. . .Bk. X. Pt. 1: Pyatt Mrs. Mary 186. . .
Bk. O-Q: Philips Mrs. Elizbth 16. . .Accts. Aud. : Paggett Mrs. Sarah 35.

R ************************** R

Bk. I: Reeves Mrs. Ann 86. . .Rickenbacker (Riconbaker) Mrs. Ann 86. . .Bk. B:
Robinson Nancy 102. .Roulain Mrs. Susan 163. .Bk. L-N: Ravenal Elizbth 29. . .
Reiley Mrs. Ann 30. .Ross Mrs. Elizbth 58. .Bk. Y-Z: Ravenal Mrs. D. Elizbth
275. . . .Rhodes Mrs. Elizbth 96. . .Rouse Mrs. Deberah 95. . .Bk R-T: Roberts
Mrs. Mary 208. . .Bk. U.W: Reading Mrs. Hannah 149. . .Ravenal Mrs. Elizbth
153. .Ritchie Mary 51. .Rowdus Elizbth 79. . .Rushing Sabrina 294. . .Bk. X. Pt.
1: Ravenal Mrs. Demaris Elizbth 24. .Ravenal Elizbth 23. . .Reggs Mrs. Elizbth
104. . .Robinson Mrs. Ann 83. . .Rows Mrs. Deborah 25.

S ************************ S

Bk. I: Seigler Mrs. Mary 88. . .Smith Mrs. Catherine 70. . .Snider Mrs. Mary
89. . . .Sucuck Ursala 91. . .Spurlock Mrs. Elizbth 89. . .Syfrett (Suffrett) Mrs.
Rebecca 88. .Bk. B: Saunders Mrs. Ann 20. . .Savage Martha 85. . .Savage Ruth
100. .Scanlan Deborah 129. .Scott Mrs. Frances 118. . .Screven Rebecca 162. . .
Simmons Mrs. 45. . .Simmons Mary 46. . .Skirving Elizbth 233. . .Skirving Mrs.
Sarah 87. .Smith Anna M. 237. .Smith Elizbth 196. . .Smith Mrs. Elizbth 236. . .
Smith Mary 205. . .Stanyarne Ann 83. . .St. Julien Susan 181. . .Stanyarne Mrs.
Elizbth 203. . .Stoll Mrs. Phoebe 219. . .Stone Mrs. Ruth 63. . .Bk. L-N: Smith,
Mrs. Mary 355. .Spring Mrs. Dorothy 315. .Bk. R-T: Saltus Mrs. Mary 154. . .
Sanders Mrs. 111. .Saylor Mrs. Elizbth 217. . .Shinholster Mrs. 296. . .Simpson
Mrs. Sophia 216. .Slappy Mrs. Isabella 216. . .Swan Mrs. Mary 155. . .Bk. U-W:
Shilley Mrs. Drewsella 157. . . .Singleton Ann 107. . .Snow Mrs. Hannah 139. . .
Sweet Keziah 140. .Bk. Y-Z: Simpson Sophia 182. .Smith Mrs. Catherine 103. . .
Smith Mrs. Janet 184. . .Stoll Rebecca 32,103. . .Suss or Surs Mrs. Susan 97. . .
Swan Mary 33. .Bk. X. Pt. 1: Saller Elizabeth 31. .Sanders Margt 51. . .Simpson
Mrs. Isabel 178. . .Simpson Mary 52. . .Singley Mrs. Rachel 83. . .Smith Mrs.
Christopher 181. .Smith Susan 29. . .Snellgrove(Swillgrove) Sarah 86. . .Steen Mrs.
180. . .Stuart Isabel 53. . .Stuart Mary 48. . .Bk. O-Q: Shoemaker Mrs. Elizbth 92,
248. .Singleton Mrs. Ann 131. .Smith Mrs. Mary 132. . .Summerford Mrs. Sarah 95.

T ************************ T

Bk. I: Tanseller Mrs. Mary 91. . .Bk. B: Tennent Mrs. Catherine 91. . .Thomas
Mrs. Ann 53. . . .Thomas Mrs. Mary 22. . .Trezevant Charlotte 78. . .Bk. L-N:
Tennant Mrs. Susan 313. . .Terrell Mrs. Sarah 34. . .Tyson Mrs. Sarah 35. . .
Bk. R-T: Teague Mrs. Alee 157. . .Toller Mrs. Mary 218. . .Bk. U-W: Thomas
Mrs. Mary L. 162. .Thompson Mrs. Sarah 161. . .Bk. O-Q: Thomas Mrs. Mary
Lambel 250. . .Bk. Y-Z: Taylor Sarah 9. . .Trapier Mrs. Elizbth 145. . .Bk. X.
Pt. 1: Taylor Jane 35. .Thompson Mrs. Elizbth 185. .Thorn Mrs. Elizbth 185. . .
Bk. O-Q: Taylor Mrs. Ann 194. .Terrell Mrs. Elizbth 96. .Bk. X. Pt. 2: Tebout
Mrs. Sarah 56,82.

U **** V ********* Y **** Z

Bk. U-W: Undean Mrs. Mary E. 196. . .Bk. Y-Z: Underwood Mrs. Naomi 60. . .
Bk. Y-Z: Vaux Mrs. Ann 201. . . .Verre Mrs. Mary 208. . .Bk. O-Q: Vanbibber
Mrs. Margt 134. .Bk. R-T: Young Elizb 250. .Bk. U-W: Zimmerman Mrs. Mary
151. . .Zuber Mrs. Rachel 142 in X. Pt. 2. . .Bk. B: Villepontoux Mrs. Jane 5. .

W ************************ W

Bk. I: Walker Mrs. Bersheba 14. . . .Weaver Mrs. Hannah 92. . .Williams Mrs.
Elizbth 93. .Williams Mrs. Mary 15. .Winckles Mrs. Elizbth 13. . .Wisher Mrs.
wid. 38. . . .Accts. Aud 3: Wilson Mrs. Winifred 55-7. . .Bk. B: Walker Elizbth
245. . .Walker Susan 31. . .Walter Mrs. 88. . .Warham Mrs. Mary 187. . .Waring
Dorothy 14. . .Waring Juliet 14. . .Waring Mary 61. . .Watson Mrs. Mary 107. . .
Watts Mrs. Rachel M. 183. .Wilkins Rebecca 61. .Williams Mrs. Elizbth 163. . .

Wood Mrs. Ann 101...Wood Martha 101...Bk. L-N: Walters Mrs. Mary 35...
Watson Mrs. Mary 318...Watsone Mrs. Catherine 36...Wheeler Mrs. Mary 70...
Wilson Mrs. Mary 37...Williamson Mrs. Celia 37...Bk. U-W: Williams Mrs.
202...Williams Mrs. Henry 148...Winkler Mrs. Mary 149...Withers Mrs. Mary
200...Wright Sarah 60...Bk. Y-Z: Walker Eleanor 222...Walker Mrs. Elizbth
177...Welch Mrs. Eleanor 129...Wilson Mrs. Martha 241...Bk. X. Pt. I: Watson
Mrs. Margt 58...West Mrs. Jane 188...Williams Elizbth 38...Williams Mary.
58...Wilson Martha 40...Wilson Mrs. Winifred 100...Wood Mrs. Mary 87...
Wood Catherine 42...Wragg Henrietta 108...Wright Elizbth 107...Bk. O-Q:Ward
Mrs. Susan 252...Watts Mrs. Rebecca 196...Weston Mrs. Barbara 195...Weston
Mrs. Sarah 195...Whitfield Mrs. Christy 100...Williamson Mrs. Mary 104...
Wooters Lilly 254.

Mrs. Rebecca Motte giving the
soldiers fire arrows with which
to burn her home.

PIONEER WOMAN

Arrest of Emily Geiger.

From D.A.R. Magazine, April 1937

Some Women of South Carolina in the Revolution

Mary Adair	Sarah Reeve Gibbes	Mrs. Samuel Otterson
Mary Alexander	Mary Anna Gibbes	Sarah Overstreet
Kate Barry	Mrs. Thomas Heyward	Rebecca Pickens
Mrs. John Beckham	Mrs. John Jolly	Eliza L. Pinckney
Mary Booth	Nancy Jackson	Dorcas Richardson
Martha Bratton	Dicey Langston	Joyce Callihan Scott
Behethland Butler	Esther Marion	Isabella Sims
Cateechee	Elizabeth, Grace and Rachel	Jane Thomas
Mrs. Dillard	Martin	Jane Elliot Washington
Anna Elliot	Mary McClure	Martha Watson
Susannah Smith Elliot	Jane McJunkin	Jane White
Sabina Elliot	Rebecca Motte	Eliza Yonge Wilkinson
Esther Gaston	Jane Morrow	Isabella Wylie
Emily Geiger	Mary Musgrove	

Rosemont, Home of Ann Pamela Cunningham, Savior of Mt. Vernon.
(Laurens County)

MARY MUSGROVE'S TRUNK. PRESENTED TO THE SOUTI
CAROLINA STATE CONFERENCE BY MRS. W. S. ALLEN,
TO BE PLACED IN THE D. A. R. MUSEUM, OLD EX-
CHANGE, CHARLESTON

THIS BRIDGE HONORS MARY MUSGROVE, REVOLUTIONARY HEROINE, WHO RENDERED CONSPICUOUS SERVICES
TO PATRIOTS DURING THAT PERIOD. BRIDGE SPANS ENOREE RIVER AT MUSGROVE MILL BATTLEGROUND.

WORLD'S "MOST BEAUTIFUL SPOT"

Glimpses of the Beauties and
Glories of Magnolia Gardens

St. Michael's Episcopal Church—S. E. corner Broad
and Meeting. Corner stone laid in 1751. Occupied
1761. Its bells have crossed the Atlantic five times.

ANNCESTRAL ROLL, S.C. Daughers of the American Revolution
Compiled 1938 by Mrs. E. T. Crawford, State Registrar.

A ☆ A

Abercrombie, Charles, Major
Abney, Paul
Abney, Nathaniel, Captain
Abney, Samuel
Adair, James Jr.
Adair, James, Sr.
Adair, John, Major
Adair, Joseph, Jr.
Adams, David
Adams, David, Jr.
Adams, Joel
Adams, Jonathan
Adams, Jonathan, Jr.
Adams, Thomas
Adams, Timothy
Adams, William
Albergotti, Anthony
Alexander, Adam, Colonel
Alexander, Abram, Lieutenant
Alexander, Elias, Jr., Colonel
Alexander, Dr. Isaac
Alexander, Jno. McKnitt
Alexander, Samuel
Alford, Jacob
Allen, Charles, Jr.
Allen, George
Allen, James
Allen, John, Captain
Alston, John Captain
Alston, William, Captain
Anderson, David, Major
Anderson, David
Anderson, Denny
Anderson, James, Captain
Anderson, Joseph
Anderson, Robert, Colonel
Anderson, William, Captain
Andrews, Sylvester, Captain
Archer, John, Lieutenant
Arnett, Hannah White
Arnold, William
Askins, William
Atwood, Joshua
Austin, William, Colonel
Avlett, William
Ayer, Thomas, Captain
Ayers, Thomas

B ☆ B

Bacot, Samuel, Lieutenant
Baer, Jacob, Lieutenant

Bailey, John, Colonel
Bailey, Samuel
Bailey, Thomas
Baker, Richard Bohun, Captain
Baker, William
Ball, William
Ballenger, James
Barker, William, Captain
Barkley, John, Major
Barnett, Joel
Barnwell, Edward, Major
Barnwell, Robert Gibbes
Barr, Martin
Barre, Jacob, Lieutenant
Barron, Archibald
Barry, Andrew, Captain
Bartlett, Josiah, Colonel
Baruch, Rufus
Baskerville, William, 2nd Lieutenant
Baskin, Andrew
Bates, Zealous, Sergeant
Baxter, Andrew, Major
Baxter, Daniel
Baxter, John, Captain
Beaty, John
Beatty, Thomas, Colonel
Beck, Jeffery
Bedford, Thomas, Sr., Lieutenant
Bedford, Thomas
Beers, Gresham
Belk, John
Bell, Samuel, Jr.
Bellinger, Edmund
Bellinger, John
Benan, James, Colonel
Benton, Felix
Benton, Lemuel, Lieutenant-Colonel
Bentham, James, Lieutenant
Berdsall, Benjamin, Lieut.-Col.
Berrian, John, Major
Berry, Hendson
Bethea, John, Jr.
Bethea, John, Sr.
Bethea, John
Bethea, William
Bethel, William, General
Billen, Stephen
Bird, Mark, Lieutenant-Colonel
Bissell, Ebenezer Fitch, Captain
Black, John, Sr., Lieutenant
Black, Joseph
Blackburn, Ambrose, Captain
Blackensderfer, Christian
Blackstock, William, Jr.
Blackwell, Samuel

Blair, James, Colonel
Blake, Isham
Blakely, William
Bland, Robert
Blassingame, John
Bledsoe, Bartley
Blythe, Samuel, Lieutenant
Boevie, Rhoda, (Rhody or Rhodi)
Boddie, Nathan
Boggan, Patrick
Boggs, Aaron
Bolling, Samuel
Bolling, William, Colonel
Bolton, Matthew
Bolton, Robert
Bonham, Absolone, Captain
Booth, John
Bostwick, Littleberry, Colonel
Botsford, Reverend Edmund
Bouchellon, Joseph, Captain
Bounethran, Peter, Lieutenant
Bowen, Robert, Captain
Bowers, David
Boyce, John
Boyd, David
Boyd, John
Boykin, Burwell
Boys, Nathan
Bracey, Sackfield M.
Bracket, Samuel
Bradford, John, Colonel
Bradford, Joseph B.
Bratton, William, Colonel
Brent, James, Major
Brewster, William
Brian, James
Brock, Reuben
Brockman, John
Browne, Henry
Brown, Archibald, Colonel
Brown, Bartlett
Brown, Bernard
Brown, Charles, Lieutenant
Brown, Daniel, Surgeon
Brown, John
Brown, John, Jr.
Brown, John, Sr.
Brown, Samuel
Bruce, Donald
Bryan, Nathan
Bryan, Simon
Bubier, John, Corporal
Buck, Jonathan, Colonel
Buddin, James, Second Lieutenant
Buford, William, Major
Bugg, Sherwood, Captain

Bull, John, Sr.
Bullock, Hawkins
Burkhalter, David
Burn (Burns), John
Burnley, Henry
Burress, Solomon
Bush, Daniel
Bussey, Edward, Lieutenant
Butler, James
Butler, Thomas
Butler, Thomas, Sergeant
Butler, William, General
Butterick, Joseph
Byrd, George, Second Lieutenant

C ☆ C

Cade, Drewry B. (Drunery) Captain
Caldwell, David, Reverend
Caldwell, James, Captain
Caldwell, John, Captain
Caldwell, William, Lieutenant
Calhoun, John
Calhoun, Patrick
Calloway, John, Major
Calmes, William, Jr. Lieutenant
Calvert, John
Camp, John
Camp, Thomas, Sr.
Campbell, David, Major
Campbell, Whittaker, Captain
Campbell, William, Colonel
Cannon, Daniel
Cannon, Isaac
Cantey, James, Captain
Cantey, Samuel
Cantrell, Thomas
Capers, William, Captain
Carey, (Cary), James
Carey, (John), Captain
Carothers, Andrew, Lieutenant
Carr, Dabney
Carroll, James
Carson, James, Lieutenant
Carswell, John, Lieutenant
Carter, Abraham
Carter, Churchwell
Carter, Dale
Carter, Giles
Carter, John, Captain
Carter, Samuel, Corporal
Carter, Thomas A.
Cartwright, Robert
Carwile, Zachariah
Casey, Levi, General

Cater, Thomas, Captain
Cave, John
Chambers, John
Chandler, Matthew
Chandler, Mordecai
Chapin, Benjamin, Surgeon
Chaplin, William, Jr.
Chaplin, William, Sr.
Chappell, Hix
Chappell, James
Chappell, Robert
Chappell, Thomas
Chase, Nathaniel Low
Cherry, Samuel, Lieutenant
Childs, Abraham
China, John
Chivesman, Samuel
Chloe, Michael
Clapp, Earl, Captain
Clark, James, Lieutenant
Clark, Timothy
Clark, William
Cleveland, Benjamin, Colonel
Cleveland, Robert, Capt
Cline, Michael
Coalter, Michael
Cobb, Jesse, Captain
Coe, Ebenezer, Sergeant
Coffin, William
Colbertson, Robert
Colburn, James, Brigadier General
Coles, John, Colonel
Coleman, John H.
Coleman, William
Collier, Joseph, Lieutenant
Collins, John, Captain
Collins, Joseph
Collins, Thomas
Connor, James
Conrad, Steven, Captain
Converse, Amos
Conyers, John
Cook, Burrell, Sergeant
Cook, James
Cookley, Benjamin, Lieutenant
Cooner, Jacob, Sr.
Cooper, Ezekiel
Cooper, George, Lieutenant
Cooper, James
Cooper, John
Copeland, John
Cornwall, Benjamin
Corrigan, William
Corry, Nicholas
Cosnahan, Joseph
Council, Henry, Captain

Covington, Benjamin
Cowen, Henry
Coxe, Samuel
Craig, James, Captain
Craig, John
Craig, Isaac, Major
Craighead, Alexander
Crane, Stephen
Crawford, James, Captain
Crawford, James
Crawford, Patrick
Creswell, James
Crittendon, Nathaniel, Second Lieut.
Cropper, John, Lieutenant-Colonel
Crossland, Edward
Culler, Benjamin
Culp, Benjamin
Cunningham, Arthur, Lieutenant
Cunningham, John
Cureton, William, Jr.

D   ☆   D

Dalrymple, John
Daniel, James
Daniel, John
Daniel, William, Sr.
Dantzler, Jacob
Darby, Asa
Darnall, Joseph
Darrant, Charles, Sr.
Davenport, Jas. M.
Davenport, William, Captain
Davis, Amos, Captain
Davies, Samuel, Colonel
David, William, Captain
Davidson, John, Major
Davidson, William, Major
Davies, Myrick
Davis, Andrew
Davis, George
Davis, John
Davis, T. Joseph
Davis, William, Lieutenant-Colonel
Davis, William, Colonel
Davis, William, General
Dean, Joel
DeGraffenried, Techarner, Sergeant
DeLeon, Jacob
DeLoach, David
Dennis, John
deSaussure, Daniel
Devlin, James
Dew, Thomas
DeWitt, William

Dial, Martin
Dickson, Matthew
Dillard, James, Captain
Dobson, Coillion
Doby, John
Dodge, Oliver
Dominick, Henry
Donelson, William, Captain
Dorn, George
Dorsey, Basil
Doty, Silas
Douglas, John, Lieutenant
Douthit, John
Dowling, Robert
Dowling, William
Downes, William, Adjutant
Dozier, John, Captain
Drake, Albrittain
Drake, Alberlain
Drake, Augustus Matthew
Drake, Oliver
Drayton, William Henry
DuBose, Samuel, Lieutenant
Duckett, Joseph
Dudley, Ambrose, Captain
Dunbar, William
Duncan, James
Dukes, Joseph
Dukes, Thomas
Dunklin, Joseph
Dunlap, George
Dunlap, William
Dunn, Jeremiah
DuPuy, John, Captain
Durant, Henry
Durham, Charnel, Captain
Durkins, John
Dusenburg, Charles

E ☆ E

Earle, Baylis
Earle, John, Captain
Earle, John, Colonel
Earle, Samuel
Easterling, William
Edings, Benjamin
Edwards, Richard
Edwards, Thomas
Elam, William
Eldridge, Christopher
Ellerbe, Thomas, Captain
Ellerbe, William
Ellison, Robert, Captain
Ellsworth Charles, Captain

Emerson, John, Captain
Ensign, John, Captain
Epes, Peter
Epting, Adam
Ervin, John, Colonel
Erwin, James, Lieutenant
Erwin, William
Espey, Samuel, Captain
Estill, William
Evance, Thomas
Etheredge, Henry, Sergeant
Evans, Batte
Evans, Ezekiel
Evans, John
Evans, Nathan
Evans, Nathan, Lieutenant
Evans, Roland, Captain
Evans, William, Lieutenant
Everett, Thomas
Ewell, James, Lieutenant

F ☆ F

Fain, William, Second Lieutenant
Farquhar, Robert
Farr, William, Captain
Farrow, Rosanna Waters
Faust, Burrell
Fayssoux, Peter Dott, Surgeon
Fearn, John, Second Lieutenant
Feaster, Andrew
Felder, Henry, Captain
Felder, Henry, Sr., Captain
Felder, Jno. Henry
Ferguson, Samuel
Few, William, Sr.
Finlay, James, Reverend
Fishburne, William, General
Fishburne, William, Lieutenant
Fisher, Adam
Fisher, Samuel, Captain
Fitts, John, Captain
Fladger, Charles
Fladger, Henry
Fleorl, John, Captain
Flewellyn, Abner, Captain
Flinn, William
Flood, Thomas
Flornay, Matthew
Floyd, John, Lieutenant
Foard, John
Folger, Frederick
Folger, Reuben
Forney, Peter, General
Forsythe, Robert, Captain

Foster, Abiel
Foster, James
Fox, William
Frasier, Alexander
Frazier, Thomas
Friday (or Fridig,) Gabriel, Captain
Frierson, John
Fripp, John
Fuller, John
Fullerton, John, Captain
Furman, Wood

G ☆ G

Gabeau, Anthony, Sergeant
Gadsden, Christopher, Brigadier
    General
Gaillard, Charles
Gaines, Joseph
Gaither, Burgess
Gale, Matthew
Gamble, Robert, Colonel
Gardner, William
Garry, John
Gary, Thomas
Gaston, John
Gaston, Joseph
Gaston, William, Captain
Gause, William
Gayle, Matthew
Geiger, Jacob John, Major
Geiger, John
George, Gotleib
Gervais, John Lewis (Louis)
Gibbes, William Hasell, Captain
Gibson, Erasmus
Gilbert, Amos Alling
Gilbert, Asabel
Gilchrist, John
Gile, Noah
Gilder, Reuben, Surgeon
Giles, James
Giles, William
Gilkey, William
Gill, Archibald, Colonel
Gillespie, George
Gillian, Robert, Major
Gillian, Robert, Sr., Major
Gilliland, James
Girardeau, John
Givens, Samuel, Captain
Gladney, Samuel
Glasgow, Robert
Glazier, John
Glenn, David, Lieutenant-Colonel

Glenn, James
Glenn, William C.
Glover, Joseph, Colonel
Godbold, Stephen, Captain
Goforth, Preston
Goggans, David
Goldsmith, William
Goldwire, James, Captain
Golson, John
Golson, Lewis, Major
Gooding, John
Gordon, David
Gordon, Roger, Lieutenant
Gordon, William, Captain
Gough, Richard, Captain
Grady, John
Grady, William
Graham, William, Colonel
Graham, William, Qm. Sergeant
Grant, James
Grant, William, Lieutenant
Gray, James
Grayson, John, Lieutenant
Green, George, Captain
Green, John, Colonel
Green, Isaac
Greene, Peter
Gregg, James, Captain
Gregg, Joseph
Gressett, William, Colonel
Grier, Thomas
Griffin, Charles, Sergeant
Griffin, James, Corporal
Griffin, Joseph
Griffin, Richard
Guin, John Nicholas
Gumeas, Elias
Gutekunsh, Frederick

H ☆ H

Hailey, William
Halbert, William
Hall, Jesse
Hall, William, Captain
Hall, William
Haltiwanger, John
Hambright, Frederick, Colonel
Hambright, Frederick, Lieut.-Col.
Hamett, Thomas
Hamilton, Andrew, Major
Hamilton, Ann Kennedy
Hamilton, David
Hamilton, John, Sergeant
Hamilton, John, Lieutenant
Hamilton, Thomas

Hamilton, William
Hammond, Abner, Captain
Hammond, Charles, Lieutenant
Hammond, LeRoy, Sr., Colonel
Hammond, Samuel, Lieutenant-Col.
Hampton, Thomas
Hanson, Walter, Captain
Harchfield, Henry
Hardir., Henry, Second Lieutenant
Hardy, John, Captain
Hardy, Thomas
Harnsberger, Conrad
Harrell, Lewis
Harrington, Henry W., General
Harris, Arthur
Harris, Hugh
Harris, John, Captain
Harris, Matthew
Harris, Robert, Colonel
Harris, Sherwood, Sr., Captain
Harris, Walter
Harrison, Benjamin
Harrison, James
Harrison, Richard, Maj.
Harvey, Arnold
Harwell, Landson
Harwood, Thomas, Captain
Haselden, William
Hatch, Benjamin
Hatch, Joseph
Hatcher, Benjamin, Captain
Hatcher, Josiah
Houser, Andrew
Hay, Ann Hawkes
Hay, Melchior, Captain
Hayes, John
Hayes, Joseph
Hayne, Isaac, Colonel
Haynes, John, Captain
Haynesworth, Henry
Hazel, Henry
Hazzard, William
Heath, Jordon
Hempsted, Stephen
Henderson, Samuel
Henderson, Thomas, Lieutenant
Henry, William, Sr
Heriot, Robert, Colonel
Herndon, Benjamin, Lieutenant-Col.
Herrick, Ebenezer
Herrick, Israel
Heyward, Nathaniel
Heyward, Thomas, Jr., Captain
Hickman, William
Hicks, George, Colonel
Higgins, John
Hill, Joshua

Hill, Lodowick, Sergeant
Hill, Squier
Hill, William
Hinds, Bartlett, Captain
Hinman, Elisha
Hodges, Joshua
Holbrook, Nathan
Holland, Reverend Moses
Holland, Thomas
Hollingsworth, Enoch
Hollingsworth, Jeptha
Hollister, Deacon Elijah
Holman, Conrad
Holmes, Orsamus
Holtzclaw, Catherine Russell
Hook, Martin, Sergeant
Hopkins, David, Lieutenant
Hopkinson, Francis
Horlbeck, John
Houscal, William, Captain
Houser, George, Lieutenant
Houston, Samuel
Howard, Groves
Howard, Seth
Howe, Daniel
Howe, (How), Samuel
Hubbard, William
Hudgens, Ambrose
Hughes, Joseph, Captain
Hughes, Thomas
Huggins, John, Captain
Hunt, Samuel
Hunter, Andrew
Hunter, Henry
Hunter, James, Colonel
Huntington, James
Hutchins, Drury, Captain
Hutson, Thomas, Captain
Hyde, Jedediah

I   ☆   I

Inabinet, John
Ingles, William, Major
Ingram, Edwin, Captain
Ingram, John
Irby, Joseph
Izard, Ralph

J   ☆   J

James, Benjamin
James, Daniel
James, Elias
James, John

Jarvis, Nathaniel
Jeffries, Nathaniel, Captain
Jenkins, Benjamin, Jr.
Jenkins, Benjamin
Jenkins, Reverend James
Jenkins, Joseph, Lieutenant
Jernigan, Jesse
Jeter, James
Jeter, Henry, Lieutenant
John, Thomas
Johnson, James, Captain
Johnson, Noble
Johnson, William
Johnston, John
Johnston, Nathan, Captain
Jolly, Joseph
Jones, Abraham Parman, 2nd Lieut.
Jones, Adam Crain, Jr.
Jones, Charles
Jones, Daniel
Jones, Jeremiah
Jones, John
Jones, John, Lieutenant
Jones, Peter, Lieutenant
Jones, Samuel
Jordan, Henry E.
Jordon, John

K ☆ K

Keeler, Jeremiah
Keels, John
Keith, Alexander
Keith, Cornelius, Captain
Kendrick, John
Kendrick, Samuel
Kennedy, James, Lieutenant
Kennedy, John
Kennedy, John, Sr.
Kennedy, Samuel, Surgeon
Kennedy, William
Kennerly, James
Kent, Phineas
Kershaw, Joseph, Colonel
Kerr, Daniel
Ketchen, Joseph
Kilgore, Benjamin, Captain
Kilpatrick, Reverend Robert
Kinard, Michael
Kincaid, James, Captain
King, Benjamin
King, Charles
King, John M.
Kirby, James
Kirk, Lewis
Kirkland, Reuben

Knight, John
Knotts, Benjamin
Knox, James, Jr.
Knox, Sara
Koger, Joseph, Captain
Kolb, Abel

L ☆ L

Lake, Thomas
Lamar, Thomas, Jr.
Land, William
Lane, Jessie
Lane, Job
Langston, Laeodicia
Langston, Solomon, Lieutenant
Langston, Solomon
Lanier, Burwell
Larray, Michael
Lawrence, Benjamin, Second Lieut.
Lazarus, Marks, Sgt.-Major
Lea, Gabrielle
Lea, James, Sr.
Leach, James
Leach, Nehemiah
Leary, Cornelius
Lecesne, Charles Frederick, 2nd
    Lieutenant
LeCompte, John, Lieutenant
LeConte, John Eaton
Lee, Andrew
Lee, Joseph
Lee Joshua
Leech, David, Captain
Leeland, John, Jr., Captain
Leeland, John, Sr.
Leonard, Laughlen, Captain
Letcher, William, Colonel
Lewis, Andrew, General
Lewis, Anne Montgomery
Lewis, John, Major
Lewis, William, Colonel
Libby, Nathaniel
Lide, Robert, Major
Lide, Thomas, Colonel
Liddell, Andrew
Lindley, Ziba
Lipscomb, Thomas
Lipscomb, William, Major
Little, James, Colonel
Livingston, Henry
Livingston, John
Livingston, Thomas
Locke, Richard
Lockwood, Joshua
Logan, Hugh, General

Logan, John
Logan, William
Long, Felix
Long, Henry
Long, Jacob
Love, Alexander
Love, Andrew, Colonel
Love, David, Lieutenant-Colonel
Love, Robert, Lieutenant
Lovell, James, Sr.
Lowell, James, Jr.
Lowell, James, Sr.
Lucas, John
Lunsford, Swanson, Captain
Lyne, William
Lymme, John, Colonel
Lyles, Aramanus, Captain
Lynn, David, Captain
Lynn, John

M ☆ M

Machen, Henry, Sergeant
Mack, John
Mackay, James, Sergeant
Manning, Lawrence
Manson, Frederick
Marbury, Thomas
Marion, Joseph
Marques, Isaac
Marsh, William
Marshall, James
Marshall, Thomas, Colonel
Martin, David
Martin, Edward
Martin, Gatlop, Lieutenant
Martin, Isaac
Martin, James
Martin, Kitchen
Martin, Matthew
Martin, Richard
Mason, David
Mason, George
Massey, William, Sr., Lieut.-Col.
Matlock, Timothy
Mattison, James
Matthews, Sampson, Colonel
Mauldin, Rucker, Preacher
Mauney, Valentine
May, John, Captain
Maybank, Joseph, Colonel
Maxwell, William T.
Means, James
Meetze, John Yost, Reverend
Mellichamp, St. Lo.

Mengel, Adam
Merchant, William
Meredith, Elisha, Captain
Meredith, Samuel, Colonel
Merrill, Benjamin, Sr., Captain
Merriwether, Thomas
Mershimer, Sebastian
Metze, John
Meyers, John F., Major
Mikell, John, Major
Milledge, John
Miller, Charles
Miller, David
Miller, Jacob
Miller, James, Colonel
Miller, Robert, Sr., Captain
Milner, John, Captain
Mills, John, Captain
Mims, Drury
Mitchell, Nazarath
Mitchell, Wm. Wilbur
Mobley, Jeremy, Captain
Moffatt, John, Captain
Monday, Jeremiah
Monroe, Malcolm
Montague, John
Montague, Peter
Montague, Thomas
Montgomery, Hugh, Lieutenant
Montgomery, James
Montgomery, John
Moore, Alexander
Moore, David
Moore, Eliab
Moore, James, Major
Moore, Phillip
Moore, Stephen, General
Moore, William, Lieutenant
Moorehead, William
Moorer, John
Mordecai, Samuel
Morehead, Charles, Captain
Morgan, Benajmin
Morgan, David
Morgan, George, Colonel
Morgan, Spencer
Morris, John
Morris, Joseph
Morrow, John
Morrow, Samuel
Morton, John, Captain
Morton, Oliver
Mosely, Azariah
Mosely, Benjamin, Lieutenant
Mosely, Samuel
Moses, George
Moses, Myer

Mosse, George, Doctor
Most, George, Doctor
Moultrie, William, Major-General
Moye, George
Muckenfuss, Michael
Mullin, James
Mulloy, Edward
Munnally, John
Murff, John
Murray, William
Myers, Jacob, Lieutenant

Mc ☆ Mc

McArthur, Daniel
McBee, Vardy, Captain
McCain, William
McCants, Nathaniel
McCants, Thomas
McCalla, David
McClendon, Travis, Captain
McClung, John, Lieutenant
McClure, John, Colonel
McColl, George
McCord, Charles, Corporal
McCord, Mark
McCormick, John
McCoy, John
McCoy, William
McCravy, Thomas, Sr.
McCrea
McCurdy, John, Jr.
McDavid, James
McDonald, Daniel
McDowell, Charles, Brig.-General
McDowell, Joseph
McDowell, Margaret O'Neal
McElwee, William, Lieutenant
McFadden, Robert
McGarrough, Joseph, Major
McGee, Michael
McGill, Samuel
McGregor, John, Lieutenant
McGrew, William
McIntosh, William
McIver, Evander
McJunkin, Joseph, Major
McJunkin, Samuel, Captain
McKinsey, William
McLean, Ephriam
McMaster, Hugh
McMaster, Hugh
McMaster, James
McMorris, William
McNeil, Hector

McNeill, Hector, Captain
McRaw, Francis
McWhorter, John

N ☆ N

Nason, Joshua, Captain
Natch, Edward
Neal, Henry, Captain
Nelson, Samuel, Sr.
Nesbitt, Jonathan
Nesmith, Robert
Nettles, George
Nettles, William, Captain
Nettles, Zachariah, Lieutenant
Neufrille, John
Neville, Jessie
Newcomb, Daniel
Newton, Younger
Nicholson, Wright, Lieutenant
Nimmons, William
Nims, Ariel, Sergeant
Nixon, Hugh Alexander
Norris, John, Sergeant
Norris, William, Sr
Norton, Ichabod, Captain
Norwood, George W.
Nuckolls, John
Nuckolls, John, Sr.

O ☆ O

Oakes, Daniel
Odill, Thomas
Ogier, Lewis, Captain
Ogletree, William
Oliver, Alexander
Orr, James
Osborne, Ephram, Jr.
Osborne, Ephram, Sr. Sergeant
Otis, Ephriam, Doctor
Ott, Abraham, Lieutenant
Outz, Peter
Outze, Peter
Overall, Nathaniel
Owen, Jesse, Captain
Owens, James

P ☆ P

Pace, Newsom, Sergeant
Page, John, Colonel

Paine, David
Palmer, John
Palmer, Jonathan
Parcival, Benjamin, Corporal
Parham, Drury
Parker, David
Parker, John
Parker, Moses
Parkinson, John
Parks, Samuel
Parrott, John, Sr.
Pate, John, Lieutenant
Pate, Matthew, Lieutenant
Patrick, Cain, Jr.
Patterson, Josiah
Patterson, William Joseph
Patton, Matthew
Paulling, William
Payne, John
Payne, Josiah
Payton, John, Lieutenant
Pearce, Joshua, Jr.
Pearman, William, Sr., Sergeant
Pearson, John, Major
Pearson, Moses, Lieutenant
Pech, Bela
Peeples, Henry
Pegues, Claudius, Captain
Perse, Silas
Perry, Benjamin F.
Peters, John
Pettigrew, Alex
Pettigrew, James, Sr.
Pettigrew, James
Petty, Absolom
Phelps, Elijah
Phillips, John
Phillips, Jonas
Phillips, Hugh
Phillips, Levi
Phillips, Mourning
Pickens, Andrew, Brig.-General
Pinckney, Charles
Pinckney, Hopson
Pitman James,
Pocher, Samuel
Poindexter, Joseph, Captain
Polk, John, Captain
Polk, William
Pollard, Robert
Pool, William
Pope, Barnaby
Pope, Folgu
Pope, Solomon
Pope, Solomon, Captain
Porcher, Peter
Porter, William, Lieutenant

Postell, Benjamin
Postell, James, Colonel
Postell, John, Lieutenant
Potter, John
Powell, Absolem, Sr., Captain
Powell, James
Powell, Sevin, Lieut.-Colonel
Poyas, Jean Ernest
Poyas, John Ernest
Preston, Walter
Price, Charles
Prior, Seth
Pritchard, George
Protho, Evans
Pruitt, Joshua
Purser, William
Purvis, George
Putman, Israel, General
Pyles, Reuben

Q ☆ Q

Quarteman, Robert

R ☆ R

Raeford, John
Ragsdale, John
Ragsdale, Peter, Sergeant
Rainey, Samuel
Rall, Thomas, Reverend
Ralston, John
Ramsburgh, James, Sr.
Rankin, Thomas, Captain
Rasor, Christian
Ravenel, Daniel
Redding, Anderson
Reed, Benjamin, Corporal
Reed, Samuel
Reese, Joseph, Reverend
Reeves, Enos, Captain
Reid, Francis
Reid, Joseph, Lieutenant
Reid, William, Jr.
Renfro, Mark Ensign
Rice, Aaron
Richards, Amos
Richardson, Amos
Richardson, John Richard
Richardson, Richard, Captain
Richardson, Richard, General
Richardson, William, Captain
Richardson, William, Colonel
Riddick, Joseph

Rinker, Jacob
Ripley, Jeptha
Risher, Benjamin
Rivers, Samuel
Roberts, John
Roberts, Reuben
Robertson, Thomas
Robertson, William
Robinson, Isaac
Robinson, Peter
Robinson, Thomas, Colonel
Robinson, William
Rogers, Benjamin, Colonel
Rogers, Lot
Rosa, Petru
Roseboom, Garrett
Ross, David, Sergeant
Rothmahler, Erasmus, Lieutenant
Rouse, William, Colonel
Rowe, Christopher, Lieut. Colonel
Roy, Beverly, Captain
Royal, William
Ruff, David
Rumph, Abraham
Rumph, David
Rush, David
Russell, Thomas, Lieutenant
Russell, William, Brig. General
Rutherford, James, Major
Rutherford, Robert, Colonel
Rutledge, George, General
Rutledge, Robert, Colonel

S   ☆   S

Sadler, David, Sr.
Salley, John, Captain
Salter, Edward
Sanders (Saunders), Peter
Sartor, William
Sass, Jacob, 2nd Lieutenant
Saunders, Nathaniel, Lieutenant
Scott, John
Scott, Joseph James, Captain
Scott, Joseph, Lieutenant
Scott, Joyce Jane Callahan
Scott, Samuel
Scovell, Elisha, Lieutenant
Seddall, Stephen
Sellers, Gordan
Setgreave, John
Sevier, John, Lieutenant Colonel
Sevinton, Hugh, Sr.
Shackleford, John
Shakleford, William, 2nd Lieutenant

Sharp, William
Sheldon, Whiting
Sheppard, James, Sr.
Shingler, George
Shiving, James, Captain
Shubirch, Richard, Captain
Shuford, John, Sr.
Simons, Keating, Asst. Brig. Maj.
Simonton, John
Simmons, James
Simmons, John, Lieutenant
Simpkins, Arthur, Captain
Simons, James Col.
Simpson, John, Commander
Simpson, John, Reverend
Sims, Charles, Lieut. Colonel
Singletary, Ebenezer
Singleton, John, Captain
Singleton, Matthew
Singleton, Ripley Nicholson
Singleton, Thomas
Skirving, James, Jr., Captain
Sloan, David, Captain
Smith, Aaron
Smith, Annanias
Smith, Charles
Smith, John, Colonel
Smith, John, Lieutenant
Smith, Jonathan, Jr., Reverend
Smith, Joshua
Smith, Merriwether
Smith, Roger Moore, Lieut. Colonel
Smith, Samuel
Smith, Samuel, Colonel
Smith, Stephen
Smith, Thomas, Lieutenant
Spann, James, Lieutenant
Sparks, Daniel, Captain
Spencer, Calvin, Lieutenant
Spencer, Thomas, Colonel
Spigner, Frederick
Spofford, Joseph
Sprague, Joseph, Captain
Spratt, Thomas, Captain
Spootswood, Alexander, General
Stackhouse, William
Stanley, Samuel
Starr, Daniel
Steadman, John
Steedman, John
Steele, Elizabeth
Steel, Francis
Steele, John, Captain
Steele, Joseph, Captain
Steen, James, Lieut. Colonel
Sterns, Josiah
Stevens, John, Lieutenant

Stevens, Simeon, Lieutenant
Stiles, Benjamin, Captain
Stillwell, John
Stock, John
Stokes. Jeremiah
Stone, Jacob, Sr.
Stone, John
Stone, Jonathan, Lieutenant
Stoncipher, John
Stoney, John
Storrs, Joseph, Major
Stratton, John
Streit, Christian, Chaplain
Strickland, Jacob
Strobel, Daniel, Lieutenant
Stroman, Jacob
Stroman, John Jacob
Stroman, Paul
Strong, Christopher
Strother, George, Lieutenant
Stuart, David
Stubbs, Lewis
Stubbs, William
Sullivan, Hewlett, Sr., Lieutenant
Summer, Francis
Summer, John Adam
Summer, John Adam, Lieutenant
Sumner, David
Swearingen, Van, Captain
Sweedy, David
Swink, John Little
Swinton, Hugh
Switzer, Henry

T ☆ T

Talbert, Richard, Lieutenant
Talbird, Thomas, Captain
Taliaferro, John, Doctor
Tarver, Absalom
Tatnall, Joseph
Taylor, Eldad
Taylor, Francis, Colonel
Taylor, George, Lieutenant
Taylor, James, Colonel
Taylor, Othneil, Sr., Adjutant
Taylor, Samuel, Major
Taylor, Thomas, Colonel
Taylor, Thornton, Lieutenant
Teer, William, Captain
Tennant, William, Reverend
Terrell, George, Major
Terry, Nathaniel, Major
Thatcher, Obediah
Thomas, Jane Black
Thomas, John, Colonel

Thomas, John, Sr., Colonel
Thomas, Jonathan
Thomas, Stephen
Thomas, William
Tompkins, Stephen, Captain
Thompson, John, Captain
Thompson, Matthew
Thomson, William, Colonel
Threewitz, John, Brig. Major
Thelkeld, John
Tillman, Frederick
Tillotson, Daniel, 2nd Lieutenant
Tinsley, Golden
Townes, William
Tozer, Julius
Treadwell, Reuben, Lieutenant
Trent, Thomas
Treutlin, John Adams
Trezevant, Theodore
Trott, Benjamin, Sergeant
Tucker, Harbert
Turner, James
Turner, John, Captain
Turner, Zadoc

U ☆ U

Ulmer, John Jacob
Underwood, Joseph

V ☆ V

VanAuken, John
Vance, Nathaniel
Vance, Samuel, Colonel
Vandiver, Edward
Varden, Steven
Vaught, Matthias
Venable, Nathaniel
Verner, John, Jr.
Vince, Joseph, Captain

W ☆ W

Waddill, Edmund
Wade, George
Waldo, Samuel
Walker, Adam
Walker, Alexander
Walker, Daniel, Jr.
Walker, Esther
Walker, John, Sr.
Walker, Nathaniel, Sr.

Walker, Samuel
Walker, Thomas
Walker, Thomas, Doctor, General
Wall, Wright, 2nd Lieutenant
Wallace, James
Wallace, John, Sr.
Waller, George, Major
Waller, John
Waller, Thomas, Sergeant
Wannamaker, Jacob, Lieutenant
Wannamaker, Jacob, Lieutenant
Wansley, John
Ward, Enoch, Captain
Ward, William
Warren, Josiah, Captain
Warriner, James, Captain
Waters, Boardwine
Waters, Philemon, Captain
Watson, David
Watson, Hezekiah
Watson, Michael, Captain
Watts, James, Lieutenant
Watts, James, Sr., Lieutenant
Watts, John, Colonel
Way, Moses, Captain
Weed, Reuben
Weedere, Augustine, Sergeant
Welch, Thomas, Sergeant
Wells, Richard
Wells, Robert, Lieutenant
Wertz, George Henry
Wertz, John
West, William, Colonel
Westbrook, Samuel, Captain
Whaley, Thomas
Wharton, Samuel, Colonel
White, Anthony
White, James
White, John
White, Vassel
White, William
Whitfield, Needham
Whitfield, William, Sr.
Whitner, James
Whitner, Joseph
Whitney, James, Rex
Whittaker, Thomas
Wideman, Adam
Wilfong, George, Major
. nkie, Lieutenant
Wilkie, William, Lieutenant
Wilkins, William, Captain
Wilkinson, Morton
Wilks, Thomas
Willard, Jonathan, 2nd Lieutenant
Williams, Benjamin
Williams, Elijah

Williams, James, Colonel
Williams, John, Major
Williams, Stephen
Williams, William
Williamson, Samuel
Wingo, John
Wilson, James P., Surgeon
Wilson, John, Captain
Wilson, John
Wilson, John Robert
Wilson, William
Winslow, John, Captain
Winston, Peter
Witcher, William, Sr., Major
Withers, Elisha
Witherspoon, David, Captain
Witherspoon, David, Captain
Witherspoon, Gavin, Corporal
Witherspoon, James, Captain
Witherspoon, John, D. D.
Witherspoon, John
Witherspoon, John
Withrow, James, Captain
Wofford, Joseph, Captain
Wood, Benjamin
Wood, Reverend Henry
Wood, John
Wood, Leighton, Jr.
Woodward, John, Lieutenant
Woodward, Thomas, Captain
Woodward, William
Wooten, Shadrack
Wooten, Shadrack (Patriot)
Warnock, Joseph
Wright, Joseph
Wright, Issac
Wright, Nicholson, Lieutenant
Wyatt, William, Jr.
Wyles ,William, Sergeant

Y ☆ Y

Young, James
Young, Thomas

Z ☆ Z

Zackary, John A., Sergeant
Zane, Isaac
Zenn, Jacob, Lieutenant
Zubers, John

ADDITIONAL ANCESTORS TAKEN FROM THE SUPPLEMENT TO THE
ROSTER OF S.C. D.A.R. COMPILED BY THE STATE REGISTRAR
MRS. JAMES T. OWEN IN 1944

Arnold, Jonathan
Anthony, James
Ayers, John
Adair, Jasper
Boykin, Maj. Francis
Bridgeman, Erasmus
Bennett, Reuben
Blount, Charles W.
Blanding, Capt. Wm.
Boozer, Henry
Bartlett, Capt. Wm.
Blassingame, Julien
Burris, Wm.
Beverly, Capt. Ray
Bowie, Maj. John
Brumbaugh, Jacob
Brush, John
Corley, Caleb
Cantalou, Capt. Louis
Chappell, Laban
Crosby, Thomas
Carruth, Robert
Conyers, Charles
Conyers, James
Crawford, Robert
Carmichael, Jno. Duncan
Cole, Capt. Abram
Cox, Henry
Cosnahan, Joseph
Croom, Major
Dick, William
DePriest, Wm.
Dorland, Garrab
Dukes, William
Deyo, James
Epperson, David
Fambrough, Thos.
Finley, Paul
Fayssoux, F.
Fullton, Jasper P.
Farrabe, Caleb
Gunnungust, Fred
Gray, John
Gaines, Richard
Gause, John
Grigsby, E
Graham, Michael
Garvin, Thomas

Gunnell, Henry
Gough, Capt. Richard
Gay, James Jr.
Goodman, William
Haselaw, Wm.
Hodges, John
Halbert, Wm.
Hayes, James
Hope, James Sr.
Hough, Joseph
Hilton, James
Huske, John
Hutto, Henry
Harris, Tucker
Hopson, Capt. Henry
Hoyle, John
Hearst, James
Johnston, Dr. Thos.
Johnston, Charles
Jarvis, Solomon
Knight, James
Kirkland, Francis
Kershaw, Jasper
Kirkpatrick, Jno.
Kennamer, George
Koger, Capt. James
Lewellyn, Capt. Abram
Lowe, Jno. Peter
Lowe, Robert
Lathrop, M
Lampkin, Stephen
Lowe, Basil
Lewis, Col. Fielding
Lennart, Wm.
Lee, Arthur
Lipscomb, James
Little, Col. James
McCalla, David
McKeown, Alexander
Messenger, David
Masters, David
McAbley, Wm.
Mackey, Thomas
Massey, Henry
Mosher, John
McMurray, Wm.
Morris, Julien
Moorer, James

McCattry, Robt.
McMullen, John
Nagel, Philip
Neel, Vol. Thos.
Orr, G
Oliphant, John
Orr, Jehu
O'Heak, James
Parsons, Wm.
Phelps, Capt. David
Pyron, Wm. C.
Pugh, Elijah
Query, Alexander
Rister, Benj.
Rose, Russell
Richards, Richard
Royse, Solomon
Scott, David
Sanders, Thomas
Sexton, Chap. O.
Sharp, Col. Starkey
Sweargengen, Capt. D
Springs, Richard
See, John Daulbit
Taliaferro, Jack
Tousinger, James
Tillingast, Col. D.
Twitty, Wm.
Ulmer, Jacob
Van Meter, Abram
Vance, Capt. David
Vaughan, John
Vigneron, Charles
Warren, Isiah
Watson, Col. Saml.
Waddle, William
Webb, Francis Jr.
Willis, Richard
Wilkinson, David
Windley, Maj. Thos.
Williams, Maj. Jno
Wings, John Sr.
Whitaker, Hudson
Wooten, Shadrach
Yancey, Capt. Thornton
Young, Capt. William

MONUMENT AT SITE OF ANDREW
JACKSON'S BIRTHPLACE

FORT MOULTRIE. On Sullivan's Island. This fort, originally called Fort Sullivan, has played a great part in two wars. From here the first decisive victory of the Revolution was won when the British fleet was repulsed in the engagement which made Sergeant Jasper nationally famous.

Jasper Replacing the Flag.

109

MAIN BUILDING (1828), COLLEGE OF CHARLESTON
The Oldest Municipal College in America

Williamsburg County Court House, Designed by Robert Mills who designed the United States Treasury Building and the Washington Monument.

GENERAL FRANCIS MARION

One of the great Partisan Leaders in South Carolina, was of Huguenot descent. He was known as THE SWAMP FOX, because he operated in the swampy forests of the Pedee region and lower part of the state. His strategy was to dash out quickly with his superbly mounted men, surprise and cut the enemy's supply lines, kill their men and release American prisoners, then swiftly back again to "the thick recesses of the deep swamps." Ramsay says of his equipment that "the pruning hook was converted into a spear; and the saw, under the hands of a blacksmith, became a terrible sabre." Marion's ORDERLY BOOK, 1775, has this item: "Every officer to provide himself with a blue coatee, faced and cuffed with scarlet cloth, and lined with scarlet; white buttons; and a white waistcoat and breeches...also, a cap and black feather..."

Below I list a few of Marion's soldiers that were connected with my family or else lines that I have worked on as a genealogist:

Arnold, Wm. . .Adair, Jas. . .Boyd, Jno. . .Conyers, Jas., Jon., Chas. . .Dickey, Jno. . .Ervin, Col. John, Col. Hugh, Saml. . .Ellerbe, Thos. & Robt. . .Fleming, Jno., Jas., Wm. . . .Frierson, Philip, William, John, George, Robert, William, Gordon, John, James, Wm. . .Gillespie, Andrw. . .Hamilton, James, John, Wm. . Knox, H ugh, Robt. . .McGill, Saml, Jno. . .Patton, Matt, Jacob. . .Nelson, John Saml, Thomas, Robert, Wm. . . .Wilson, John, Hugh, Wm. . . .White, John. . . . Witherspoon, Gavin, David, James, John, Robert. . .James, Major Jon, Alex, Geo, Robt., Wm.

Also the women: Dunklin, Mary. .Ervin, Mrs. Eliz. James. . .Ervin, Eliz. Ellison. . . .Ervin, Jane Witherspoon. . . .James, Mrs. Sarah. . . .Wilson, Mrs. Mary. . .

OLD STONE CHURCH

A few miles south of historic Pendleton. It was here that General Robert Anderson and General Andrew Pickens attended services and served as elders. Completed in 1802, this structure of rough native stone still stands as one of the oldest landmarks in upper South Carolina.

"HALCYON GROVE"—Historic Home of Gov. Andrew Pickens

St. David's Church at Cheraw, used as a hospital during the Revolution.

MISCELLANEOUS NOTES AND DATA

One hundred and forty-six actions were fought in the state during the Revolution and for almost three years, South Carolina was a battleground. This is stated in an article published in the D.A.R. Magazine of April 1937, by A.S. Salley, State Historian of South Carolina. Quoted in the article is General Knox, first Secretary of War, and the Historian, George Bancroft, neither of whom were South Carolinians and had no reason to be partial to this state, - Knox as saying that South Carolina furnished more troops to the general cause in proportion to population than any other state, and more money, regardless of population. Bancroft is quoted as saying that South Carolina suffered more and achieved more than the men of any other state. For almost three years civil war raged and there was no constituted government. Chapman in his History of South Carolina says that General Greene's Army outside Charleston, was for three months, half-naked and over 700 of them had no clothing except a small strip of cloth about the waist. In Johnson's Life of Greene we read, "...hundreds...were naked as they were born...the bare loins of many brave men...were galled by their cartridge boxes, while a folded rag or tuft of moss protected the shoulders...from injury (of) ...muskets." Chapman says that "after Charleston...had fallen, and the men who so bravely defended it had become prisoners of war, the British soon overan the whole state; for after the loss of Lincoln's Army, there were no Americans in arms in the state, except a few small detached bodies..." Quoting White, The Making of South Carolina, "...the region of the waters of Broad and Saluda...filled with companies of armed patriots...(they) planned attacks upon the enemy in their own way, captured forts in a manner not spoken about in books...did more than any other people of equal numbers to win freedom for America." Simms, History of S.C. states that "vapacious plundering and outrages (were the order of the day) ...volunteer bands...sprang up like mushrooms...officers without commissions, pay or provisions or necessary clothing (for their men) were leading (them) daily to little victories...many leaders...not mentioned in history, with troops of volunteers, achieved the salvation of South Carolina." Again, "after the battle of Eutaw Springs...William Cunningham (Tory leader) took advantage of the absence of any large American force, penetrated the interior, broke his force into small bands...gave no quarter..." Ninety-Six District alone had "1400 widows and orphans."

Chapman tells us that "Major Cunningham...led (a band) ...sole object... seemed to be to plunder, burn, murder. In the dead of night... they entered the solitary farm homes and sacrificed to their revenge the heads of families... these and other cruelties, compelled parties to arm and associate in self-defense." The Colonial and Revolutionary History of Upper S.C., by Landrum, states that "the unexpected appearance of Cunningham and the consternation that spread rapidly over the country on account of his cruelties, caused small parties here and there, to get together and take up arms in self-defense." Simms says that "soon small parties headed by outraged fathers were upon the heels of the marauders." Among the best known of the Partisan Leaders were Generals Francis Marion, Andrew Pickens, Thomas Sumter, Colonel & Brig-Genl. Williams. of Ninety-Six District, hero of Musgrove Mills and who fell at Kings Mountain. Major James was a well-known leader in Williamsburg county and organized the battalion that became the nucleus of Marion's Brigade. There were many other local leaders throughout the state. Ninety-Six District, embraced what is known as the Up-Country or Piedmont section and in 1785 was composed of what was later the following counties: Laurens, Edgfield, Abbeville, Newberry, Spartanburg, Union. This district claims 30 Revolutionary battles within her borders and 7 more on the Cherokee Indian lands which later became Up-country counties.

MISCELLANEOUS LIST OF S.C. SOLDIERS

Andrews Saml. . .Arnold Wm. . .Arnold Benj. . .Anderson Jno. . .Bolling Wm. . . Burton Jno. . .Choice Wm. . .Craig Jno. . .Cureton Jno. . .Gayle Josiah. . .Giroud David. . . .Holley Rich. . . .Kilgore Henry, Benj. . . .Knight Jno. . .Lewis Chas. Crawford. . . .Mahaffey Martin. . .Miles, Jno. . .McCauley Jas. . .Moore, Gully, Jeremiah, Chas, Jno. . .Moon, G--- . . .Paine Thos. . .Perrin Theus. . .Patton, Jacob. . .Pinson, Moses. . .Rodgers, Edward, John, Robt. . .Ridgeway, John Jr. & Sr. . .Susack Adam. . .Smith Eleazer. . .Simons, Cor. Jas. . .Sullivan, Moses, George, Patrick, Johnathan, John, Daniel, Hulet, Charles. . . .Tucker Rich. . _ Waller Benj. . .Watson, Michael, David, James, Joh, Robert, Gavin.

LIST OF SOUTH CAROLINIANS WHO CAME TO RELIEF OF BOSTON

The historian Ramsey says that people from every part of the state met in Charleston on 6 July 1774 to consider plans to support Boston. For the following list see D.A.R. Mag. Mch. & Aug. 1945. Also, McCrady, Under the Royal Gov; Gregg, Hist. of Old Cheraws; Drayton, Memoirs of Revo. South Carolina was the first to minister to the need of Boston. "By account pub. by Comm. appt. by Boston to receive donations...July 18, 1778, it appears that (those of) S.C. exceeded both in money & supplies, any other, not excepting Mass. itself":

Alston, Joseph, John, Joseph, William, Josias, Francis. .Andrews, Jno. .Barnard, Noble. .Bingham, Thos. .Butler, Thos. .Bonneau, Anthony. . .Boykin, Burrel. . . Buchanan, Peter Simons. . . .Clyf, Saml. . . .Cuttino, Wm. . .Council, Henry. . Corgill, Magnus. .Downs, Walter. .Donaldson, Jno. . .Dwight, Nathl. . .Edwards, Abel. . .Ellerbe, Thos. . .Godfrey, Thos. . .Gordon, Jas. . .Gillespie, Francis. . . Hazel, Thos. . .Hennery, Saml. . .Henry, Futhy. . .Hart, Arthur. . .Harrington, H. W. . .Huger, Ben. . .Horry, Alex. . .Hardwick, Wm. . .Hariot, Robt. . .Hicks, Geo. . .Lide, Thos. . .Lessenee, Peter. . .Mitchell, Anthony. . .Murfee, Malachi Jr. .Parks, Abram. .Pledger, Philip. .Pyatt, John. .Pegues, Wm. & Claudius. . . Pawley, Col. George, Memb. Prov. Cong. & Benj. & Wm. . .Roche, David. . . Rogers, Ethelred. . . .Reed, James. . . .Sparks, Danl. . .Scriven, Benj. . .Smith, Saml. . .Saunders, Jas. & Nathl. . .Trapier, Benj. . .Williams, Thos. . .Wright, Thos. . . .Wragg, S. . .White, Arthur. . .Warden, John. . .Wright, Geo. . .Young, William. . .Withers, Jno. . .Young, Benj. . .Hennery, Thos. . .Wright, Thomas.

MISCELLANEOUS

Soon after Battle of Lexington, following men chosen a COUNCIL of SAFETY: Henry Laurens, Chas. Pinckney, Rawlins Lowndes, Thos. Ferguson, Miles Brewton, Arthur Middleton, Thos. Heyward Jr., Thos. Bee, John Huger, James Parsons, Wm. H. Drayton, Benj. Elliott, Wm. Williamson, David Oliphant, Thos. Savage. Also Henry Middleton & John Rutledge were on a Council in 1775.

DELEGATES TO FIRST PROVINCIAL CONGRESS, JAN. 1775, from the DISTRICT BETWEEN THE BROAD & SALUDA, were: Jonathan Downs, James Williams, Maj. Jno. Caldwell, John Colcock, Rowland Rugely, John Satterwhite, John Williams, John McNees, Chas. King, George Ross. On DISTRICT COMMITTEES were: James Creswell, Saml Savage, John Satterwhite, John Ford, John Thomas, John Gordon, John Prince.

PROVINCIAL CONGRESS voted themselves the GENERAL ASSEMBLY 1776 and elected the following members a Legislative Council: Thos. Beem, Stephen Bull, Thos. Ferguson, John Kershaw, LeRoy Hammond, Wm. Moultrie, Henry Middleton, Rawlin Lowndes, Chas. Pinckney, Richard Richardson, David Oliphant, Thos. Shubrick, Gabriel Powel.
    MEMBERS OF THE PRIVY COUNCIL: Jno. Edwards, Wm. H. Drayton, Jas. Parson etc...ORDINARY: Wm. Burrows...ASST; JUDGES: John Matthews, Henry Pendleton, Thos. Bee. ATTY. GEN'L: Alex. Moultrie. PRESIDENT: John Rutledge and VICE-PRES., Henry Laurens.

THE S.C. LEGISLATURE MET IN JANUARY 1782 at JACKSONBOROUGH

    Members from the Districts named were as follows:
NINETY-SIX----Senator: John Lewis Gervais. Representatives: Robt. Anderson, LeRoy Hammond, Patrick Calhoun, Jno. Ewing Calhoun, John Murray, James Moore, Hugh Middleton, Andrew Simkins, Andrew Pickens.
LITTLE RIVER, between Broad & Saluda rivers----Senator: Col. Levi Casey. Representatives: Benj. Kilgore, Dr. Ross, Cpt. Wild Montgomery.
LOWER DISTRICT, Broad & Saluda----Senator: Maj. Gordon. Representatives: David Glynn, Philemon Waters, Michael Leirner, George Roof.
SPARTAN DIST.------Senator: Simon Berwick. Representatives: Col. Wm. Henderson, Col. Thos. Brandon, Col. John Thomas Jr., Saml McJunkin.
ST. JOHN, BERKELEY-----Senator: Francis Marion. Representatives: John Frierson, Thos. Giles, Richard Gough, Alex. Broughton, John Cordes, Gabriel Gigailliat.
                (Taken from Diary of Josiah Smith Jr.)

    Provisional Articles of Peace between Great Britian and the United States were signed in Paris 15 Nov. 1782 but war was not legally terminated until 1783. Under an Act ratified 12 March 1783 the Governor of South Carolina was authorized to appoint an auditor for each judicial district to adjust all claims arising out of the Revolution. These were for fol. Dists:
NINETY-SIX, Robt. Anderson; CAMDEN, Wm. Tate; GEORGE TOWN, Peter Horry; BEAUFORT, Wm. Hazard Wigg; ORANGEBURG, Wm. Arthur; CHERAW, Thomas Powe.   ----------

PETITIONERS TO COMMON HOUSE ASSEMBLY FOR RELIEF BECAUSE OF STAMP ACT 7 May 1776
Ash Jno. . . .Ash Cato. . . .Andebert Philip. . .Atkinson Jos. . .Bruce Donald. . . Boone Wm. & Thos. . .Baker Jon. & Wm. . .Blake Wm. . .Bedon Jno. . .Bothwell Jon. . .Banpfreed Wm. . .Bounetheau Peter. . .Berwick, Simon. . .Bocquet Peter Jr. .Banbury Wm. .Butler Peter. .Cope Brian. . .Chapman Jon. . .Carson Jas. . . Cannon Danl. . . .Crington Jos. . .Crosby Timothy. . .Capers Chas. . .Dawson & Dudley. . . .Dodd Jon. . .Dill Jos. . .Downs Arthur. . .Farr Thos. . .Fitzsimmons Christpr. . .Grimke Jon. P. . .Godfret & Gadsden. . .Grimke Fredk. . .Gibbes Wm. . . .Guern & Williamson. . . .Harvey Robt. . .Hinds Patk. . .Horn Alex. . . Hartly Thos. .Hopton Wm. . .Holson Christpr. . .Hutcheson & Elfe. . .Hall Wm... . Holiday Wm. . .Hutchins Jos. . .Hogan Jas. . .Ingles Lloyd. . .Kinlock Francis. . . Jones Edw. . .Logan Wm. . .Lyford Wm. . .Lightwood Edw. . .Legaree Danl. . . Learmouth Alex. . .Legaree Sol. . .Legaree Jas. . .Marr Andrew. . .McCall Jon. Jr. .Morris Mark. .Mill Thos. .Marley Jon. .Martin Edw. .Matthews Edmund. . . . McGilivray Robt. . .Rutherford Robt. . .Neufvill Jon. . .Poyas Jas. . .Prue Jon. . . Odingsell Chas. . .Pockron Jon. . .Pike Thos. . .Perdriau & Fabre... .Pendergrass Darby. . .Prioleau Saml Jr. . .Smith Thos. . .Scott Jno. . .Stockton & Jackson. . . Richardson Rich. . .Savage Wm. . .Robinson Thos. . .Sarrazin Jonathan. ...Roberts

115

Benj. .Scott Nathl. .Tebout Tunes. .Sharp Jas. . .Tufts Simon. . .Trustler Wm. . .
Theus Jeremiah. .Toux Villepou. .Townsend Paul. .Tidyman Phil. . .Vanderhorst
Elias. . .Ward Jon. . .Warley Melchoir. . .You Chas. . .Wagner Jon. . .Wish Jon. . .
You Thos.

First 'Tea Party' Was Held Here

The Old Exchange building at East Bay and Broad streets in Charleston was the scene of the first tea tax revolt against the British before
the Revolution and here also was where the Provincial Congress met in
July, 1774, to set up the first independent government in America.

Historical Prince George Winyah church, built
1742-46

CHARLES BREWTON HOUSE
(BUILT BEFORE 1733)

The Funeral Procession of the Stamp Act
From an old print

HAMPTON (1735), NEAR McCLELLANVILLE

MISCELLANEOUS RECORDS

A Muster Roll of the Grenadier Company in the Second Regiment of South Carolina Infantry, on The Continental Establishment, commanded by Colonel Isaac Motte.

August 25, 1778.

Names	Date of Commissions

Commissioned Officers

Thomas Dunbar, Captain	November 9, 1777
Albert Roux, 1st Lieutenant	December 15, 1777

Staff-Commissioned Officers

John Downs, Adjutant	March 12, 1778
Rev. Henry Purcell, Chaplain	May 7, 1776
John Hall, Quarter-Master	July 1, 1776
Henry Gray, Pay-Master	December 16, 1777
Jeremiah Thews, Surgeon	August 2, 1777
John Henry Rusche, 1st Mate, do.	June 11, 1778
Silvester Springer, 2d Mate, do.	June 27, 1778

Staff Non-Commissioned Officers

Lewis Coffer, Sergeant-Major	June 16, 1778
John Wickom, Sergeant-Major	October 5, 1778
William Fletcher, Qr.-master Sergeant	July 15, 1778
Daniel Simpson, Qr.-master Sergeant	During the war
James Arnold, Drum-Major	September 16, 1779
Hugh Campbell, Fife-Major	June 16, 1778

Non-Commissioned Officers	Enlistment Time	Time of Service

Sergeants

William Jasper	July 8, 1775	July 8, 1778
John Marlow	June 26, 1775	June 26, 1778
John Gemmell	July 18, 1775	July 18, 1778
Robert Watt	Aug. 5, 1777	During the war
William Brown	July 6, 1778	July 6, 1781

Corporals

Samuel Butler	July 7, 1775	July 7, 1778
John Roberts	Nov. 26, 1776	Nov. 26, 1779
Robert Watt	Aug. 5, 1777	During the war
Frederick Simons	July 27, 1777	During the war

Drummers

John Wheeler	July 1, 1775	July 1, 1778
Peter Uptegrove	July 18, 1778	Jan. 18, 1780

Privates

William Ashford	July 11, 1777	During the war
William Arnold	July 8, 1775	July 8, 1778
Barnaby Bryan	Aug. 5, 1777	During the war
John Cook	July 13, 1775	July 13, 1778
Charles Cox	July 1, 1778	Mar. 1, 1779
John Baptist DeLaney	June 25, 1775	June 25, 1778
Owen Griffin	July 11, 1777	During the war
Silas Gibson	July 16, 1778	July 16, 1781
Loami Husbands	Aug. 2, 1775	Aug. 2, 1778
John Humphreys	June 18, 1775	June 18, 1778
Aaron Harris	Jan. 31, 1777	Jan. 31, 1780
James Hooper	Aug. 5, 1777	During the war
William Jones	July 7, 1777	During the war
Robert Ivey	July 8, 1775	July 8, 1778
Charles Lucas	July 19, 1775	July 19, 1778
Joseph Martin	July 10, 1775	July 10, 1778
Martin Moore	July 8, 1775	July 8, 1778
Jacob Murphy	July 8, 1775	July 8, 1778
John McCaid	Aug. 5, 1777	During the war
John McDowell	June 16, 1778	During the war
James McClean	Aug. 5, 1775	Aug. 5, 1778
Archibald McDonald		During the war
James Oliver		During the war
Edmund Penrice	July 2, 1775	July 2, 1778
David Parsons	Aug. 1, 1775	Aug. 1, 1778
Richard Richardson	Aug. 3, 1777	During the war
William Roberts	Aug. 7, 1775	Aug. 7, 1778
Frederick Simmons	July 27, 1777	During the war
Thomas Stafford	Jan. 4, 1777	During the war
John Steele	July 9, 1778	During the war
Anthony Uhthoff	July 6, 1775	July 6, 1778
John Whitely	July 11, 1777	During the war
Robert Whiley	Mar. 11, 1778	During the war
Shadrack Williamson	July 8, 1775	July 8, 1778
Richard Williamson	July 9, 1777	During the war
John Kelly		During the war

We do swear the above Muster Roll is a true state of the Company, without fraud to the United States or any individual, according to the best of our knowledge.

THOS. DUNBAR, Captain
ALBERT ROUX, 1st Lieutenant

Sworn before me this 25th August, 1778.
FRANCIS MARION, Second Colonial Regiment
Then mustered, as certified by

THOS. JERVEY, Deputy Muster Master.

*   *   *

A Muster Roll of Capt. Richard B. Roberts' Company of the South Carolina Continental Corps of Artillery, Commanded by Col. Owen Roberts.

Head Quarters, Purysburgh, March 19, 1779.

Com. Officers' Names	Rank	Date of Commission
Richard B. Roberts	Captain	June 4, 1777
John Gorgan	Capt.-Lieut.	May 30, 1778
Frederick Von Plater	1st Lieut.	October 28, 1778

Non-Commissioned and Private Names	Date of Enlistment	Time of Service
John Smith, Sergeant	June 3, 1777	3 years
Brice Mathews, do.	Nov. 24, 1777	3 years
Joseph Hull, Corporal	June 25, 1777	The war
John Sessions, do.	June 29, 1778	3 years
Edward Conner, do.	June 29, 1778	3 years
Robert Goodall, Gunner	Sept. 17, 1777	The war
Benjamin Williams, do.	June 2, 1777	3 years
Alexander McMullan, do.	Feb. 3, 1779	16 months
Aaron Baroth, do.	June 3, 1777	3 years
David Cunningham	June 3, 1777	3 years
John Driver	July 14, 1778	3 years
Joseph Johnson	June 2, 1777	The war

117

John Causey	Sept. 5, 1778	3 years
John Murrow	July 16, 1778	3 years
Samuel White	Sept. 25, 1777	The war
Jacob Paul	June 2, 1777	The war
John Porter	June 19, 1777	The war
Aquilla Sing	July 18, 1778	3 years
John Colby	Aug. 10, 1778	The war
James Roe	July 22, 1778	The war
Lewis Cornyorck		The war
Charles McIver	Aug. 2, 1778	3 years
James Hughes	June 1, 1777	3 years
John Conner		The war
Nicholas Glossom		The war
James Lewis		3 years
Michael Lewis	Sept. 17, 1778	The war
Isaac Garrick	Feb. 16, 1779	16 months
Wm. Maloy		3 years
James Causey	Sept. 5, 1778	3 years
Denis Choloque		The war
Joseph Antonio	Sept. 17, 1778	The war
Samuel Hickman	July 21, 1778	3 years
Robert William	May 28, 1778	The war
Hill Hewet	June 2, 1777	3 years
Nicholas Prince	Aug. 3, 1778	3 years
Samuel Jefft	July 16, 1778	The war
William Read, Drummer	Sept. 21, 1777	The war
Wm. Fleming, Fifer		The war

I do swear that the within Muster Roll is a true state of the Company, without Fraud to the United States, or to any individual thereof, according to the best of my knowledge.

R. B. ROBERTS, Capt. Artillery.

Sworn before me this 19th March, 1779.
J. WISE.

Then mustered as certified by

F. BREMAR, Deputy Muster Master.

• • •

From Documentary History of American Revolution from originals in possession of the Editor—by R. W. Gibbs. Maryland, 1857.

Appeared in the D.A.R Magazine.

CONTINENTAL PAPER MONEY.

CPT. WM. BUTLER'S COMPANY OF VOLUNTEERS, EDGEFIELD DIST., S. C.

Allen Jas. .Berry Jno. .Butler Jno. . .Butler Wm. Lt. . .Bledsoe Bartlett. .Bledsoe Berryman. .Butler Jas. Sr. . .Corley Abner. . Corley Sherod. . . .Corley Jno. Lt. . . . .Corley Nathl. . .Corley Zacheus. . .DeLoach Saml. . .Davis Robt. . .Davis Thos. . .Davis Zachariah. . . .Douglas Jno. . . . .Edson Jas. . .Edson Jno. . . .Fort Dunn. . .Foy Peter. . .Eskridge Burdett. . .Jones Danl. . .Jone s Matt. .Jones Danl C. .Mason Bledsoe. .Nuun Joseph. . .Nicholson Gideon. .Laggett Josiah. . .Padgett Joel. . .Richardson Amos. . . Sissoin Fredk. . .Sison Wm. . .Smith Jno. . .Smith Smallwood. . . Turner Starling. . .Troop, James. . .Wilson Russell. . .Warren Josiah. . . .Wilson Jno. . .Watson Zakiah. . .Watson Richman. . . Watson Willis. . . .Williams Saml. . . .Webb Handley. . .Watson Hesekiah. .Cate. .two Harrisons. .Humphreys. .Whittle Burrows.

SOLDIERS OF OTHER STATES
INCLUDING LISTS OF MANY FROM SOUTH CAROLINA

REVOLUTIONARY SOLDIERS BURIED IN MISSOURI

Allen, Jno. .Boles, Saml. .Boyd, Thos. .Burks, Saml. .Berry, Wm. .Brann, Wm. .Casey, Christopher. .Chambers, Jno. .Cooper, Col. Benj. .Conway, Saml. .Dodd, Abel. .Finnell, Chas. . .Franklin, Maj. Thos. .Goodson, Wm. .Harding, Geo. .Hawkins, Jno. .Headlee, Elisha. . .Hill, Abram. . .Jamison, Robt. .Kennedy, Thos. .Kirkpatrick, Robt. .Leake. . Lemon, Robt. .Lumbley, Wm. .Majors, Jno. .Martin, Lewis. .Moore, Maj. Zechariah. . Musick, Elder T. R. .Overly, Henry. .Parks, Jas. .Paul, Jno. .Peers, Maj. Valentine. . Quarles, Maj. Robt. .Ramsey, Capt. Wm. .Reading, Geo. .Robertson, Edw. .Scruggs, Timothy. .Russell, Robt. S. .Sewell, James. .Sims, Richard, .Sims, Rodem. .Steele, Saml. . Snowden, Jas. .Stuflebeau, Jno. .Taylor, Benj. .Thomas, Edw. .Talbot, Haile. .Taylor, Danl. .Tomb, David. .Truesdale, Nathan. .Wells, Jas. .Woolfolk, Jno. .Walker, Jesse. . Walton, Wm. Ward, Col. Wm. .Watson, Saml. .Wells, Col. Saml. .Brock, Uriah. .Nicholson, Wm. .Miller, Geo. .Wyatt, Thos. .Baylis, Cpt. Wm. .Lambley, Wm. .Mason, Benjamin.

REVOLUTIONARY SOLDIERS BURIED IN TEXAS

Jas. Wilson Henderson, bur. at Shilo Cem. Wife drew a pension. .John Abston, bur. in Lavon, Collins Co. Applied for pension. .James Thompson, bur. Peacock Cem. .Stephen Williams, bur. near Jasper. .Alexander Hodge. .John Archer Elmore, bur. New Waverly. . Jonas Chaison, bur. near Beaumont.

REVOLUTIONARY SOLDIERS WHO EITHER LIVED, DREW
A PENSION OR BURIED IN IOWA

Bell, Benjamin. .Bean, Danl. .Breese, Timothy. .Brown, Nathan. .Brown, Timothy. .Bell. Timothy. Baine, Danl. .Crockett, Wm. .Scarrem, Richard J. .Caldwell, Saml. .Dow, Danl. . Fellows, Nthl Sr. .Garricks, Wm. .Harry, Chas. .Kincaid, John B. .Leeper, Jno. .Linn, Martin. .Morgan, Jno. .Kincaide, Wm. J. .McDonald, Jno. .Lewis, Saml. .Osborn, Jno. Perkins, Geo. .Poole, Sherman I. .Price, Samson, .Price, Saml. .Rogers, Achilles. . Rhodes, Thos. .Shepard, Chas. .Stubbs, Chas. .Smith, Joseph W. .Ware, Fredk. .Wiley, Jacob. .Winton, Nathan. .Woody, James. .Woody, Jonathan. .Woody, Wm.

SOUTH CAROLINA SOLDIERS WHO REMOVED TO ALABAMA

Arnold, Thos. .Barnet, Thos. .Barton, Jno. .Brown, Hamilton, Dav. .Broughton, Thos.. Bussey, Zadoc. .Campbell, Geo. .Casey, Wm. .Clement, Thos. .Clements, Culliver. . Chandler, Jno. .Crenshaw, Stephen. .Darden, Geo. .Day, Wm. .Dickey, Geo. .Du Bais. . Eddins, Benj. Elliot, Elizbth Knox. .Embrey, Jos. .England, Wm. .Files, Abner, Jeremiah.. Franks, Marshall. .Gill, Jas. .Garrett, Thos. .Gary, Thos. .Gayle, Matt. .Godbold, Zach. . Graham, Jno. .Green, Jacob. .Holland, Jacob. .Hamilton, Thos. .Hanna, Robt. .Harrington, Drury. .Hill, Hiram, Lewis. .Hogg, Thos. .Holloday, Danl. .Houston, Saml. .Howard, Jos. . Hughes, Jos. .Johnson, Wm. .Kelly, Gresham. .King, Jos. .Kirkland, Wm. .Lofton, Thos.. Lavender, Hugh. .Lipscomb, Joel. .Littlejohn, Chas. .Lynn, Jas. .McCutcheon, Jno. .Mc Gaughey, Saml. .Majors Benj. .McGuire, Elijah. .Malone, Cornl. .Mangum, Jno. .Morgan, Jas. .Morrow, Saml, Davis. .McWhorter, Jno. .Norris, Patk. .Nollen, Stephen, Geo. .Oden, Alex. .Outlaw, Alex. .Owen, Jno. .Pettigrew, Jas. .Poe, Jas. .Pool, Jno. .Queen, Thos. . Randolph Abram. .Reese, Geo. .Robertson, Jas. .Rolison, Wm. .Ross, Isaac. .Roy, Jos.. Russell, Thos Sr., Wm. .Sample, Jno. Sr. .Sawyer, Jos. .Scott, Jas. .Stone, Reuben, Wm. . Storey, Henry. .Strothers, Wm. .Sutton, Jacob. .Stephenson, Hugh. .Tarrant, Jas. .Tribble, Jas. .Tubb, Jno. .Turner, Lewis, w. Nancy. .Walton, Wm. .Vaughan, Joel. .Ware, Robt. .

Weston, Robt. .Winn, Gallenus. .Witherspoon, Mary. .Wright, Danl. .Wylie, Wm. .Wynee, Williamson. Susp. Claims: Duncan, Jno. .Hawkins, Thos. .Hollis, Wm. .McFerrin, Archb. . Murcer, Jas. .Petty, Theop. .Riley, Jno. .Robuck, Jno. .Sterling, Silas C. .Thompson, Wm. . Williams, Thos. . .Walker Matthias. .Covington, Susan wid. Jno. .Hart, Martha wid. Henry. .Ponder, Violet wid Amos. .Turner, Nancy wid. Lewis. .(Above abstracted from : Ala. Histl. Quart. Winter Issue 1944. Editor Marie B. Owen, Pub. by State Dept. Archives & Hist; also recds. from D.A.R. Magazines; DaA.R. Lineage Books.)

SOUTH CAROLINA TO GEORGIA

Addington, Wm. .Bryan, Jonth. .Buchanan, Benj. .Buckhalter, Marion. .Baker, Jon. .Brown, Jno. .Bullock, Hawkins. .Brown, Bartlett Jr. .Boykin, Fran. .Barnet, Wm. .Butler, Jno. . Bratton, Martha R. .Cante, Jas. .Cook, Jno. .Clark, Thos. .Craps, Jno. .Crawford, Joel Sr. .Bugg, Sherwood. .Brisbane, Adam. .Daniel, Jno. .Dickson, Dav. .Davis, Wm. .Ezell, Hartwell. .Edenfield, Dav. .Edwards, Wm. .Elbert, Sam. .Floyd, Chas. .Farrow, Rosanna W. .Garrard, Jacob. .Griffin, Jno. .Garrison, Jed. .Gillham, Ezek. .Gibson, Jno. Jas. . Graves, Lewis. .Howard, Jno. .Hardwick, Wm. .Hatton, Fran. .Hardin, Wm. .Hartwell, Ezell. Hames, Jno. .Harvey, Thos. .Jackson, Dan. .Jeter, Levi. .Jones, Jas. .Kelly, Lloyd . . Lindsay, Jno. .Lamar, Basil. .Martin, Wm, Elijah. .McCall, Jas. .Middleton, Hugh. . Montgomery, Jas. .Milner, Jno. .McMullen, Jas. .Matthews, Jas. Moses. .McClure, Mary G. .McCalla, Sara. .Morris, Thos. .Mallette, Gideon. .Newton, Moses. .Oliver, Jas. B. . Pittman, Jas, Jno. . .Prothro, Evan. . .Quarterman, Rob. Thos. .Randall, Robinson. . Rutherford, Jno. .Rushin, Jno. .Stevens, Jno. .Slappy, Henry, Saml. .Scott, Walter Jr. . Strickland, Jacob. .Storey, Anthy. .Stutstill, Jno. .Sparks, Danl. .Spann, Jas. .Taylor, Wm. . Tharp, Vincent. .Watson, Jno. .Winn, Jno. .Williams, Isaac. .Young, Jas. .(From: Memb. Roll & Reg. Ancestors Ga. Soc. D.A.R; D.A.R. Lin. Bks; D.A.R. Magazines.)

SOUTH CAROLINA SOLDIERS WHO REMOVED TO FLORIDA

Bessent, Jno. .Bird, Jno. .Brown, Jno. .Bozeman, Ralph. .Edwards, Henry. .Fletcher, Jno. . Harbison, Geo. .Hudson, Hall, r. .Liles, Jno. .McCall Sherrod. .Osteen, Sol. .Rawls, Wm. . Singletary, Jos. .Taylor, Jeremiah. .Snowden, Aaron & Ester. .Weeks, Levi. .Wood, Dempsey. .(From: D.A.R. Lin. Bks. & Mag; Pen. Recds. of Sold. removed to Fla., By Jessie Robinson Fritot, Jacksonville Chpt. D.A.R. 1946.)

SOUTH CAROLINA--MISSISSIPPI

Brown, Jno. .Buckholtz, Abram. .Brent, Jno. .Crane, Mayfield. .Chambers, Jos. .Downes, Wm. .Davis, Saml. .Farrar, Thos. .Fitzpatrick, Thos. .Hillhouse, Wm. .McBee, Silas. . May, Jos. .McCaleb, Wm. .Murphy, Jno. .Neely, Saml. .Portman, Jno. .Purvis, Gilbert. . Raley, Chas. .Turner, Noel. .Smith, Chas. .Wigington, Geo. & sons. .Whittington, Grief. . Wilson, Jas. .(D.A.R. Lin. Bks. & Magazines.)

SOUTH CAROLINA--ILLINOIS

Gaston, Wm. .Gill, Thos. .Woods, Jno. .Means, Wm. .McClurkin, Thos. .McMillian, Danl. . Lusk, Jas. .Gilliham, Issac. .Land, Moses. .Warnock, Jos. .(From: D. A. R. Lin. Bks. & Magazines.)

SOUTH CAROLINA SOLDIERS BURIED IN OHIO

Barr, Christopher. .Berryhill, Alex. .Campbell, Jno. .Caldwell, Wm. .Cunningham, Jas. . Dickey, Robt. .Farley, David. .Hale, Wm. N. .Morton, Jno. .McGaw, Wm. .Stephenson, Jno. .Stewart, Wm. Sr. .Stone, Benj. .Strain, Dav. .Williamson, Rev. Wm. .(From: "Offic. Roster Sold. Amer. Revo. Bur. Ohio"; D.A.R. Lin. Bks. & Magazines.)

SOUTH CAROLINA SOLDIERS TO TENNESSEE

Armstrong, Robt. .Barnett, --. .Bostic, Jno. .Blair, Jno. .Burns, Laird, .Carter, Danl. . Davis, Andrew, Absolom, Fredk. .Dial, Jeremiah. .Frierson, Wm. .Franks, Marshal. .

Fenner, Rich, Robt. .Goggans, Wm. .Houston, Jno. .Kennedy, Wm. .Kaigler, Andrew. .
Lee, Thos. .Love, Hezek. .Mayes, Saml. .McClosky, Jos. .Miller, Adam. .McDearman,
Thos. .Meek, Adam. .Martin, Matt. .McGowan, Wm. .Pickens, Wm. .Pinckney, Chas. G . .
Queen, Thos. .Sample, Jesse. .Suddoth, Benj. .Thomas, Jas. .Teague, Wm. .Taylor, Geo. .
Wilson, Jno. .(D.A.R. Lin. Bks. & Mag.)

SOUTH CAROLINA SOLDIERS TO KENTUCKY

Adair, Jno. .Brothers, Jno. .Connall, Jesse. .Clinton, Jas. .Ford, Wm. .Jeffries, Nathl,
Wm. .Lynn, Jas. .Love, Wm., Mark. .McDougal, Alex. .Prince, Wm. .Pickens, Wm. .
Petrie, Peter. .Ringo, Corn. .Renick, Jas. .Ramsey, Jno. .Scott, Wm. .Tanner, Josiah. .
(D.A.R. Lin. Bks. & Mag.)

SOUTH CAROLINA SOLDIERS TO INDIANA

Abney, Geo. .Adair, Jas. .Alcorn, Geo. .Archer, Robt. .Bell, Thos. .Benbow, Edw. .
Brown, Matt. .Cain, Jno. .Campbell, Wm. .Cannon, Jas. .Culbertson, Josiah. .Dowell,
Geo. Evans, Jno. Floyd, Abram. .Garretson, Jno. .Gibson, Wm. .Griffin, Ralph. .Hammond,
Job. Hanna, Robt. Harrel, Jeremiah. Horton(Hooten) Thos. .Irvin, Saml. .Kever, (McKever)
Jas. .Kellar, Devault. .Lanman, Jas. .Lawrence, Isaac. .Lipperd, Wm. .Logan, Wm. .
Martindale, Wm. .Moore, Wm. .McCammon, Matt. .McClure, Robt., Wm. .McMillom,
(McMullen), Rowley. .Palmer, Jno. .Parr, Arthur. .Sample, Thos. .Sanders, Henry. .
Shores, Christian. .Still, Murphy. .Tramel, Sampson. .Veale, Jas. Carr. .Williams, Isaac. .
Young, Jaret. .Youngblood, Jacob. .(Abstracted from "Roster Sold. of Amer. Revo. Buried
in Ind" by Mrs. Roscoe C. O'Byrne -- 1938; D.A.R. Lin. Bks.)

SOUTH CAROLINA REVOLUTIONARY ANCESTORS OF ARKANSAS D.A.R.

Arnold, Thos. Adair, Jno. Addington, Wm. .Bennet, Thos. .Brown, Sims. .Bobo, Sampson. .
Blakeney, Jno. Sr. .Bullock, Hawkins. .Casey, Randolph. .Collins, Jno. .Crawford, Joel. .
Carroll, Saml. .Cowan, Andrw. .Cherry, Lamuel. .Darby, Benj. .Evins, Alex. .Felder,
Henry. .Hawthorne, Jos. .Harrison, Reuben. .Haile, Benj. .Hamilton, Paul. .Hall, Wm. .
Hallam, Jno. .Holcombe, Phil. .Knight, Jno. .Kalb, (Kulp) Benj. .Lining, Chas. .Longmire,
Wm. Moores, Henry. Maxwell, Edw. Mayson, Jas. McIntosh, Wm. .Moss, Jno. .Martindale,
Wm. Jr. Nisbit, Wm. Nicholson, Wright. .O'Neall, Wm. .Pickens, Andrw. .Prothro, Evan. .
Russell, Wm. .Strobel, Danl. .Snoddy, Jno. .Shirley, Thos. .Saxon, Lewis. .Smith, Aaron. .
Sloan, Alex. .Thomas, Jas. .Trammel, Thos. .Ward, Jno. .Williams, Moses, H. .White, Wm.
(From: D.A.R. Year Bk. State of Ark. 1948-9; D.A.R. Lin. Bks.)

SOUTH CAROLINA REVOLUTIONARY ANCESTORS OF OKLAHOMA D.A.R.

Adams, Dav. Alexander, Jnl, Elias. .Barnett, Jno. .Benson, Thos. .Barry, Andrw. .Bonner,
Jas. .Butler, Wm. .Bobo, Sampson. .Bumpass, Jno. .Bryan, Jas. .Black, Jos. .Cannon,
Henry. .Choice, Tully. .Coleman, Jas. .Cooper, Geo. .Davis, Surrey. .Dunklin, Jos. .Dodd,

Jesse, Jno. Sr. .Drewery, Fletcher. .Findley, Jno. .Felder, Henry. .Foster, Wm. .Gamble,
Jno. .Gough, Rich. .Gowan, Jno. .Gilliam, Robt. Sr. .Gaston, Wm. Robt. .Hall, Wm., Thos. .
Harrel, Zach. .Hamilton, Wm. .Henry, Malcolm...Howle, Wm. .Head, Jas. .Irby, Jos. .
Jaudon, Jas. .Jaggers, Nathan. .Kilgore, Benj. .Kennedy, Jas. .Keith, Corn. Jr. .Know, Jas .
Knox, Jno. .LaGroue, Adam. .Liddell, Wm. .Lee, Wm. .Lucas, Jno. .Martin, Salathiel. .
McAbee, Vardrey. .McKinney, Jno. .McIntosh, Wm. .McDaniel, Edw. .McDill, Thos. H. .
Michau, Jacob. .Milner, Sol. .Miller, Mordecai. .Mitchell, Sol. .Marion, Jos. .Moore,
Henry. .Moberly, Edw., Saml. .Nicholson, Dav. .Neal, Thos. .O'Neall, Wm., Saml. .
Patton, Jno. .Pinckney, Chas. .Pittman, Philip. .Polk, Ezek. .Reynolds, Saml. .Salmon,
Geo. .Simmons, Maurice. .Selman, Jeremiah. .Sibert, Jno., Dav. .Stone, Jas. .Switzer,
Henry. .Tandy, Archilles. .Tennant, Wm. .Terrell, Geo. .Tisdale, Jno. .Tracey, Nathl. .
Walker, Alex. .Winn, Rich. .Wilson, Dav., Jas. .Weyman, Edw. .Wingo, Jno. W. .Walkup,
Jno. .Van Arsdale, Simon. .(From: N.S. D.A.R. of Okla. Year Bk. 1948-9; D.A.R. Lin.
Bks.)

The records of many S.C. Revolutionary soldiers have never been published.
Some of the lines have not been proved by descendants. Consent has not been given
to publish others.

The first State House, built in
Charles Town in 1753-1760.

St. Philip's Episcopal Church— Church
Founded 1670. First church corner Broad and Meetir
(where St. Michael's now stands), built in 1681. Move
to present site, 1723.

REVOLUTIONARY
POWDER-HORN AND
CANTEEN.

General Pickens.

Middleton Place Gardens, Oldest Landscape Gardens in America

122

GENEALOGIES OF FAMILIES DESCENDED FROM S. C. REVOLUTIONARY SOLDIERS

JAMES ABERCROMIE md. twice. ISSUE, viz: Isabel md. a Blackwell in Va. . . 2-Mary md. a Dial in NC. . .3-Thos. md. Mrs. Rucket SC. . .4-Isaac, grant in Laurens SC 1769(wit. by Jas. & Jno. A-) to NC. . .5-JOHN of Laurens had-Jas. Jr., Alex, Jonathan, Wm. . .6-James of Laurens b. abt. 1740. . .7-Alex. . .8-Chas.NC-Ga. . .9-Colvill. . .10--Rebecca 1738-1825 md. Hastings Dial. . .11-Crystie md. Martin Dial. . . .ALEXANDER SR. of Laurens had w. Susan & sons-John, Alex, Henry, Hugh, Lewis, Jonathan; drts-Hannah, Susan, Polly. . .COLVILL, abv. CHN: Harriet Nash, Mary Sims, Rebecca Babb, Elizbth Campbell, Christy Ridgeway, Ruth Sims, Jonathan, Lindley, Colvill, James to Ga., John. . .Colvill Abercromie Jr., md. Sara Mahaffey. . . .JAMES ABERCROMIE of Laurens, no. 6 abv. md. twice. CHN: (1) Mary md. 1st Benj. Williams: 2nd Wm. O'Daniel. Had-Josiah, James, Abercromie, Mary, Rhoda, Lucinda, Pamelia, Elizbth (2) Isabella md. Josiah Blackwell, is in Tex. (3) Rebecca md. 1797 Gabriel Jowell to Miss. (4) Susannah Matthews (5) Hannah md. Elias Brock (6) Elizbth Andrews (5) James had w. Cynthia.

JAMES AGNEW settled abt. 1737 in Pa. md. twice. ISSUE, viz: John, Janet Scott, David**Saml**James**, Martha, Margt, Rebecca, Sara, Anna, Abram. The son David md. Mary Irwin. The son James md. Mary Ramsey & was 1st to SOUTH CAROLINA. I- Samuel abt. 1770 md. Elizbth Seawright & had-Mary, Andrew, Jane, Elizbth, Saml, James. The son Samuel had-Elizbth, James, Andrew, Joseph, Alfred, Malinda, William, Dr. Wash who md. Elizbth Sullivan, Dr. Enoch who md. Letitia Todd of Laurens to Miss. . .JAMES AGNEW, s. of Saml & Elizbth, md. Mahala Dodson. ISSUE five: Saml, Elizbth, Mahala, Andrew, & Dr. Enoch who md. 3 times. 1st-Sara Sullivan, 2nd-Jane Waters, 3rd-Ella Waters. Had-Anna Smith, Jennie McCarley, Ena Sullivan James.

BENJAMIN ARNOLD & w. both**. He b. Va. d. SC 1796. ISSUE to maturity, viz:. . . 1-Wm. md. twice & left-Benjamin, Anderson, William, Polly. . .2-Edward to Ky & left chn. . .3-Charity Martin had-Nancy Townsend, Temperance Smith Gunnels. . . 4-Hendricks of Laurens, SC had-Mary Townsend, Nancy Taylor, Ira who md. Polly Saxon; William who had-Jeff, Hendrick, Billy. . .5-Temperance md. Thos. Hamilton** 6-John from Laurens to Tenn. Chn: Benjamin, Rickerson Lem. . .7-Thomas** had-Temperance Ross, Ann Dunklin, William, Thos. H., Sally. . .8-BENJAMIN JR.** d. in SC. ISSUE: Alston, Martin, Benjamin, Ann H. Sullivan, Temperance Sullivan, Winifred Camp, Clara Grace, Sara Pinson, Malinda Arnold.

CHARLES ALLEN SR. md. Lucy Bacon Va-SC. ISSUE, viz: CHARLES JR** md. Susan Garner; Lyddall md. Milly L. Downs; Sara K. md. 1st Lewis Saxon; Cynthia Catherine md. Jno. Williams; Isiah & possibly Mary, Drury, Richard, Joel. The son Lyddall Allen of Laurens, SC had Issue: Isaac md. twice, to Ga; Jonathan, Milly Frances Atkin; Lucy Bacon Arnold; Chas. Walter, Mary Drury, Sara Jane(Nancy). Four Revo. S. in this line.

ANDERSON--JOHN, WM, JAS, & THOS. ** filed Revolutionary claims, Camden Dist., later Chester. James &. Thos. appeared to be bros. James Anderson Sr. & sons-John, James, William & prob. Quinton, moved from Chester area to Greenville, lands on Horse creek, while William had lands on Rabun & Lick cks. JAMES ANDERSON who d. 28 Oct. 1807 md. Nancy Ewing. ISSUE 9, viz: Robt. Quinton d. 1852, Jane d. 1857 Mary, John, Anny, Elizabeth, William, James, Ewing. . .I.-James Anderson II (s. of Jas & Nancy) md. Martha Young (Fulton) & had 4 sons, viz: Thomas, Daniel, Robert Quinton, George. (1)Thos. md. Jane Williams (2)Danl md. 1st Lucinda Smith, 2nd . Fanny Miller. Had-Emmie, Cora, Lizzie, Mattie, md. Albert Todd. (3) Robt. Quinton md. Frances Louise Smith. Had 11 chn: Nan, James, Oscar, Walter, Mary, William, Alice, Thomas, Clara, Louise, Sally. Of these (a) Nan md. Martin (b) James md. Minnie Williams & had-Ruth; Ann md. Dr. H. A. Pruitt; Lois md. W. W. Sullivan Jr., Maj. Saml (c) Oscar md. Ida Williams (d) Walter md. Zella Campbell (e) Sally md. Sam

Bowen (f) Louise md. Cape McPhail (7) Thos. unmd. (8) Mary md. 1896 Edw. H. Anderson, desct. of Maj. Dav. of Nazerath community, had-John, Frances. . .II.-MARY ANDERSON, drt. of Jas. I & Nancy, md. Austin Williams. ISSUE; 5: Nancy J. md. Thos. F. Anderson; Jno. Lewis md. Helen Featherstone & had 8 chn; Jas. unmd; Saml md. Ann Archer; Harriet md. W. S. Blake. . .III.-JOHN ANDERSON, s. of Jas. I Nancy, 1784-1837, md. Mary Terry (drt. Thos. T. &-w. a Harrison. 2 md. w, Rebec. McDowell) ISSUE, 10, viz: Anna G., William, James, Thomas, Ewing, John, George, Robert, Mary, David. (1) Anna Gibson md. Hewlett Chapman, had-Bill, John, Mary (2) Wm. of Ala. had-Thomas, John, Cassy, others (3) James of Fairview, Grv Co. SC md. Rachel Stenhouse. Had 11: (a) Geo. C. md. Hattie Sprouse (b) Margt L. md. J. Wister Stewart & had-Leila, Mrs. Cath Rachel Peden; Anderson H. Stewart (c) Lawrence md. Evelyn Thornberry of Ala. Had 4: Forest M. of NY City md. 1915 Grace F. Barnum & had-Eleanor, Virginia, Mary; Marvin s. of Lawr. of Okla. has 2 chn; Mrs. Julius Bujol of Baton Rouge, drt. Lawr. (d) Sara J. drt. Jas. & Rachel, md. Lawrence Garret. Had-Jody A. md. Geneva West; Talmadge Miles Garret md. Lila Cameron Witherspoon & had: Talmadge (e) Ann md. Charlie Smith. . .(4) Thomas, s. of Jno. & Mary, md. Carrie Gray, Woodruff, SC. Had-Pierce, Mittie, Ida, Berry, Lillian, Jeff (5)-John d. 1865 bur. Fairview md. Sara Blakely. Had 4: Chas who md. Anna Knox; Lina md. M. Prince; Mattie md. Jno. Savage; Wm. P. md. Carrie Peden (6) Ewing d. 1842 bur. Fork Shoals (7) George s. Jno. & Mary, bur. Williamston, SC md. Nancy N. Nesbitt. Had 10 chn. viz: (a) Geo. L. md. Ida Holland (b) M. Jane md. W. D. Hutto (c) Dr. James Nesbitt of Univ. Fla. md. Janie drt of Cpt. C. W. Sullivan of Williamston (d) Jno. L. d. 1928 (e) Mary N. (f) Annie (g) Bertha md. D'Arcy P. Gray (h) Wm. (i) Albert (j) Lillian Andrea md. Dr. Jno. W. Parker Jr. . .(8) Robert, unmd. . .(9) Mary Jane, drt. of Jno & Mary, md. Wm. L. Hopkins. Had-(a) Robt. md. Mattie Ramsey & had-Wm, David, Fred, Ethel (b) Jas, unmd. (c) Jno. H. md. Minnie Wright. . .(10)-David Quentin, md. Parnecia Griffith. Had-John, William, S. Griffith of Woodruff, SC. David md. a 2nd time, had chn.

ANDERSONS of Laurens, SC: George, William, Andrew & probably Joel, bros. GEORGE ANDERSON 1740-1808, Capt. of Militia Co. raised in Laurens, pro. to Major. His 12 yr. son David served with him & recvd Pen. 1838. Maj. George md. 3 times, 1st Miss Anderson; 2nd Miss Lewis (mother of D. Lewis A- who served as Prob. Judge of Laurens 30 yrs) 3rd-Molly Saxon 1773. By her 13 chn. viz: Chas 1774, Margt 1775, Judith 1778, James 1780, Geo. 1783, Wm. 1785, Tabitha 1787, Lewis 1789, Jno 1791, Molly 1794, Saxon 1797, Elizbth 1797, Sally 1802. The son JAMES md. 1801 Nancy Saxon & had 11 chn: Parmelia, Joshua, Geo. David (Ga. descts) Wm. C. Saxon, Lucinda, Jno. Saml, Jas. M., Sara Ann, Saxon Mills, Mary C.

WILLIAM ANDERSON**bro. of Maj. George, d. 1795, md. Elizbth Cobb. ISSUE, 9-viz: Margt md. Jno. Middleton, s. of Ainsworth M-of Laurens; Mary md. Robt. Stevens; Sara Ann; Saml md. Mary Hinton, drt. Robt. H-of Laurens; Ambrose; James md. Elizbth Middleton, s. of Jno. & to Mo; Andrew; Joel; Robert. The son SAMUEL ANDERSON & wife Mary Hinton, had 10 chn. Viz: Robt. W. 1812; James md. Nancy Wilson Poole; John, Malinda, Nellie, Rachel, Margt, Larkin, Samuel.

NATHAN & SAMUEL AUSTIN among first Greenville county settlers, near Enoree & Gilder's ck 1761. Nathan High Constable, but later he & 10 sons in Revo. One was Col. Wm. . .Dr. Thos. C. Austin had son, Hon. J. Thos. Austin, rep. Grv. 1876 in "Wallace House". . .Dr. Manning Austin had s. Jno. W.

THOMAS BELL md. abt. 1744 Jane-ISSUE, viz: Adam, Robert, William, Thomas. REVO. claims filed for last three. ADAM BELL d. bef. 1805, Laurens, SC w. Mary, Chn: David, John, Adam, James, Robert, Mary, Isabel, Esther, Elizbth. . .JAMES Bell of Laurens d. bef. Sept. 1824, w. Sara, CHN: John, Robert, Adam, James, Elizbth Milan, Susan. . .WILLIAM BELL** Laurens, SC md. Rachel Waters & had-Thomas, Peter, md. Lucinda Eddins, Jane md. Mr. Vandiver, William md. Mary Crews, David to Ga. . . The William Jr. lived first in Laurens then Ala. His chn. were-Francis M. to Miss; Mary Warton, Martha Henry, Dorothy Gann, Benjamin, Jonathan, Jas. William, Thomas, Joseph N.

JOHN BETHEA** md. Mary Pearce. ISSUE, viz: 1-William md. 1st Olivia Pearce, 2nd Sara Hargrove. .2-Tristram md. 1st Mrs. Ann Pearce Bethea, 2nd Margt McCall. . 3-John md. Hannah Walker. .4-Cade md. Kitty Bethea. .5-Martha md. John Bradley. . 6-Sara md. Timothy Rogers. .7-Betsy md. Jerry Walter. The above John's son, DAVID md. Sara Manning. . .WILLIAM BETHEA** 1725-1799 md. Sara Goodman. ISSUE, viz: 1-John md. Mary Hanagan & had-Elizbth. Mary Council. . 3-Philip md. Ann Bethea. .4-Jesse md. Celia Harrelson. .5-Charity ,md. Henry H. Hybert. .6-Martha md. Athneil Trawick. .Members of our D. A. R. chapt. on this line- Mrs. Cornelia Bethea Harris*, Mrs. Evelyn Peele Sullivan*.

WILLIAM BLACKSTOCK SR. 1720-1799, w. Euphemy, had-Wm. Blackstock Jr.**1750- 1841 md. Mary Yarborough b. Laurens Co. Chn: Polly md. Berry Poole; Jane md . Mr. Foster. . .D. A. R. on this line: Ruth Todd Waldrop*.

WILLIAM BOLLING OF VA.** ISSUE, viz: Samuel**, Archibald, John, Amelia, Matoaka (Mata). The son SAMUEL BOLLING b. Va. d. SC Laurens county. ISSUE, viz: Nancy Sullivan, Elizbth Dunklin, Lucinda Johnson, Mary Perritt, Mehitabel Tarrant, Robert md. Rachel Tarrent, Tully md. Mary Ann Smythe Mimms, John md. Sara Rabun, Thornberry unmd. The dau. NANCY md. James Sullivan II & had-(1) Edny Cunningham (2) Lucinda (3) Henderson Whitlow md. Grace Downs (4) Tully Francis md. Sara Berry & had-James, Robert, Sara Ann. The son James Bolling Sullivan md. Elizbth Griffin & had-Arthur, Ann. Descts in Ga. . .D. A. R's this line: Lee Hunt Pinson*, Cecile Moore Mallory*, Patti Willis*, Florence Trapp Smith*.

BOYD the bros-Jame, Samuel & William   settled in Laurens Co., SC bef. Revolution. JAMES BOYD I md. Bonnie Luray & had-John 1753-1827 md. Rebec. Amelia Watson. Had 9 chn. viz: 1-Abram md. Annie Gray, to Tex. .2-John D. 1775-1859. .3-Wm. II md. Fannie Bullock,. to Va. Had Alfred. .4-Edney. .5-Mary md. John H. Boyd. Had-Louella, Rebecca W., Jno. Abram. .6-Martha md. Joel Allen. Had 10 chn. .7-Nancy md. Frank Ross. .8-Sallie md. Raymond Fuller. .9-Rebecca-----WILLIAM BOYD(bro. of Jas.) wife Eva(says one recd). . .A Wm. Boyd is bur. abt. 2 mi. w. Madden Station, Laurens Co., stone marked 1738-9. He said have md. 1st Miss McClanahan & had 2 drts, one of whom md. Mr. Brock. William md. 2nd Miss McClurkin. ISSUE, nine, viz: 1-Catherine md. Isaac Pinson, had-Lucinda, Elizabeth, Gabriel, others. .2-James md. Elizbth Parks, had-David, William, Isaac, Sara K. Simpson, Nancy, Catherine Pitts, Jane Peden, Elizbth Hipp,James F., Margaret. .3-David was gr-father of the two "Todds". .4-Samuel md. Nancy Henry. .5-Eleanor Henderson. .6-One to Tex. no heirs. .7-Isaac. .8-Bradford md. Margt Watkins. .9-Prob. Jane, 2nd. w. Jno. Henry-----SAMUEL BOYD(one of the 3 bros) md. Nancy Valentin Mace or Macey. Had chn: Samuel II, Bradford...The son Saml II md. Miss Henry of Laurens Dist, SC. Had-David, Jno. Bradford, Sanford, Harrison (These data from Miss Hitt, a Boyd desct). . .The following Boyd data from Rev. T. S. Mosely. . .A Boyd b. abt 1762 had chn: William b. 1787, Joseph 1791, Mary 1793, Hugh 1797, Jennet 1799, James 1802, Robt 1805, Rosannah 1807, David 1810, Frances 1812, Jeff 1817, John 1795-1872. Later md. Elizbth Blackburn, to Ala. Had chn: Nancy Canon, Rosanna Tramill, Emily Tubb, Mary Hall, George, Rachel Ellis Hurley, William, Matilda Mackey, Sara Mackey Turner.

ELIAS BALL founder SC family, md. Elizbth Harleston. Had-Bartholomew, w. Elizbth. ISSUE, viz: Bartholomew II b. 1736, Edward 1744**, Sampson, William, Sara Giles 1754, drt. md. Thomson, drt. md. Mikell. Wm. Ball md. 1769 Sara Martin(He s. of Wm. Ball** 1750-1805, d. in Laurens Co.)

ROBERT BOLT**, will 1795, had-John, Lewis, Peggy, Sally, Polly. SQUIRE JOHN BOLT & wife Nancy had-Samuel md. 1848 Ellen Kennedy. . . .JOHN BOLT & Nancy of Va. Had-Asa, Robert. .Asa Bolt md. Hannah Crombie. ISSUE 13, viz: William, Toliver, John H., Thomas, Crombie, Abram, Lewis, Martin, Edmund, Oliver, Elizbth, Mary C., Theresa. The son Abram b. LAURENS 1839, d. 1909 md. 1856 Mary M. Clark. Had- Martha, Lawson A., Thos. L., Dolphus J.

JOHN COOK** from Va. to SC 1770 md. 1st-Betty Brown; 2nd-Martha Pearson. ISSUE ,

125

viz: Elizbth McCrellis, Mary Hutchinson, Burrell, John md. Ellen Hampton., Nathaniel P., Phillip to Ga; Isaac, & several drts. The son BURRELL** md. Mary Pope & had among others, Burrell md. Mary Kirkland.

JEREMIAH COOPER from Pa. to SC abt. 1774, Indian Trader, md. Charity Clark. (Clark, Columbus, Micajah, Saml-bros.) Clark was b. in Laurens 1818, youngest of 11 chn., md. 1847 Alice Reed. ISSUE, viz: Samuel P., Marion, Georgey md. Robt. G. Center, Jerome, William S., Eliza Clark, Julia D., Alice, Lillian. The son, Wm. S. md. Augustus Faust.

THOMAS CAMP SR.** 1717-98 md. twice. ISSUE 24. Of these, Nathan & Thos. settled in Laurens, SC; John & Benj. in Grv., SC. .1-Edmund md. twice & had 21 chn. d. in Ga. .2-Joseph md. Miss Rountree. .3-John md. Mary Tarpley. .4-Nathl md. Winifred Tarpley, had Hosea md. Elizbth Jordan. Desct in La. .5-Thomas md. Nancy Tarpley. One child, Sara Calhoun. .6-Starling. .7-Hosea. .8-William, descts. Spartanburg, SC. . 9-Alfred NC-SC. .10-Benjamin md. Elizbth Dykes, had-Joseph, John, Benjamin, Winifred Ackins. .11-Elizabeth md. Reuben Brock. .12-Joel NC. .13-Crenshaw NC. .14-James md. Sara Jennings. .15-Daniel md. Sara McKinney NC. .16-Adam, bach. .17-Lewis md. Joanna Neel. .18-Stephen. .19-Larkin. .20-21--Uriey & Ruth no is. .22-Aaron md. 1st Miss Terrill; 2nd Sara Suttle. .23-George md. Mary Norman. .24-Joshua md. Nancy Gregory NC-SC. THE SON JOHN CAMP**bur. in SC. ISSUE nine, viz: 1-Thos. had-Nancy Smith, Violet Stroud, Patience Thompson, Elizbth Camp, William. .2-Abner md. Miss Ragsdale (drt. of Revo S) to Ga. had-Edmond, Russell, Arthur, Hiram, Satira, Martha, Mary, Thomas, John. .3-Starling. .4-Wm. .5-John. .6-Kizziah md. Benj. Arnold & had is. .7-Sara Grayson. .8-Winifred Kinman. .9-Annie Hill. (Sullivan-Dunklin D. A. R. on this line-Mrs. Sara Ervin*, Mrs. Albert Stephens*, Mrs. Thos. Baldwin*, Mrs. Jack Agee*, Mrs. Jno. Allbritton*, Mrs. Wm. Horton*, Miss Mary Jean Knight*.)

REV. THOMAS CRAIGHEAD died 1739 Pa.The Rev.Alex Craighead 1705-1766, had ISSUE: Rachel Caldwell, SC., Nancy Richardson SC., Jane Calhoun SC., Margaret Carruth, Mary Dunlap, Elizbth Crawford, Agnes Alexander, Thomas.

COL. JOHN CRAWFORD had sons-Robert, James, Joseph from Pa. to Waxhaws, SC abt. 1760. Joseph or Joel said to have settled in Edgefield, SC but moved to Ga. & father of William H. Crawford. . . .2-ROBERT CRAWFORD** md. Jean White. ISSUE: Sara Donnon, Mary Dunlap, Isabel, Martha Williams to Ala., Elizbth Vaughan, James, William, John. . . .3-JAMES CRAWFORD; w. at Charleston, SC., d. 1779, md. Jennett Hutchinson. ISSUE: James; Alex md. Elizbth Craighead; George; drt. md. Jno. Martin; drt. md. Isaac Smith; drt. md. Wm. Henderson; drt. md. Jno. Parton (drts. were-Mary, Jean, Martha, Margt); John md. Miss Snead, Thomas.

JOHN CURETON** 1731-1803 from Va. 1788 to SC. He md. in Va. 1st w. Winifred Heath. Appears 1790 census SC. Records at Newberry & Laurens Courthouses. Will, Laurens prv. 1803. Bur. Beaverdam church-yard, grave marked. ISSUE(all wives): John, Louisa, Susanna, Frances, Martha, Charles, Nathl, David, George W., Heath, Jinny, S. Hunter, E. Sheppard, Danl, Thos. T. . . .The son JOHN (1757-1821) named in will, md. in Va. 1778 (Bond no 113) Sarah Moon. Sells out in Va. 1797 (Lunenburg recds). Wife dying, he follows relatives to SC with two sons, John Moon age 18 & Abner Heath, 12. They settle near county line Spartanburg-Greenville, Enoree river & were associated with the LESTER family in the old factory there. (The son Abner, md. Matilda Lester) The newspaper, The Greenville News (Oct. 1948) had article on early cotton mills in US, which says in part: "Wm. Bates b. R. I. came to this county 1819. BY THAT TIME, Spartanburg county already had a small textile manufacturing plant-LESTERS- at which Bates worked until he & associates were able to establish BATESVILLE on the Greenville county side on the Enoree riv. . ." Here at Lester Factory, on the Spartanburg side of the Enoree river, lived John Cureton (1757-1821) & sons, Jno. Moon & Abner Heath.About a mi. away, in prv. cem. the fath. John is buried. The two sons later removed to Sandy Springs Section of Greenville county, lived adjoining plantations & Abner bur. Sandy Springs. John Moon Cureton md. Mary Adkins Dacus & both bur. on plant(still owned by desct), graves marked.

ISSUE: M. Layfatte, Mary E., Harriet D., Claudia C., John M., David T., Pascall, Sarah, Ann, William. . .CHN. OF ABNER(md. 2) were: Thos. Jeff, George W., David, William, John M., Sally, Mary, James, Pascal, Tandy, Robert, Abner, Walker, Lizzie, Caroline.

CAPT. HENRY ARTHUR DIAL md. Isabella Hastings. ISSUE, viz: Hastings, James of NC., Isaac, Isabella, Albert, John, Martin. .The son, Col. Hastings Dial, d. in Laurens, SC md. Rebecca Abercromie. ISSUE: 1-Hastings md. Miss Allen. .2-Isaac md. 1st Amanda Coker, 2nd Mary Coker. Had 15 chn. Most of whom to Tex. .3-James md. Elizbth Stallworth. .4-Rebecca md. Jas. Johnson. .5-Isabella md. Jno. Woody. .6-Jane md Abram Madden. .7-Mary md. Mabra Madden (These two had bro Wm. Madden md. Sara Pinson). . . .MARTIN DIAL (s. of Cpt. Henry Arthur) d. in Laurens Co. md. 1st Christy Abercromie: 2nd Hannah--ISSUE, viz: 1-John md. Chrystie Thomason. .2-Hannah md. Cpt. Jno Armstrong. .3-Colvill md. Lidia Eastwood. .4-Isaac md. Sara Thomason.. 5-James md. 1st Sara Stoddard; 2nd Jane East. .6-Martin Jr. md. Jane Eastwood. .7-Jonathan unmd. .8-Wm. md. Hannah Hellams. Members of our chapt. who joined on this line: Mrs. Marcelle Babb Quillen*, Sara Frances Abercromie*, Mrs. Lucile Baldwin Hellams*.

JOSEPH DUNKLIN of South Carolina** md. Jean Warthen** (variously spelled) ISSUE, 7-viz: Joseph, Elizabeth, Nancy Ann, John, Mary, William, James. .1-Joseph II md. Sara Margt Sullivan. Had-Mary Gregory, Jane C. Hicks, Joseph who md. in SC Sara Parkins to Miss; Stephen T. md. Rachel McGuire to Mo: Gov. Daniel of Mo. . .II-ELIZABETH DUNKLIN md. Mr.Sweeny in Ky.. .III-NANCY ANN DUNKLIN md. 1st Wm. Shipp** Had-William, Joseph, Harriet. She md. 2nd Nat Sullivan to Ala. . .IV-JOHN DUNKLIN** md. Polly Bowman from SC to Ky-Mo. Had-William, Nancy, Jeff, Madison. . . .V-MARY DUNKLIN**md. Hewlett Sullivan**(See Sullivan). . . .VI-WILLIAM DUNKLIN md. Anne Hendricks Hamilton, from SC 1819 to Ala. Had-Hance, John, Dr. Wm., Dr. James, Thos. W., Temperance, Caroline, Elizabeth, Mary, Margaret. Of these, Hance md. Miss Arnold, some descts to Tex; Dr. William md. in Miss., moved Tex; Thomas had 7 chn. Three descts members our D. A. R., viz: Joyce Dunklin*, Patricia Smith*, Mrs. Olen Delany*. .Temperance abv. marr. Wm. B. Haralson Ga-Ala. .. Thomas of Ala. Had-Mary Rast, Elizbth Hardy, Martha Dudley, Emma Rast, Frank, Wm. John CA. .Caroline md. Hugh Caffey, Ala. Had-Hugh, Thomas, Mary Dunklin of Tex; Irene Caffey. .Elizabeth md. J. A. Pierce, Ala. Had-Dr. Dunklin, Dr. Wm., Annie, John. .Mary & Margt unmd. . . .VII-JAMES DUNKLIN, s. Jos. & Jean, lived on Reedy River near Laurens-Grv. line, md. four times, 1st in Laurens, Elizbth Bolling; 2nd in SC., Marjorie Law; 3rd Martha Irby; 4th Catherine Lee Gafford. He moved to Ala. 1819. ISSUE, ten, viz: John, Joseph, Abigail, Nancy Ann, Lucinda. By 1st w: James Law, Caroline, Turner. By 3rd w: Dr. Irby Dunklin of SC. By 4th w: Daniel Gafford. . .1-JOHN DUNKLIN. ISSUE: James H., Joseph, Dock, Nord, Thomas, Lucinda, Caroline, others. . .2-JOSEPH DUNKLIN SC-Ala., md. Mary C. Judge. ISSUE: James H., Elmira, Abigail. (1) Gen. James Hilliard Dunklin, C. A., had Revo. ancestors in Cook, Hutchinson & Bolling families. He md. 1st Abbie Reid; 2nd Mary Jane Reid. ISSUE: Mollie, Elizabeth, Anna, Jas. H., Joe, Jennie, Erin, Lora, Judge. .(2) Elmira md. Judge Fletcher Johnson, M. C. Had-Jennie Whittington, Fletcher Jr., Mary May. .(3) Abigail md. Capt. Holden Wade, Montgomery, Ala. . .3-Abigail md. Dr. Hillory Herbert SC-Ala. ISSUE: George, James, Elizabeth, Lucinda, Martha, Fannie, Cornelia, Abigail, Margery Catherine. . .4-Nancy Ann Warthen md. Dr. George Herbert in Ala. ISSUE: Richard, Nancy, Curtis Burke, M. D. . .5-LUCINDA md. Ennis McDaniel. ISSUE: Two. . .6-JAMES LAW DUNKLIN md. Mary Amanda Burnett. ISSUE: William Turner, Catherine, Susan Florence, Daniel Edward, Almira, Ida, Caroline F., Irby J., Ellen Reid. The dau. Susan Florence md. 2nd 1869 Joel Flanagan Thames & had-Ruby Florence* md. 1899 Levy John Beeland & had-Florence Perdue* & Marjorie Steele*. Ellen Reid, drt. of Jas. Law Dunklin md. 1882 Thos. Wm. Peagler & a drt. Myra W.* md. 1921 Wm. S. Blackwell. . .7-Caroline md. S. A. Mears. . .8-William Turner md. Mary H. Cook, had-James, Ella, Margery, George, Herbert, Irby. . .9-Dr. Irby Dunklin md. late in life, Harriet F. Montgomery. He was for many years a prominent physician in Laurens, S. C. Had chn. (1) Mary M. (2) James W. who md. Zelene, drt. of Hugh E. Gray & wife Susie (drt. of Hon. Chas. P. Sullivan & wife Zelene Boyd). . .

10-Daniel Gafford Dunklin C. A., md. 1st Susan C. Burnett. Had-Walter unmd. He md. 2nd Hannah Pickett Patton. Had-Patton, d. unmd.

I.---JAMES IRVINE (Ervin), md. Elizbth, drt. Capt. John William James. ISSUE, viz (known): Rebecca, Jean, Robert, Elizbth Shaw, Hugh Sr., John. . .1-The son Hugh md. 1st Mary Ellison; 2nd Elizbth James & his chn. were-Susannah md. 1st Cooper, 2nd Jos. Wilson. . .2-Elizbth McClure. . .3-Mary Cannon. . .4-Isaac. .,.5-Jane, md. cous. Robt. Ervin. . .6-Sara. . .7-Margt. 2nd w. Col. Jno. Ervin. . .8-James md. Elizbth Witherspoon. . .9-Wm. to Miss. . .10-Col. Hugh md. Drt. Gavin Witherspoon & had-Robert, Mary Wilds. . .II.---JOHN IRVINE SR., md. Elizbth, drt. Robt. Ellison Esq. ISSUE, viz: 1-Elizbth md. Jno. Fulton & had-Elizbth md. Robt. s. of Col. Hugh Ervin. Descts in Darlington,SC. . .2-Robert md. Jane, drt. Hugh Ervin Sr. . .3-Sara Dobbins. . . 4-Jeane Matthews. . .5-Mary James. . .6-James. . .7-Col. John. . .8-Margaret. . . .III.-COLONEL JOHN ERVIN** md. 1775 Jane Witherspoon; md. 2nd 1791 his cous. Margt Ervin. Colonel John Ervin commanded Britton's Neck Regiment under General Francis Marion. ISSUE to maturity, viz: 1-Samuel 1776-1823 md. 3 times. . .2-Elizbth md. Mr. Ford of Miss. Had drt. md. Mr. Cooper, parents of Tim Cooper, Chief Justice of Miss. . .3-James Robt, next in line. . .4-Hugh 1792-1815. . .5-John md. Harriet Glenn Pope. . . .IV.-COLONEL JAMES ROBERT ERVIN md. 1813 Elizabeth Powe, drt. of Genl. Erasmus Powe & wife Esther Ellerbe** (Erasmus s. of Thos. Powe**. Father of Esther was Wm.) ISSUE, viz, 8: 1-Saml James md. twice & had-James Robert, Erasmus Powe, Elizbth, Samuel J., Clarence. . .2-Erasmus Powe md. 1847 Mary McCollum & had-Nellie, Gavin, Robert James, Maxy Gregg, Thomas Powe, Jane, Mary, Erasmus. . .3-Elizbth 1819-22. . .4-John Witherspoon, next in line. . .5-Jane md. 1851 Wm. S. Harris & had-Ervin, Everard, Charles, Jane, Brevard. . .6-Jas. Robert killed battle 1864. . .7-Mary Caroline md. cous. John Fulton Ervin, Lt-Gov. of SC. Had-(among others) Mary md. Colonel Evander McIver. Darlington, SC. . .8-Anne Davis by Col. Jas. Robert Ervin's 2nd wife, md. 1851 Dr. H. K. W. Flinn. . . .V.-JOHN WITHERSPOON ERVIN removed from Manning, SC to Morganton, NC md. 1844 Laura Catherine Nelson (drt. of Jared Nelson & wife, Susanna Magill Conyers & gr-drt. *Fighting Capt John Nelson** who lived on Black river, now Clarendon Co., SC) ISSUE, nine, viz: 1-Lawr. Nelson, next in line. . .2-Rev. Erasmus Ellerbe md. 1st Lillias Blair McPhail; 2nd Mary Guthrie. Had-Lilly Blair, John Witherspoon, Belle Walker. . .3-John Conyers Ervin md. Louisa Morgam. . .4-Donald McQueen Ervin md. Sue Barr. . .5-Susan Elizbth md. James E. Kennedy. Had-Katie, Louisa, Crawford, Harry, Thomas. . .6-Samuel J. Ervin md. Laura T. Powe & had-Laura W; Catherine E; Margt T; Edw. Powe; Saml James; Hugh Tate; Joseph Wilson; Eunice Wood; John W; Jean C. . .7-Louisa Nelson md. Wm. C. Ervin & had-Flora, David W; Eliza; Dorothy C; Mary W. . .8-Annie D. md. James L. Michie & had-Margt, Mamie, Elsie, Donald McQueen. . .9-Henry Flinn, inf. . . .VI.---LAWRENCE NELSON ERVIN b. Clarendon Co., SC. d. Indiantown, SC. Confederate Soldier, wounded in battle, md. 1871 Elizbth Gotea Wilson (drt. of Harvey Wilson & Jeannette Witherspoon who had chn: Clara md. F. E. Taylor 1868 of Charleston, SC; Mary, Emma, Harvey, Gotea) ISSUE of Lawr. Nelson Ervin, viz: Mary, Jno. W., Robt. W., Laurie N., Clarendon, Annie Louise, Eras. Powe, Samuel J., Jane W. . . .Descendants in Laurens county, S. C., are: Houston S. Ervin; E. Felicia Ervin Stephens*.

SAMUEL FLEMING, est. settled 1805 in Laurens, SC. Sons-Robert, Saml. Big Robert Fleming 1771-1826 md. Elizbth McClintock, had among others, Mary. . .SAMUEL FLEMING JR., 1763-1843 md. Rebecca Hall. One child was Joseph H. md. Elizbth Jane Bryson.

WILLIAM FULLER md. Jane Griffin, had 14 chn. . .CALVIN L. FULLER b. 1848 Laurens md. Carrie Philips. ISSUE five, viz: Benj. R. md. Mrs. Antho Watt Dial; Calvin M. md. EffieWinebrener;Clementine md. Dr. J. H. Teague; Rosa md. J. H. Motes; William P.

CHARLES GARY OF VA. had sons: Thomas, Absolom, West. 1-THOMAS md. Rebecca Jones, SC-Ala. Had-Thomas, William, Arthur, Isaac, Dr. Martin, Jesse, Charles (last three of SC). Jesse had a son Dr. Thos who had-Gen. Martin W. Gary. . .2-Absolom of SC md. Hetty Griffin, had-Some descts in Tex. . .3-West of SC md. Frances Griffin, had-Charles, Wash, Dr. John K.

JOHN GWIN(Guinn), Va. to SC as wid'r, d. aft 1756, md. 2nd 1739 Catherine Ricketts. ISSUE (known) 7, viz: Jno. Nich., Richard, Mary, George, Roger, Catherine, Elizbth An...The son, Jno. Nicholas Gwin(Guinn)** md. Mary Elizbth Bland. Known ISSUE: Jno. Lancelott Bland Guin md. Mrs. Eliza Ann(Moore) Henderson; Jos. Maurice Guin md. twice, 1st w. d. in SC. He migrated to Tenn-O...D. A. R: Dorothy Humbert*, Louise Humbert Milburn*, Emma L. H. Nash*.

JOHN HARRIS** b. Md. 1763 md. Mary Pickens. ISSUE: 7 sons, 4 drts. One son was John Jr., had a gr-son Benjamin md. Orpha Harris. Had 5 girls, 4 boys, two served CA. Bonneau Harris md. Nannie Hudgens of Laurens. Had-8 sons, 3 drts.

LT. THOMAS HERBERT, settled Old Dutch Fork, SC by 1772, md. Jemima Dawkins. ISSUE: 1-John b. abt. 1760/3, had-William, John Thomas, Amanda...2-George...3-Hardy who Bishop Abury ments as accomp. him from Charleston to Ga., to Finches ck 1794. Had-drt Alice Dameron...4-Thos. Sharp md. Elizbth Hampton. ISSUE, 10: Harriet Cook, Elizbth McDaniel, Nancy Hampton, Mary Wade, Hardy, John, Thos. S., Edward, Richard, ?Preston....GEORGE HERBERT (no 2 abv) md. 1787 Elizbth Finch, to Ala. Had-Martha Page, Ann Cook Oliver, Dr. Hillary who md. Abigail Dunklin; Geo. who md. 1st Anne W. Dunklin; Thos. E. md. Dorothy Teague Young & had-Aurelia Calhoun d. in Miss; Theodora Adams Royal; Flora A. Buel; HILLARY b. in LAURENS , SC., M. C., Secretary Navy, md. Ella Smith. They had three chn. but only Ella Micou left issue.

TIMOTHY KELLY & sons, Saml, John with drt. Abigail, set. in SC near Camden. John md. abt 1755 Mary Evans, lived in 1762 on Bush riv. ISSUE: Isaac md. Merrie Gaunt; Anna md. Abijah O'Neal; Saml d. 1851 aged 91 md. 1788 Hannah Pearson. They had-Mary Whitacre, John, Timothy, Saml, Moses to Ohio, Anna.

JAMES WILLIAM KILGORE md. Elizbth Jack in Pa. had 19 chn. of whom nine believed in Revolution. The son BENJAMIN moved to NC & later SC md. Ann McCreary, land deed recd, Laurens. ISSUE, viz: James, & fol. to Ala-Miss: David, William, Martha Elizbth, Anna Isabel, Saml. The drt. Martha Elizbth md. John Walker...JAMES, s. of Benj. Kilgore, md. Kizziah Greer. ISSUE: 1-Elizbth Stone SC...2-Mary Brockman SC. .3-Dr. Ben had-9 chn. .4-Margt. Barry to Miss...5-Jesse...6-Malinda Barry... 7-Lavinia Borum to Miss...8-Dr. James...9-Josiah...JOSIAH KILGORE md. Harriet Benson. ISSUE, seven: Dr. Benjamin; Mary Stokes, Harriet Hunter, William C., James B., Jesse, Isabel....CHARLES KILGORE (one of the 19) md. 1st. Winnie Clayton; 2nd Martha McIllhaney. He d. in Tenn. 1823. ISSUE: 1-Chas. Jr. md. Avirilla Simpson...2-Rev. Robt. md. Jane P. Green...3-William md. Va. J. Osborn...4-Mary Culbertson...5-Hiram md. Rebecca Renfro...6-Ralph md. Miss Gray...7-James... 8-Jno...9-Martha Walker...10-Rebecca Shirl...11-Sara Henderson.

WILLIAM KENNEDY** md. Ann Brandon. ISSUE, 11. Two drts. Letitia, Ellen, md. Brandons; James md. Mary Snowden; Ann md. Thos. Hamilton; Elizbth md. Saml Clowney; Mary md. Wm. Hamilton; Jesse md. Mary Hughs; Benjamin md. Lucy Gilbert; William Jr...The Rev. John Brandon Kennedy md. Rebecca Ross, Laurens County, S.C.

HENRY LAURENS b. 1724 Vice-Pres. of SC 1776 & Pres. Continental Congress of U.S. He signed Preliminary Peace in Paris 30 Nov. 1782 in conjunction with Jno. Adams, Dr. Franklin, Jno. Jay. "One of the Founding Fathers of this Nation." Was sent to borrow 10 million from the Dutch, ship captured by British & he confined in Tower London 1780. He md. Elinor Ball. ISSUE 4: John killed in Revo; Henry; Mary Pinckney, & a dau. md. Dav. Ramsey.

LIDE: John, Thos., Robt** bros. abt. 1740 to Cheraw Dist. SC...Robt. md. Hannah Hart, had 5 sons; one was Hugh who had sons: Rev. Thos. P. & Jno. M. Latter had Jno. Miller md. Eliza Edwards; Rev. Thos. md. Martha Hawkins, & a s. was Robt. Lide of Greenville.

WILLIAM LIPSCOMB** from Va. bef Revo. to Cherokee Co., SC(Sptg) had s. John. Had Edw. md. Melissa Littlejohn & had-Hamlet S. md. Alice Wood. . .Nathan, CA 1842-1918 md. Mary Wilkins.

ALEXANDER LOVE of York Co. Pa. md. Margt Moore, to SC. abt 1765. Set. near old Yorkville & memb. Prov. Cong. 1775. A desct was: Robt. Mitchel Love who had s. Dr. Robt., md. Jane Hemphill.

PATRICK MARION md. Jane McNeel, had-Jno. Alex Marion md. Margt. J. Sterling, had-James Taylor Marion 1845-1911 CA md. Jane A. Hardin, had-Hon. Jno. Hardin Marion md. Mary P. Davidson (drt. Col. Wm. D.-& Ann Irvin Pagan. Col. Wm. Davidson was gr-son of Maj. Jno.**) GENERAL FRANCIS MARION** 1732-1795, the "Swamp Fox" was son of Gabriel & Esther Cordes Marion & youngest of six chn. Gabriel was son of Benjamin Marion & Louise d'Aubrey, French Huguenots, to S. C.

JAMES MARTIN 1723-1792 md. 1745 Amy Holt. Their son, KINCHEN MARTIN** 1762-1841 md. Chloe Hough. ISSUE: 1. William md. twice,-Parker, McBride. . .2. John md. twice,-Parker, Boswell. . .3. Jas. H. md. Charlotte Kirby. . .4. Lucy md. three times,-Morton, Ingram, Kendred. D.A.R: Lena J. Abercromie*.

JOHN MATTISON McDAVID, w. Anna, had (known) chn: 1-John Allen md. Nancy Acker & had 11 chn. . .2-Patrick** descts Ky-O. . .3-Rosannah md. McKay,SC. . .4-David** of SC. . .5-Jennie md. Mr. Rutledge. . .6-JAMES md. Penelope Rodgers. ISSUE to maturity: (1) Abner (2) Hiram (3) William to Miss. (4) Anny Shumate, (5)Nancy Mattison Graham (6) John md. Miss Davenport (drt. & gr.drt. of Revo. S.) Chn: James,William Jackson, Richard, John, Adeline Roberts to Tex., Robert, George, Mary, Andrew,Nancy, Benjamin, Rosannah Williams, Nancy Graham to Ga., Mary Arnold, SC. (7) Jas.

JESSE McGEE located in Anderson Co, had s. Elias md. Sara Landrum, had s. Julius F. md. Mattie J. Jones. . .One Michael McGhee**. Desct. Hon. Saml Hodges McGhee of Cokesbury md. Laura Harrall of Bennettsville.

WILLIAM, JOHN & JAMES McGOWAN filed Revo. Claims in S.C. . .William McGowan]md. Jane McWilliams, Laurens County. They had a son, SAMUEL McGOWAN who md.Susan Caroline Wardlaw. He was Brig-General 1863 in command of McGowans:Brigade ISSUE: Lewis, Samuel, Sara E., William C., Alex M., Lucia R. . . .Capt John Jackson McGowan md. Mary Wells. Had-Franklin Pierce, b. Laurens Co. md. 1887 Mattie Calhoun.

ROBERT MOSELEY 1725-1796, b. in SC md. 1st Mary; md. 2nd Penelope Talley. Fol. Moseleys filed Revo. Claims in SC: Robert, John, Thomas, Benjamin, William, James. Robert by 1st w. had-Rachel Davis, Elizbth Vann, Sara Hagood, Martha Stallings, Susan Adams,Mary Holsonbacke, Edward 1771-34 md.in SC Miss Butler,John. . .Robt. Moseley Sr. had by 2nd w. issue: Anna Jeter, Lydia Williams Moseley, Robert S., Jesse, Daniel, Grace, Thomas, Penelope Copeland. The son, EDWARD MOSELEY md. 1793 in SC. Miss Butler, d. in Ala. . . .A GEORGE MOSELEY** of Laurens from Va. md. 1st Lucy Moore; 2nd Mary Moore.

THOMAS NEAL SR, md. Susannah Harrell, had-SAMUEL NEAL** md. Patty McCormick 1786 in SC. ISSUE: Polly Pruitt, Betsy, John, Sara, Thomas, James who md. 1st Elizbth Beal, 2nd Elizbth Rawlings Davenport.

WILLIAM O'NEALL Va-SC 1766, Mudlick Ck. Laurens. Son Hugh b. 1767 was father of Judge O'Neal, historian.

RICHARD OWINGS** & wife Ann, Laurens Co., SC. ISSUE with descendants: 1-Richard** & wife Sara, had-Richard, William, Archibald, John. . .2-Edward to Tenn. . .3-Butler md. in Laurens abt. 1787. . .4-Archibald to Kershaw Co. . .5-William to Va-Ky. . .5-Jonathan of Laurens County.

WILLIAM PARSONS** md. in Va. Mary Goolsby. ISSUE: Samuel, Joseph,, Archibald, Isiah, others. D.A.R. members: Margaret Brockman Fowler*, Rosemary Fowler*.

HENRI PATRICK, M.C. & REVO. Patriot, Orangeburg Dist. HAD-Mary & twin sons, George, Lewis. Geo. md. Hannah Lee of Edgfield (drt. Andrw Lee** & Nancy drt. Russel Wilson & Susan Rutherford.)

PHILIP PENDLETON of New Kent, Va. ISSUE: Elizbth Clayton; Rachel Vass; Cathryn Taylor; Henry. Latter md. Mary Taylor & had-James, Philip, Nathl. Latter md. in Va. dau. of Philip Clayton. They had-Henry b. 1750 d. in SC 1789; descts in Pendleton Dist.

GENERAL ANDREW PICKENS** b. Pa. d. SC. md. Rebecca Calhoun. ISSUE, viz: 1-Mary md. John Harris & had-Andrew, Rebecca, John, Ezekiel, Mary, Nathl, Thomas, Joseph, Eliza, Benjamin. . .2-Ezekiel Pickens had (by 1st w. Elizbth Bonneau): Ezekiel Saml, Elizbth. by 2nd w. (Eliza Barksdale): Thomas, Mary, Andrew. . .3-Ann md. Jno. Simpson, Ala. Had-Leah, Andrew, Rebecca, John, Ezekiel, James. . .4-Jane, 2nd of that name, md. Dr. John Miller. Had-Robert, Eliza, John. . .5-Margaret md. George Bowie, had-Louisa Smith. . .6-Andrew md. 1st Miss Wilkinson, had-Frances W., Susan Calhoun. . . 7-Rebecca md. Wm. Noble. Had-Andrew, William, Ezekiel, Samuel, Joseph. . .8-Catherine md. Dr. Jos. Hunter, had-Margt-Eliza, Maria, Ezekiel, Andrew, Joseph. Res. Ark. . . 9-Joseph md. Miss Henderson. Had-Sara McQueen, Joseph, Rebecca Green, Anderson, Andrew.

COL. CHAS. PINCKNEY 1731-1782 md. Frances Brewton. A son was Chas. (2nd cousins: Chas. Cotesworth Pinckney & Thos. P.) The son Chas. md. 1788 Mary Eleanor Laurens: "It is believed that at least 31 of Chas. Pinckney's ideas went into the Constitution of U.S." [Every time we are reminded of the Constitution under which we live in freedom & independence, we might remember this great South Carolinian who did so much to bring about that freedom, which makes of us the most fortunate people in the world.] (Hennig)

AARON PINSON of Va. left w. 1758. He md. twice. Some of his chn. migrated to NC. Aaron Pinson left w. in NC naming wife Delilah. his chn. were: Thomas, Joseph, Zachariah, William, Aaron, Isaac, Ann Cunningham, Mary Evans, Elizbth Campbell, Dorcas Austin, Sara Head. Descts of Thomas to Ga. . .Both Aaron & Joseph Pinson belonged to Rabun Creek church, St. Marks Parish, Craven Co., SC in 1771 (the present Mt. Pleasant section of Laurens Co) AARON had land grant 1766. This Rev. Aaron Pinson of Laurens, w. Elizbth, had chn. 10, viz: Aaron, Joseph, Marmaduke, John, Moses, Isaac, Mary Cole, Jemima Henry, & drts. who md. Thos. Shirley, Joseph Fowler of Tenn. There is Revo. Service for 3 this family. . . .JOSEPH PINSON md. Mary Omehundro. He appears 1790 census, 7 in family, one being the son, MARMADUKE PINSON SR, will at Laurens, SC 1820. Chn: Abijah md. an Arnold, all to Ark. except youngest son to Ala; Isaac J. to Ga; Edith McDaniel; Huldah Cunningham; Polly Strain; Jerusha (Ruchey); Ruth; Sallie Madden; Marmaduke Jr. . . .The Rev. Marmaduke Pinson, w. at Laurens, md. Elizbth Sullivan 1805-1847. Had 8 chn, viz: 1-Mary Harris of Waterloo, had 6 chn. . .2-Louisa Brown. . .3-Dr. Washington. . .4-Elizbth Blain. . .5-Virginia Dora Edwards. . .6-Martha Charles. . .7-Joseph who md. 1871 Mary Luana Cox. Had 8 chn, viz: James Abner, John S., Mildred E., Joseph C., Washington, Clincie W., Clara M., Corrie L. . .The son JOSEPH ABNER PINSON md.1895 Emmie Shirley. Had 6 chn. Of these, following members our D. A. R. chapter: Annie Laurie Pettus*, Lydia Pinson Thomas, Shirley Perry, & a gr.drt. Vera Higeria*, dau. in-law, Lee Hunt Pinson*.

RAZOR, CHRISTIAN of Va. Had-Ezekiel Razor, CA md. Pamelai Barmore & had 11 Chn: James C., E. B., others. JAMES CHRISTIAN RAZOR of Laurens Co., md. Lucy Ann Agnew. Among their chn. were: Elizbth, Maggie, Emma, Ida, Wm. C., Ella, James, Samuel, Sally, John B. The son, William Christian Razor of Laurens Co., md. 1884 Ella L. Clardy of Laurens. . .E. B. Razor, md. Eliza, drt. of Dr. Harrison Latimer.

131

AMOS RICHARDSON** 1741-1815 md. Mary Elizbth Peterson. ISSUE: (1) David md. Fannie Williams (2)Susanna md. Mr. Allen (3)Rush md. Amanda Boulware. . .D. A. R. Louise Holmes Motes*.

JOHN RIDGEWAY** had a son JOHN** md. Fanny Ragsdale (drt**) ISSUE: 1-John had a son John. . .2-Betsy Lindley. . .3-Richard, had-David, Elijah, John. . .D. A. R. member-Agnes Ruth Babb.*.

DR. JOHN RUTLEDGE & ANDREW RUTLEDGE, bros. to SC. 1730-5. ANDRW md. Sarah Boone Hext. No chn. ment. will. . .DR. JOHN RUTLEDGE md. 1738 Sarah Hext (her mother md. Andrw) ISSUE, 7 viz: (1)Com.-in-Chief & Pres. of SC John md. 1763 Elizbth Grimke. .(2)Edward, SIGNER Declaration Independence md. Henrietta Middleton. . (3)Andrw. md. Elizbth Gadsden. . .(4)Thos. md. Margt Deveaux. . .(5)Sara md. Gov. Jno. Matthews. . .(6)Hugh md. Ann Smith. . .(7)Mary md. Roger Smith. . .Pres. of SC Jno. Rutledge had ISSUE, viz: Martha Kinlock; Sarah; Gen. John md. 1791 Sara Motte; Edw. md. Jane Harlestone; Fred'k md. Harriet Pinckney Horry; Chas. md. Caroline Smith; Elizbth md. Henry Laurens; Thos. d. young; Wm. md. Ann Coslett; States md. Julia Haskell.

CHARLES SAXON d. 1816** Cpt. Revo. Will at Laurens. Chn: Polly Anderson, Sally Rodgers, Lewis. . .The son, CAPT. LEWIS SAXON** md. Sally Allen. ISSUE, viz: 1-Clarissa Downs who had-Phoebee Farley, Mary Grace Sullivan, Susan T. Griffin, S. Caroline Downs. . .2-Charles md. twice-Pierce, Wolf. Had-J. F. W., Lewis, G. W., Robt. C. . .3-Mary Arnold. . .4-Joshua had-John, Sara Craig, Dr. Charles A., Mary E. Dorrah, others. .5-Lydall P. Saxon to Ala. .6-Tabitha Cleveland. .7-Susannah Thurston. . 8-Samuel. . .9-Allen. . .Others unmd. Following Saxons of Revolution granted Bounty Lands: Samuel, James, Wm. Follqwing filed Revo. Claims: Joshua, Charles, Hugh, Lewis, John, Archille, Yancy, Thomas & Edmond Sexton. D. A. R. members: Bernice Abercromie George*, Ruth A. Cain*.

I.--OWEN SULLIVAN II(s. Owen I, s. Jno) md. 1721 Mary Margt. Hewlett (Hughlett) ISSUE 5 to SOUTH CAROLINA; viz: James, Oen, Margt, Charles, Pleasant. . .I-JAMES OF LAURENS, SC** md. 1st Meta Bolling; 2nd Sara Harrison Choice. Had 10 chn: Sara Godfrey; Elizbth Burton to Ga; Larkin; Harrison; Delphy Osborne; John to Ga; Priscilla Moore; Jas. Jr; Rebecca Roland; Nancy Vaughan. . .2-OWEN III**, grant SC 1773, d. 1797 SC md. Sallie O'Dell Nelson. Had-(1)Fanny md. a Gore, Grv. Co, had 2 drts. One was first per. bur. Lebanon. Other md. a Lowe (2)Sallie md. a Croft, had Dr. Geo. of Ala. (3)Elizbth Jackson to Ky (4) (5)Wm & Nelson to Ky. (6)Charles md. 1816 Jane Ressell to Ala. 1824, had 6 chn: Abigail md. Thos. A. Lanford; Caroline md. Henry Harte; Dr. Oen md. 3 times, d. 1897, Waterloo, Ala. Had-Jane, Hewlett, Mary, James, Lizzie, John & Charles. Latter prac. medicine with father. . .3-MARGT or MAUDLINE md. Col. Saml Wharton b. 1740 d. SC. Had: (1)Betsy Burts (2)Patsy Grimes (3)Lottie Davenport (4)Nancy Lowe (5)Sam who had Edw & Geo. (6)Pleasant who had Wm. . .Wm. Nelson md. Leanna Fuller & had-Wm. & Jno. of Laurens. . .Jno. md. 1869 Laura Harris & had 8 chn. . .4-PLEASANT** ancestor Anderson, SC branch, md. Milly Kelly. Pen. papers give chn, viz: Kelly, Nimrod, Hudson Berry, Mary J., Sara, James, Maria, Mosby, Frances. The son Kelly had: Nimrod b. 1829 md. Emily K. Mattison & had 5, viz: James M. b. 1855 md. Mary A. Wannamaker; Nimrod B. 1863 md. Lila Simpson; Charles S. b. 1868 md. 1890 Lutie Bewley; William W. md. Anne Patrick; H. K. . .5-CHARLES.

II.--CHARLES SULLIVAN** md. 15 June 1749 wid. Mary Charlton (Johnson)** b. Va. 1722, d. SC. 1837. ISSUE 5 to South Carolina, viz: Moses, Sara, Claiborne, Stephen, Hewlett. . .1-MOSES** d. abt 1810 SC md. Milly Chandler d. 1832 Ala. Had-Joel md. a Johnson; Martha md. Joel Ferguson; Matilda md. Jas. Webb; Agnes md. Vardy Bonds; Nancy md. Isaac Littleton; Mary md. Robt. Scott. All to Ala., except Mary. . .2-SARA MARGARET md. Joseph Dunklin in SC**. . .his d. sc to Ky. with bros. Stephen & Claiborne & bro-in-law Jno. Dunklin. ISSUE 5, viz: Mary H. md. David Gregory in SC to Ala; Jane Caroline md. Isaac Hicks in SC to Ky; Governor Daniel md. Emily W. Haley in Ky. to Mo. 1810; Joseph Jr. md. Sara Parkins in SC to Miss. 1834 & wid. to

La-Tex; Stephen Tomplat md. Rachel McQuire to Ky. 1816...3-CLAIBORNE to Ky. 1806 to Mo. d. 1860 very old, md. Mary Harvey in SC. He with bro. Stephen & sister Sara Dunklin, helped blaze trail across mts, belongings on pack-horses, joined Danl Boone. Had 10 chn. viz: (1)Rev. James who had 4 (2)Mark had 6 .chn (3)Stephen b. 1795 md. Dorcas Pinell & had 13 chn. viz: Claiborne to Ohio; Blassinggame md. Elizbth Burton & lived Phelps Co. Mo. & had-Herbert, Blassinggame Jr., Mary, Lily, Fanny; Anna, drt of Stephen & Dorcas, d. in Cole Ridge; Sara md. a Mitchell to Miss; Elizbth md. a Magee & had 3 boys & 1 girl; Lettie of Crawford Co. Mo. md. J. Huitt & her drt. Elizbth md. N. W. Gibbs; Mary md. a Huit or Hewitt & a drt. md. Thos. Tune... Claiborne Sr. md. 2nd a Davis. A gr.son was Saml b. 1813 md. sister of Genl. Geo. Crook, Indian Fighter & had a son Thos. C. (Genl. Thos. C. Sullivan USA). Going to Ky-Mo. with Sullivans & Dunklins was Joseph Shipp & other relatives...4-STEPHEN to Ky. 1806 had a s. Charles md. a Hammett...5-HEWLETT;

III.--HEWLETT SULLIVAN(s. Chas. s. Owen II)** md. 19 Dec. 1787 Mary Dunklin**, drt. Jos. D-**. Hewlett entered army age 15. With father's assistance some 4 yrs. later in fall 1781, he organized a company of Scouts or Rangers, composed of relatives & neighbors. They caught & hung many Tories & cleared their section of Red Coats. He d. Grv. Co., SC. 1830. ISSUE 12, viz: Judge Dunklin, Dr. John C., Joseph P., Hewlett Jr., George W., T. Jefferson, Dr. James M., Jane, Elizbth, Frances, Mary, Charles P....1-JUDGE DUNKLIN SULLIVAN 1791-1837 md. Mary Mayberry, lived Perry Co. Ala. Member Convt. organized State Gov. One of founders Judson Col. Had 6 chn: (1)Mary Jane md. E. G. Byrne of Selma, Ala. & had Edw. md. T. King & had-Emma Harris*, Mary, Gonzella, Ida, Edw. (2)Lumley md. Jos. P. Walker & had 2 daus. She md. 2nd Elam Parrish. Chn: Maud & Ida Walker; Emma, Lona & Elam Parris (3)Hewlett md. Eliza Reid, Leon Co., Tex. Had-Dunklin, Lumley, Dunklin md. & had-Terrell, Marion, Harold, Herman; Lumley md. a Davidson & had- Wm., Lewis, Arthur, Dunklin, Ira, Clyde. (4)Dunklin md. Margt Griffin, Ala. Had-Dunklin, Jeff, Griffin, Bessie, Mary (5)Monroe md. Mary Griffin to Miss. Had-James, Tolbert. . . .2- DR. JOHN C. SULLIVAN, s. of Hewlett, 1793-1864 md. 1828 Anne Hendricks Arnold, Fork Shoals, Grv. Co., SC. Had 7 chn, viz: (1)Jno. D. md. Penelope McDavid & had- Allen md. Lula Garrison; Benj. md. Mabel Mendenhall; Caroline* md. H. H. Newton; Mark md. Elizbth Frierson; Mary md. F. M. Royall (2)Sara md. Dr. Enoch Agnew of Abbv., SC & had-Janie; Anna md. Chas. Smith (3)Jane md. Capt. Jno. McFall & had- Mary Elizbth md. Lt. H. L. Odiorne USN & drt. was Mabel* md. Hugh S. Macglashan; Rachel* md. J. R. Shannon & had-Marjorie Lawry*, Lilou McLane* (4)Elizbth md. Dr. W. Agnew (5)Emma md. Col. Mark Hardin, had-Blanche McCoslin*, Mattie Garner*, Virginia* (6)Martha md. Adam Eichelberger (7)Clara md. Dr. I. Cannon. Also descd. through this line: Mrs. Henry White* of Chester, SC; Jean McFall White*, Mrs. Ann White Leith*, Mrs. Jno. Edwards* of Seneca. . . .3-GEO. W. SULLIVAN, s. of Hewlett, of Sullivan Township, Laurens Co. 1809-1887, md. Jane Washington Brooks of Edg. Co. Had 6 chn, viz: (1)Addie md. J. C. Featherstone & had-Judge C. C. Featherstone of Greenwood (2)Mary md. Robt. Goodgion & had-Maida*, Geo., Brooks (3)Jane md. Saml. Todd of Laurens & had-Rev. Charlton (4)Lizzie md. Chas. Garlington. One drt. is Janye Pruitt* (5)Geo, Jr. md. Mary E. Chiles of Abbv. One son, Wash, md. L. Moseley & had among others, Mary Louise* (6)Joseph md. Mary Pelham, Laurens, SC. . . .4- JOSEPH PINCKNEY SULLIVAN, s. of Hewlett, 1796-1820 md. Temperance Hamilton Arnold, Laurens Co. Had 8 chn. viz: (1)Jno. Hewlett md. Mary D. Cureton (2)Milton CA. Bach (3)C. Pleasant, md. Mary E. Gilkerson & had-Be Pure, Linda M. Wood* (4) Keziah J. md. Col. Jas. McCullough (5)Mary Ann md. James M. Eppes. One son, Jas. md. Emma Davenport & had-Jesse Goode*. Others: Temp. md. Capt. James L McCullough; Mary Ann md. Wash Sharp; Lina md. Saml Dent; Lucia md. Saml Eppes (6)Malinda C. md. 1st Dr. Wm. C. Kilgore; 2nd B. D. Kay (7)Temperence md. 1853 Jesse C. Kilgore & had-Mary, Jesse, Josiah, Frances. Fol. descts this branch, charter members Sullivan-Dunklin D. A. R: Mrs. Mary L. Leonard*, Mrs. Frances Wood*, Mrs. Edna Hodges*, Mrs. Mary Hassell*, Mrs. W. M. Melton*, Miss Clara Kilgore*, Mrs. W. C. Smith*, Mrs. W. E. McKamy*. . .(8)William Dunklin 1838-1931 Laurens Co. md. 3 times, 1st Elizbth Humbert & had-Elizbth Johnson, Gainesville, Ga; Zelene Wells* who had-May Smith*. He md. 2nd Harriet G. Humbert & had-(1)Joseph Giroud of Laurens md. Lidie Miller. Had-Bob, Herbert, Cecil, Hattie, Anna, Dunklin (2)Felicia A. md. 1884 Thos.

133

J. Sullivan II & had 6 chn. WDS. md. 3rd Mary E. Quarles & had-Anges West, Margie Culberson, William, Richard, Keziah McKelvy, Thomas, Milton. .5-HEWLETT SULLIVAN Jr-. bach. . . .6-ELIZABETH (drt. of Hewlett Sullivan Sr.) md. Marmaduke PINSON (see Pinson Geneal). . . .7-FRANCES (drt. of Hewlett Sullivan) md. SQUIRE CALHOUN. ISSUE, viz: (1)Dr. John of Summerville, Ga. (2)Thos. of Crackett, Tex. (3)Jane md. Judge Glenn of Laurens (4)Elizbth md. Dr. E..C. Ragsdale of Grv. Co. SC to Tex. (5)Lucinda md. Jos. Beavers, Houston Co., Tex. (6)Hewlett md. Miss Smith, Cook Co., Tex. (7)Fanny unmd. . . .8-JANE (drt. of Hewlett Sullivan) md. SAMUEL L. MOORE; Grv. Co., SC. Had-(1)Hewlett md. Esther Benson & had Saml. Then he md. Temp. Shepherd & had-Hewlett, Maggie, Annie Fanny, Shepherd, Orph (2)Dr. D. D. Moore md. Eliza Barber & had-Mrs. H. H. Blalock, Charlton D., J. H. S., Claud (3)Mary Jane md. Jno. D. GRAY & had-Mrs. Ransom, Oscar, Thomas, Jane (Chapt. D. A. R. members: Mrs. Ann W. Gray*, Mrs. Alice M. Taylor*). . . .9-MARY (drt. of Hewlett Sullivan) 1813-83 md. Jas. M. Latimer of Abbv. ISSUE: (1)Helen md. Wm. Shumate of Grv. Co. & had-Albert, Lillie, Frank, William, Helen. .D.A.R. Helen Fawcette*. (2)Amanda md. Dr. Jno. Groves of Ga. & had-Sallie, James, Bessie (3)Frances md. Jno. Jordan & had-Isabel, Lallah (4)Elizbth md. Thos. Cosby of Atlanta (5)Emma md. Capt. Jno. Austin of Grv. & had-Joseph, William, Hattie, Gertrude (6)Dr. Joseph P. md. Hattie Mooney of Grv. & had-Annie, Lullie, Jos. Jr., Jean (7)Jno. Henry md. Molly Lites, near Troy, had-Jno. H., Mary (8)James H. md. 1884 Mary L. Ramsey, Grv. Co. Had-Mary, Andrew, DeWitt, Charles, James, Frances, David, Jno. Austin. . . .10-THOS. JEFFERSON SULLIVAN (s. of Hewlett) 1807-1866 md. 12 Sept. 1833 Sara Cureton of Grv. Co. 1817-82. Res. Sullivan Township, Laurens Co., SC. ISSUE, 8 viz: (1) Henrietta md. Capt. C. H. Parkins 1866. Res. Grv., SC. Had-Paul C; Elizbth Norris; C. Allen; Mark D; H. Jeff; Cora; John H. (2)Frances A. md. 1880 Capt. J. W. Goodgion (3)Adelaide md . 1865 Pascal D. Huff & had-Dr. Junius of Hodges; Agnes Childers; Swan B. of Grv. Co; Vilonia Garrison; Warren; Corrie Bozeman (4)Sarah md. 1868 L. T. Mahaffey, Laurens Co. Had-Sara md. 1895 R. L. Mears & had-Dr. G. M; Carrie E; Prof. Jeff md. Ruth Harrelton; Walter md. Rosa Wham 1897 & had-Margt, Sara Grace, Bonnie; Claudia was 2nd w. R. L. Mears & had-Robt, Herman, Edw;' Pauline* md. 1897 W. M. Nash & had-Sara, Hortense Ropp had-Helen*; J. W. Walter md. Mary Austin; Lois Parsons, Alfred, Pauline Corden, Annett Hellems, Ellen* md. Robt. C. Wasson. (5)John D. Sullivan md. 1st Ellen Clinkscales & had-Florence md. W. W. Smith & had-Dr. David; Jno. S; Ellen Rippy, William, Thomas. JOHN D. 2nd w. Florence Allen 25 Feb. 1880 & had-(a)Ella md. Izzy Gray (b)Allen J. md. Mary T. Humbert & had-A. Carlisle, Lois W. (c)Jno. D. Jr. md. Sidney Harris & had-Jno. D. Elliott H. (d)Grace md. Rev. J. H. Brown & had-James H; Grace, Ella, Rebecca, Annette, Elizbth. . . .(6)CLAUDIA C. md. 1877 Aug. Huff & had-Ernest A. md. Catherine Blake. . . .(7)Chas. Pascal McLeod md. 1882 Arrah J. Watts. . .(8)THOMAS J. Sullivan II b. 24 Dec. 1853, d. 5 Nov. 1923 md. 11 Nov. 1884 Felicia Arnold Sullivan b. 1 Aug. 1865, d. 26 May 1927, drt. of Wm. D. Sullivan & Harriet Humbert. ISSUE 6 to maturity, viz: (a)Jos. Giroud, bach. (b)Claudius A. Vet. WWI (c)Sara Lucile* md. 6 Mch. 1907 E. P. Ervin & had 2 chn: Houston S. Vet. WWII; Elizbth Felicia* md. 24 May 1935 Albert Stephens, Laurens, SC. Chn: Sara, Albert E., Robt., John (d)Rev. C. H. Sullivan, Meth. Conf. SC & Vet. WWI & Chap. & Cpt. WWII md. Grace Pitts & has-Joan, Jack (e)Dr. Charlton H. Sullivan md. Evelyn Peele* & had-Giroud, Earl (f)M. Catherine' b. 1899 md. A. F. Holley. Has-Linda Frankie* & adopted son Billy. . . .II.--CHARLES P. SULLIVAN, s. of Hewlett, 1811-1876, md. 1st Sara Smith of Newberry d. 1845. He md. 2nd Zelene Boyd of Laurens. His chn. were, viz: Jno. M.; Warren P.; Jarred D.; James; Charles, Hewlett, Arthur, Addiso¬, Alice, Zelene, Susan. The son Jared md. Rosalie Moore & some of chn. were: Blanch Bostic, Sara Milan, James H., Rosalie Burnside. The son Charles to Miss. Arthur md. Cornelia Herndon. Susie md. Hugh E. Gray & had-Zelene md. J. W. Dunklin & others. Hewlett was father of Mrs. Joe Sparks of Grv; Mrs. H. A. Jennings of Grv. & others. Alice md. John Grier. The descendants of CPS not complete. . . .12-Dr. JAMES M. SULLIVAN, s. of Hewlett, 1816-75, Res. Grv. Co., SC. md. 1st Sara Mimms of Abbv. Had-(1)M. Frances md. Peter A. McDavid (2)Sarra md. Mack Harrison (3)Harriet md. Wm. Holland (4)Capt. Mimms md. Mary Stokes (5)Joseph md. Emma Earle (6)Jane md. John W. McCullough. One ch. was Sara md. John J. McSwain, M. C. . .DR; JAMES M. md. 2nd Lizzie Vaughan of Fla. Had-(7)Paul of Honea Path, SC. md. Ena Agnew (8)Marion md. J. Agnew (9)Elma md. 1st

Hankins, 2nd Martin (10)Belton md. Jane Walsh (11)Virginia md. W. M. Waterfield (Some branches of this family more complete because we had the cooperation of members of Sullivan-Dunklin D.A.R.)

Among SIMPSONS who filed Revo. Claims are: John, William, James, Hugh. .Dr. John Wells Simpson of Laurens had two sons: John Wister 1821-1893 md. Ann Patillo Farror; Governor Wm. D. Simpson & Chief Justice Supreme Court. There was also a drt-Cornelia F. md. Henry P. Farrow. John Wister & Ann Simpson md. 1847. Chn: John md. Annie Knox; Wm. Wells md. Francis Jane Kilgore of Laurens; Stobo J. md. Elouise, drt. of Gov. Simpson; Elizbth md. Chas. W. Zimmerman; Paul md.Flora Cates; Richard & Casper unmd; Dr. Frank.

WILLIAM SPEER** 1747-1830. (Mother was drt of Wm. Houston) 1776 moved to Abbeville, md. 1784 wid. Mrs. Eleanor (Little) Norris, had 4 chn: John, Alex, Margt md. Jos. Rucker, Wm. He md. 1811 Mary S. Gill. Had 8 chn. One was Dr. Andrw, surg. C. A. md. Sophia Verdell.

WM. THOMAS SUMTER & w. Patience of Va., had: THOMAS SUMTER 1734-1832, Landowner in SC 1763 md. 1767 the wid. of William Jameson (Polly). ISSUE: Mary. . . . THOMAS b. 1768. Two of Gen. Sumter's gr.sons were: Charles & Etienne de Fontenay. Sumter built his home at Statesburg which he hoped would be the state capital. He owned 150,000 acres land. Sumter District named for him. He was one of South Carolina's famous Partisan Leaders.

THOS. TAYLOR of Culpepper, Va. w. Johanah, will 2 Dec. 1787. Thos. Taylor Jr's will names w. Elizbth; Daus: Mary Ann Burress, Sara Obriant, Johannah S. Campbell, Frances & a son Edw. A Thos. Taylor sold land on Horse ck to Wm. Arnold 1822 & to Jas. Riley 1825. . . .NANCY (sd to be dau. of Thos. Taylor Sr) 1782-1856 md. James Riley, lived near Tumbling Shoals, Laurens County.

JAMES THOMAS** 1757-1803, SC, md. Elizbth Calaham. Had 1-John C. to Miss.-Ala. abt. 1816. . .2-Joyce md. Thos. Williams to Miss. . .3-Silas unmd. . .4-Wm Shepperd, w. Mary. . .5-Elizbth md. 4 times, to Miss. . .6-James, w. Lucy. . .7-Sara md. Wm. Brunson.

BARRETT TRAVIS md. Elizbth Deloach. Res. Edgefield, SC. Two known sons, Mark, Alex. I--Rev. Alex 1790-1852 md. Polly Williams. ISSUE: (1)Jno. D. md. Mary Stallworth (2)Martha md. Nich Stallworth (3)Jas. md. Mary Ann McCreary (4)Philip md. Adriane Calloway, Ala-Tex. . .II. MARK TRAVIS 1783-1836 SC-Ala. md. 1808 Jemima Stallworth. ISSUE: (1)Col. Wm. B. perished at the Alamo 1836, md. Rosanna Cato. Had-Chas E., Susan I. (2)Mark B. md. Louise A. Bradley. Had-Pierce, Butler, Mason (3)James C. md. 1st Saphronia Davis; 2nd Mary E. Green. Had-Louise, Mark (4)Sara A. md. Francis Brantley (5)Emily C. md. Jos. Brantley (6)Nancy md. Rufus Kilpatrick. Others were: Jemima, Calloway, Alex'& a dau.

NATHANIEL VANCE SR.** Laurens Co., SC. md. Mary Dunbar McTier. ISSUE who left descts: 1-Samuel md. 1st Mrs. Elizbth Kincaid Armstrong & had-Mary Simms; Major James. The latter md. twice & had some 15 chn. A drt. Mary A. Dorrah had-Griffith V. who md. Richard Mimms Sullivan Jr. . .2-Frances md. Wm. Greer. . .3-John md. Nancy Wright Watson. . .4-Mary Caroline. . .5-Allen. . .6-William md. Elizbth Edington. Had-Mary, Sara, William, Martha, Eliza, N.W., Susan. . .7-David md. 1st Sara Eddington, 2nd Matilda Tinsley. Had-Mary Rivers, Sara Godbold, Eliza Copeland, Permelia, Martha Ferguson & 3 sons to La., viz: Dr. Roseborough, Dr. Samuel W. and Harrison.

ALEXANDER VERNON to Spartanburg Co. SC 1755, md. Margt Chesnee. ISSUE: James, had-(1) Dr. Jas. J. md. drt. of Judge Jas. Jordon. . .(2)Judge Thos. O. P. Vernon 1818-1877 md. drt of Elisha Bomar, had chn: 7. . .Was holding court when LAURENS RIOT occured, Writ of Habeas Corpus suspended, to give prisoners hearing.

JOHN WATTS** b. Va. d. Laurens, SC md. 1788 Margt (Peggy) Pollard (She drt.)**

ISSUE, viz: Beaufort, Matilda, William, Eliza K., Braxton, Richard, Louisa, Narcissa who md. 1829 John Ball, John, Cornelia, Elvira, Peggy. . .The son JOHN WATTS md. 1841 Elizbth Cannon (Drt.**) & had Chn: 1-William A. of CA. . .2-Arrah md. 1882 Chas. M. P. Sullivan. . .3-Richard, Chief Justice SC md. 1st Alline Cash; 2nd Lottie (drt. of Chief Justice Henry McIver) He was surv. by drts: Mrs. Bessie Royal, Mrs. J. D. Sullivan, Mrs. Frank Stokes. .ˑ. WILLIAM DENDY WATTS md. 1828 Miss Young; md. 1837 Sara Speake Cannon. ISSUE: Nancy, Phoebe, William, John W., Laurens, Susan Young, Lucy Nance, Eliza who md. B. W. Ball, Lucy Boyd, William Mills, Arrah N., James Dunklin, Rhoda B., W. D. . .The son James D. Watts md. Harriet Frierson. The unmarried drt. Betty made her home with niece Mrs. M. L. Copeland.

COL. JAMES WILLIAMS** 1740-1780, settled Laurens Co., 1773. Hero of Up-country, fell at Kings Mt. md. Mary Wallace 1762. Had among others-Washington Williams 1777-1829 md. 1797 Sara Griffin (drt.**).

WILLIAM WYATT JR.** md. twice, 1st Frances Newton. Had 6 chn. viz: Frances Mattison, SC; Macajah, Va; Lettice Smith, SC; William, Elizabeth English, Elijah. . . Wm. Wyatt Jr. md. 2nd Elizbth Snoe. Had-Talitha Payne, Malinda Dumington, Frances Wyatt, Mahala Rosser to Mo., Malissa Rosser. . . .The son ELIJAH WYATT md. 1793 Mary Grigsby Foster, to SC 1800. ISSUE 9 chn. viz: Eliza Mattison, Esther Mitchell, Jas. F., William N., Redmond G., Mildred Cox Susan C. Kay, Harriet Mauldin, Malinda Alexander. . . .MILDRED LUANI WYATT became 2nd w. of Abner Cox. They had, among others, Mary Cox md. Joseph D. Pinson. From this line 4 D. A. R. members, Sullivan-Dunklin chapter.

In these brief genealogies,** signifies Revolutionary service, and *, D. A. R. member. There are no doubt some errors, but in every case, the data was obtained or checked by a member of that family or a family connection. No attempt has been made to give all the descendants of any family, but only the ones that were available through the cooperation of members of the Sullivan-Dunklin D. A. R. chapter. These data should furnish enough "clues" so that further research can develop many new D.A.R. and S.A.R. lines.

GRAVE OF GENERAL THOMAS SUMTER, WITH SMALL CATHOLIC
CHAPEL BUILT FOR HIS WIFE, IN THE BACKGROUND

ABSTRACTS OF WILLS----1775-1855
LAURENS COUNTY, SOUTH CAROLINA,
PART OF OLD NINETY-SIX DISTRICT

In the early days, all courts were held at Charleston, so the oldest records were filed there. However in 1768 by Act of the South Carolina Assembly, seven Judicial Districts were created for the province, one of these being Ninety-Six. The old log Court-house was located at the town of Old Ninety-Six (about 2 1/4 miles south of the present town) and here in the summer of 1783, from the steps of this building was read "the Treaty of Peace between his Brittanic Majesty and the United States of America." At the Court of General Sessions held there on Nov. 20, 1784, the Treaty was duly recorded. It appears that no courts were held at Ninety-Six during the Revolutionary Period of July 1776 to the Spring of 1783. The Court of General Sessions convened there 1783-1799 and Courts of Equity, continued for some years. In 1785 the twenty-six counties were formed from the Judicial Districts. County courts of limited jurisdiction, were now held and continued for fourteen years. Members of the Court were drawn from among the leading citizens. In 1799 the counties were called Districts and were not again called counties until "Reconstruction." About 1800 the General Assembly abolished Old Ninety-Six Court and formed Equity Districts. Division two of the Western District included Laurens and Newberry with Court being held at Laurens. At the Court House, rooms of Clerk of Court, is found the first written record of a court for Laurens in Book I, page 1, dated 12 Sept. 1785. The gentlemen Justices were: Jonathan Downs, James Montgomery, Silvanus Walker, William Mitchelson, Charles Saxon. On 15 May 1792 Samuel Saxon sold four acres to "the Judges of the County Court of Laurens, to wit: Jonathan Downs, John Hunter, Thomas Wadsworth Esquires, for the use of the County Court of said county," also the right to use a certain spring. The price paid was two guineas.

ABBETT, Abbott-Daniel--"I have soldier claims for lands in the western state of Pa., & 850 A. in Laurens Co., S.C.--all to wife during widowhood or until oldest ch. Betsy be lawful age or marry.." Chn: Lewis M., Wm. McClanahan, Danl. Marshall, James Smith youngest, Betsy Pagett...EXR: Wife Ailsey, Danl. Wright, Reuben Kelly...30 Oct. 1800--16 Mch. 1801...Bk. A, p. 285...WIT: Austin Moore, Nelson Kelly, M. E. Stallard.

ABERCROMIE Alexander--Chn: Martha Jane, Susannah S., Lucretia, Elizabeth, Richard A., Hugh, Robert, Wingfield B...EXR: John Woods, R. Alex. Abercromie son...28 Apr. 1852--25 Mch. 1853...Bk. A...WIT: M. P. Evins, Arthur Roger, Thos. A. Saden.

ABERCROMIE Alexander Sr.--Wife Susannah...Sons: Lewis, John, Alex, Henry, Hugh, "Unfortunate son Jonathan".."other sons already recv'd share"..Daus: Hannah, Susannah, Polly...EXR: Sons John, Alex...28 Dec. 1830--16 Apr. 1831...Bk. F, p. 344...Wit: John Harris, Jno. Woods, Matthew P. Evins.

ABERCROMIE Calvin, Colvin--Wife Mary & at her death prop. div. bwt. fol. chn: Harriet w. of Jno. W. Nash; Mary w. of Hiram Sims; Rebecca w. of Kellet Babb; Calvin Jr; Elizabeth w. of Halway Campbell; Christy w. of Wm. Ridgeway; Ruth w. of Alfred Sims. John dec'd & wid. Elizabeth & heirs; Johathan; James; Lindley to take care of mother...EXR: Sons Johathan, Lindley...21 Sept. 1837--Bk. A, p. 96...Wit: Asa Garret, Isham Bolt, William F. Davis.

ABERCROMIE James-Son James..Step-son Archibald McDaniel..gr. son Jas. Abercromie... Daus: Mary wife of Wm. Odaniel (?McDanl); Isabella Blackwell; Rebecca wife of Gabriel Jewell; Susannah Mathews; Hannah Brock; Margaret Blackwell; Elizabeth Andrews...

137

EXR: Son James, Elias Brock Jr...29 Nov. 1819--8 Feb. 1820Bk. E, p. 56...WIT: E.L. Rowling, David Bell, John Neel.

ABRUMS Abrams, Martha--Chn: Thomas, Joseph, James, George, William, John, Mary Montgomery, Elizabeth Jones, Margaret?Siddar, Anna, Lucky or Leah...EXR: Friend John Whitmire, Whitmore..4 Apr. 1840--8 Nov. 1842..Bk. A, p. 24..WIT: Thos. Whitmore, Geo. Young Jr; Byrd B. Allen.

ADAIR Hannah---Living Chn: Eleanor Ramage, Hannah Meadows, Nancy Langston, Susannah wife of Wm. Castle, James Adair...Gr. ch: Patsy Gamble, Jinny Beavors... EXR: James Adair...25 Oct. 1826--4 Dec. 1826...Bk. F, p. 65...WIT: Thos. Leek, Isham Milan, Susannah Prater.

ADAIR Joseph--Wife Susannah...Sons: Joseph, Benjamin, James "my cooper's tools belonging to my trade"...Daus: Sarah, Jean Ramage, Mary & hus. John Owins...S.L. Robt. Long...EXR: Sons Joseph & James...9 Jan. 1788...Bk. A, p. 19...WIT: Jas. Montgomery, Wm Bourland, Jas. Greek.

ADAIR Joseph--Sons: John, James, Robert, Elisha & Gr. son Joseph Adair...Daus: Jane & hus. Thomas Holland; Elizabeth & hus. John Hutson; Casey & hus. ThomasMcCrary; Charity & hus. David Little...EXR: Elisha & John Adair...20 Jan. 1812--15 Jan. 1813... Bk. D-1, p. 105...WIT: Richard Holland, Wm. Adair, George McCrary.

AKINS Lewis--Sons: John, Ezekiel, Archer, Frank...Daus: Sally, Patty Petty...Two Gr. sons; Wm. & Thos. Petty...16 July 1791...Bk. A, p. 40...WIT: Joel? Leagill, Thomas Feevil, John Meadon...EXR: Son Ezekiel & S.L. Benj. Feevil.

ALLISON James--Wife Nancy, home place dur. widowhood...Son James, land with grist & saw-mills...Daus: Polly, Elizabeth...EXR: Son James...10 Nov. 1788--9 Mch. 1789... Bk. A, p. 9...WIT: R. R. Bowen, Saml. S. C. Campbell, Joseph Lyon.

ALLISON Robert--Sons: James, Robert, William, Joseph, Samuel, Francis, Watson, Moses Lewis "land on n. side Beaverdam," Joseph...Daus: Margaret, Mary, Ann & her son William Hellans...Gr. S. James Allison...EXR: Wife Frances, son Joseph.... 5 Jan. 1791...Bk. A, p. 53...WIT: Wm. Turner, Emanuel York, Wm. Higges.

ANDERSON Philip--Wife Elizabeth...Sons: Allen, Reuben, Lewis...Daus: Elizabeth, Ann Davis, Lucy Davis..."Three youngest chn"...EXR: Son Allen & friends Joseph Jones, Moses Whitten...27 Mch. 1814--19 Apr. 1814...Bk. D-1, p. 152...WIT: John B. Bennett, Moses Whitten, Joseph Dunkin (Dunklin?).

ARMSTRONG John--Wife Elizabeth...Daus: Artemesus wife of Saml. Austin; Cresy Ann wife of Wm. Owens. Syntha wid. of Isaac Hollingsworth; Mary w. of Edward Martin; Haney or Hannah "place where I live provided she does not marry John R. Fuller son of Solomon & Phoebe Fuller," Elizabeth, wid. of John Fuller & apparently wife of Dr. Robert Austin...TRUSTEES for dau. Artemesus, Edmond Martin & Wm. Owens...EXR: Wife Elizabeth but in case of her death or marriage, friends: John & Henry Burton, Travis Hill...Prv. 26 Apr. 1845...Bk. A, p. 39...WIT: John & A. C. Garlington, W. D. Watts, R. Campbell.

ARMSTRONG Joseph--Wife, land on Mudlick ck...Two sons minors...Dau. Mary Ann... Also named, John Williams & James Burnside...EXR: Wife Rebecca & friend Robt. Gilliam Sr...30 Jan. 1790...Bk. A, p. 37...WIT: James & Andrew Burnside, Jno. Butler.
ARNOLD Hendrick--Wife Ruth (Cash)...Sons: William, Ira...Daus: Mary, Nancy.."my living chn. & their heirs"...15 July 1795...Bk. A, p. 142...(Note: Ira md. a Saxon; William was father of Jeff, Hendrick & Billy).

ARNALL (Arnold) Joshua--Wife Leanna...Only dau. Martha...200 A. div. bwt. Joshua Arnall & Joshua Franks...Gift to Joshua Millenor...EXR: Joshua Franks, Charles Smith.. 5 Mch. 1792...Bk. A, p. 34...WIT: Robert, Poley & N. Franks.

ARNOLD Zachariah--Sons: Lewis, William minors...Daus: Rebecca Flynn, Sara Arnold, Nancy Arnold, Juda West & chn: Georgeberry West & Mary West...Bequest to Jim B. Moseley...EXR: Wife Mary, John West...15 Nov. 1826--11 Mch. 1829...Bk. F, p. 210...

WIT: Reubin Powell, Reubin Arnold, Mark Moseley.

ATKINSON Henry--Wife Mary "all until oldest son John is 21"...Youngest chn: William, Alexander...EXR: Wife Mary & John Dacus...22 Apr. 1799...Bk. A, p. 199...WIT: John Davis, Mansfield Walker, Barthlomew Craddock.

ATWOOD James--Son William..Son-in-law Wm. Ball..EXR: Wife Polly, William Atwood, Wm. Ball...17 Jan. 1816 --Bk. D-1, p. 257...WIT: John Clemons, William Pollard, Tobias Cook.

AUSTIN Alexander Sr--Wife Agnes...Chn: Alexander, Samuel, Robert, John, James, William, Jennet, Henrietta, Sarah...Gr. Chn; David & Agnes Whiteford...EXR:Sons James, ?Alexander, Samuel...18 Sept. 1826--28 Nov. 1826...Bk. F, p. 59...WIT: Alsey Fuller, John Cook, F. D. Cook.

AUSTIN James--Wife Henrietta...Son James..."my children"...EXR: Alex Austin....30 Mch. 1832--14 Apr. 1832...Bk. F, p. 416...WIT: R. C. Austin, John Moore, Thos. Austin.

AUSTIN Samuel--Sons: James, Thomas, Alexander, William...Daus: Elizabeth Munro, Mary Caldwell, Nancy Carter, Nelly Streight...EXR: Major James Austin, John Moore Sr., Son Thomas Austin...10 Nov. 1826--21 Apr. 1827...Bk. F, p. 106...WIT: John Moore, James Carter, Daniel Downmond.

AVARY Joseph--"Joseph & Cynthia as much as others had when they left me"...balance "bwt. all my chn. except Joel who has his"...EXR: Wife Rhoda, son Joseph,..27 Sept. 1848...Bk. A, p. 108...WIT: E. B. Gambrell, A. McKnight, Joseph Sullivan.

BABB Sampson (Simpson?)--Chn. of dau. Polly who md. Wm. Boyce...Balance "bwt. all chn"...EXR: Sons Alston, Martin & Simpson Babb...30 Oct. 1847--Bk. A, p. 145... WIT: Hosea Mahaffey, Thomas A. Peden, John Woods.

BAILEY James--Sons: William, Zachariah, James, Silas...Daus: Polly Brown, Sally Ducker, Winifred, Betsy, Levicy or Givety...William's part div. bwt. his chn: Madison, Susanna, James,Broth...EXR: Benj. Brown, James & Silas Bailey...19 Jan. 1826-- 14 Nov. 1826--Bk. F, p. 51...WIT: John Snead, James Nickles Jr., Wm. Bailey.

BAILEY William (Revo. S.)--Wife Ann...Chn: John, Zachariah, Margery, Mary, William, James, Lucy..Gr. chn: Wm. son of David Bailey..EXR: Sons Zachariah, William, James... 27 Jan. 1787...Bk. A, p. 48...WIT: A. Rodgers Jr., Thomas & John Rodgers.

BALL George--"Children"...EXR: Wife Memima, John Ball, Lewis Ball Sr...28 Dec. 1807--10 Mch. 1817...Bk. D-1, p. 359...WIT: James Ball, Jas. Neely, Henry Hitt.

BALL Jeremiah--Sons: Stephen, Harris, John, ?Minyard, Young..Daus: Elizabeth Garrett, Nancy Abercromie, Frances Owen's chn...EXR: Son John...18 Nov. 1850--8 Mch. 1856... Bk. A, p. 180...WIT: S. Knight, Z. C. Garrett, James A. McDowell.

BALL John--Father...Bros. & Sisters: Martin, Reubin, James, Katherine, Peter...20 Dec. 1824--7 Mch. 1825...Bk. E, p. 480...WIT: Ben & Reubin Martin, Thos. Garrett.

BALL Martin--Wife Hannah...EXR: Thos. Garrett...4 Sept. 1827--4 Mch. 1828...Bk. F, p 172...WIT: Jeremiah Ball, Benj. Martin, Reubin Ball.

BALL William--Wife "estate that came with her"..Chn: John, George, William, Jeremiah, Elizabeth Stephens, Frances Hitt, Martin Peter, James Lewis, Mary Sadler, Pamelia & heirs (names not separated)...EXR: Wife Lillian, Reubin Martin...23 July 1805--5 Apr. 1806...Bk. C-1, p. 169...WIT: Reubin Martin, Stephen Garrett.

BARKSDALE Nathan--Sons: Allen, John, Nathaniel, Colyar (Collier)....Daus: Nancy, Leannah...EXR: Wife Mary, sons Colyar & Allen...8 Sept. 1812--17 Nov. 1812...Bk. D-1, p 92...WIT: L. Saxon, Charles Allen, Sam Dason.

BARKSDALE Jol ̄--Bros. & sisters: Nancy, Martha, Polly, Lennah, Nathaniel, Collyar... EXR: Allen Barksdale, Thos. F. Jones...14 Apr. 1830--4 Oct. 1830...Bk. F, p 283... WIT: Andrew Kennedy, Francis Ross, John Garrett.

BAUGH William--Sons: John, William, David, Jonathan...Daus: Elizabeth, Margaret, Mary, Agnes & "rest of chn"...Wife Agnes & son John EXR...4 May 1787-Rec. Bk. A, p. 21...WIT: James Abercromie, Wm. Obannon, John Pinson.

BEASLEY Thomas--Wife Patsy - At death wife, est. div. bwt. 5 daus, eldest Polly Ferguson; Nancy w. of Abram Holland & son Edmund; Elizabeth Ferguson; Jinsey Williams; Dolly Chambers & Dr. Alex. Chambers...EXR: S.L. Dr. Alex. Chambers, Maners Williams...23 Feb. 1831--27 Mch. 1832...Bk. F, p. 407...WIT: Perry Jeans, Elizabeth W. Ferguson, Cary Bell.

BELL Adam--Sons: David, John, Adam land purchased of Saml Erving..."if my son Robert ever returns..." Daus: Isabel, Mary, Esther, Elizabeth...EXR: Wife Mary... 16 Dec. 1801--18 Nov. 1805...Bk. C-1, p. 180...WIT: Robt. Long, Jas. Bell, Thos. East.

BELL James--Sons: John, Robert, Adam, James...Daus: Elizabeth Milan, Susanna: EXR: Wife Sarah...27 Mch. 1824--5 Sept. 1824...Bk. E, p. 413. (Note-These Bells evidently descendants of Thos. B. Ire abt. 1726 to S.C. 1762. Descendants in Laurens, Abbeville, Greenville cos.)

BENNETT Richard--Wife Sarah...Chn: Anna, Miles, Jennette...EXR: Thos. Hendrick, Lewis Jones...3 Dec. 1820--4 June 1821...Bk. E, p. 165...WIT: Jesse Prater, Jenes Jones, John B. Bennett.

BLACKWELL Richard--Wife Margaret....Sons: James, David, Joel, Richard...Daus: Nancy, Elizabeth, Rebecca, Hannah, Margaret, Caroline, Susan Frances...EXR: Charles Brook Jr...25 July 1832...Bk. F, p. 427...WIT: J. Abercromie Sr., John Coats, John Morgan.

BLAKELY William Sr---Chn: Jonathan, John, William, James, David, Thomas, Samuel, Catherine, Isabel...EXR: Wm. Blakely...13 Dec. 1845...Bk. A, p. 82...WIT: James L. Young, F. N. Folker, Henry M. Bryon.

BOBO Absolum--(Revo. S.) Wife Amey...Dau. Betsy Gaines...S.L. Wm. Powell & fol. Powells: Fanny, Sarah, Ann, Belinda, Milly, Virginia...Roddy Waits...? Perady Posey... Polly Delph...EXR: Friends David Anderson, Lewis Graves...8 July 1808...Bk. D-1, p. 159...WIT: John Golding Sr., Andrew & James Anderson, Wm. Anderson.

BOBO Dr. E. M.--Chn: C. D., Mary Ann, Susan Jane Springs...EXR: C. D. Bobo & S.L. .R. A. Springs...3 May 1853...Bk. A, p. 313...WIT: Thomas W. Holloway, Drayton Nance, James A. Graham.

BOLLING Samuel (Revo. S.)--Sons: Robert, John, Tully, Samuel, Thornberry...Daus: Elizabeth Dunklin, Lucinda (Johnston), Polly (Perritt) youngest, Nancy Sullivan, Mehitabel (Tarrant)...EXR: Wife Abigail, sons Robert, Tully, John, Saml...9 May 1808--5 Sept. 1808...Bk. C-1, p. 318...WIT: William, Mary, Tully Choice.

BOLLING Thornberry--Mother Abigail..."to Thornberry (s. of Saml. Jr) my share & interest in the Fork Shoals Library Society...to Samuel Perrit (son of Alfred & Polly)... to Saml. Bolling (son of John) land in Ala."...4 bros: Robert, Tully, John, Samuel... 4 sisters: Nancy (Sullivan) Strange, Lucinda Johnson, Polly Perritt, Elizabeth Dunklin... balance to Henderson Sullivan & Joseph N. Johnson...EXR: Tully Bolling, Henderson Sullivan, Jos. N. Johnson...13 June 1822--3 Sept. 1827...Bk. F, p. 125...WIT: Micajah Berry, Tully Bolling, Sophia Choice.

BOLT Robert Jr--Sons: John, Lewis...Daus: Peggy, Sally, Polly & "if wife be with child"...EXR: Neighbor Joseph Downs...20 Oct. 1795...Bk. A, p. 143...WIT: James & Thomas Parker, Susanna McHarg.

BONDS James--Daus: Jinny Welsh & son James; Mary Welsh; Nancy Murphy & dau. Mary...Sons: James, son Colvin's chn...EXR: Sons John & Richard...22 June 1820--3 Sept. 1820...Bk. E, p. 87...WIT: Robert Long, James Bell, Sarah Bell.

BROCKMAN, Borockman, Backman John--Chn: Anny Parks, Mary Deen, Franky Mullens, Henry "lands on Enoree riv"...Dau. Lucy Dec'd w. of John Owens Sr. left chn: Betty,

Amely, John H; Dau. Frankey w. of Thomas Mullins, no issue as yet...Son Henry & his son John Brockman...EXR: Wife Ameley, Son Henry...27 Nov. 1800--13 Feb. 1801... Bk. A, p. 274...WIT: Daniel Wright, Robt. Burton, Asa Wright.

BOULAND, Bourland, Bowland John--Wife Mary...Sons: John, Thomas James...Daus: Mary Scott, Martha Ramage, Sarah, Jane, Charlotte..EXR: John Ramage, Robert Bouland.. 10 Jan. 1820--17 Apr. 1820...Bk. E, p, 70-72...WIT: Robt. Ramage, Samuel Young, Edward Wasson.

BOURLAND William Sr--Chn: John, William, James, Andrew, Ruby ?Welburn dec'd; Elizabeth Ramage & dau. Jennet; Rebecca Fowler; Peggy Harper; Sara Grace; Jennet Dooland; Mary Odle; Nancy Whetford...EXR: Son John...6 Jan. 1804--6 Feb. 1804...Bk. C-1, p. 95...WIT: Robert Long, John Wilson, Elizabeth Langston.

BOWLEN, Bolen Martha--Sons: William H. & Albert D..Daus: Elizabeth, Patsa, Matilda, Nancy, Polly...EXR: Son William, Bro. Wm. Green...25 Aug. 1834...Bk. A, p. 4...WIT: Elisha Watkins, Franklin Glen, John C. Watkins.

BOX John--Wife Rachel...Sons: Shadrack, Robert, Abraham, Benjamin...Daus: Nelly South, Rachel Banks, Jemima Sneid..Gr. chn; Rachel & Louisa Box, Elisha Williamson... EXR: Elisha Williamson...22 Nov. 1815--5 Feb. 1821...Bk. E, p. 137...WIT: William Arnold, Robert Nabors, Joseph M. Ewen.

BOYCE Drury--"all my chn"...Sons: Drury, James...Daus: Nancy, Polly..."to Anderson Arnold as his share of his father's est., which came to me in consequence of my marriage with Adminstrx. of said est.",..EXR: Wife, or at her death, Dempsey Nesbitt... 1 July 1830--20 Dec. 1830..Bk. F, p. 311..WIT: John Anthony, Nathan & Thomas Nesbitt.

BOYCE John--"Present wife, Nancy E. Boyce"...Chn. by present wife equal share... other chn. recv'd from est. of their dec'd Gr. father John Robertson...Gr. chn: Sarah I. & John B., chn. of Elizabeth Craig dec'd...8 Sept. 1841--7 Aug. 1843...Bk. A, p. 36...WIT: Rowland Jennings, John F. Kern, A. R. Boyce.

BOYD Isabella--Sons: William H., Samuel A...EXR: Gr. son Abram Miller Johnson... 25 July 1842--16 Dec. 1850...Bk. A, p. 135...WIT: William W. Floran, Archilles Dendy, Elihu Watson.

BOYD Margaret--Dau. Jane w. of Samuel R. Todd...EXR: Saml R. Todd...4 Nov. 1843-- 3 Apr. 1860...Bk. A, p. 329...WIT: John W. & S. D. Simpson, W. E. Templeton.

BRADEN David--Wife Peggy...Sons: William, Isaac, Reubin...Daus; Betsy, Margaret, Peggy, Susan, Polly Ann, Sary...EXR: Sons William, Isaac...11 Aug. 1822--10 Sept. 1822...Bk. E, p. 234...WIT Benjamin F. Tearce, James Wardlaw, Jesse E. Clardy.

BRADY Charles--Wife Eleanor...Sons: William, John, Alexander "land on Reedy riv," Charles & George youngest sons...EXR: Wife Eleanor, friend John Cochran...3 Oct. 1793...Bk. C-1, p. 167...WIT: Anna Wadkins, Deborah Barns, John Cochran.

BRAMLETT Nathan--Wife Elizabeth....Sons: James, Billy...TRUSTEES, William H. Kennedy, Henry Bass, David Derrick...EXR: Thomas Brownlee, William Henderson... 11 Mch. 1839...Bk. A, p. 12...WIT. James B. & D. Higgins, Washington French.

BREAZEALE Enoch--Wife Ruth..Daus: Hulda Johnson, ?Hamutal Hall or Hill, Caroline.. EXR: S.L. Wiley Hill, George W. Johnson...10 Apr. 1826--2 Oct. 1826...Bk. F, p. 45... WIT: Zachariah Bailey Jr., Tobias Cook, Robt. Campbell.

BREAZEALE Ruth---Dau. Hulda w. of George W. Johnson...Gr. daus: Frances & Hemital Johnson, Frances & Caroline Hill...EXR: James Davis...30 Aug. 1831--17 Nov. 1831...Bk. F, p. 420...WIT: Matthew Gamble, James Davis, Barbara Casey.

BROWN Benjamin--Wife Polly...Dau. Ann...Gr. son Thomas Jeff Tygart...EXR: Wife & in case of death, friend J. M. Young...19 Feb. 1847...Bk. A, p. 84...WIT: J. M. Young, Ross Benham, A. C. Young.

BROWN James (Revo. S.)--Wife:..Daus: Rachel, Elizabeth, Jane, Peggy, Mary...Son

141

William & friend Robert Creswell EXR...17 Feb. 1822--15 Apr. 1823...Bk. E, p. 280...
WIT: William & James F. Wright, R. Creswell.

BROWN Roger--"gave all my chn. that's married..." Daus: Lydia, Annie, Judy, Rebecca,
Mary, Ferebe, Matty, Bexee, Cennee, Fanny, Genney youngest & Rachel a min., Elizabeth
Gill...Sons: William & Roger minors, "in case son James never settles here"...EXR:
Wife Bexey...Dec. 1818--20 Mch. 1826...Bk. F, p. 11...WIT: William Adair, Joseph
Hitch, L. Hitch Sr.

BROWN William (Revo. S.)--Wife Frances..Chn: John, William, Joseph, Ursley Thompson,
Mary Wood, Frances Brook, Susannah Nix, Sara Gilbert...EXR: Son Joseph...16 July
1811--5 Jan. 1818...Bk. D-1, p. 426...WIT: Wm. Gilbert, John Meadows, Thos. Jones.

BROWNLEE Esther, Easter--Dau. Alsey Babb..TRUSTEE & EXR: James B. Brownlee...
19 Nov. 1828--6 Apr. 1829...Bk. F, p. 212...WIT: John Martin, Mary & F. Richardson.

BRISON William--(also Bryson)--Sons: John, James, Robert...Daus: Jean, Sarah "the
watch I fetched from Ireland"...EXR: William Blakeley, Charles Little...7 Dec. 1807...
Bk. C-1, p. 285...also Bk. D-1, p. 411.

BRYSON John--Wife Martha...Dau. Margaret & hus. Wm. Fleming...Bro. Wm. Bryson
& chn...EXR: Col. John Simpson, William Fulton...27 Mch. 1804--Apr. 1804...Bk. C-1,
p. 110...WIT: Archibald Lewis, John Fakes, Agnes Boyd.

BURGESS Joel--Wife Ellen...Sons: Elijah, Walter, Thomas, William, Roland, Joel, John
"to be schooled"...S.L. Wm. Hendrick & dau. Tabitha min...Daus: Jenny, Sally, Nelly,
Tatty (Tabitha?) ...EXR: Wife, sons Roland, Joel...11 Feb. 1803--2 Mch. 1803...Bk.
C-1, p. 32...WIT: E. S. Roland, Thomas Babb, William Nelson.

BURNSIDE Ann Jane--Bros: William, Thomas...Sisters: Elizabeth, Martha, Hannah...
EXR: William & George Burnside (sons of Andrw)...29 Jan. 1827--18 Nov. 1828...Bk.
F, p. 185...WIT: James Hollingsworth, Daniel & Nancy Jones.

BURNSIDE Elizabeth--Sisters Esther, Martha, Ann Jeane, Hannah...EXR: William &
George, sons of Andrw. Burnside...7 Nov. 1828--4 Feb. 1829...Bk. F, p. 203...WIT:
James & Anna Young, Mary Burnside.

BURNSIDE James--Sons: John, William T., James "lands in Laurens Dist"...Wife Anna
to "school & settle younger chn."...EXR: Wife & son James...10 Dec. 1801--Mch. 1803...
Bk. C-1, p. 34...WIT: Joseph & Goerge Hollingsworth.

BURNSIDE James Sr--Sons: James, William, Thomas, Andrew (Revo. S)..Daus: Jennet
Anderson, Margaret, Elizabeth, Martha, Ann Jane, Hannah...EXR: William & Thomas
Burnside, Margaret Burnside...17 Aug. 1797...Bk. A, p. 179...WIT: Wm. & A. Rodgers,
James Cook.

BURNSIDE Martha--All est. to 3 sisters: Elizabeth, Ann Jean, Hannah...EXR: William
son of Andrew Burnside, Geo. A. Burnside...29 Jan. 1827--18 Nov. 1828...Bk. F, p.
186...WIT: Daniel & Nancy Jones, James Hollingsworth.

BURNSIDE Thomas--4 youngest sisters: Elizabeth, Martha, Ann Jeane, Hannah...neph.
Thomas son of Andrew Burnside...EXR: James Hollingsworth, Thos. Burnside...7 May
1826--16 Oct. 1826..Bk. F, p. 47..WIT: James Young, Mary Burnside, Andrw. Rodgers.

BURNSIDE William--4 youngest sisters: Elizabeth, Martha, Ann Jeane, Hannah...EXR:
Bro. Thomas & friend John Kennedy...14 Nov. 1808--23 Mch. 1826...WIT: Wm. Black,
Enos Cook, James Moore...Bk. F, p. 12.

BURTON John--Chn. of dau. Edny Wells dec'd; dau. Susannah w. of Wiley Hardy; S.L.
James Henderson...19 Dec. 1853...Bk. A, p. 344...WIT: W. D. Watts, H. R. Shell,
J. H. Rose.

BURTON Thomas--Wife Rachel...Sons: William, Charles..."all my chn"...EXR: Sons
William & Charles...12 Feb. 1827--13 Feb. 1630...Bk. F, p. 257...WIT: Isaac Pinson,

James Lowery, Augustin Marshall...the two sons named "had by me in the evening of my life."

BURTON Thomas--Chn: Samuel, Robert, Benjamin, Ann, Rebecca Ford, Judah youngest. Last two "until of age or marry"...EXR: Wife Lillian, Sons Benj. & Henry Box...4 May 1802--28 June 1802...Bk. C-1, p. 2...WIT: Jno. Puckett, Jno. Garlington, Thomas Grace.

BYRD Benjamin--Wife Jane Downs....Sons: William, (md. a Barksdale), George (md. a Kern), Purnelly...Daus: Leah (md. Benj. H. Allen & had Benj); Sarah, w. of Wm. Hill; Mary Jane..Wm. Hill & son Purnelly or Purnall, trustees for Sarah & also EXR... 14 Nov. 1828--21 Mch. 1831...Bk. F, p. 338...WIT: John Cargill, R. Freswell, Robt. Anderson.

BYRD Elizabeth--Dau. Hannah w. of Danl. Cook (&David Cook named); Martha Mitchell; Eliza Coleman; Dorothy Blum (all apparently daus); part to James C. Lasley or Lesley for his family & heirs, one being the dau. Elizabeth...EXR: Henry, Austin & Edmond Lesly (?sons-in-law)...9 Dec. 1844--9 Jan. 1845...Bk. A, p. 42...WIT: Wm. & Jemima Cook, Daniel Carter.

CABANESS, Cabiness Amey--Neph. Elijah Cabiness & he EXR...4 Oct. 1823--18 Nov. 1823...Bk. E, p. 331... WIT: John G. Viern Jr; P. D. Dern or Dorn; John Davis.

CABANESS Elizabeth--Son Elijah EXR...4 Oct. 1823--18 Nov. 1823...Bk. E, p. 332... WIT: John B. Kennedy, John Henderson, John David.

CALDWELL James (Revo. S.)--Bro. David Robert Caldwell, min...EXR. Bro. George Forrest Caldwell, friend Dr. John Simpson...24 Apr. 1827--3 Sept. 1827...Bk. F, p. 126...WIT: Drayton Nance, R. C. Caldwell, C. D. B. Higgins.

CAMPBELL Angus--Son & dau-in-law Angus & Milly Campbell & their chn., the Jones Plantation; son Robert, place where I live & books; dau & S.L. Sarah & Robert Cunningham; S.L. & dau. Jonathan & Jane Johnston; dau. & S.L. Polly & Jesse Paine; son Sullivan Campbell....1 Aug. 1809--17 Aug. 1809....Bk. C-1, p. 358...WIT: John Nickles, Wm. F. Burnside, James Ward.

CAMPBELL John M.--Sister Mary Aikin two chn. viz: John & Elizabeth...EXR: James Aiken...26 Apr. 1846...Bk. A, p. 85...WIT: John R. Spearmand, Wm. Hitt. H. Carter.

CARGILE, Cargill William--Mother Sally...Sisters: Elvira, Rebecca, Rachel, Nancy... EXR: M. T. Evins Esq....20 Jan. 1844-27 June 1844...Bk. A, p. 26...WIT: Arch I. Owings, Amelia Owings, M. P. Evins.

CARLISLE Coleman--Chn: James J., Thomas A., Gideon N., Sarah H., Elizabeth L., William H., Jonna...EXR: Wife Sarah, John Abel, Thos. A. Carlisle...11 Jan. 1824-- 6 Dec. 1824...Bk. E, p. 440...WIT: William Wright, James Leake Sr, John Able.

CARTER John--Wife Rachel...Son William...S.L. Wm. McCrary & his sons John & James...EXR: Wife, sons Wm. Carter & Wm. McCrary...14 Apr. 1798...Bk. A, p. 180... WIT: John Rowland, J. Johnson, Robert Carter.

CARTER John--Sons: Joel, Benjamin...Daus: Elizabeth Garner, Mary Nelson, Ruth Brown, Margaret Bailey...EXR: Son-in-laws Benj. Garner, Andrw. Nelson...3 Apr. 1818...Bk. D-1, p. 120...WIT: John Johnston, Howard Pinson, Elizabeth Brown.

CARTER Robert--Wife Betsy...Sons: Robert, Richard, Zimry, James...Daus: Patsy Osborn, Polly Perkins, Sarah Riley, Elizabeth ?Bagley...EXR: Sons Zimry & Robert... 6 Dec. 1825--4 Feb. 1826..Bk. F, p. 3..WIT: Nancy Carter, Mary Pinson, Jonah Johnson.

CARTER William--Wife Martha, "the Cross Hill tract"..."all my surv. chn. as they come of age or marry"...EXR: B.L. Daniel Ligon & bro. Henry N. Carter...20 Nov. 1845--27 Nov. 1845...Bk. A, p. 65...WIT: J. H. Coleman, Wm. Lindsay, Jno. Watts.

CASON (?Carson) Mary--Bros: William, Thomas...Latter's chn: William, John, James,

Samuel...EXR: Sister Sarah Miller, friend David Green...15 Jan. 1812--5 Feb. 1821. Bk. E, p. 136...WIT: John & Wm. Miller, Anderson Hill.

CHANDLER John--Wife Mary & son Asey EXR: Son ?Wiltt...Daus: Elizabeth Leek, Patsy Griffin, Polly Clardy, Nancy Martin...8 Sept. 1820--2 Sept. 1822...Bk. E, p. 229...WIT: William & John Dunlap, Thomas Stone.

CHARLES John--Prop. div. bwt. wife & chn...EXR: Wife Margaret, William Fulton... 14 Mch. 1808--10 Aug. 1808...Bk. C-1, p. 316...WIT: Wm. & Andrew Burnside, Jas. Donald.

CHEEK Ellis--Chn: William, Richard, Sally Sentall, Mary Rhodes, Jane Rhodes, Casey ?Farrow, Willis D., Linvey Riddle...EXR: Willis Cheek & Friend William Ross...12 Jan. 1838--17 Sept. 1838...Bk. A, p. 115...WIT: James B. & Benjamin B. Higgins, Samuel Willis.

CHEEK Willis--Wife Eliza & her two chn: James William & Willis Abram Cheek... First wife Jemima's chn. viz: Randal, Silas, Austin, Ellis, Anna Garret; Rebecca Hammond & her 4 chn; Dau. ?Levi, Levy Riddle's pt. in trust...EXR: Friend Wm. M. Dorrah...7 Nov. 1845...Bk. A, p. 154...WIT: Joseph Sullivan, Hastings Johnson, Andrew McKnight.

CHEEK Willis D--Wife Priscilla..."Small chn. & all my chn"...EXR: Wife, son John... 5 Oct. 1849...Bk. A, p. 113...WIT: James Nesbitt, W. W. Hitch, Wm. A. Todd.

CHILDRESS Richard--Wife Martha...Sons: Richard, John, Robert, Abraham...Daus: Nancy, Sarah, Patsy, Melinda, Betsy, Lucy...23 Mch. 1825--15 Nov. 1830...Bk. F, p. 301...WIT: George Fuller Sr. & Jr., Robert Tuater.

CLARDY James--Wife Sarah...Sons: Jesse E., James, Michael..."have given to heirs of son William dec'd"...Daus: Nancy Wright, Suky Tierce...EXR: Sons Jesse, James, Michael...2 Sept. 1830--14 Oct. 1846...Bk. A, p. 37...WIT: Philip Waite, Jeremiah Bailey, James Daniel.

CLARDY Jesse E.--Wife Rachel...Chn: Michael, William, Katy, Sarah, ?Mahaby, Jesse Ellis James Andrew Jackson, Zachariah, Derrock Smith, John Wesley, Zedikiah Henry (names all run together)...EXR: James & Michael Clardy brothers of Jesse E...29 July 1832--17 Sept. 1843...Bk. A, p. 32...WIT: Philip Wait Sr., John C. Wait, William P. Delph.

COKER Drury--Wife Betsy...Son Joseph & wife & chn...Daus: Menice Coker, Polly Dial...EXR: Dau. Menice or Mencie...Prv. 21 Dec. 1830...Bk. F, p. 312...WIT: Samuel & William F. Downs, James Bruster.

COKER Joseph--Wife...Sons: Drury, Colvin, Thomas, youngest John...EXR: Sons Drury &Colvin..20 Mch. 1792...Bk. A, p. 71...WIT: Wm. Hellams, Thomas Coker, Martin Dial.

COLEMAN Absolom--Sons: John, Larkin, Alfred, Alsey...Guardian for John is Bro. William & Zachariah Bailey...Dau: Decorah Ann...EXR: Wife Sarah, friend Parson Fuller...17 Nov. 1814--10 Dec. 1814...Bk. D-1, p. 179...WIT: James Young, William Bailey, W. Walker.

CORLEY, Coley Charles--Wife Henrietta...Sons: James, John, Spencer, Jackson...Dau. Sally Smith...EXR: Wife...25 July 1818--5 Sept. 1818...Bk. E, p. 4...WIT: John & Elijah Walker, Samuel Boyd.

COOK Abraham--Wife Henrietta...Son William...Daus: Martha E., Henrietta Frances, Mary Louise...EXR: Friend Alsey Fuller...30 May 1843--11 Oct. 1843...Bk. A, p. 19 ...WIT: John Young, Silas M. Bailey, Henry Miller.

COOK George--Chn: James, Joshua, Nancy, Allen B., John, William E., Mary Martha Abram, George (no commas bwt) Elizabeth Knight...EXR: Sons Joshua & James with wife Polly...23 July 1845--15 Aug. 1845...Bk. A, p. 58...WIT: J. J. Atwood, R. Thomas, William Rose or Ross.

COOK James--Wife Ursula & Sons Mitchel & Daniel...EXR: Sons Clayton & his son James a min; John, Tobias, William...Gr.chn: Emily, Matilda, Eliza, Mary Teague... 28 Feb. 1815--15 Aug. 1816...Ek. D-1, p. 330 ...WIT: Agner Pyles, Wm. Black, Allen Pitts.

COOK John--Wife Catharine Sons: James, William, Franklin...Daus: Edny Ligon dec'd; Mary Ann Babb...EXR: s.l. Alsey Fuller, son William...16 July 1835--24 June 1844... Bk. A, p. 19...WIT: David Owen, John Hitt, A. C. Griffin.

COOK William--Chn. of sister Ann Fuller viz: Franklin G., Anthony C., Mary Smith, Edny Richardson, Augustus, ?Lalessie, John C., Edward P...EXR: Wife Jamima...19 May 1850...4 Oct. 1853...Bk. A, p. 197...WIT: Henry W. Pasley, Duke Goodman, Jones Loyd.

CROUCH Isaac--Wife Susannah...Chn: Samuel, Becky w. of John Stroud; Susannah w. of B. Roberson...EXR: Son Samuel...Bk. F...22 Mch. 1817--2 May...WIT: William, Nancy & John Young.

CROCKER James--Dau. Sarah dec'd wife of Meredith Brison & gr.chn: Henry & White-field Brison...Sons: James, John, Joseph, ?Athenion...EXR: Wife Elizabeth & sons William, James, Atharion...12 Jan. 1808--12 Oct. 1822...Bk. E, p. 238-9...WIT: David Anderson, John Cruz, Ebenezer Starnes.

CRAGE(Craig) Eleanor--Sons: John, William, James, "balance div. bwt. chn. not herein named"...EXR: Thomas Logan, James Craig...17 Oct. 1785...Bk. A, p. 79...WIT: Robert Hanna, James Craig, Thomas Logan. (An Eleanor wid of Jno. Craig, filed a Revo. claim.)

CRAIG James--"my chn"...EXR: Wife Elizabeth. Bro. William, Dr. George Ross...2 July 1813--2 Nov. 1813...Bk. D-1, p. 132...WIT: Jno. Briggs, Danl Long, Jno. Craig.

CRAIG John (Revo. S.)--Niece Jane dau. of Joseph Harland...Neph. George Craig...Also ment. fol. Craigs: Wm. Perry, Saml G., William W., Thomas, Robert, William; also Thomas Little...EXR: Thomas & Robert Craig...18 Oct. 1843--30 Oct. 1843...Bk. A, p. 31...WIT: Thos. B. Rutherford, N. C. Nance, W. D. Byrd, Samuel H. Murell.

CRAIG William--Sons: John, William, Thomas, James...Dau. Eleanor...Gr.son: William C. Harlen; Gr.dau. Jane E. Harlen...EXR: Sons John, James & Rev. Wm. Alexander... 10 Oct. 1824--3 Jan. 1825...Bk. E, p. 480...WIT: James & John Craig, John Templeton.

CRAWFORD John--Son: John, James...EXR: Friends John Young, John Black...4 Aug. 1824--3 Dec. 1826...Bk. F, p. 66...WIT: G. W. Young, George Teague, Daniel Cargill.

CREECY John (Creece)--Wife Elizabeth & "her chn. by Zachariah Sims dec'd"...Son of wife, James Sims...Joel Sims...Son Zachariah S. a min...Fanny w. of Jacob Clemmans...John Wait...EXR: Friends David Anderson, Robert Cunningham...15 Jan. 1812...Bk. D-1, p. 64...WIT: John & Frances Wait, John Midleton.

CROSSEN(Croson) Thomas--Dau. Mary w. of Zimry Carter...Son Thomas, wife Martha EXR...5 May 1800--30 July 1800...Bk. A, p. 243...WIT: John Wiseman, Joseph Hollingsworth, J. Reed.

CUNNINGHAM James--Sons: Thomas, James, John, William, George, Samuel...Daus: Margaret, Dorcas, Catherine, Ann Allison & chn: Mary, Saml...Named also David Allison, William Hall, Joseph Dean (prob. son-in-laws)...EXR: Sons John, Thomas, wife...15 Oct. 1788...Bk. A, p. 17...WIT: David Dunlap, James Dorroch or Dorrah.

CUNNINGHAM John--EXR: Wife Nancy, James & Wm. Cunningham, Joseph Dean...8 Mch. 1814...Bk. D-1, p. 172...WIT: John D. & Thos. Cunningham, Hannah Dean.

CUNNINGHAM John--Wife Mary Louise...*all my bros. & sisters*...son Samuel James Cunningham...EXR: Bro. Thomas...27 June 1832--6 Aug. 1832...Bk. F, p. 422...WIT: H. G. Young, R. C. Campbell, A. Kennedy.

CUNNINGHAM, John D.--Wife Mahala...*All my chn. as come of age*: Thomas, Mary, Elvery, Sintha, Margaret, Laursay, Nancy...EXR; Wife...13 Dec. 1832--10 Aug. 1833... Bk. F, p. 495...WIT: Philip Wait, I. Culberson, Allen Johnston.

CUNNINGHAM Patrick--Wife Ann...Sons: William land on mid. fk. br. of Reedy & Saluda; John tract on Beaverdam ck; Robert home place...EXR: Sons John & William... 22 Oct. 1796...Bk. A, p. 153...WIT: Lewis Graves, M. Walker, Sarah Clarey.

CUNNINGHAM Sally--Bros: Elihu & Jacob Cunningham...Sisters: Jane, Mary, Elizabeth, sister Margaret Norris' chn; sister Anna Bolt, Wm. Bolt & 8 daus; neph. Franklin Cunningham...EXR: Elihu Cunningham & neph. James Hudgins...Prv. 30 Jan. 1855... Bk. A, p. 184...WIT: M. Madden, Benjamin Yeargin, Sarah C. Ray.

CUNNINGHAM Thomas--Sons: Thomas, Samuel, John Dean & *each of my chn. as come of age*...EXR: Wife Mary, bro. Samuel, Joseph Dean...2 Apr. 1796--3 Feb. 1806...Bk. C-1, p. 201...WIT: James S. Dorrah, John & William Cunningham.

CUNNINGHAM William--Sons: John, William...EXR: Martha Cunningham, son John...1 Sept. 1822--2 Dec. 1822..Bk. E, p. 242..WIT: Wm. Pitts, L. Cunningham, Henry Marzen.

CURETON David--Neph. Elihue & his 4 chn. viz: James G., Richard, Levington, Mary A....EXR: Elihue Payne, George Wells...29 Dec. 1846...Bk. A, p. 95...WIT: Wm. H. Adams, James A. Foshee, David F. Foshee.

CURETON John (Revo. S.)--Sons: John, Nathaniel, David, George Washington, Thomas, Daniel...Daus: Jinny Paine, Elizabeth Barnette, Heath...EXR: Wife Hannah, Edward Cureton, Thos. Taylor Cureton, David Cureton...31 Aug. 1802--9 Jan 1803...Bk. C-1, p. 19...WIT: James Young, Blagrove Glenn, Stephen Jones (Note: John Cureton is buried at Beaverdam Church, Laurens Co., grave marked. He md. (1) Winifred Heath.

DALRYMPLE Ann--Chn: Benjamin C., John, Henry H., Ephraim, Susanna Jones; Mahala Benjamin & dau. Anna; Lucinda Hitt dec'd & dau. Susanna; Lucretia Jones dec'd... EXR: Lewis D. Jones...3 Feb. 1846--15 Nov. 1852...Bk. A, p. 246...WIT: John Jones, Thos. W. & Thomas Dalrymple.

DALRYMPLE John G.--Wife Sarah..*Bros. & sisters*..EXR: Friends-Dr. James Dillard, Joshua Saxon, George Byrd, John Craig, John F. Kern, John Henderson, W. D. Byrd & wife...22 Sept. 1842--6 Nov. 1843...Bk. A, p. 22...WIT: David Templeton, Berry C. Beasley, W. D. Byrd.

DANDY, Dendy Daniel--Dau. Irene...*Equal div. when youngest chn. of age*...EXR: Marcus & William Dendy...9 Sept. 1829--20 Nov. 1829...Bk. F, p. 239...WIT: John W. Smith, Jack S. Godfrey, J. Chapman.

DANDY, Dendy Thomas Sr.--Sons: Cornelius, Thomas, William...Daus: Elizabeth w. of Samuel Powell, Sarah w. of James Young, Molly w, of William Mitchell, Patsy w. of M. Walker...EXR: Wife Mary, son William...20 Sept. 1797--3 Mch. 1800...Bk. A, p. 229...WIT: John Hunter, William Dendy, Samuel Leek.

DANDY, DENDY William--Wife Clary..Sons: John, Joel, William, Thomas, Daniel, James H...Daus: Priscilla, Sally Motes, Betsy...EXR: Sons John, William, Joel, Daniel...12 Aug. 1800--9 May 1801...Bk. A, p. 294...WIT: D. Hill, Wm. Smith Jr., Jeremiah Sadler.

DAVENPORT John--Sons: John Ransom, Thomas, William, Richard, David..Wife Mildred. EXR: John Roberson, Frederick Purty...5 Feb. 1806--19 June 1807...Bk. C-1, p. 268... WIT: Jonathan Johnston, William Roberson, Howard Pinson.

DAVENPORT Thomas--First wife Sally, *present wife Lathee*...Son Burket...Dau. Lucy Harris...14 Sept. 1812--25 May 1816...WIT: William Nelson, Nathan Sims, Stephen Wharton...Bk. D-1, p. 295.

DAVIS John--Wife Ann...Sons: John H., James...Daus: Mary Creswell, "unfortunate dau. Elizabeth" & trustees for her viz: Robt. Creswell, Dr. James Davis, John McClellan, Benjamin James...Son John to have "land in Kentucky conveyed from Littleberry Sullivan to me"...EXR: Sons John, James, Robt. Creswell, Dr. James Davis...22 Apr. 1823--7 Nov. 1823...Bk. F.

DAY Jemima--All to Charles Simmins, Pamela his wife & their chn: Pamela Adeline & Charles Young Lafayette Simmons...23 Aug. 1850...Bk. A, p. 134...WIT: William Graves, Wm. W. Graves, Wm. E. Caldwell.

DAY Philip--Wife Frances...Chn: William, John, Philip, Daniel, Benjamin, Nathaniel, Mary, Elizabeth, Jemima, Nancy, ?Amy...EXR: William Cason Jr. of Bush riv., John Watts...9 Jan. 1793...Bk. A, p. 118...WIT: Robt. I. Smith, Thos. W. & Margaret Fakes.

DEAN Easter--Lands on Indian ck. bounded by John Mason, David Martin...Sister Polly Dean & aft. her death, bros. Thomas Sr. & Job Dean to have all est. because "they lived near us & saw to us in old age"...Other bros. & sisters: Isham & Wm. Dean, Dan Dean's heirs, Sarah Dalrymple's heirs...EXR: Friend John Mason...28 Mch. 1844--7 June 1844...Bk. A, p. 44...WIT: William Hutchinson, H. R. Metts, C. James.

DENDY John--Chn: Elizabeth Tinsley; Nancy w. of Branch Ligon; Posey w. of Langford Power; Sally w. of David Craddock (Craddoah); ?Youngsets Dendy; Share to Daniel I. Dendy...EXR: Son Thos. N. Dendy...24 Sept. 1847...Bk. A, p. 73...WIT: Charles & L. G. Williams, James A. Hood. (See also Dandy)

DIAL Hastings--Wife Rebecca (Abercromie)...Sons: Hastings, Isaac, James & his chn. Hastings & Joseph...3 sons-in-law, Mabra & Abraham Madden & John Woody...EXR: Wife, Sons Isaac, Hastings...17 Apr. 1809--5 June 1809...Bk. C-1, p. 349...WIT: John Godfrey, Asa Turner, John Cochran (Note: Chn. not named: Isabella, Mary, Rebecca, Jane)

DIAL Martin--Wife Hannah...EXR: Son Jonathan...30 June 1827--5 Feb. 1844...Bk. A, p. 14...WIT: Elihu Abercromie, Jonathan Abercromie, J. G. Sims.

DIAL Rebecca--Sons: Hastings, James, Isaac...Sons-in-law: Mabra Madden, Abraham Madden, John Woodie, James Johnson...EXR: Isaac Dial, Robert McNees...16 Apr. 1825--18 July 1825...Bk. E, p. 511...WIT: Samuel H. Lockhardt, David Hellams.

DILLARD Ann (Hus. Samuel)--Prop. div. bwt. surv. chn: George, John, Polly w. of Capt. N. C. McCrary; Nancy wid. of William Parks; Mildred w. of Reubin Jordan; Sarah...Gr. son Thomas McCrary...the plant. orig. granted Jas. Dillard 1784 & from him went to Saml of Laurens...EXR: Sons John, George...20 Dec. 1821...Bk. E. p. 201... WIT: John B. Bennett, Charles Thuber, John Dillard.

DILLARD George--Wife Martha...Chn: Susan Johnson, Elizabeth, A. I. Dillard, Elvira, J. B., ?Sebran...Gr. son Samuel Packer...Wife to keep amt. recv'd from est. of Susan Dillard dec'd...Dec. 16, 1846...Bk. A, p. 69...WIT: James Hill, L. T. Rhodes, N. Harris.

DOLLAR, Doller Sarah--"husband"...Chn: Susan Colley, Rhoda Biges, Elizabeth Baker, John dec'd., William, Reubin...EXR: Charles G. Franks...26 Oct. 1841...Bk. A, p. 11... WIT: J. D. Hopper, Joshua Burns, Thomas Luvens.

DONAHOE John--"her children & my children"...EXR: Wife Eleanor, Peter Roland... 25 Dec. 1801--23 Mch. 1802...Bk. A, p. 316...WIT: Peter Roberts, Mary Kellett, Eliza Sarah Donahoe.

DORROH, Dorrah James--Wife Jane...Son James EXR...23 Apr. 1810--2 Oct. 1820...Bk. A, p. 12...WIT: John Taylor, George Pearce, A. Downs.

DORRAH James--Sons: William M., John F., Lewis C...Daus: Margaret, Nancy, Martha, Mary..."7 oldest chn"...EXR: Wife Sarah & son David...25 Jan. 1840--5 Mch. 1842... Bk. E, p. 94...WIT: John B. Simpson, Daniel & Samuel Todd.

DORROH James--Wife Martha EXR....17 Oct. 1850--6 Oct. 1857...Bk. A, p. 288...WIT: W. D. Simpson, Alexander McCarley, H. M. Young.

DOWNS Jonathan--Daus: Jane w. of Benj. Byrd; Milley (Mildred Lucy) w. of Lydell Allen; Frances w. of William Kelly; Phoebe w. of James Bruster (Brewster); Louisa w. of John Bruster...Son William F. Downs...(md. Clarissa Saxon)...Gr. son Jonathan Allen...EXR: Wife Sarah (Gary), son William F...18 Aug. 1818...Bk. E, p. 9...WIT: John F. Wolf, C. Saxon, D. T. Saxon.

DOWNS Joseph--Wife Jane (Alexander)...Daus: Arrabella Lewis, Rebecca Alexander, Sarah Gary, Nancy (Anne) Barksdale, Mary L. Downs (md. Mr. Alexander)...(Note: Joshua not named but he set. in Miss.)...EXR: Sons Samuel, Jonathan, neph. William F. Downs...26 Dec. 1818--5 July 1819...Bk. E, p. 32...WIT: E. A. Saxon, G. F. Wolf, J. Allen.

DOWNS Sarah--To Wm. Byrd in trust for dau. Phoebe Brewster wife of James & for gr.son Jonathan D. Brewster...to trustees for dau. Claricy (Clarissa) Brewster...to Wm. R. Farley & Dr. Hugh Saxon, trustees for family of Wm. F. Downs...EXR: William D. Byrd, Allen Barksdale...17 Aug. 1842--27 Dec. 1844...(the gr.son Jonathan died bef. 14 Feb. 1844)...WIT: N. D. & C. Barksdale.

DREW William Sr.--Ninety-Six Dist., S. C...Sons: Langston, William 300 A. on forks of Beaverdam by Wharton's cabin...Daus: Lucy, Polly, Sarah, Elizabeth...Rem. div. bwt. "all chn. males at 21, fem. 18"...Wife Sarah EXR...14 Feb. 1777--15 Mch 1786... Bk. A, p. 1 (part of p. 1 destroyed)...WIT: A. Rodgers Jr. John Lucas, Edw. Philpot.

DUNCAN James--Sons: Joseph, Jonathan, chn. of dec'd son David...Daus: Elizabeth w. of Whitman Jones; Margaret w. of John Jeans; Sarah w. of Fred Jones...Aft. abv. beq. rem. est. div. bwt. "all my chn"...20 May 1820--5 Sept. 1828...Bk. F, p. 174...WIT: Mary, Reubin & James Flanagan...EXR: Benj. Ducket, Bardywin Roberts.

DUCKET Sarah--6 chn: Martha, Alcey Robertson, Liday Dillard, George Young, John, Thomas (names all run together)...EXR: John & George Duckett...13 Jan. 1832--3 Dec. 1832...Bk. F, p. 455...WIT: John Whitmore, Joseph Garrett, George Dillard.

DUNLAP David--Sons: James, Brill, Mitchell, Robert, David, John..Daus: Mary, Christen, Jane, Martha, Elizabeth...2 gr. sons David Bishop, Robert Green...S.L. Caleb ?Earp... EXR: Wife Jane, Wm. Miller, James Dunlap, James Powell...26 July 1805--15 Apr. 1807...Bk. C-1, p. 262...WIT: John McDavid, Mary Dunlap, Leanna Powell.

DUNLAP Samuel--Wife Nancy...Sons: James, Samuel, John land on Rabun ck...Daus: Catherine, Susannah, Sarah, Nancy, Mary ?Jeather...EXR: John Dunlap, Wm. Hellams, Martin Dial...5 Feb. 1791...Bk. A, p. 43...WIT: Martin Dial, John Dunlap, Wm. Hellams.

EAGERTON Charles--Wife Frances "not allowed to dispose of prop. to Benj. Holt & wife Amelia & chn; nor to Nathan Chapman & wife Sophia & chn"...adopted son & neph. John Edw. Jones...to John Josep h, Frances & Matison chn. of Robert Gates dec'd.. "my sisters: Clarissa Scott, Elizabeth Oliver dec'd & her chn"...EXR: Friend Anthony Y. Golding...26 June 1846...Bk. A, p. 91...WIT: Patrick & Wm. Todd, Sarah Wright.

EAKINS Lewis--Sons: John, Ezekiel, Anker, Frank...Daus: Sally, Fannie...S.L. Benj. Kevel...2 gr. sons: William & Thomas sons of Patty Petty...EXR: Son Ezekiel, Benj. Kevel...16 July 1791...Bk. A, p. 60...WIT: Joel League, Thos. Kevel, Jno. Medder.

EAST Josiah--Daus: Sarah Drake, Nancy East...EXR: Son Langston, Sarah Drake...27 Aug. 1818--16 Nov. 1824...Bk. E, p. 434...WIT: William Neil, Richard Davis.

EAST Shadrack--Wife Mary...Chn: Kesiah, John, Thomas, Ann "as they marry or come of age," oldest son Allen, min...EXR: Thomas East Sr., James Cook...12 Nov. 1792... Bk. A, p. 78...WIT: Samuel Henderson, William Young, Thomas Wordsworth.

EVANS John--Wife land on Cane ck...Sons: Josiah, William, John...Daus: Mary Edwards, Frances & Rachel mins...rem. to chn. living or their heirs at death of wife...EXR: Wife Sarah...16 Feb. 1779--8 Feb. 1785...Bk. C-1, p. 141...WIT: Mary Edwards, Martha & James Puckett.

FAIRBURN, Fairbern Alexander--Of Durkin's ck...Wife Crissey...Dau. Geney Wood...

148

EXR: Son James...2 June 1798...Bk. A, p. 197...WIT: Roger Brown, Samuel Laid, B. Holland.

FARLEY Mary--Son Thompson...18 Dec. 1817...Bk. E, p. 133...WIT: John Wallace Sr., William Ross, Benjamin Griffin.

FARROW John--Everything to Eupemia Brown & William Winder Hitch...EXR: Joshua Saxon, William C. Byrd, Dr. James H. Dillard...23 July 1841--22 Jan. 1844...Bk. A, p. 21...WIT: Joshua Saxon, Isaac B. Henry, James J. Newman, T. F. Murphy.

FARRAR, Farrow Patillo--Wife Jane S...Sister Mrs. Nancy Farrow to have judgment on late Dr. Samuel Farrow...My chn: James, Susan W., Thomas, Henry P., Rosannah, Lilly, Anny w. of Wister Simpson...John L. James is named...EXR: Sons James, Thomas, S.L. John W. Simpson...16 Oct. 1849--19 Nov. 1849...Bk. A, p. 104...WIT: Samuel R. Todd, William Anderson, John Garlington.

FARROW Thomas F.--Wife Sophia EXR.."my chn"...29 Mch. 1852--23 Jan. 1855...Bk. A, p. 185...WIT: J. H. Thomson, John R. Lyons, W. H. Langston.

FELTS John--Wife Mary...Daus: Mary J. Finley; chn. of dec'd dau. Susannah Houlditch viz: Wm. H. & Jno. F...EXR: Son John, s.l. Wm. T. (?J) Finley...11 Dec. 1852...Bk. A. . . WIT: Alsey Fuller, James F. Coleman, Matthew Bryson.

FERGUSON Nehemiah--Sons: John, William, Jeremiah, Joseph, James, N. B...Daus: Elizabeth, Margaret, Sarah, Mary...EXR: Sons Joseph & James...9 Sept. 1787...Bk. A. p. 16...WIT: Joseph Wood, R. Roland, John Dalrymple.

FERGUSON Richard--Sons: Miles, John & his chn., Charles, ?Wara...Daus: Tabitha Motley, Mary Vaughan, Franky McCravey, Elizabeth...EXR: George McCravy, Samuel Ferguson...25 July 1807--6 June 1808...WIT: T. A. Elmore, N. T. Martin, Turner Richardson...Bk. C-1, p. 315.

FILLSON Alexander--Cousin Robert Fillson & his son...EXR: Henry C. Young...8 Oct.. 1842 prv...Bk. A, p. 14...WIT: Milton Pyles, M. I. Lockhardt, W. Leak.

FINLEY John--Wife Polly....sons Hampton, his w. Susan & dau. Mary Frances;Dau Elizabeth w. of Larkin Coleman & gr. ch. James T. & Nancy Elizabeth Coleman; Gr. ch: Sara Frances Tyler...At death wife, est. div. bwt. son James, Margaret Miller, Jane Walker, James F. Coleman, Sara Frances Tyler, Nancy Elizabeth Coleman... Mary Frances Finley equal with chn...EXR: Son James, in case death, Albert Miller, Azariah Walker, James F. Coleman...20 Feb. 1851--30 Aug. 1852...Bk. A, p. 148... WIT: John Wharton, Moses Griffin, J. H. Coleman.

FINLEY Paul--Wife Mary...Chn: Hampton, John, Margaret, Nancy Hank, Anne Coleman, Lettice Coleman, Jane Houlditch, Elizabeth Cargill dec'd; Sarah Wait dau. of Nancy Arnold a legacy...EXR: Son Hampton...15 June 1843--12 Sept. 1843...Bk. A, p. 25... WIT: Larkin Coleman, Alsey Fuller, F. G. Fuller.

FINNEY John--Wife Nancy...Daus: Elizabeth, Ann, Polly, Sarah, Peggy, Martha...Son John...24 Jan. 1820--19 Apr. 1825...Bk. E, p. 494...WIT: Jason & Polly Meadows, Wm. Copeland.

FORGY, Forgey, Forgie, Peggy--Sons: Menoah, Ase...Dau. Rachel McPherson...EXR: George Anderson...9 June 1828--11 Apr. 1829...Bk. F, p. 216...WIT: Elijah Elmore, Rachel & D. Anderson.

FOSHEE Benjamin--Wife Susannah, son Benjamin EXR...Chn: Nancy, Sally Turner, Abby Turner, Jancy Turner, Benjamin, Daniel...25 Nov. 1807--14 Aug. 1824...Bk. E, p. 409...WIT: H. Walker, Ephraim Knight, Daniel Foshee.

FOWLER John--Chn: James, Wade, Millicent, Wesly, Linsa, John, Jesse a min; William & his chn; Nancy Thomas; Elizabeth Gowesy (names all run together)...14 Jan. 1790-- 4 June 1791...Bk. A, p. 32...EXR: Wife Elizabeth, friend John H. Henderson, son William...WIT: G. Thomas, William B. Boyd, Moses Williams.

149

FOWLER John--Wife Elizabeth...Chn: William, Wade, Wiley Y., John, Wesley, Jesse, Elizabeth w. of James ? Lawry, other daus...EXR: Son William, friend John Henderson... 16 Aug. 1851...Bk. A, p. 112...WIT: Wm. B. Gary, Henry H. Watkins, Wm. Burgess.

FOWLER Josiah--Wife Sarah...Sons: Thomas, Newton...EXR: Sons Richard, Thomas, Alhanan Crocker, Alsa Fuller...21 Feb. 1817--7 Apr. 1817...Bk. D-1, p. 370...WIT: Abner Pyles, Thomas Burnside, Isaac Mitchell.

FOWLER Nathan--Wife Martha...Dau. Sarah Ann...EXR: Thomas Owins, George Young Jr...8 Apr. 1827--17 Sept. 1827...Bk. F, p. 127...WIT: Thomas Young, John Whitmore, John Addington.

FOWLER Richard--Wife Elizabeth...Chn: Joshua, Richard land on Durbin ck; Ann Neuel, Elizabeth Flannigan, Rebecca ? Barton...EXR: Sons Richard, Joshua...5 Oct. 1790...Bk. A, p. 42...WIT: Hudson Berry, Joseph Burchfield, John Armstrong (Descts. claim also William & John as sons.)

FOWLER William--Wife Agnes...Sons: John, James, William, David, Charles...Daus: Nancy, Peggy Parks & her son William...EXR: Wife Agnes & son John...22 June 1800-- 5 Sept. 1803...Bk. C-1, p. 68...WIT: James McClintock, Jas. Hutchins, Jas. Fowler.

FRANKLING, Franklin Mathew--"wife, negro woman Dinah & her chn"...EXR: Friends Stephen & Jesse Garret srs...30 June 1821--7 May 1822...Bk. E, p. 215...WIT: W. F. Downs, G. F. Wolf, Mary Wolf.

FRANKS Joshua--Wife Prudence...Sons: Robert P., Niles, Joshua S., Abner C., George... Daus: Mary Hellams, Nancy Bolt...six Saxon gr. chn. named: Samuel, Joshua, William N., John W., Mary, Thomas L...EXR: Sons Joshua, William...17 Nov. 1847--30 Jan. 1848...Bk. A, p. 102...WIT: William Clardy, Lewis Saxon, Arch Henderson.

FULLER Avent--Nieces: Rebecca A. & Delphy Fuller...Son John T...EXR: Delphy Fuller, Henry ? One...31 Aug. 1838--6 Sept. 1841...Bk. A, p. 9...WIT: James Leaman, Justiman Henderson.

FULLER Henry--"chn"...EXR: Wife Charlotte, worthy friend Zachariah Bailey Esq... 28 Sept. 1813--3 Sept. 1814...Bk. D-1, p. 167...WIT: James Fuller, John Holt, Sarah Holt.

FULLER John--EXR: Elizabeth G. Fuller wife...12 Sept 1842--29 Oct. 1842...Bk. A, p. 25 WIT: Abraham Thompson, Anthony F. Golding, I. I. Brownlee.

FULLER Solomon--Sons: Solomon, William, John ? Avent, Ransom, Alsey...Daus.: Charlotte, Sarah Coleman...S. L. William Green & gr. dau. Gilley A. Green...EXR: Wife Gilley, son Solomon...26 Feb. 1816--19 Nov. 1821...Bk. E, p. 191...WIT: David Stephens, Joseph Hodges, Richard S. Drake.

FULLER Solomon--Wife Phoebe...Chn: Ellison I., John R., Harrison M., Solomon T., Mary--two sons-in-law & their chn. & "those that have already recv'd their pt."... EXR: Bro. Alsey Fuller, sons John & Harrison...27 Aug. 1844--2 Sept. 1844...Bk. A, p. 48...WIT: Henry W. Pasly, William Fuller, George Robert.

FUNK George--Wife Nancy...Chn: Hampton, Elizabeth Ann Watson, Albert W., Ann Wood...EXR: Sons Albert, Wade...17 Dec. 1842-7 Jan. 1843...Bk. A, p. 37...WIT: J.A. Coleman, John Wood, Robert Brady.

GAMBLE James--Son John...Wife...EXR: William Fulton, John Williamson...20 Apr. 1799--13 Oct. 1800...Bk. A, p. 250...WIT: Charles Witson (? Wilson), John O'Neel; also Bk. D-1, p. 107.

GARLINGTON Edwin--Wife Eleanor...Son Johnny Motes..."all my chn"...EXR: Son John Garlington...31 Oct. 1823--7 Jan. 1824...Bk. E, p. 341...WIT: John Cook, Wm. Ball.

GARNER Thomas--Sons: John 640 A. at Rocky Mt..Benjamin min...Daus: Molly Roberts, Sarah ? Laffold, Elizabeth youngest & min...niece Sally Garner...EXR: David Anderson, Joseph Downs...13 July 1791--Bk. A, p. 44...WIT: Jonathan Downs, James Floyd, J. F. Wolff.

GARNETT (?Garrett) Ambrose--"Chn"...EXR: Wife Nancy, friend Fountain Martin...
9 May 1840--9 July 1840...Bk. A, p. 3...WIT: Stephen Garrett, Jesse Davis, B. Davis.

GARRETT Hannah--Sons: Elisha, Charles, Jesse...EXR: Elisha & Chas. Garrett...3
Dec. 1818--4 June 1821...Bk. E, p. 166...WIT: Joseph & Nathan & Wm. Harris.

GARRETT Jesse--At death of w. Elizabeth, div. 7 pts...Sons: John, Thomas H., Edward,
Jesse, Stephen & wife Polly, William...Daus: Polly Cook; dec'd dau. Fannie Martin ;
Betsy Ashley...EXR: Thomas & Jesse Garrett...22 Sept. 1847--30 Oct. 1853...Bk. A,
p. 161...WIT: Willis Wallace, William Clardy, Calvin Abercromie.

GARRETT John--Sons: Joseph, Henry, Elisha, Jesse, Charles (last 3 youngest)...Daus:
Abby, Sarah Prude, Rebecca, ?Minorah..EXR: Wife Hannah, son Joseph...12 Aug. 1805--
4 Apr. 1806...Bk. C-1, p. 215...WIT: John & Rachel Carwell (Caldwell).

GARRETT Silas--Wife Ann..Sons: Enoch, Joab, John, Silas..Daus: Mary, Martha Harris,
Elizabeth Yarborough, Margaret....EXR: Son Enoch...3 May 1796--7 Jan. 1805...Bk
C-1, p. 140...WIT: Roger Brown, John Garrett, William Doller.

GARRETT Edward(Garrot)--Wife Anny..Sons: James (no pt. until he reforms), Stephen...
S.L. Stephen Mullins...a dec'd dau. had md. Pleasant Sullivan & her ch. Garret
named...Will in the form of statement...EXR: Nelson Kelly, Stephen Mullins, Stephen
Garrett...23 Aug. 1794...Bk. A, p. 102.

GAREY Charles--Friend Milly Coker..."my natural dau. Cason Coker to have est.
at Milly's death or marriage"...EXR: Bro. David Garey, friend Drury Coker...... 22
Feb. 1805--5 Feb. 1806..Bk. C-1, p. 202...WIT: John Armstrong, John Coker, Wm. Gary.

GARY David--Sons Joseph, Warren...EXR: Wife Sarah...23 Sept. 1832--3 Dec. 1832...
Bk. F, p. 456...WIT: Samuel Downs, Henry R. Brewster, William F. Downs.

GARY Newman--Wife Elizabeth...to Daniel Mangum one-third as trustee for my dau.
Mary R. wife of Thomas McDowell; gr. dau. Elizabeth dau. of dec'd son Jesse R.
Gary; chn. of dec'd dau. Pamela C. Pyles...EXR: Addison T. Martin...25 Nov. 1848...
Bk. A, p. 119...WIT: Daniel & Belsa Magnum, Asa B. Davis.

GILBERT William--Wife Sarah....Dau-in-law Catherine Gilbert...Sons: James, John,
William, Jeremiah, Joshua, Harvey Austin...Daus: Elizabeth ?Collins, Mariah Wilson,
Rebecca Burchfield...EXR: Son William Jr...29 July 1822--7 Oct. 1822...Bk. E, p. 237...
WIT: Hartwell Lester, Joseph Gilbert, Isaac Liedham.

GILBERT William--Chn: William H., Edward, Matilda Austin, Lucinda Atkins, Nancy
Cooper...EXR: William Gilbert...30 Apr. 1842--22 Mch. 1843...Bk. A, p. 23...WIT: G.
B. Teague, W. H. Hughes, J. P. Sarett.

GLENN Alexander--Dau. Nancy T. Rice & her chn...EXR: Dr. Hezekiah Rice, James
Young, Richard F. Simpson...5 Jan. 1826--5 June 1826...Bk. F, p. 28...WIT: Langdon
East, James Crawford, James Young.

GLENN David--Chn: Anna, Rebecca, Elizabeth, James, George, John, David...EXR:
Wife Elizabeth & bro. Francis....28 Feb. 1821--3 Sept. 1821...Bk. E, p. 176...WIT:
John Stuart, J. T. Citch, James Fleming.

GLENN James--Sons: Francis, James, John...Daus: Catherine...EXR: William Cowan,
David Glenn...17 Apr. 1815--17 June 1816...Bk. D-1, p. 313...WIT: Alexander Mills,
Francis & Elizabeth Glenn.

GLENN Jeremiah--Sons: Blagrove, Jeremiah, William, Tire...Daus: Frances Craighead,
Sarah Garland Walker, Martha Newstep Moon, Mary Williamson, Elizabeth Walker,
"rest to all my chn"...EXR: Wife Anne, sons Jeremiah & William...22 Dec. 1807--
5 June 1809...Bk. C-1, p. 347...WIT: John Davis, Richard Shackleford, Robert Pasley.

GLENN Reuben--Wife Elizabeth all prop...EXR: Alexander Glenn...26 Oct. 1808--11
Nov. 1808...Bk. C-1, p. 327...WIT: John Caldwell, Michael Frantman, Wm. Wright.

GOFF Hugh--Son Thomas...Dau. Christeen Mears...EXR: Wife Rebecca, Ira Arnold...

151

22 Jan. 1823--7 July 1823...Bk. E, p. 293...WIT: J. L. Maddox, Wm. Arnold, Joel Ellison.

GOLDING Anthony--Wife Isabel...Sons: James, John, Anthony Foster, Thomas min... Daus: Elizabeth, Rachel, Permelia Nancy...EXR: Friend Charles Griffin, neph. Jacob Crastwhite...27 Dec. 1800...Bk. A, p. 282...WIT: James Tinsley, James Williams, John Leonard.

GOLDING Anthony F.--Wife...Trustees: Dr. R. E. & A. C. Campbell...Daus: Caroline Matilda Elizabeth Golding, Pamela Cunningham Golding, Clementine B. wife of Dr. Wm. Philips...Sons: John Brown Golding, chn. of dec'd son Anthony R. Golding....gr. son Calvin Foster...EXR: Nephs. B. R. & A. C. Campbell, wife Caroline Matilda.... 27 Sept. 1853--23 Apr. 1858...Bk. A, p. 303...WIT: H. G. Dean, O. P. Vernon, E. I. Henry...Named in codicil: Son-in-law Dr. Wm. Philips, neph. Dr. Robt. E. Campbell... A. C. Campbell died bef. Oct. 1857.

GOLDING Temperance--Hus. James...3 sons: Foster, John Franklin a min...EXR: Dr. Wm. Philips friend..24 July 1845...Bk. A, p. 60...WIT: Wm. & Christina Philips, Anthony Golding.

GOODGION Joseph--"chn"...EXR: Wife, Micajah Berry...4 Aug. 1837--7 Dec. 1840... Bk. A, p. 5...WIT: Garland Lewis, Thomas Pedero, Jonathan Downs.

GOODMAN Duke--Place stones at graves of father, mother, bro. Bluford, sister Sally Goodman & all my other bros. & sisters...sister Kitty Goodman named, also sister Rebecca w. of Humphrey Willis & their heirs--25 Oct. 1851...Bk. A, p. 147...WIT: James Parks, J. J. Atwood, W. D. Watts.

GOODMAN Samuel Sr.--Wife...Sons: James, Samuel, Gilliam, David...Daus: Rhoda w. of James Nickles; Maria w. of James Cook; Jamima w. of Wm. Cook; heirs of my chn. that may be dec'd...EXR: Friend John D. Williams...9 Oct. 1829--3 Jan. 1831... Bk. A, p. 61...WIT: M. W. Cristman, James G. Williams, E. D. Williams. Also Bk. F, p. 314.

GOODMAN William--Wife Mary...Bro. Claborn, all prop. at death wife...Bro. James... 28 Sept. 1793...Bk. A, p. 86...WIT: Mary Goodman, Nicholas Vaughan, Saml. Warthis.

GORDON Ann I.--Daus: Catherine Alexander, Charlotte Fulton, ?Join...EXR: William Dunlap..9 May 1823--3 Apr. 1826...Bk. F, p. 15...WIT: Joseph Griffin, William Milligan, Sarah E. Saxon.

GORDON Jane---Sisters: Charlotte Fulton, Catty or Cetty Hannah ?Maxleds, & to William Dunlap in trust for Charlotte...29 June 1832--10 Sept. 1832...Bk. F, p. 428... WIT: Edward Jones, Robert Johnson, James Lip.

GRANT Isaac--Wife Jane...Son Marion...Dau. Ariahah...'prop. been given chn. married & left me"...EXR: Son Marion, William A. Sten...6 Sept. 1832--22 Oct. 1832...WIT: John Boyd Sr., Thomas Salmon, Sally Golding...Bk. F, p. 452.

GRANT John--Wife Mildred...Son Milton two-thirds & if he leave no heir, to the daus. of Robert Whiteford...Bk. A, p. 151...WIT: Henry Whitmire, C. D. Smith, Wm. S. Shell.

GRAY Isaac--Dau. Sally Roundtree...Gr. chn: Bethia w. of Thomas Meadows; Jenny w. of John Gray; Mahala dau. of Abraham Gray; Melepa w. of John Taylor...other Gray gr. chn: Eliza, Lesly, Josiah, Polasky, Abelina, Mekona, Madison, Archer, Tallson...EXR: John Taylor...26 Mch. 1829--1 Mch. 1830...Bk. F, p. 261...WIT: Starling Tucker, Samuel Parsons, Elias Cheek.

GRAY James--Dau. Elizabeth's 2 chn; dau. Sarah's chn. viz: Agnes ?Rearnaghan; dau ?Phelu & her son James Cochran...rest div. bwt. 4 chn. viz: Andrew, John, Robert, Mary ?Lewers & heirs...EXR: Sons Andrew & John, S.L. Thos. Lewers...23 Apr. 1824-- 9 Jan...Bk. A, p. 267...WIT: William Hobody, Joseph Downs.

GREEN James--EXR: Friend Mary Nisbett, Richard Blackwell...19 Apr. 1818--6 July 1818...Bk. E, p. 2...WIT: Robert & Sally McNeer, Elizabeth N. Pool.

152

GREEN William--Wife Agnes...Daus; Sarah Rogers, Elizabeth Motes, Martha Boling... EXR: Son William...5 Oct. 1823--4 Dec. 1824...Bk. E, p. 439.

GREEN William--Wife Frances...Sons: N. A., E. B., J. F., Wm. W., Washington, S. R., S. C...Daus: Nancy Simms, Gilly A. Pasley...14 June 1847...Bk. A, p. 140...WIT: Wm. C. Nickles, Willis Dendy, Benj. M. Wells.

GREEN Zachariah--Chn: James, Elizabeth Eastwood...neph. Elisha Casey...EXR: Gr. son James Green, Elisha Casey...11 Feb. 1793...Bk. A, p. 73...WIT: William Hellams, Elizabeth Atkins.

GRIFFIN Anthony--Sons: Asa, Abia, James...Daus: Betty Butler, Caty Cook, Suky Griffin...EXR: Wife Mary, Richard Griffin, John Cole...20 Aug. 1798...Bk. A, p. 178... WIT: Robert Russell, Robt. Cleland, John Armstrong.

GRIFFIN Anthony--Chn: Dr. W. H., Richard F., Frances Amanda, Jane L. Fuller, Martha F. Higgins, Mary W. Watts, Sarah A. Phinney...EXR: Relative Ino D. Williams, friend W. D. Watts...4 Nov. 1849...Bk. A, p. 133...WIT: John D. & Willis Brown, James Babb.

GRIFFIN Richard Sr.--"Ellinor McClain my present wife 'cert. prop. provided she release right to balance willed' to my heirs"...Est. div. bwt. chn. & their heirs.... EXR: Charles Griffin, James Caldwell of Newberry...2 Feb. 1800--5 Nov. 1805--Wife renounces claim & signed 8 Feb. 1805...Bk. C-1, p. 185-6...WIT: John Cook, George Ball, Jemima Ball.

GRIFFIN William Sr.--Wife Rachel...Sons: William, James (Cason's ck. boundary bwt. them)...Daus: Jane, Peggy, Caty...EXR: Bros. Richard & Anthony & son James...Bk. A, p. 50...27 June 1791...WIT: Charles & James Griffin, Jane Dogharty.

GRIZZLE, Grisel, Grisels John--Daus: Nancy, Judah Garey, "all rest my chn"...EXR: wife Elizabeth...6 May 1810--6 Aug. 1810...Bk. D-1, p. 18...WIT: William Craig, Wm. Grizzle, Stephen Gary.

HAIRSTON Peter--Wife Sarah EXR..Chn: John Speak, William Peter, Elizabeth Calmers, Sarah Frances, Martha Catherine...20 Sept. 1844...Bk. A, p. 137...WIT: John Whitten, John W. Owens, John F. Kern.

HALL William--Sons: Abraham, Henry land; after death wife, personal prop. bwt. Elizabeth Carter, Frankie Carter, Sarah Clardy, Mary Bailey...27 May 1797...Bk. A, p. 200...WIT: T. Moore, Abram Hall, James Clardy.

HALL William--EXR: Wife Alsey, William Franks, Adam Potter...26 Jan. 1821--21 Feb. 1821...Bk. E, p. 145...WIT: Charles Allen, John Pope, John Dollard.

HAMBLETON, Hamilton Robert--At death wife Elizabeth, prop. div. bwt. all chn. & gr. son Marshall Hill..EXR: Robert Hollingsworth, Reubin Hill..WIT: Robt. Hollingsworth Samuel Goodman, John Owens...25 Dec. in 35th yr. Amer. Indep...18 Apr. 1812...Bk. D-1, p. 74.

HAMILTON Andrew--To neph. James Downey a minor & niece Eliza Downey both chn. of Samuel Downey....Rem. bwt. Saml. & Alexander Hamilton, Mary Downey, Martha Dorrah, Elizabeth Scoles....EXR: Saml. Downey...Bk. A, p. 114...WIT: Nancy Pitts, Robt. McDaniel, W. R. Molloy...30 Oct. 1848--8 Oct. 1849.

HAMILTON Jane--Daus: Elizabeth Taylor;Margaret w. of William Mills; Nancy McClintock & son John....Gr. chn: Jane & Elizabeth Taylor, Mary Julia Mills...EXR: Son John McClintock...10 May 1834--16 Apr. 1839...Bk. A, p. 5...WIT: John Dean, J. Hutchinson (Hutcheson), F. Dean.

HAMILTON Jane--Chn: Martha Dorrah, Mary Downy, Elizabth Downs, ?Eliza & s.l. James Coles "should he come to this country," Alexander, Andrew, Samuel the tract bought from Jas. Dorrah & Alex. Culberson...EXR: Sons Saml, Andrew...6 Oct. 1842-- 30 July 1844...Bk. A, p. 41...WIT: H. C. Young, Chas. Smith, J. I. Culberson.

153

HAMMOND Joseph--Sons: Macky, John, Joseph...Gr. son Jos. Hammond...Daus: Nancy, Elizabeth w. of Jack Grizel...EXR: Jesse Childress, Thomas Goodwin...11 Jan. 1817... Bk. D-1, p. 420...WIT: William Owings Jr., Thomas Childress, Rachel Spelse.

HAMMOND Peter--Wife Ann..Sons: William, Isum, Peter...Daus: Riody Robertson, Sally Garrett, Nancy McChurg, Betsy Barrett...EXR: William, Peter & Isum Hammond... 26 Jan. 1816...Bk. D-1, p. 264...WIT: Isiah Couch, Saml Couch, Reuben Roberson.

HANCOCK William--Mother...Dau. Fanny a min...William son of sister Sally Rhoades... Patsey & other surv. chn. of Clement Hancock...James & other surv. chn. of John Hancock...surv. chn. of James Hancock...EXR: Abner Pyles, William Burnside...WIT: James Hancock, William Young, Betsy Pyles.

HAND Robert R.--Chn. 9...Dau. Polly & hus. Robert Thomason & their chn: Sally, Polly, Nancy...EXR: Son Robt. Hand, later changed to Elizabeth w. of Robt. Hand Sr... 9 Nov. 1827--24 July 1840...Bk. A, p. 8...WIT: Arch & E. Young, Thos. Wright.

HARDING, Hardin, Harden William--Sons: Abraham, William, George, Nicholas, Henry's 2 chn. Isaac & Abram; Abner's wid. & his chn. when of age...Daus: Sally, Elizabeth, Susanna & her min. chn...EXR: Sons Nicholas, George...22 May 1809--5 June 1809... Bk. C-1, p. 345...WIT: Zadoc Wood, Jno. M. Clery, John C. Cole.

HARLAN Aaron--Sons: Samuel eldest, George, Joshua, Aaron, Joseph, Isiah (last 3 youngest)...Daus: Sarah, Jane, Mary, Rebecca a min..."married chn. already have theirs"...Wife Elizabeth...EXR: Son Samuel...24 July 1806--17 Nov. 1806...Bk. C-1, p. 239...WIT: Benet Langston, Wm. Sparks, Joshua Galmer...the wid. died bef. 7 Dec. 1835 & Samuel was living in Fayette Co., Ind., so son Joseph appt. Exr.

HATHORN James--Wife Edny...Daus: Nancy Caroline, Mary Ann...EXR: Joseph Neely of Laurens Dist. & Lewis Mitchell of Abbeville...6 Apr. 1817--18 June 1817...Bk. D-1, p. 393...WIT: J. L. Neely, Sam J. Hopper, James Reddon.

HAZLETT Guzzlet--Bro. Robert...Nephs. William McDaniel, Mathew & Nathan & Adam NcDonnold (McDonnal), David Nelson...EXR: Charties Nickles...1 Dec. 1815--18 May 1816...WIT: William Reed, James Strain Esq..Bk. D-1, p. 294.

HELLAMS William--Wife Constant...Dau. Rachel Allison & her son John P...gr. son Jonathan son of Jonathan...other gr. chn: Sons & daus. of William, Jonathan, W. P., Nancy, Rachel...Chn. are EXR--2 July 1788...Bk. A, p. 8...WIT: John Childress, Richard Owings, John Hellams.

HENDERSON Anne (wid. of James)--Sons: James, Samuel, William...Daus: Polly Irby, Petsy, Fanny, Sarah (last 3 min)...beq. to Nancy & ?Retter Irby...S.L. Wm. Hancock... EXR: John Hunter, William Dunlap, Samuel Henderson...25 Aug. 1801--19 Oct. 1801... Bk. A, p. 308...WIT: Abner Pyles, Saml Henderson, William Dunlap.

HENDERSON Mildred A.--Bro. Abner G. Gary...Sister Peunesy Frances Martin to "take my dau. Frances & raise her"...B.L. John A. Martin of Fairfield...Step. chn: William T., Robert Y., Sarah C., (all Hendersons) get legacy from their gr. father John Boyce dec'd..25 June 1845...Bk. A, p. 78...WIT: Wm. Young, Thos. Wier, Jno. Kern.

HENDERSON Samuel--Chn: Nancy, Justiniana, John, Sally...EXR: Wife Susanna, friend James Young...4 Mch. 1817--15 Apr. 1817...Bk. D-1, p. 378...WIT: James & Anne Young, Alexander Glenn.

HENDRICK Margaret--Sons: Mujah, William...Daus: Fanny Turner, Rachel Hendrick, Mary Burgess, Elizabeth Wright, Martha Willard...EXR: Friend Lewis Graves...2 Jan. 1797...Bk. A, p. 158...WIT: John Middleton, Jacob Clemens, Elizabeth Simms.

HEWIT Charles--Wife Susannah...Sons: John, William, Ashley...Daus; Catherine, Ruth, Susannah Null...EXR: Son John...22 Feb. 1816--4 Mch. 1816...Bk. D-1, p. 263...WIT: William Dunlap, Samuel Bardsdale, George Lick.

HILL Elender, Eleanor--Sons: William, Stephen, Isaac & dau. Anne; David with wife Mary & dau. Mary Turner; Benjamin with wife Susie & chn. Jacob William & Elizabeth Emmeline...Daus: Mary Burns, Catherine Flynn...EXR: Son Benjamin...30 Aug. 1828-- 2 Nov. 1829...Bk. F, p. 235...WIT: John L. Kennedy, Alfred A. Kern, John F. Kern Jr.

HILL Silas--Wife Rebecca...Three bros: Thomas, James, John..."sons & daus."...29 June 1845--18 Dec. 1845...Bk. A, p. 55...WIT: Saml. R. Todd, Jno. D. Wright, Jno. Klink.

HILL Thomas--Fol. Hills named: William, Sarah, F., Robert, James...EXR: Wife Polly, friend Robert Malone, William B. Smith...30 Nov. 1820--14 Dec. 1820...Bk. E, p. 106... WIT: Marshal Pollard, Daniel Jones, Josiah Cason.

HINTON Robert--Wife Elizabeth "& her chn"...Sons: John, Robert, Thomas a min... gr. son Robert Anderson...Daus. Hannah Moore, Elander Hinton...EXR: Wife, son John.. 20 Oct. 1797...Bk. A, p. 173...WIT: Thad. & Wm. Owen, Samuel Anderson.

HITT Elizabeth S.--Sons: Jesse, William, Henry, Benjamin, Martin..."my clothes to son's wives"...EXR: Son William...18 June 1844...Bk. A, p. 141...WIT: J. W. Johnson, John R. Spearman, H. N. Carter.

HITT Henry--Wife Elizabeth Stevens Hitt...Sons: Jesse, Henry, Benjamin, Martin... Dau: Elizabeth Hollingsworth & chn. viz: Mary, Elizabeth, Susan, John R...EXR: Son Jesse, Lewis Ball...3 Mch. 1828--27 Sept. 1830...Bk. F, p. 282...WIT: Martha & Willie Ball, Peter H. Boyd.

HOLCOMB Casea (?Cassey)--Sister Phoeby Holcomb EXR..Bro. John & chn: Cassandra, Alfred, Kevel, ?Martral...1 Apr. 1835--10 July 1843...WIT: Peter Simpson, Nathl. Thackston, E. Lyon, Thos. Wright, Stephen & Lucy Griffith...Bk. A, p. 33.

HOLCOMB Richard--Wife Sarah lands on mid. fk. Durbin's ck...EXR: Friend Jacob Robards...22 June 1794...Bk. A, p. 102...WIT: Elisha Holcomb, Reubin Higgins, Joseph Lonins.

HOLDER Jesse--Sons: Solomon eldest, Jeremiah, Willie, Jesse, John...Daus: Delia, Rebeka, Martha, Sarah, Mary, Elizabeth youngest...F.L. Solomon Langston & wife Mary EXR...16 July 1798...Bk. A, p. 200...WIT: Roger Brown, Henry & Sarah Langston.

HOLLAND Jane--Prop. div. 5 pts...Son Thomas, three daus. names..."chn. & gr. chn"... EXR: Son Thos., S.L. John Leek...23 Aug. 1830--9 Nov. 1830...Bk. F, p. 287...WIT: John B. Kennedy, Thomas Wier, John Little.

HOLLAND Regin, Rezin--Sons: John, Thomas, Jeremiah min...Daus: Sarah, Elizabeth, Rachel, Marah, "unborn chn"...EXR: Wife Mary, Joseph Adair...30 July 1802...Bk. C-1, p. 11...WIT: William Saxon, Thomas Holland.

HOLT Sarah--Sons: Larkin, Alfred, Alsey all sur-named Coleman...Daus: Elizabeth Robertson, Gilley Braden, Charlotte Nelson, Deborah Bailey..EXR: Son Larkin Coleman.. 17 Oct. 1843--2 Dec. 1843...Bk. A, p. 31...WIT: Alsey & A. D. Fuller, Jones Miller.

HOOD Robert--Wife Jane...Dau. Jenny Cunningham...gr. father Kelly Cunningham... EXR: Wife, son Thomas, friend John Cochran..20 Aug. 1796..A, p. 201...WIT: Thomas Richardson, Thos. Harris, John Cochran.

HOPKINS Solomon--Sons: Francis, John, Jeremiah, James...EXR: Wife, son Francis ... 19 July 1814--19 Apr. 1815...Bk. D-1, p. 198...WIT: James & Wm. McDonald, Jno. Smith.

HOPPER William--Wife Lettuce...Sons: Joseph, Samuel dec'd & his chn...Dau. Polly Brown...EXR: Saml. G. Williams, James S. Rodgers...19 Nov. 1830--17 Jan. 1831... Bk. F, p. 320...WIT: John S. Osborne, Samuel Irby, H. S. Beadel.

HORTON Enos, Enas--Bro. Rolphly..Neph. John Horton...Niece Mary Ann Horton...EXR: Wife Reobee...8 Sept. 1820--2 Oct. 1820...Bk. E, p. 90...WIT: Robt. Long, Richard Bonds, James Bell.

HOULDITCH William--Chn: 7-James, ?Lily, Zachariah, George, William, Lucy, Polly (last 5 min.)...EXR: Friends James & William Bailey...6 Aug. 1805--19 Oct. 1805... Bk. C-1, p. 74...WIT: Jas. Bailey, James H. Dendy, Jas. Young.

HUGHES Aaron--Wife Margery...Sons: William, Elijah...22 May 1806...Bk. C-1, p. 23.. WIT: Richard & Jesse Childers.

HUNTER Andrew--Land to bro. Robert...Andrew Hunter a horse...cows to sisters Elizabeth & Jane...a verbal will in form of conversation bwt. James Parks & Andrew Hunter & heard by Martha Miller & Margaret Parks...24 Aug. 1795...Bk. A, p. 141.

HUNTER John--Sons: William, John, Samuel, James & his son John B. a min...Daus: Nancy, Mary or Margaret McClintock, lands of Duncan ck (sons lands on Warrior)... EXR: Son Saml..6 June 1818--5 Mch. 1819..Bk. C-1, p. 36...WIT: Alexander Kirkpatrick, Samuel Mills; also Bk. E, p. 19 which names a dau. Peggy & gr. son Wm. Hunter.

HUNTER Langhlin--Wife Esther....Daus: Mary, Esther McDowall, Hetty Simpson, Margaret, Abigail...EXR: Thomas McDowall or McDonald, Jiles Cason...24 Feb. 1798-- 12 Jan. 1803...Bk. C-1, p. 20...WIT: James Young, Wm. Golighly, John Lyon.

HUNTER Matthew--Mother Elizabeth....Bro. James...Neph. Matthew Henry...Chn. of dec'd sister Mrs. L. Henry, viz: Robert, Elizabeth, Sarah, James, Matthew, Ibly, Nancy, Jane...EXR: Capt. John Hunter, William F. Downs...13 Nov. 1813...Bk. D-1, p. 139... WIT: R. Briswell, I. Dunlap, - Richardon.

HUNTER Matthew Senr---Wife Elizabeth...Sons: Matthew, Andrew...Daus: Margaret, Nancy, Betty Jean, Sarah..EXR: James McMahon Esq..Charters Nichels...12 July 1815 -- 8 Sept. 1815...WIT: Alexander Austin, Hugh & Samuel Leamon. Bk. D.1.

HUNTER Robert--Wife Isabella...EXR: Matthew Hunter, Andrew Parks, James Parks Jr...26 Jan. 1820--5 Mch. 1821...Bk. E, p. 148...WIT: Charlotte, Thos. Jr., & Wm. Fulton Sr.

HUNTER Thomas--"My chn."...EXR: Wife Maryann, son John...24 Feb. 1824--29 Oct. 1824...Bk. E, p. 426...WIT: William Nelson, Charles W. King, F. Richardson.

HUNTER William--Wife Mary with John, Matthew & William Dunlap EXR...Chn. to get education...21 Mch. 1802...Bk. A, p. 322...WIT: George Miller, Thomas Cason, Andrew Middleton.

HUTCHESON, Hutchinson William Sr--"Each of chn."..EXR: Son James...28 May 1804-- 10 Jan. 1805...Bk. C-1, p. 141...WIT: Wm. Hutcherson, James Fowler.

HOLLIDAY William--Sons: William, Robert, Matthew...Daus: Margaret, Nancy Rush or Rusel, Polly w. of James Mulaham..."all my chn"...EXR: Wife Jenny, son Robert... 12 Jan. 1822--14 Nov. 1826...Bk. F, p. 53...WIT: Philip West, M. Hood, R. Wait.

IRBY William--Sons: William, Joseph, James H., Samuel...Daus: Nancy w. of John Dice; Frances Cheek; Elizabeth Benham; Henrietta Cook; Sarah Clink...gr. son Irby Dunklin...EXR: James Irby...17 Sept. 1828--20 Oct. 1828...Bk. F, p. 179...WIT: Thomas Jones, William Davis, P. Farrow.

JOHNSON Abraham--Wife Anny...4 single chn: Andy F., Abraham, Mary, Jesse...Others: Sarah Munro, William, Andrew, John...EXR: William Neel Langston...19 July 1829-- 7 Sept. 1829...Bk. F, p. 234...WIT: Andrew Cable, John Hewitt, Wm. Haran.

JOHNSON George--Wife Martha...4 sm. chn: George Washington, Willard Simpson, Sara Ann, John Wesley...other chn: William, Abram, Margaret w. of John Miller Sr... EXR: Bro. Anderson Johnson...21 Feb. 1847...Bk. A, p. 93...WIT: Elihu Watson, Larken S. Monroe, Jesse ?Enterkin.

JOHNSON Jabez, Jubez W.--Chn: William, Jubez, Ann...EXR: Ann W. Johnson...6 July 1842--29 June 1843...Bk. A, p. 33...WIT: Wm. Donnan, Archilles Dendy, Jno. Godfrey.

JOHNSON John--Of Mudlick settlement...Daus: Janet, Agnes, Mary, Margaret...EXR:

Son Douglas, Charles Wilson, - McClintock...25 Nov. 1793...Bk. A, p. 84...WIT: William Fulton, James Wilson, John Wilson.

JOHNSON John--Wife Nancy...Chn: Ezekiel, Aaron, Lofton, Frederick, Isaac, Mary, Elizabeth, Katherine, Martha, Jennette...EXR: Son Isaac...3 Feb. 1844--15 Nov. 1844... Bk. A, p. 52...WIT: James Blackburn, George H. Brown, Susannah King.

JOHNSON Matthew--Son Thomas, dec'd...Daus: Elizabeth Barnett, Fanny Smith, Mary Grant...gr. dau. ?Ethaling Johnson...EXR: William & James sons...14 Nov. 1820 Prv... Bk. E, p. 98...WIT: Robert & Sally B. McNees.

JOHNSTON Abner--Sons: Jabus (Jabuz), Jeremiah, Joseph, Benjamin, George W...Daus: Turnely Neighbors, Mahala, Elizabeth...EXR: Wife Rebecca, friend-Beeks...20 Oct. 1826--4 June 1827...Bk. F, p. 112...WIT: Richard Cannon, Thos. Butler, Jas. Neal.

JOHNSTON Thomas--"youngest chn"...EXR: Wife Ann...23 Mch. 1813--4 Oct. 1813... Bk. D-1, p. 130...WIT: B. Nabers, James H. Lawry, William Burton.

JOHNSTON William--Wife Sally...fol. recv. legacies: Sally Monroe, Larkin Shepherd, Abraham Johnston, Elizabeth ?Guttery, John Munro min...4 Apr. 1798...Bk. A, p. 181... WIT: James & Isabel Gray.

JONES Abner--Wife Esther L...Sons: R. A. & J. M. "land on Durbin ck," & John H. Jones...Daus: Alethia w. of A. W. Harris; Mary Caroline Cooly; Sarah D. Westmoreland; Eliza...EXR: Sons Oliver H. P. & William R. Jones...12 Nov. 1842--13 Nov. 1853... Bk. A, p. 166...WIT: John Jones, Richard H. Vaughan, C. P. Sullivan.

JONES Elizabeth, wid. of Edward...Sons: Gabriel, James, Joseph...Daus; Frances Ward, Mary Burnside, Nancy Burnside (these get money)...fol. 7 get the est: Edward, John, Thomas, Elizabeth, Sarah, Mary or Margaret, Lucy...EXR: Sons Edw. & John...6 Apr. 1809--27 May 1809...Bk. C-1, p. 344...WIT: John Cook, Elijah & Nancy George.

JONES James--Wife Lucy...Sons: Benjamin, Miles, Whitemire, Jesse, Joseph..Daus: Angelia Philips, Jane Duncan, Sarah Bennett...EXR: Son Joseph...23 Oct. 1804--6 Dec. 1804...Bk. C-1, p. 127...WIT: George Whitmore, Joel Whitten, Elizabeth Wason.

JONES John--Niece Joyce w. of Robert Ward...Nephs. Jones & Moses Foster...EXR: Wife Joyce, friends Robt. Ward, Jones Foster...7 Sept. 1804--7 Mch. 1811...Bk. D-1, p. 38...WIT: Thomas Hill, Donel Shell, Samuel B. Shepard, Charles McGeher.

JONES Joseph--Sons: Joseph, John...gr. son Leander Duncan, min...legacy to Nancy & John Watson...EXR: Joseph Jones, John Watson...21 July 1826--7 Sept. 1826...Bk. F. p. 43...WIT: Benjamin Duckett Sr., William Duckett, George Smith.

JONES Joseph--Wife Margaret...."my chn"...Son Samuel...EXR: George Ball, James Neely...3 Nov. 1831--10 Nov. 1831...Bk. F, p. 367...WIT: John Ball, Nathaniel Nickle, Cornelius Puckett, T. B. Leeke.

KIRK, Keirk James--Son John & gr. chn: James, Sarah...S.L. William Brison & his 5 chn. viz: Robert, Sarah, John, James, June...Cousin James Keirk of N. C...EXR: John Kirk, John Hunter...30 July 1799--3 Mch. 1800...Bk. A, p. 231...WIT: John Puckett, Agnes Creswell, Daniel Chawleton (Charlton?).

KELLETT Joseph (Revo. S.)--Wife third pt. while wid. or until youngest ch. of age... Dau. Mary...Son John land along Indian Line...William land over Reedy riv...Div. bwt 4 youngest land where Hugh McHaffy lives, viz: Martha, Ann, James, Martin...EXR: Wife & son William...9 Oct. 1785...Rec. Bk. A, p. 4...WIT: Martin Mahaffy, Corn. McKent.

KELLETT William--Wife Aorna? land Greenville Co...Mother Gennet Kellet lands in Laurens...Sisters: Jennet, Margaret...Div. rest est. bwt. all my bros. & sisters...EXR: Mother...13 Aug. 1795...Bk. A, p. 140...WIT: Edw. Scarborough, Hannah & Jane Kellett.

KERN Elizabeth--Dec'd hus. John F. Kern...Sons: John F., Alfred A., dec'd son P. Daniel & his son Benjamin Daniel & gr. dau. Elizabeth Susan Kern...Daus: Louise
157

Lucy, Eugenia Caroline, Mary Ann Perry, Elizabeth Amelia ?Dason (Deason)...EXR: Sons John, Alfred...23 Mch. 1833--3 Mch. 1834...Bk. F, p. 530...WIT: John Whitmore, Thomas R. Ferguson, Benjamin Hill.

KEVIL Thomas--Wife Agga...Sister Mary Glazebrook...Bro. Benjamin Kevil...EXR: Friends John Westmoreland, Jack Teague...18 Jan. 1813--12 Apr. 1814...Bk. D-1, p. 149...WIT: Joseph Compton, John Edwards, Jinny Edwards.

KINARD Martin--Wife...Sons: H. H., M. T., J. P...Daus: Catherine, Elizabeth Sumner, Martha Garee (Gary), Sarah Dalyrymple, dec'd dau. Huldah M. Henson & chn.—requests that est be settled at Newberry...EXR: Son H. H. Kinard...14 June 1849--30 Aug. 1854.... Bk. A...Codicil 16 Oct. 1852 names gr. son Henry Oliver Henson..WIT: Jacob Eichelberger T. R. Pratt, Jacob Kibler.

KINMON, Kenmon James--Daus: Nancy Cook, Rachel Willison or Williamson...EXR: wife Elizabeth, son Thomas...28 Mch. 1815--2 Feb. 1818...Bk. D-1, p. 432...WIT: Benjamin & Nancy Arnold, George Grace.

KIRKPATRICK Alexander--"As chn. come of age"...EXR: Wife Susan, bro. Thomas, F.L. William Ligon...27 Dec. 1832--4 Feb. 1833...Bk. F, p. 469...WIT: R. Cunningham, R. Hooker, E. Kirkpatrick.

KNIGHT Ephraim--Sons: William, Ephraim, Joel...Daus: Polly, Lucinda...EXR: Son William...27 June 1826--14 Oct. 1826...Bk. F, p. 48...WIT: James & Levi Hill, Joseph Pollard.

LANGSTON Solomon-Wife Sarah..Sons: Henry, Solomon, Bennett..Daus:Amey Christopher, Leodicea Springfild (w. of Thos.), Sarah Miller, Selah Stily, Patty Jones...EXR: Sons: Henry, Solomon...25 Feb. 1810-15 Aug. 1825...Bk. E, p. 513...WIT: John Hitch, John Styles, Basil Wheat (Note: Leodicea, Revo. Patriot).

LEAKE Jeremiah--Wife Jane...Sons: William J., Jeremiah...Daus: Rachel B., Lucinda, Jane Emeline, Isabella, Margaret L. Bonds & dau. Jane E...EXR: Son Jeremiah...4 July 1851--1 Mch. 1853...Bk. A, p. 189...WIT: H. C. Young, B. R. Campbell, Wm. Mills Jr.

LEEK, Leake William Sr.--EXR: Wife Providence & sons Samuel & William...7 Jan. 1807--1 Apr. 1816...Bk. D-1, p. 277...WIT: James Holley, William Carter, Newman Gary.

LEEK George--Wife Margaret..Chn: Samuel, Johnny, William, James, Margaret,Malinda, Jinna, Alzira, Anne a min...EXR: Friends Jeremiah Leek, Samuel & Abner Young, also recv'd bequests..23 Oct. 1819--7 Feb. 1820...Bk. E, p. 61...WIT: Thomas Fulton, Mathew Hunter, Theris Odell.

LEEMAN Samuel--Sons: James, Hugh...Daus: Elizabeth, Mary Bryson, Jane Thomson, Sarah Austin...EXR: Sons Hugh & John, friend James McMahon...8 May 1819--13 Nov. 1821...Bk. E, p. 185...WIT: James & John Hollingsworth, James McMahon Jr.

LEONARD John--Mother Mary...Sister Nancy Pearson...Nancy wid. of G. Leonard... B.L. Ephraim Andrews...EXR: Friend John K. Griffin, neph. Allen Andrews...25 May 1810--26 Apr. 1823..Bk. E, p. 282...WIT: Charles Griffin, Mary Cole, Leonard Andrews.

LEWIS Ellinor--Bros. George, John & Samuel Dalrymple...Samuel's chn. viz: Ellinor & Rosanna; George's dau. Ellinor a min; niece Ellinor Davis; neph Thomas Davis & son John...Sister Rachel Smith & dau. Ellinor...EXR: Bros. John & George...11 Sept. 1787...Bk. A, p. 22...WIT: John Teague, David Mason, John Hill.

LIGON Susannah--Daus: Polly Holman, Susannah Grier..."div. bwt. all chn. or heirs"... EXR: Sons William,Joseph...28 Aug. 1827--15 Feb. 1828...Bk. F, p. 149...WIT: Anthony Golding, Reubin Hill, Eliza Ligon.

LIGON William--Wife Elizabeth...Chn: Thomas, Susan Milan, Patsy Carter, William, Daniel, Joseph T., Robert B., John W., George A. (last 4 youngest), chn. of James dec'd; chn. of Elizabeth Henderson dec'd...EXR: Son Daniel, Henry O'Neal, John Milan... 20 June 1847...Bk. A, p. 130...WIT: James E. Lockart, Aaron Wells, Thomas Nelson, Silas Walker.

LINDLEY Thomas--Sons: James, William 5 youngest, viz: Thomas, Aqula (Acquilla), John, Jonathan, Henry....Daus: Elizabeth, Hannah, Sarah, Mary Abercromie, Nancy Bolt.. EXR: Wife Elizabeth, sons James & William...18 Oct. 1808--Pvd. 6 Jan. 1810...Bk. D-1, p. 5...WIT: Charles Smith, Colvil & John Abercromie.

LITTLE Charles--Sons: Robert Henderson, James ?Clendier, Charles, David...Daus: Catty (Katy) w. of James Kirk & their dau. Sarah; Jean Taylor & dau. Margaret Wier; Ann Mary Bonds & chn. viz: Henry & Caroline of Ga..."minor chn"...EXR: Wife Ann, sons Robert, Charles..19 Sept. 1831--5 Dec. 1831..Bk. F, p. 373...WIT: Robert Creswell, Andrew Kennedy, Jeremiah Leek.

LITTLE David--Wife Charity..."chn"...Step-dau. Mary Farmer...EXR: Wife & Chas. Little...12 Oct. 1812--17 Nov. 1812...Bk. D-1, p. 94...WIT: Robert D. & C. Little, Robert Fleming.

LITTLE David--Wife Sarah..."Son George F. be equal with wife's other chn. had by John"...EXR: J. F. Dorrah...23 July 1850--13 Mch. 1852...Bk. A, p. 151...WIT: W. D. Byrd, E. C. Simpson, J. L. Williams.

LITTLE James---Wife Agnes....Chn: Robert, Mary, Isabel, James, William, David, Thomas....Cousins: Charles & David Little....EXR: Friend James Nickles, Col. John Simpson..29 May 1808--6 June 1808...Bk. C-1, p. 313...WIT: John Munro, James Simpson, David D. Grier.

LOGAN David--Son David...Daus: Polly, Hannah, Cate...EXR. & guard. dur. minority of chn: Angus Campbell, James Caldwell, Pat. Cunningham...Bk. A, p. 14...WIT: Reuben Pyles, Jacon (?Jason) & Mary Gibson.

LONG Elizabeth--"all my chn. consisting of 2 families,--the Mattox & the Long" viz: John & William Maddox(Mattox); Sally Gwin & her son John; Polly Simpson; Elizabeth Davis; Nancy Long; Reubin & Daniel Long & latter's 2 sons, Perry & Micajah..."Nancy lived with me & nursed me"...EXR: Thomas Garrett...9 Nov. 1831--16 Jan. 1832...Bk. F, p. 392...WIT: Ambrose & Hollingsworth & Bennett Garrett.

LONG Robert--Son Daniel...Daus: Susanna, Jane w. of Col. David Cole; Nancy Wier; Rebecca Cargil w. of Dr. John W. Cargil...EXR: John Kern, Dr. Thos. Wier...8 Mch. 1830...Bk. E...WIT: Robt. Owens, William W. Kennedy, Pascal M. Meadows.

LOWE William--Sons: James, Allen, Pleasant...gr. son William Lowe...Daus: Martha C. Crymes; Elizabeth w. of John Young & gr. son. James..EXR: Sons James & Pleasant... 20 Jan. 1844--23 July 1844...Bk. A, p. 20...WIT: James C. Bailey, H. C. Young, Henry Fuller.

McCAIN James--Son John...Dau. Mary...5 Aug. 1786...Rec. Bk. A, p. 3...WIT: John & Henry Hollingsworth.

McCARLEY Thomas--Wife Martha...gr. son Thos. Augustus McCarley...EXR: Son Alexander...13 Dec. 1839--23 Mch. 1840...Bk. A, p. 7...WIT: William & Alexander Power, & C. Williams

McCELLAR Bridget--Dau. Janie Dendy...EXR: son John...1816...Bk. D-1, p. 392... WIT: John Davis, Jno. H. Davis, B. H. Allen.

McCLINTOCK John--Sons: James, John...Daus: Peggy Hunter, Mary Mills, Martha, Betty Fleming, Nancy...EXR: Wife...12 Aug. 1796--1 Aug. 1799...Bk. C-1, p. 66...WIT: Margaret, John and James McClintock.

McCLURE William--Chn: William, John, James already had their pt..."other chn. equal"...EXR: Wife Ruth, son William...13 May 1806--7 Jan. 1822...Bk. E, p. 195... WIT: William Craig, William & John Brigg.

McCLURKEN James--Sons: Samuel, John, James...EXR: Wife Catherine...6 Jan. 1828-- 22 Jan. 1831..Bk. F, p. 323...WIT: Florence & Geo. Washington, Mancil Owings, Sam Cunningham, Sr.

McCONEHY (McConely) Samuel--Daus: Ruth, Amy Scott, Martha Bebe, Peggy Wilson...
EXR: Sons Joseph, James...29 Aug. 1818--2 Nov. 1818...Bk. E, p. 7...WIT: James Bonds,
James Murphy, Peter William Gautier.

McCRADY William--Son James..chn. of son John, viz: Jane, Mary Ann, Caroline....
EXR: Wife Mary, Son Robt. Carter McGrady...3 May 1826--19 June 1826...Bk. F, p.
30...WIT: William & Alsey Fuller, George Nickles.

McCRARY George--Chn: Elizabeth, Lucinda Furgeson, Frances Sheldon, Sara Owens
& Her chn. Robert & Sara, Sophy Smith dec'd & chn.: son Chastine, Edwin home place..
EXR: Edwin McCrary...1845...Bk. A, p. 71...WIT: Edmond Adair, Robert I. & James H.
Adair.

McCRARY Thomas--Sons: Matthew, Charles, Moses, Christopher, Andrew...Daus:
Elizabeth Young, Jean w. of Jno. Greer, Mary Catherine...EXR: Wife Letty, Thos.
Brandor, Geo. Young...9 Jan. 1790...Bk. A, p. 71...WIT: Thos. McCrary, Geo. Bush,
David Bailey.

McCURLEY John--Daus: Nancy Davis, Peggy Shirley, "as 5 single daus. come of age
or marry"...EXR: wife Polly, son George...6 Mch. 1825--11 Feb. 1826...Bk. F, p. 4...
WIT: Martin Graves, Nathan Long, Lemarcus Deale.

McDANIEL Archibald--Wife Mary...Wade McDaniel...Sons: Thomas, Matthew, Joel...
Dau. Elizabeth Moor...EXR: Elizabeth Brook, Jno. Burton, Jas. Boyd...5 Oct. 1825-
2 Jan. 1826...Bk. F, p. 2...WIT: Turner Richardson, Joel Weathers, Polly Strain, Jas.
Boyd.

McDOWALL Benjamin--Wife's dau. Patsey Jinnings in Ga. & Anton Jennings, carpenter
tools...30 Aug. 1790...Bk. A, p. 25...EXR: Wife Elizabeth...WIT: Reuben Pyles, John
Tyner, Pat. Riley.

McDOWELL James--Son James EXR...Dau. Jinny Blakely & her son Jas...27 Apr.,
1808--7 Nov. 1814...Bk. D-1, p. 170...WIT: Robt. Creswell, Wm. & Polly Atkins.

McDOWELL James--Wife Jane...Chn: Permelia Hollingsworth, Elizabeth Cannady,
Telitha Bryson, Jane Taylor, Isabella Martin...to wid. Jane McDowell & chn...EXR:
Friend C. P. Sullivan, son James, Jr...20 Feb. 1850--6 Jan. 1855...Bk. A , p. 203.
WIT: Edw. & T. W. Anderson, B. R. Campbell.

McGIN Dannel (Daniel)--Wife Catherine...Dannel Son of Wm. James...Rebecca & Mary,
daus. of Jas Caldwell...EXR: Jas. & Wm. Caldwell...30 Apr. 1806...Bk. C-1...WIT: Jno.
Griffin, Jas. Simpson, Jas. Hamilton.

McGOWN (McGowan) John--Wife Jane..."all my gr. chn."...These named: John McWilliam's
6 chn. viz: Wm, John, Saml, Patrick, Martha, Mary...Dau. Elizabeth Reed's chn:
Jonathan, David, Elizabeth, Martha, Jane...EXR: Son William, Jonathan Reed...27 Apr.
1829--18 July 1830...Bk. F. p. 276...WIT: Jas. '& Alex. Austin, Jno. C. Campbell.

McKELVEY John--Chn: James, George, Peggy w. of Jno. Dalrymple, Saml, Hugh, Jabez,
Thos, Rachel Alexander, Nelly, Polly, Isaac, ?Anna..."minor chn. share equal with
those written"...EXR: Wife Mary...29 Sept. 1824--5 Feb. 1827...Bk. F, p. 93...WIT: Jas.
Leak, Jr., Jabez McKelvy, Wm. Fulton.

McKITTRICK George--Wife...Sons: Saml, James, John...Daus: Isabel, Jane, Sarah,
Elizabeth...EXR: son Saml...19 Oct. 1844--12 Nov. 1844...Bk. A, p. 44...WIT: Jas. F.
& Wm. Blakely, Wm. C. Leek.

McKNIGHT Andrew, Sr.--Wife Abigaile EXR:...Daus: Abigail, Jennet...Sons: Andrew,
Archibald "land w. side Rabun ck"...8 Feb. 1787...Bk. A, p. 15...WIT: Martin Huey,
Ino Alexander, David Morton.

McMURTY William (Murtry)--Sons: Wm., Nathan, Campbell, Min...Daus: Jenny Bryson,
Susan Hall, Elizabeth McClussey...Wife Mary...EXR; Friends David Grue, McSeres
Easte...23 Feb. 1808--7 Mch. 1808...Bk. C-1, p. 298.

McNEERS (McNees) Robert--Sons: Saml, Richard, James dec'd...Daus: Susannah w. ol

160

Jno. Milner, Margaret Babb dec'd, Agnes w. of Joshua Teague, Sabra White...EXR: Jos. Babb, Jno. S. James...30 Mch. 1833--23 Jan. 1840...Bk. A, p. 1...WIT: David Dorrah, Jno. Phillips, Elijah Saunders.

McNEES (McNeese) Sally--(dau. of Chas. Allen, who md. 1st Cpt. Lewis Saxon).. "grave of hus. marked"...Daus: Clarissa Downs, Susan Thurston, Polly w, of Ira Arnold & chn. Ruthy, Tabitha w. of Benj. F. Cleveland & chn. Robt. L...gr. dau. Sally Arnold... to Elizabeth w. of Lewis Arnold of Ala...Sons(Saxons): Hugh, Joshua, Lydall, Allen, & his ch. Isabel Weatherall...Other sons: David, Charles...Trustees for daus. Clarissa & Polly were: W. R. Farley & Saml Barksdale...EXR: Sons Hugh, Joshua...25 Nov . 1847 ...WIT: Wm. Leek, Jas. McNinch, Geo. Saxon...Bk. A, p. 175.

McTEER Frances--Daus: Elizabeth, Frances, Margaret ? Olton, Mary Vance & chn. Saml & Wm...EXR: Bro. James Griffin, friend Jas. Simpson...10 Sept. 1803--7 Nov. 1803...Bk. C-1, p. 77...WIT: Alex. Simpson, Wm. Spears, Milling Olton or Alton.

McTEER William--Sons: Nathl, William...Daus: Margaret, Elizabeth, Frances, Jeane, Mary...Chn. & wife to "go to Nathl Vance," all prop. sold...EXR: Nathl Vance, Chas. Griffin...20 Mch. 1800--June 1800...Bk. A, p. 238...WIT: Jno. Simpson, Jas. Wallace, James ? Leffam.

McWILLIAMS Alexander--Chn: David, John, Andrew, Robert, Jane, Mary, Esther & hus. Wm. Crawford...EXR: Saml Leeman, Jno. Wiseman...30 Mch. 1813--7 Apr. 1813...Bk. D-1, p. 117...WIT: Jno. Wiseman, Andrw Hunter, Wm. Crawford.

McWILLIAMS Samuel--Wife Martha...Daus: Martha, Mary...Son Alexander land on w. Cane ck...EXR: son Alex...7 Feb. 1845--10 Mch. 1845...Bk. A, p. 48...WIT: Saml & Mary McWilliams, Jas. Ball, Wm. McGowan.

MADDEN George-- Wife Nancy....Chn: Nancy N., Lacklin L., Fanny, Sarah, Rebecca, Polly, Anny, ? Lewey, Elizabeth Wilbon...EXR: Wife, son Lacklin...3 Oct. 1842--28 Aug. 1844...Bk. A, p. 46...WIT: Wm. & Wait Graves, Thos. Dison.

MADDEN John--Wife Susanna...Chn: Charles, Abraham, William, John, David, George ? Martha..."rest prop. bwt. all my chn."...EXR: Wife, son George...20 Aug. 1795...Bk. A, p. 142...WIT: Richard Pugh, Ann Madden.

MADDEN William--Wife Sarah...Chn: Moses, ? Malso, Eliza Graden, Polly M., Sophia, Hulda...EXR: Sons Moses, Malso...13 Oct. 1849...Bk. A, p. 103...WIT: J. S. Coleman, Hampton Findley, B. F. Madden.

MAHAFFEY Hugh--Daus: Cynthia, Clarinda, "all my chn"...EXR: Friends Wm. & Hosea Mahaffey...31 Dec. 1846...Bk. A, p. 89...WIT: Lewis, Sanford & Cynthia Mahaffey.

MAHAFFEY Martin--EXR: Wife Mary, son Martin...Bk. A, p. 69...WIT: John McMahan, Elisha Hunt.

MAHAFFEY Nancy--Sons: Wm., Lewis, Hosea...Daus: Polly Babb, Sally Cunningham, Cynthia Nesbit, Unice...EXR: Son Hosea...7 July 1832--7 Feb. 1833...Bk. F, p. 466... WIT: James Y. Coker, Wm. T. Downs, E. H. Garrett .

MANLEY (Manly) John--Sons: William, James, John...Daus: Christiana, Jane...EXR: Wife Jane, son Jas...3 Apr. 1808--5 Sept. 1808...Bk. C-1, p. 370...WIT: J. D. Wright, Jas, McDaniel, B. Smith.

MANLEY William--Sons: Joseph, Washington home place..Chn: Ephraim, Vincent, Nancy, Jeremiah...gr. dau. Dedamia Evans...EXR: wife Elizabeth...11 Sept. 1788--1 Jan. 1801... Bk. A, p. 265...WIT: Joel Burgen, Thos. Burton, John Cochran.

MARTIN David--Wife Nancy...Dau. Levinia Frances Martin...EXR: son Addison P. Martin...30 June 1846--21 Aug. 1846...Bk. A, p. 54...WIT: A. L. Wilson, Wm. Rook, Jr., W. H. Dillard.

MARTIN Edward--Wife Mary...Trustees: Jno. Armstrong, Jas. Davis...Chn: Robt. Jefferson, Margaret Caroline...EXR: David Martin, John Armstrong, James Davis...18

Jan. 1845...Bk. A, p. 66...WIT: Edw. Martin, Turner Milan, W. A. Waldrop.

MARTIN Mary--"Fam. burying ground at father's place"...Friend Robt. Vance Trustee for my step-dau. Margaret Caroline Martin...Est. div. 3 pts. one pt to ea. fol: sister Cynthia Whitworth; William D. Watts in trust for sister? Artemasia Austin & her hus. Saml; Dr. Wm. Philips for sister Elizabeth G. & hus. Robt. Austin...EXR: Friend Dr. Anthony F. Golding...26 Aug. 1846--26 Oct. 1846...Bk. A, p. 56...WIT: T. G. & Rhoda Williams, Eliza Goodman.

MARTIN Reuben--Sons: Reuben, Joseph, Benjamin, Saml, Stephen, John...Wife Joanna... EXR: Sons Henry, Reuben...25 July 1808--5 Oct. 1812...Bk. D-1, p. 88...WIT: Stephen & Sally Garrett, Robertson Moore, Wm. Craig.

MASON David--Wife Isabel...Chn: Mary, John, James, Doritha Ellinor, Samuel, Hannah & chn. of last 3...Needley Davis...Mary Ann Gray...Abner & Saml Young..."ea. of my son-in-laws"...EXR: Sons John James...8 May 1820--20 Oct. 1829...Bk. F, p. 236...WIT: Joshua Teague, Nesby Davis, Elijah Teague.

MATHEWS John--Daus: Olley, Polly, Sally Garrett...EXR: wife Hetty, Jesse Garrett, Jr.. 27 Jan. 1826--1 May 18 26...WIT: Jno. Bolt, Tho. Parker, Andrw. Garrett...Bk. F, p. 22

MAYERS(Mayar) John--Put stone to grave of mother in Columbia...Cous: Rachel & Wm. Brown, Edw. Flannagan...EXR: Edw. Flannagan, Moses Leake, Thos. Craig, esq... 14 May 1829--9 July 1829...Bk. F, p. 230...WIT: Matt. E. & Nancy Cunningham, Sarah Carlisle, Dorcas Leake.

MAYHON Joseph L.--Wife Rachel...son Joseph...EXR: Friend Jas. Powell, son Joseph... 28 Feb. 1819--24 Apr. 1819...Bk. E, p. 25...WIT: Jno. Walker, Jno. Shaw, Isaac Reed

MEADOWS James--Wife Susannah...Sons: Reubin, Jason, ?Ichru...EXR: Wife...28 Sept. 1803--13 Sept. 1804...Bk. C-1, p. 128...WIT: A. Elmore, Reuben Jordan, Polly Saxon.

MEADOWS Mary--Daus: Susan, Polly, Elizabeth..."my husband's & son William's wearing apparel div. bwt. all my sons, viz: Wash, John, Henry, James, Warner, Morris"...EXR: Son Warner...13 Oct. 1827--3 Nov. 1827...Bk. F, p. 137...WIT: Henry & Elizabeth Neel, Thomas Young.

MEADOWS Reuben--Chn. Susannah Prather, Paschal, Polly Pearson, Martha, Reuben, James...EXR: Wife Hannah, son Paschall...9 July 1829--15 Sept. 1829...Bk. F, p. 238. WIT: Isham Milan, Robert Adair, H. S. Neel.

MEADOWS Susannah--Son Reubin & his dau. Anne; sons Jason & John...Dau. Ann w. of James Saxon, Esq...EXR: Son Reubin...18 July 1823--7 Aug. 1826...Bk. F, p. 38...WIT: James Bryson, Wash Meadows, Wm. Fulton.

MEDLEY Edward--Mother Sarah...Bro. James Medly's son Edward Newton Medley a min....Joel Walker's son Thomas Milton Walker a min...EXR: William Coleman...6 Dec. 1821--7 Jan. 1822...Bk. E, p. 194...WIT: John H. Coleman, Alsey Fuller, Jno. Hendley.

MEEK Jno--Chn: William, Betty, Nancy, Jenny, Samuel, John, James "share equally as they marry"...EXR: Wife Ellinor, Charles C. Neall, William Rowe...13 Dec.1802-- 6 Apr. 1803...Bk. C-1, p. 44...WIT: John Cook, Drury Sims, Benjamin Cason.

MEREDITH Henry--Son Samuel...Dau. Nancy Arnold...Mentioned: Fleming? Mosely, Thomas Waters, Broadwin & Permelia Waters, Sally w. of Benj. Martin, Jane w. of Wm. Bowen, Nelson Meredith, James Meredith's two chn. viz: Amealy, Henry...EXR: Son Samuel...15 Dec. 1842--3 Feb. 1843...Bk. A, p. 34...WIT: William Robertson, John H. Templeton, I. F. Dean.

MIDDLETON Answorth-Sons: Andrew, Thomas, John, James, Hainsworth...Daus: Margaret Hunter, Ann Williams, Judith Sarah, Jane...EXR: John Middleton, Matthew Hunter.... 1 Mch. 1798...Bk. A, p. 119...WIT: William Saxon, Thomas Roberts, James Cobb.

MIDDLETON Jane--dec'd hus...Sons: Andrew, Ainsworth "died in west, no heirs"...

Dau. Jane...EXR: Jane Middleton...8 Jan. 1823--4 June 1827...Bk. F, p. 113...WIT: Coleman & Gideon Carlisle, R. C. Creswell.

MILAN John--Chn: Bartlet, Isam, Wm. A., Henry, John, Milton, Leander I., Betsy Braddock, Ferrie Milan, & fol. Brysons: Patsy, Polly, Jimmy, Nancy...EXR: Feral or Ferrie & Leander Milan...13 Jan. 1857--21 Apr. 1857...Bk. A, p. 272...WIT: William Bailey, Joseph Vance, Robert Bryson.

MILLER Hanse--Youngest son Joseph home place aft. death mother, or if childless, to his sister Betsy, latter also gray mare giving her sister Ellinor 1st colt...Sons: John, Jacob, Jesse, George, James & s.l. James Huddleston...EXR: Wife Susanna & friend John Brown...14 Apr. 1788...rec. Bk. A, p. 7...WIT: Joseph & James Adair, Thomas Ewing.

MILLER John--Wife Margaret...Chn: Nancy Garret, Rachel Addington, Mary Harris, Matthew, Mark, Charles, Wash...EXR: William Hendricks...8 July 1846...Bk. A, p. 75. . . WIT: C. P. Sullivan, Wm. Hance, R. E. Todd.

MILLER Martin--Wife Martha..."all chn. equal with those who have recv'd..." EXR: sons Franklin, Albert...Mgr. of est: Jones Fuller...William Fuller to be schooled...6 Oct. 1827--7 Apr. 1828...Bk. F, p. 159...WIT: Solomon Fuller, Robert & William Bryson.

MILLER Sarah--Bro. Thomas Cason's chn. viz: William, John, Samuel & Elizabeth Buckwalter; Bro. William Cason & dau. Nancy; step-daus: Rebecca Cason & Mary Smith; Sally dau. of Sally Brooks; William Miller; cousin Jeremiah Cason...EXR: Stepsons: John Miller, Joshua Smith...19 Sept. 1828--3 Nov. 1828...Bk. F, p. 173...WIT: Fred Foster, Henry W. Garlington, Alfred Nance.

MILLWEE William--Dau. Margaret...Sons William & James div. home place....Wife Sarah to leave her est to "the child use her best"...Gr. son: Wm. Hudgins schooled... EXR: Wife & son William...26 Jan. 1784...Bk. A, p. 7...WIT: George Ross, James Henderson, William Irby.

MILNER Richard--"all my chn"...EXR: Joshua & James Milner...9 June 1812--3 Aug. 1812...Bk. D-1, p. 79...WIT: Drury Coker, Salathel Shaklee.

MIMS, Mimms John--Wife Martha & only child Charles Ellison Mims. If son leave no issue, one third to neph. Josiah Coggins, same to Sally dau. of Richard & Frances Sims, same to John Strobel Jr...EXR: & Trustees: John F. Carns of Laurens, Josiah Coggons of Newberry, John Strobel Jr. of Colleton Dist...2 Oct. 1831--20 June 1833... Bk. F, p. 466...WIT: Dave, Jesse & Rachel Felder.

MITCHELL Judith--Sons: Thomas, Charles, John, James all "Cobbs"...Daus: Suky Wilson, Susannah Owins...31 Mch. 1826--14 Oc. 1826...Bk. F, p. 46...WIT: James & Temple Cooper, Richard Gaines.

MITCHELL William--Wife Nancy...Chn: Permelia Pyles, Sinthey, Thomas, Isaac, Lewis (sons mins)...EXR: Isaac Mitchell, Wm. Dunlap, Wm. Burnside...15 Oct. 1808...WIT: John ? Casgillva, James Cook, Wm. Dendy...Bk. C-1.

MONRO(Munro) John--Wife Sarah...Daus: Jenny eldest, Sally, Betsy Nancy...Sons: Robert, Alex, Andrew, John (Shepard), Larkin youngest...EXR: Col. Jno. & James Simpson, David Green...WIT: Thomas Fakes, Thos. Witson(? Wilson), Geo. Miller...Prv. 4 June 1821... Bk. E, p. 163.

MONROE Jane--Three chn. now living viz: Margaret, Danl A., John H...EXR: Bro. Larkin S. Monroe & son Danl A. Monroe...22 May 1847...Bk. A, p. 86...WIT: Elihu Watson, Wm. East, James Joye.

MONROE Larkin S.--Wife Rebecca...4 chn...EXR: Friends Anderson Johnson, Elihue Watson...25 May 1849--30 June 1849...Bk. A, p. 107...WIT: William East, R. W. Vance,

James M. Oxner.

MONTGOMERY James--Wife Margaret...Rebecca w. of James Adair; Isabella w. of George Ross...names land in Greenville Co. & in Laurens on Harold Br. of Enoree orig. granted Wm. Lacey...EXR: s.l. Jas. Adair, wife...17 Aug. 1791...Bk. A, p. 52... WIT: John & Isabel Crag(Craig).

MOORE James--Chn: Jesse, James, Jinny min...Wife Valley & her chn...EXR: Cornelius Tinsley...22 Dec. 1805--25 Jan. 1806...Bk. C-1, p. 200...WIT: Jas. Holley, Joel Dendy.

MORRISON(Morison) Alexander--Cous. Alan McDougall...Neph. Alex. Turner...EXR: Benjamin Boyd, Maj. John Simpson...25 Mch. 1799--4 Apr. 1816...Bk. D-1, p. 289... WIT: Arch. Smith, William Boyd, John Luke.

MOSELEY George--(Revo. S.)...Wife Polly(Moore the 2nd w...1st was her sister Lucy)... Chn: George, Robertson, Fleming, Nancy, Tully, Sophia, Thomas, John, Eliza Austin, Elizabeth Moore, Polly Young, Frances Belcher...EXR: Robertson & Fleming Moseley... 10 Nov. 1823...Bk. E...WIT: John Walls, Wm. Ross, James Hunter, Saml Mills.

MOTES Jesse--Wife Sarah...Sons: Jesse Milford, ?Machlin mins..."all that rec'v nothing My lifetime on equal footing with those who have"...EXR: Sons Dendy & Hogan, Alsey Fuller...1 Aug. 1827--25 Aug. 1827...Bk. F, p. 124...WIT: Robt. Campbell, Joseph Willcut, Solomon Fuller.

MOTES Jonathan--Wife Susan...Daus: Dicy Ann Reynolds w. of Benj; Betsy w. of Chesley Motes; Minerva w. of John Pinson...EXR: S.l. Benj. Reynolds...30 Dec. 1845... Bk. A, p. 57...WIT: G. Thomas, Reubin Griffin, H. Finley Sr.

MUNFORD Hugh--Sons: James, Johnston...Daus: Nancy Finney, Margaret Scott, Hannah Bell, Anny...EXR: George Whitmore...30 Oct. 1802...Bk. C-1, p. 238...WIT: Thomas Gibson, William Law, William Dillard.

MUSGROVE Edward--Of Enoree, Laurens Co...Sons: Edward Banks Musgrove, William the home place & mill...Daus: Rebecca Cannon, Mary Berry...Wife Ann plant. lifetime "for self & her 7 chn. viz: William, Margaret, Ann, Hannah, Rachel, Liney, Leah"... EXR: Wife...25 Aug. 1790...Bk. A, p. 28...WIT: George Gordon, Alex. Morrison, John George.

NEELY George--Of Liberty Spgs. & Laurens Co...Dau. Agnes...EXR: Wife Anne, son James...1 July 1793...Bk. A, p. 82...WIT: Joseph Hollingsworth, Henry Hitt, John McCosh.

NEELY James--Wife Mary...Sons: Saml, James, George...Daus: Nancy or Mancy, Betsy... s.l. Joseph Jones...EXR: George & James Neely...19 July 1824--1 Aug. 1832...Bk. F, p. 421...WIT: William Tinsley, William Pollard, Jabez Johnson.

NEELY Joseph--Dau. Rebecca min...EXR: Wife Nancy, son Young...19 Oct. 1824--9 Feb. 1830...Bk. F, p. 255...WIT: Robt. Campbell, Jos. Willcut, D. Anderson.

NEELY Mancy--Wife Elizabeth...Two bros. George, James...Sister Elizabeth Neely... Saml Neely...EXR: Bro. George Neely...30 Sept. 1846...Bk. A, p. 101..WIT: B. T. Watts, I. M. Hill, W. T. Nealy.

NESBITT Samuel--Wife Mary...Chn: Nancy, James, William, Nathan, Demsey, Polly, Samuel, Thomas, Elizabeth...EXR: SON Wm...4 Aug. 1824--4 Nov. 1824...Bk. E, p. 425.. WIT: Drury Boyce, John Nash, Michael Dickson.

NEWPORT Jane--EXR: Dau. Rachel Feagin...4 Oct. 1805--5 Sept. 1814...Bk. D-1, p. 167...WIT: Archeble Young, Danl Wright.

NICKLES Nathaniel--Sons: Nathl, Scott, Robert, James, John (oldest...Daus: Elizabeth, Isabel...s.l. James McDowall...Bro. Wm. Nickles...EXR: Son James, Charles Nickles...

164

22 Mch. 1804--28 July 1804...Bk. C-1, p. 114...WIT: John Johnson, M. Campbell, James Hollingsworth.

NICKLE Chartis(?Charles)--Sons: John, Robert, James, George, William, Turner, Thomas(last 4 mins)...Daus: Margaret, Polly, Catherine, Ginna, Betsy, Naomi, Sally (last 4 mins.)...EXR: James McMahan, Joseph Hollingsworth...12 Sept. 1819--19 Aug. 1826...Bk. F, p. 40...WIT: James, Joseph, William Hollingsworth.

NICKLES Dr. John--Wife Jane...Daus: Catherine N. Holmes, Mary S. Anderson, Isabella Jane Wright...EXR: Dr. John W. Simpson...25 Feb. 1848--23 Oct. 1850...Bk. A, p. 123... WIT: Willis Benham, J. H. Lockhardt, William F. Martin.

NORRIS Thomas--Dau. Matilda Sadler..."all rest chn. by 1st wife"...Min. chn: Christopher, Felise, Imma, Lewis, Azel...EXR: Wife Sarah...12 Mch. 1833--2 May 1833... Bk. F, p. 488...WIT: Saml Cunningham, J. A. Cheek, Alfred Blackwell.

NUGENT William--Daus: Jane, Martha Elizabeth...gr.dau. Emily F. Owens...EXR: Wm. Blakely Jr...15 Sept. 1836--9 Mch. 1844...Bk. A, p. 28...WIT: Nancy & Nathl Day, Willis Hill.

O'Dell John--Wife Becky...Sons: Thomas, William, John...Daus: Elender, Margaret, Martha..bound-boy Levi Rogers..EXR: Thomas Henderson...20 Jan. 1830--1 Mch. 1830... Bk. F, p. 259...WIT: Stephen Hill, James Duncan, John J. Johnson.

ODELL Rachel--Daus: Margaret w. of Edw. Scribner; Mary w. of Thos. Scribner ; Elizabeth, Rachel...Sons: Thomas, Saml, Levi..."my int. in est. of Baruch Odell...tract of land in state of Ill. Shelby Co. to 5 youngest chn"...EXR: Friend John Odell...16 Feb . 1844--12 Mch. 1844...Bk. A, p. 52...WIT: Josephus C. Babb, Richard M. Owens, John Lusk.

ONEAL Anna Jane--(Hus. John Dec'd)...EXR: Son John Cook...21 Dec. 1808--21 Mch. 1818...Bk. D-1, p. 451...WIT: R. W. Owen, Miller Ligon, William Houlditch.

ONEAL John--Wife Anna Jean...Sons: Barney, William...Daus: ?Market(Margaret?), Jane...land lying on Muclick ck...EXR: Sons Barney, Wm...5 Jan. 1803--25 June 1805... Bk. C-1, p. 160...WIT: Charles Wilson, Samuel Weir.

ONEALL (O'neil) Hugh--Sons: Hugh land on Little Riv; Charles mill & house; Thomas land on Rabun ck...Daus: Patience, Ruth, Ann, Rachel, Elizabeth wife of Thos. McDaniel...4 youngest schooled...EXR: Mearm Babb, William Pearson, Elisha Ford... 3 Oct. 1797...Bk. A, p. 268...WIT: John Hunter, Thos. Wardsworth, P. McDaniel.

OSBORNE Daniel--Sons: Danl, William, Langston, ?Ress...Daus: Amanda w. of Wm. Martin; Polly w. of Jno. Martin; Thoeba Atkins; Elizabeth; ?Eaitha w. of Duke Pinson & gr. son John...EXR: Son Langston...1 Nov. 1822--25 Apr. 1823...Bk. F, p. 6...WIT: John Dunlap, Saml Farar Jr., Addison Pyles...(A dau. or gr. dau. Milly had md. bwt dates of will to Thos. ?Cose).

OSBORNE John--Wife Delphia...Sons: Robertson, Claburn, John & his w. Jane & chn; James & his chn; Nancy Barns...EXR: Thos. F. Jones...8 Mch. 1845...Bk. A, p. 80... WIT: Collier, Beverly & Alfred Barksdale.

OSBORNE William--Sons: John, Edward, Jesse W., ?Etsal...Daus: Polly, Pricilla, Ruthy...EXR: Wife Sally, son John, s.l. Jesse Osborne...24 Feb. 1817--21 Mch. 1817... Bk. D-1, p. 369...WIT: Mitchell Cook, Saml Goggans, John Drake.

OVERLY Meshack--Wife Mary...Sons: Nimrod, Nicholas, Benjamin...Daus: Mary Wells, Elizabeth Green, Anne Edwards, Joana Ross & her chn: Elihu & Mason...EXR: Son Nimrod, s.l. Ross Wells...14 Jan. 1801--2 Aug. 1816...Bk. D-1, p. 323...WIT: Joana Johnson, William Bucks Jr., Benj. Overly.

165

OWENS Daniel--Mother Mary...Bros: Thomas, Robert...Sisters: Jennet, Elizabeth, Anne, Martha Cabaness..."land I bought of Alex. McQuary"...EXR: Bro. Thomas...29 Mch. 1811--4 June 1821...Bk. D-1, p. 44...WIT: John & Elizabeth Owens, Mary Long.

OWENS John--Wife Mary,..Sons: Daniel, John Jr., Thomas, Robert...Daus: Mary Greer, Martha, Anne, Jean & Elizabeth mins...EXR: Daniel Owens, Jno. Finney...4 Sept. 1806-- 17 Nov. 1806...Bk. C-1, p. 241...WIT: Robt Long, Manasah & Jno. Finney.

OWENS John--Wife Elizabeth..."chn"...EXR: James Watts, Nathl Day...1 Jan. 1817-- 3 May 1817...WIT: Robt. Campbell, Wm. C. Ball, Rebec. Childs...Bk. D-1, p. 380.

OWINGS Pressley--Wife Margaret...Son Lanson to live with his M...EXR: Sons Abner, Lanson...10 Mch. 1836--3 Mch. 1845...Bk. A, p. 53...WIT: Robertson Moore, Stephen Garrett, Jonathan Jones.

OWINGS Rachel--Bros. William, Richard, Archibald, John(all Owings)...Sister Nancy Childs...Bk. A, p. 4...WIT: B. K. & James & H. E. Owings.

OWINGS Richard(Revo S.)--Wife Sarah...Sons: Richard, William, Archibald, John (also Jonathan but not named)...Daus: Rachel, Nancy Ann, Sarah, Polly Thomason, Elizabeth Studdard,..EXR: Sons Ricard, William...13 Aug. 1828--17 Mch. 1834..,Bk. D-1, p. 266... WIT: R. K. Owings, Turner Goldsmith, Lavinia Owings, (also Bk. F, p. 541).

OWINGS Thomas--Sons: John, William, David, James...Daus: Jane, Margaret, Rebecca... EXR: Wife Sarah, Son John...23 July 1800--23 Oct. 1800...Bk. A, p. 251...WIT: Rodger Brown, John & Minansah Finney.

PAGE John--Sons: William, John, James...s.l.William Carter...Daus: Betty, Frances , Jenny, Hannah...EXR: Wife Anna, son John...28 July 1803--7 Mch. 1804...Bk. C-1, p. 99...WIT: William Fulton, Betty Page.

PARK Agnes--Daus: Molly Stewart; Elizabeth Blakely; chn. of dec'd dau. Isabella Fowler; Nancy Simpson oldest dau. of my son Andrw Park; Nancy who md. Mr. Pearson; dau. of my dau. Sally Hutchinson...?Celema Brewer who lives with me... EXR: Relative Dr. Jno. Simpson...8 Jan. 1842--25 Mch. 1844...Bk. A, p. 51...WIT: J. D. Wright, B. A. James, C. A. ?Lewers.

PARK Andrew--Sons: William, James, Andrw. min...Daus: Isabella & Marcey Fowler, Nancy, Sarah, Betsy...gr.son Andrw Fowler min...Neph. Andrw. Parks...EXR: Wife Agnes, son James...2 Feb. 1809...Bk. C-1, p. 360...WIT: Robert Hutcheson, James Hunter, James Parks.

PARK James--Br. Wm...Sons: Andrw, John, William, Robert Hunter, Matthew Brown, Thomas Porter...Dau. Elizabeth...EXR: Wife Rachel, James & Andrw Park...11 Nov. 1825--25 Nov. 1825...Bk. E, p. 527...WIT; James Park, Andrew Kennedy, William Fulton, Andrew Spears.

PARKS Charles--Bro. Samuel...Sister Lucinda Parks & her chn, viz: Henry, Sarah, Blueford...EXR: Bro. John Parks, James Boyd...26 Apr. 1833-ŗ3 Feb. 1834...Bk. F, p. 524...WIT: James & Elizabeth Boyd, John Coates.

PASLAY(Pasley,Paisly) Robert--"Chn"...Dau. Martha Mitchell...EXR: Wife Elizabeth... 6 July 1818--1 Apr. 1819...Bk. D-1, p. 447...WIT: Asa Chandler, Absolom & William Bailey.

PATTERSON Joseph--Wife Rebecca...Sons: Robert, Joseph...1 May 1820--2 Feb. 1824... Bk. E, p. 358...WIT: Elizabeth & Saml Workman, William Ross.

PEARSON Joel O--Sons: William, Ephias...Daus: Mandy, Mahala w. of M. S. Scruggs; Nancy w. of Osborn Coal; Elizabeth w. of Joel Edwards...EXR: Wife Elizabeth, son Ephias...17 Jan. 1830--17 May 1830...Bk. F, p. 270...WIT: Joseph Brown, Isaac &

166

Nancy Cooper.

PERRITT Alfred--Wife Mary...Sons: Bryant, Thornberry A...Daus: Nancy Caroline, Sarah A. Ashmore, Abigail C. Ellison, Lucinda F. McDonald...EXR: Wife Mary, son Thornbury...28 Apr. 1845--3 July 1845...Bk. A, p. 47...WIT: Abram Machem, G. B. Riley, Thomas J. Sullivan(Wife Mary was dau. of Saml Bolling).

PETERSON James--Son Benjamin to get all not willed to gr.daus: Patsey, Ann, Susannah Peterson...EXR: Wife Ann...23 June 1799--2 June 1800...Bk. A, p. 237...WIT: John Watts, Wm. Roberson.

PINSON Aaron--Minister...Wife Elizabeth...Sons: Moses, Isaac, John...Daus: Jemiah Kennery, Mary Cole dec'd & chn. as they come of age...EXR: Sons John & Moses... 21 Feb. 1794...Bk. A, p. 159...WIT: John Henry, Aaron Pinson Jr.

PINSON John--Sons: John, Howard, Thomas, Aaron...s.l: Wm. Strain, Richard Duty, Cornelius Pucket, Thomas Weathers...Wife Betsy...EXR: Sons Howard, Thomas...26 June 1811--11 July 1811...Bk. D-1, p. 46...WIT: Robert Carter Sr. & Jr. Richard Puckett.

PINSON M. D.--Wife Elizabeth...Chn. Wash, Mary, Louise, Elizabeth, Joseph, Virginia, Martha, Alpheus...EXR: Geo. W. Sullivan...15 Oct. 1850...Bk. A, p. 136...WIT: Wm. A. Stone, H. D. Pinson, Ruth C. Madden.

PINSON Marmaduke Sr.--Wife Molly...Sons: Bicajah(eldest), Isaac, Marmaduke (youngest)...Daus: Edee, Sally Rucky, Hulsagh, Polly Strain, Ruth(Edee or Edith, 1st w. of Arch. McDaniel had a son Pinson; Hulda md. Jas Cunningham; Sally md. Wm. Madden; Abijah md. Sara Arnold; Marmaduke Jr. md Elizabeth Sullivan)...EXR: Son Bijah, Wm. Madden...26 Apr. 1820--6 Oct. 1820...Bk. E, p. 100...WIT: Isaac Dial, James Boyd, S. Cunningham.

PITTS Milton--Wife Mary...EXR: f.l. William Lovell...13 Nov. 1844--25 May 1845.... Bk. A, p. 50...WIT: W. E. Lindsey, Noah Johnson, Chaplin Lindsey.

POLLARD William--Wife Elizabeth...Daus: Matilda, Elizabeth...EXR: Sons Marshal, Alfred, William...15 June 1817--6 July 1817...Bk. D-1, p. 396...WIT: John Robeson, James Mitchell, Braxton Watts.

POLLOCK James--Wife Ann...Sons: William J; John & his chn. including James; Samuel & his chn...Daus: Gennet Henley, Isabel, Elizabeth Gray & her son James; Sarah Darymple & her son James...gr. dau. Ann Scott...Rec. 26 June 1793...Bk. A, p. 101.

POOL Elizabeth--Chn: William, Rebecca Patterson, Nancy Compton, Mary Coleman... gr. dau. Mary E. Moseley's part in trust by son Berry P. Pool...EXR: son Berry,.. 24 Sept. 1850--23 Oct. 1850...Bk. A, p. 121...WIT: W. S. Smith, Saml Mills, A. S. Hutchinson.

POTTER Thomas G.--Chn: Weyman H., Francis A., Thomas G., Allen T., George W., Moses, Mary H. Kennedy of Ga. & chn; Elizabeth H. Potter...EXR: Son Weyman...3 Feb 1842--16 Feb. 1842...Bk. A, p. 193...WIT: Wm. Young, Thomas Wier, John H. Kern.

POWELL Samuel--Chn: Thomas, Samuel, Elizabeth Bailey...gr.chn. Oliver Powell... EXR: Thomas & Saml Powell & s.l. Zachariah Bailey...June 1820--4 Oct. 1824...Bk. E, p. 418...WIT: James & Silas Bailey, Benj. James.

POWELL Thomas--Wife Lucinda...Sons: Thomas, Samuel, William, Robert...Daus: Margaret Delia, Marietta w. of David Goodman, Elizabeth, Nancy Bailey dec'd...EXR: Sons Thos & Saml, friend R. F. Simpson...Pvd. 3 Mch 1834...Bk. F, p. 539...WIT: Hugh Buster, John T. Woody or Weedy, Thomas P. Williamson.

POWELL William--(married more than once)...Chn: Wm. Wesley, Nancy, Elizabeth Gaines, Rhody, Peachy, Polly, Belinda, Milly, Virginia, ?Avoney...EXR: Bro. James Powell, s.l. Philip Waits...19 Nov. 1816--28 Dec. 1816...Bk. D-1, p. 343...WIT: David Brademan, Wm. Braden, Martin Norman.

PRATER(Prather) Ann--EXR: Son Israel, John Allen...12 Jan. 1834--4 Mch. 1834...Bk. F, p. 546...WIT: Saml Young, Moses Baty, John Roberson, Margery McMiller.

PRATHER Josiah--Wife Ann--Sons: Israel, Thomas, Jesse, Amos...Daus: Polly, Sabitha J., Deliliah, Rachel Ensley...EXR: Joseph Duncan, Thomas & Jesse Prater...6 Apr. 1822--18 Nov. 1823...Bk. E, p. 329...WIT: John & Josiah Atcheson.

PRATHER William--Wife Mary...EXR: Dau. Dorcas...3 Nov. 1788...Bk. A, p. 12...WIT: A. Gray, John Lindsey, John Wallace.

PUCKETT James--Dau.. Susannah w. of John Pinson & her son Joel; Jean w. of John Beasley & her chn. viz: Nancy, Chainey; Patsey w. M. Walker...son James min... Others: Richard, Dabney, Neeley, Jueen or Queen...10 Feb. 1796--20 Feb. 1800...WIT: Wm. Ball, Martha Avery, Meshack Avery...also 20 Sept. 1797--3 Mch. 1800...EXR: Wife Mary, son Wm...Bk. A, p. 229...WIT: Jno. Hunter, Wm. Dandy, Saml Leek.

PUGH John--Sister Elizabeth Gilbert...neph. Jesse Pugh...EXR: Wife Nancy, Wm. Gilbert... 2 Dec. 1815--21 Feb. 1816...Bk. D-1, p. 189...WIT: Thomas Roberts, John Hezzery, James Garrett.

PUGH Richard--Gr.dau. Nancy Cochran...4 step-chn: John, Wm, Saml & Margaret McClanahan...EXR: Wife Mary, Jno. McClanahan...10 June 1796--Bk. A, p. 148...WIT: William Boyd, Saml Mattles, John Cochran.

PYLES Abner--Sons: Newton, Milton, Adison "who recv'd prop. bef. he left here," T. Jefferson youngest...only surv. dau: Susannah H. Tribble & her chn...also named: Richard & Maryann Shackleford gr.parents of "my oldest dau. Matilda Teague dec'd & Matilda's chn. Elizabeth & Eliza"...EXR: sons Newton & Jeff...12 Apr. 1844...Bk. A, p. 87...WIT: W. T. Campbell, William Blakely, W. A. Waldrop.

PYLES Hewlett--Wife Nancy, pregnant...Chn: Estha, Diadama...EXR: Father John Pyles , bro. Nathl Pyles...10 May 1834--6 Sept 1842...WIT: Joseph Sullivan, Chas. H. & Wm. Simmons(orig. not in files Prob. Judge)...Bk. A.

RAGADALE Edmond--Wife Sarah...Sons: Peter, William, Edward C., John's two sons Robert & Thomas...Daus: Marinda, Ann, Jane...EXR: Edw. C. Garrett...9 Nov. 1848-- 6 Mch. ?1856...WIT: William Bolt, Sarah Saxon, Thos. J. Sullivan.

REAFS(Reass, Rees) Nancy--Daus: Betsy Pugh, Polly Yorke & her son Jonathan Allison, min...EXR: James Allison, William Pugh...3 Feb. 1808...Bk. C-1, p. 332... WIT: Nancy Wright, Danl Wright.

REED David--Chn: Jonathan, Elizabeth, David, Matthew...EXR: wife Elizabeth & bro. William Reed...11 Sept. 1815--29 Oct. 1815...Bk. D-1, p. 229...WIT: John W. Williams, John & James Nickles.

REED Mary--Sister Elizabeth Strain(Strange)...gr.chn: Mary, Caroline...EXR: William Reed, bro...28 Mch. 1831--16 Apr. 1831...Bk. F, p. 345...WIT: Katherine Whiteford, Letty King.

REEDER(Reader) Simon--Sons: William, Thomas...Daus: Sarah, Patsy, Charlotte...9 Nov. 1818--18 Nov. 1823...Bk. E, p. 328...WIT: Robert Long, Robert & Thos. Owens... Wife ment.

RICHEY(Ritchey) John--Wife Margaret...Dau. Jane Harris....s.l. Joseph Graves...Samuel Richey...EXR: son William & friend Martin Shaw...3 July 1819--8 Nov. 1819...Bk. E,

p. 41...WIT: David Caldwell Jr., Arch Holte, Owen Fuller.

RIDDLE John--Wife Mary...Sons: Harris, Newton, Melmouth, Berry, Fealden...Daus : Catherine Garner, Elizabeth w. of Elihu Garrett; Mary w. of John Cannery; Matilda C...19 Aug. 1850--6 July 1855...Bk. A, p. 209...EXR: Berry Riddle, Wm. Power...WIT: Reubin, Jeremiah, Fountain & Benjamin Martin.

ROBERSON John--Sons: Reubin, Toliver, John with w. Marah, also Menoah, William Barnett appear to be sons...Daus: Fanny, Peggy, Polly, Melley...23 Feb. 1802--19 Nov. 1803...Bk. A, p. 321.

ROBERTS Jacob--Sons: John, Isaac, Jacob, Thomas...Daus: Elizabeth Meadows, ? Allemon Brown, Sarah Gilbert, Morah Roberts, Claresy, Copey Gilbert dec'd & her chn. viz. Miledy & Lucinda...EXR: Wife Mary, Isaac Roberts, John Meadows...3 Jan. 1804--15 Apr. 1806...Bk. C-1, p. 217...WIT: David & Jno. Wright, Ezekiel Griffin.

ROBERTS James--Sons: James, George...Daus: Susannah, Mary Ann, Patty B., Sally Fuller...EXR: Richard Shackleford, William Bailey...23 Jan. 1801--30 Jan. 1801...Bk. A, p. 272...WIT: A. Rodgers Jr., Zachariah Motes, Peter Roberts.

ROBERTS James--Wife Sarah...Bro. Edward...EXR: Jacob Niswonger, "if he fails then James Crocker"...26 Jan 1816...Bk. D-1, p. 326...WIT: Jacob Niswonger, Wm. McFerson, James Crocker.

ROBERTSON Manoah--Wife Loucreacy...2 min. daus...EXR: William Owings...18 Nov. 1844--9 Dec. 1844...Bk. F, p. 55...WIT: John Garrett, Mary Owings, E. Hilton.

ROBIRSON William--Sons: John, Thomas, Robert, ? Isor...EXR: Friends Fred Burts, Wm. Green...1 Mch. 1812--21 Mch. 1812...Bk. D-1, p. 69...WIT: John & Joseph Cook, David Caldwell.

RODGERS Andrew--Sons: Abner, Andrew & his dau. Peggy Young; chn of my son William; chn of son John...Dau. Anna Frier...EXR: Son Abner...7 Dec. 1820--3 Sept. 1821...Bk. F, p. 175...WIT: James & Matthew Henry, John Leek.

RODGERS John--Wife Sally...Chn: James L., Lavinia Brownlee, Tabitha w. of Berry Martin, Jane...EXR: Son James, s.l. Thomas Brownlee, friend Charles Allen...20 July 1827--7 Apr. 1828...Bk. F, p. 160...WIT: Wm. Pitts Jr., Mary Reynolds, Henry S. Beadel.

RODGERS Sarah--Son James...Dau. Tabitha...gr.dau. ? Menima Martin...EXR: Friend R. T. Simpson...1 June 1832--20 Aug. 1832...Bk. F, p. 424...WIT: Saml Downs, C. W. & Jonathan Allen.

ROOK William--Wife Elizabeth...Sons: Saml, Thomas I., William...Dau. Catherine w. of Benj. Lyles...1 Feb. 1848--5 Nov. 1850...Bk. A, p. 129...WIT: P. C. Caldwell, Chas. C. Wells, John Suber.

ROSS Catherine--Chn: John, Jane, Sara, Francis, Elizabeth, James youngest...EXR: Son Francis, s.l. William Cowan...11 Oct. 1826--14 Nov. 1826...Bk. F, p. 52...WIT: Samuel Fleming, James & Alex Mills Sr.

ROWLAND Christopher--"personal prop. bewt. all chn"...EXR: Wife Mary, son Robert. 29 Mch. 1796...Bk. A, p. 153...WIT: Silver Walker Sr., Matthew LeFoy, Mary Rowland

ROWLAND Henry B.--"my chn. equal"...EXR: Wife Lettice, John Whitmore...24 Apr. 1828--12 Feb. 1831...Bk. F, p. 325...WIT: James Blackburn, Aaron & John Johnston.

RUNNOLD Joseph--Chn: Polly, Betsy, Anna, Lunorda, William, ? Pearly...EXR: Wife Elizabeth, John Cook...25 Jan. 1815--16 Feb. 1816...Bk. D-1, p. 332...WIT: Reubin

Goldin, Anthony Goldin, Joseph Jones.

RUSHING Aquila--Wife Mildred...Daus: Sarah, ?Higrah...EXR: Wm. Rushing, Joseph Owen...6 Jan. 1805--11 July 1805...Bk. C-1, p. 167...WIT: A. N. Owen, W. Hollingsworth.

RUTLEDGE William--Bro. John Knight...Uncle Joseph Rutledge..Sisters: Polly, Nancy... EXR: Joseph Rutledge, Cornelius Cook Sr....Pvd. 5 Jan. 1823...Bk. E, p. 222...WIT: Larkin Gaines, Betsy Gaines, Robt. T. Duff.

SADLER John--Mother Mary...Son Pleasant..."my chn"...EXR: Wife Mary, Pleasant Sadler, Lewis Ball...15 Sept. 1812--9 Dec. 1819...Bk. E, p. 43...WIT: Henry, Hitt, George Ball, Peter Ball.

SATTERWHITE Mary--Daus: Martha Hill, Sarah Whitlow...gr.dau. Mary Hill,..EXR: Sons John & James Mitchell...2 Mch 1820--27 Nov. 1824...Bk. E, p. 437...WIT: Elihu Creswell, Benj. Hatter.

SAXON Charles Sr.--Daus: Sally w. of John Rodgers; Polly wid. of George Anderson; Sally Allen McNees; son Lewis Saxon's wid...EXR: gr.son Charles Saxon Jr...named also, Tilly Anderson, Bailey Rodgers (prb. gr. ch)...WIT: Jonathan Downs, Ezekiel & Rebecca Mathews...2 June 1816--7 Oct. 1816...Bk. D-1, p. 336.

SAXON Hugh--Sister Susan W. Thurston...to Capt. Saml Barksdale in trust for sister Mary Arnold & chn. & niece Ruth Arnold...Neph. Hugh son of Saml Saxon dec'd...to Hugh Saxon Allison son of cous. Jane...to Mrs. Omey Stone...to Hugh S. son of Wm. R. Farley...prop. of est. of Polly Harris & John L. Harris...aunt Cynthia Williams dec'd & her chn: Monima Brooks, Matilda Little, Nancy Parks...Uncle Lyddall Allen & chn: Frances Allen, Lucy Arnold(others were: Jonathan, Isaac, Cynthia N, Chas W., Mary D., Sarah)...Clarissa Downs dec'd...names mother as living...niece Mary w. of Henry Sullivan...EXR: Bro. Joshua, friend Willis Wallace...11 Nov. 1851...Bk. A, p. 142... WIT: Geo. W. Connors, N. Barksdale, Jeremiah Glenn.

SEURLOCK(Scurlock) Ann--Daus: Frankey, Dolly...2 gr.sons, Reubin & Joshua Scurlock... EXR: Friend Lewis Banton...18 Sept. 1796...Bk. A, p. 165...WIT: Sarah Arrowood, Chester Ware, Claborn Goodman.

SEILLION Hugh--Daus: Jane, Amey, Patsy...EXR: Wife Jane...July 1806...Orig. not in J. P. Of. but recd. Bk. D-1, p. 325...WIT: Basil & Keziah Prater, Z. D. Keron.

SHEA Patrick P.--EXR: Wife Elizabeth, Robt. Campbell...8 Oct. 1815--7 Aug. 1817... Bk. D-1, p. 407...WIT: Jno. Roberson, Martin Shaw, David Madden.

SHEARS Jude--Son Saml...EXR: Dau. Lethere...22 June 1830--15 Oct. 1830...Bk. F, p. 285...WIT: Ursula Brooks, Thos. Harris, Meliona Crocker.

SIMMONS Charles--Chn: Sarah, John, Mary McCas, with fol. minors: Charles, William, Elizabeth, Jean...EXR: Wife Elizabeth & son John...7 July 1791...Bk. A, p. 47...WIT: Joshua Downs, John Rodgers, James Floyd.

SIMMONS Elizabeth--(dec'd hus. Charles)...Sons: William, John, Charles...Daus: Sally Madden, Elizabeth Smith, Jane Franks...EXR: John Garlington...27 Mch. 1822--7 Oct. 1833...Bk. E, p. 338...WIT: John Dunlap, Henry C. Young, R. F. Simpson.

SIMPSON Alexander--Sons: John, James...Daus: Mary Hutcheson, Margaret Glenn, Agnes Dunlap, Elizabeth, Sarah...EXR: Sons James & John, Saml Austin...13 Apr. 1811--5 Sept. 1814...Bk. D-1, p. 165...WIT: John Blake, Ann Haron, John Sheer(Shear).

SIMPSON John--Wife Sarah...Sons: William W., John, Richard F...Daus: Jane & hus. John Nickles; Mary & hus. Capt. Anthony Griffin; Kitti & hus. Major R. Griffin; Nancy & hus. Major Thos. Wright...sister Agnes...Bros: Alexander, James...EXR: Sons W. W. & J. W. Simpson...13 Feb. 1815--2 Oct. 1815...Bk. D-1, p. 218...WIT: Ezekiel

North, Rover Gray, John Felts.

SIMPSON John--Wife Harriet...Chn: "equalpts."..EXR: Henry R. Shell...17 Aug. 1846...
Bk. A, p. 106...WIT: James & Joseph Hipp, Isaac Lovelace.

SIMMS Charles--Chn: George R., James D., Judith, Lucy Ann, Pelina C...EXR: Wife
Sarah, Clough Shelton, Bernard Glenn...25 Apr. 1813--1 Nov. 1813...Bk. D-1, p. 131....
WIT: John McCoy, Benj. Saunders, Danl Long.

SIMMS Francis--"my chn. & their heirs" viz: Starling; William; Chn of Elizabeth
Gidding viz: Wm. C., Jno. L., Elizabeth I.; Haney Fowler; Priscilla Cheek; Polly
Walker...EXR: Son William, s.l. Willis D. Cheek...4 June 1845...Bk. A, p. 128...also
named a gr.dau. Elizabeth ?Geons...WIT: Wm. Jones, R. S. Woodruff, Danl Lanford.

SIMS William--Wife prop. dur. wid.hood or until youngest ch. of age...Chn: Nathan,
Ann, Reubin, Simpson, Rhoda, John, Messor Babb Sims(confused)...EXR: Wife Rebecca,
Fred K. Burts...20 June 1805--10 Sept. 1805...Bk. C-1, p. 173...WIT: John Sims Jr.,
Lewis Graves, M. Burts.

SMITH Drury--Sons: George, James, John & "rest of chn. viz: Elliott, William, Sarah,
Elizabeth Cheek, Mary Ford"...EXR: Wife Sarah, John Smith...12 Aug. 1797...Bk. A,
p. 182...WIT: Danl Ford, Henry Vaughan.

SMITH John--EXR: Wife Susannah...20 Nov. 1807--15 June 1816...Bk. D-1, p. 312...
WIT: Nelson Sanders, John Smith, R. M. Owen.

SMITH Lucy--Daus: Sarah McNeese, Mary Harris...Son Charles Allen money due me
in Virginia, said Chas. to pay: to Sally Atkins, dau. of Lydall Allen for Schooling;
to Frances & Cynthia Allen, daus. of Lydall...to gr.son Joel Allen...to Milly wid. of
Lydall Allen...to gr.dau. Sara Crisp & her dau. Lucy...to gr.daus. Lucy Bacon Allen,
& Harriet Saxon...EXR: Son Charles...9 Feb. 1826...Bk. F, p. 250...WIT: Colvill
Abercromie Jr., Mary Marshal, E. S. Roland(apparently Lucy Smith was the former
Lucy Bacon who md. as 1st hus. Chas. Allen Sr.)

SMITH Robert--EXR: Son William...29 June 1817--16 Feb. 1818...Bk. D-1, p. 434-435..
WIT: John W. & James. Smith, Saml Kennedy.

SMITH William R.--"All my chn. & their Heirs"...chn of dec'd son Marshall...EXR:
Sons Ezekiel & Archibald Smith...24 Sept. 1850--7 Apr. 1857...Bk. A, p. 271...J. H.
Irby, C. C. Higgins, W. B. Henderson.

SOUTH William--Wife Cathy(Catherine Daniel)..Sons: Daniel, William, John, Gabriel,
James, Zedekiah dec'd & left wid. Ruth & chn...Daus: Nancy(w. of Wm. Hall) & her
chn. Wm. Fr. & Patsy Robertson; Rachel(w. of Jesse E. Clardy); Hannah(w. of Jno.
Norwood); Sarah(w. of Reuben Hall)...EXR: Son Gabriel, s.l. Jesse E. Clardy...2 Sept.
1842--5 Aug. 1844...Bk. A, p. 38...WIT: Philip Waite Sr., John C. Hall, R. L. Waite.

SPEIRS(Spears) William--Wife Elizabeth...Son Andrew & his sister..."all my chn"...
EXR: Son William...10 Jan. 1845...Bk. A, p. 100...WIT: J. P. Hutcherson, M. B. Sheldon,
John Stewart.

STARNES Ann--Sons: Aaron W., Ebenezer, John...Daus: Molly Murphy, Ann Jones,
Rachel Hughes, Rebecca Sims...28 Nov. 1800--1 Oct. 1802...Bk. C-1, p. 4...WIT: Rachel
& David Anderson.

STARNES Ebenezer--Sons: Aaron, Ebenezer, John...Daus: Mary, Ann, Rachel, Rebekah...
EXR: Wife Ann, son Aaron...4 Nov. 1789--Bk. A, p. 24...WIT: Saml Wharton, John
Field, Roger Murphy Jr.

STARNES Mary Ann--Chn: Moses, chn. of dec'd son John; chn. of dec'd dau. Ann
Sherby; Susan w. of Berryman Sherby; Rebecca w. of Lewis Graves; Elizabeth w. of

Aaron Hill; Sarah w. of Isaac Edings...EXR: Martin Shaw, friend...20 May 1843...
Codicil 28 Jan. 1851...Bk. A, p. 256...WIT: Joel Laidson, Asa Fogy, James McPherson...
Codicil names Mary w. of Wm. Cobb, apparently a dau; gr.son Joel son of Ann Sherby
dec'd & Mary Berry sister of Joel.

STEVENS John--Sons: John, James, David, Solomon...Daus: Janey, Elizabeth, Mary...
EXR: Wife Mary...8 Aug. 1793...Bk. A, p. 81...WIT: Zachariah Bailey, Elizha, Wiles..

STEWART Francis--Chn: William, Robert, John Allen, Mary...Mother of these chn:
Sarah Lipp Stewart...EXR: Friends Wm. Blakely son of Wm. Blakely, James L. Young...
6 May 1845...Bk. A, p. 63...WIT: Alex & Hugh McKeby, John Dalrymple.

STIMSON(?Simpson) Enos--Adopted dau. Mary Simpson all prop...EXR: Friend & Neighbor Saml Wharton...7 July 1798--8 Dec. 1800...Bk. A, p. 262...WIT: Thos. & John
Davenport, Benj. Watson.

STONE John--Sons: Rolley, Lewis, William, Reubin, Elin(?Elam...Dau. Nancy...EXR:
Wife Mildredge (Mildred), son Rolley...25 Jan. 1797--17 Mch. 1800...Bk. A, p. 253...
WIT: Danl & H. Wright.

STONE John--Chn: John, George, Janey, Polly Kennedy(youngest daus: Polly, Fanny)...
EXR: Rev. Zachariah Arnold, Dr. F. Conn...30 Aug. 1826--6 July 1827...Bk. F. p.
117...(John Stone renounced all claim to house at Mineral Spring, purpose of spring
bathing)WIT: Geog. & John Comer, Gable Trenton.

STRAON(Strain, Strange) David--Sisters: Susanna, Jane...EXR: Susanna Strain...20 Oct.
1831--8 Nov. 1831...Bk. F, p. 363...WIT: David Strain, Andrw. Rogers, Wm. Green,
Nathl Nickle.

STRAIN James--Sons: David, John, William...Dau. Susannah...Dau. & s.l. Ferguson...
EXR: Wife Jane, son David...9 Oct. 1812--14 June 1813...Bk. D-1, p. 104...WIT: James
Nichols, Jonah Johnson, R. Campbell.

STWART(Stewart) John--Oldest son Francis...y.dau. Nelly...s.l. David Stodard...EXR:
Charles Little...3 Jan. 1806--4 July 1806...Bk. C-1, p. 225...WIT: James Brown, Joseph
Vance.

SULA William--Son Geo. Moore Sula...wife Sarah...5 Aug. 1840--11 Sept. 1840...Bk.
A, p. 7...WIT: John Wm. Simpson, M. Garlington, Richard Denron.

SULLIVAN Joseph--Wife Temperance...Bro. Thos. Jefferson Sullivan prop. in trust
for wife permitting her reside on land, get toll of mills & labor of slaves...Chn:
Milton A., Wm. Dunklin, Chas. Pleasant, John H., Kezziah McCullough, Mary Ann
Eppes, Malinda C., Temperance(latter gets land including "the Hickory Tavern")...
Bro. Geo. Wash Sullivan trustee for son Milton, minor who gets land bounded by
Andrw. McKnight, Jno. Bolt, Willis Cheek, Pleasant Shaw, Jno. Mears, Christ'pr Posey...
all chn. to be educ...EXR: Bro. T. Jefferson Sullivan...WIT: E. B. Gambrell, W. H. &
Thos. Manly...27 May 1846--12 Nov. 1849...Bk. A, p. 109.

SUTHERLAND Joshua--Son Samuel & "rest of family"...EXR: Wife Eleanor, Wm. Leak,
Andrew Rodgers...28 Apr. 1801...Bk. A, p. 298...WIT: Elijah Edwards, Martha Leak,
Andrew. Rodgers.

SWAN Timothy--Son Alexander...Daus: Rebecca, Isabella...EXR: Wife Sarah, friend
Wm. F. Downs...21 July 1816--7 Oct. 1816...Bk. D-1, p. 338...WIT: James Hutchinson,
John Simmons, David Sloan...Mother named.

SWINDLER(Swindle) Michael--Sons: John, Daniel, George...Daus: Deliah, Susy Saxon...
EXR: Bro. George, Aaron Cloar...3 July 1809--8 July 1815...Bk. D-1, p. 210...WIT:
Philip Wait, Wm. Washington, Jones Box.

TANNEY John--EXR: Wife Elizabeth...Nieces: Peany Raney, Susannah Taney...4 Sept. 1798..Bk. A, p. 202...WIT: Thos. Honor, Ambrose Johnson, John Gamble.

TAYLOR Alexander--Wife Margaret...Daus: Jane, Margaret, Hannah, Catherine Ransom, Mary...gr.son Alex McCarley...EXR: Sons Robert, John, James...25 Dec. 1821--22 Feb.. 1822...Bk. E, p. 203...WIT: Wm. Cowan, Charles & William Taylor.

TAYLOR James--Mother Martha...Bros: Samuel, chn of bro. John ,dec'd...also ment: Mary w. of Hugh Workman, Jane Goodwin, Robert Taylor, Elizabeth w. of Wm. Speers... 19 Oct. 1843--13 Nov. 1843...Bk. A, p. 30...WIT: J. C. Wright, J. H. Irby.

TAYLOR John--Wife Barbara...Sons: Alexander, William...Daus: Barbara, Mary & step-dau. Rebecca...EXR: Alex Taylor, Wm. Cowan...22 Feb. 1818--5 Mch. 1818...Bk. E, p. 18...WIT: James Hutcherson, William Young, Hugh Crooks.

TAYLOR John--Wife..."all my chn."...6 Apr. 1833--2 June 1833...Bk. F, p. 489...WIT: Nathl Day, Samuel Templeton, Saml Taylor Jr.

TAYLOR Margaret--Sons: James, Robert...Daus: Jane Chambers, Catherine Roberson, Margaret, Hannah..."to Alex. McCorley"...EXR: John & James Taylor...21 Nov. 1829--

5 July 1830...Bk. F, p. 273...WIT: Robt. Caldwell, Saml Pearson, Sterling Tucker.

TAYLOR Martha--Chn; Robert, John, Samuel, James, Elizabeth Speers, Jane Goodwin, Mary Workman...EXR: Saml Taylor Sr...14 Feb. 1831--12 Oct. 1843...Bk. A, p. 29... WIT: John & Henry Taylor, Nathaniel Day.

TAYLOR Robert--EXR: William W. Sloan...Fol. appear to be chn: Margaret w. of Julius Martin; William Taylor's son William I; John, James, Jane...3 Apr. 1843--26 Sept. ?1851...Bk. A, p. 139...WIT:--Taylor, John & James Goodwin.

TAYLOR Robert--Sisters: Kitty Goodman, Rebecca w. of Humphrey Willis & their chn: Sally Goodman...Bro. Bluford...EXR: Duke Goodman...25 Oct. 1851...Bk. A, p. 147... WIT: James Parks, J. J. Atwood, W. D. Watts.

TAYLOR Samuel--Sons: Andrw, Kennedy, John, David, William dec'd...Daus: Martha, Margaret, Katherine w. of Robert Taylor, Mary Ann.w. of Joseph McCullum, Nancy w. of Wm. Taylor, Jane...EXR: Wife Jane, son David...3 Jan. 1842--3 Nov. 1843...Bk. A, p. 15...WIT: Andrew Kennedy, Thomas & Feril Milan, relative Robt. Gilliland.

TEAGUE Elijah--Sons: Robert, heirs of son Joshua...Daus: Elizabeth Hipps, Sarah McAdams, Mary Wilson, Catherine McAdams, Rebecca Teague...EXR: Son Abner, s.l. Joseph Hipps...2 Oct. 1824--18 Apr. 1826...Bk. F, p. 20...WIT: Elijah Teague, Charles Mchesky, John Miller.

TEAGUE Joshua--Lands from Wm. Caldwell & John Lewis, one line being Indian creek... Sons: Israel, Elisha, Isral, Abner, James...Daus: Isabel Mason, Sophia Lyon, Susan ?Mafer, Mary Adam...s.l. Wm. Gray...EXR: Sons Elijah, Israel...12 May 1804-- 2 May 1808...Bk. C-1, p. 308...WIT: Nathan Jones, Thomas Dalrymple Jr. & Sr.

TEMPLETON David--Sons: David, James, Robert, William, John...Robt. Hanna & gr.son David Hanna...EXR: Dr. George Ross, Creek William Craig...19 Apr. 1817--2 June 1817...Bk. D-1, p. 390...WIT: William Craig, James Templeton, Hezekiah Rice.

THOMAS Isaac--Sons: Evan, John, ?Jeremiah, William yg., Edward, Isaac, Abel the 3 ods sons...yg. daus: Sarah, Phoebe; ods. daus: Mary Weisner, Elizabeth Cox...EXR: Wife Mary, son John...4 June 1802...Bk. C-1, p. 164...WIT: Jacob & Mary Weisner.

THOMASON Nancy--"my 5 chn", named are James D., Cathy P., both min., Polly & Step-dau. Nancy Thomason...s.l. Wm. Thomason EXR...27 May 1837...Bk. A, p. 211... WIT: M. P. Evins, William Studdard, Gideon Thomason.

173

THOMPSON Henry--Chn: Rebecca Richey, John, Polly, Nancy, Jenny, James...EXR: Wife Catherine, son John...17 Feb. 1825--4 Dec. 1833...Bk. F, p. 503...WIT: Martin Shaw, Menoah Forgy, Joseph Irby.

THREAT(Threet, Thweatt) Sarah...Hus. Reuben...Son Tom..."5 young chn"...EXR: John & Robert Dunlap...5 Apr. 1819--6 Sept. 1819...Bk. E, p. 38...WIT: John H. Davis, Robert Bell, William Brown,

TINSLEY Abraham--Son William...Daus: Sarah, Mary..."pay Joseph Cason from money collected from Chas. Huet"...EXR: Bro. James, wife Nancy, f.l. Henry Johnson...5 Jan. 1804--5 Feb. 1810...Bk. D-1, p. 8...WIT: Frances Stewart, George Dalrymple, Elijah Teague.

TINSLEY Cornelius--Daus: Patsy Weeks, Betsy Tribble...gr.son Corn. Tinsley...EXR: s.l. Jeremiah Tribble...3 Dec. 1817--8 Dec. 1817...Bk. D-1, p. 423...WIT: Saml Vance, John Dendy, J. Underwood.

TINSLEY Zachariah--"raise & educ. chn"...EXR: Wife Betsy, John Dendy...25 Mch. 1830--18 Nov. 1830...Bk. F, p. 286...WIT: Abner Pyles, Joel Dendy, Saml Vance.

TODD Andrew--"Wife"...Daus: Letitia, Margaret...EXR: Saml B. Lewers & s.l. Enoch Agnew...6 Aug. 1835--4 Dec. 1843...Bk. A, p. 23...WIT: Joseph Cooper, James Dorrah, Charles Smith.

TODD John--Wife Nancy...Sons: James, Charles, Robert, John...Dau. Mary...s.l. Robt Bryson...22 Jan. 1821--4 May 1821...Bk. E, p. 162...WIT: Wm. McClonahan, Jas. Todd, John Hobbs.

TODD Patrick--Wife Jane, at death div. est. 7 pts...Sons: Ar 'har, William, ndrew, Dr. Patrick, James & his chn., John & 2 chn. viz: Martha Winn, Pat Todd ? lf-bro. of Martha..Daus: Jane McCall; chn. of dec'd dau. Ellen 1. McFall...EXR: John D. Williams, son Dr. Patrick...15 June 1852--11 Dec. 1852...bk. A, p. 151...WIT: Wesly Smith, Francis Hill, John H. Goodman.

TODD Samuel--Bros. John, Andrew...sister Jane Hamilton...nephs. Saml & John Hamilton & Saml Todd...nieces Martha Hamilton, Eliza'eth & Jane Todd...1818-1830...Bk. E.... EXR: Samuel B. Luers(Lewers).

TODD S.T.H--Bros: Robert E., William W., James R.--"all my bros. & sisters includ- ing chn. of dec'd sister Mary W. Higgins"...mother a legacy...EXR: Robert E. Todd... 6 Aug. 1843--30 Dec. 1844...Bk. A, p. 45...WIT: C. P. Sullivan, E. W. Simpson, Robt. Thompson.

TOMPSON(Thompson) William--Wife Nancy...Sons: William, Abraham & son Wm... Daus: Molly, Elizabeth Lemon, --Williamson...EXR: Anthony F. Yelding..11 Nov. 1826-- 22 Dec. 1827...Bk. F, p. 137...WIT: Sally M. Hall, Cynthia Armstrong, Martha Cheppbell (Chapel).

TOMPSON(Thompson) William--Chn: Sarah Ann, Isabella, Elizabeth, Nancy, Jane, Mary..."young chn. equal to those md."...EXR: Wife Jane, John W. Perry(Penny)...23 Sept. 1836--18 June 1840...Bk A, p. 2--also Bk. F, p. 2...WIT: John, Allen & Wm. Coleman.

TUCKER Lavinia--Bros: David & Ezekiel Higgins...Chn. of sister Lavinia Rofs...sister Haney & hus. James B. Higgins dec'd & chn...William son of sister Nancy Fowler... Elizabeth w. of James French...neph. Benj. B. Higgins..."balance bwt. bros. & sisters"... EXR: James B. & Benj. B. Higgins, b.l. & neph...17 Dec. 1842--Codicil 24 Dec. 1845 (She was apparently wid of Genl Wm. House Tucker & bwt. 75-80 yrs. old. Statements from Joseph Prior who talked with her 14 Mch. 1837, Wm. Fowler in 1850 & Wm. Powers in 1855)...Bk. A, p. 230

TURK Mary--Bros. & sisters: Hannah Pitts & chn. & bro. Henry Pitts...Jean & James Bolen & chn...Ordery & Jonathan Motes & Chn., one being Joseph...bro. Benj. Collier's chn...neph. Jos. Motes chn. Mary, John...EXR: Sister Ordery's son Joseph Motes, friend John Simpson...16 July 1799...Bk. A, p. 217...WIT: Wm. Rason, Zachariah Motes, Archibald Sayers.

TURK Rachel--Bros: Archibald & Matthew McDaniel & sister Margaret McDaniel; neph. Matthew O'Daniel, min...16 July 1797...Bk. A, p. 171...WIT: Matthew Johnson, Arch McDaniel.

UNDERWOOD James--Sons: Robert, James, Mathew, William, John & Isaac dec'd... Wife...Daus: Jane, Mary & step-dau. Nancy Copeland...EXR: s.l. John Blakely, son John...29 June 1822--18 Nov. 1823...Bk. E, p. 333...WIT: Robt. Caswell, John H. Davis, Watson Deen.

VANCE Mary(She was Mary Dunbar McTier & hus. Nathl Sr.)...Chn: Saml, John, James W., Joseph H., Nathl, Allen, David, William dec'd, Frances Greer, Mary(Williams)... EXR: Son Joseph...-1840--16 Nov. 1841...Bk. A, p. 9...WIT: John & J.W. Watts, Elihu Attom.

VAUGHAN Claiborn--Son John, "all my chn."...EXR: Wife Mary...11 June 1816-- 5 July 1819...Bk. E, p. 31...WIT: Coleman, Elizabeth B., & Joanna Lewis Carlisle.

VAUGHAN Walter P.--EXR: Bro. Drury Vaughan & his dau. Elizabeth, Charles Eggerton...18 July 1827--5 Nov. 1828...Bk. F, p. 184...WIT: Charles Eggerton, Arch. Todd, S. B. Cook.

WALKER Elizabeth M.--m.l. Mrs. Susannah Walker...sister Eliza Garey...Bro. John L. Young...niece Theodora dau. of G. W. Young...EXR: Bros. John & James Young... 18 Jan. 1842--11 Aug. 1842...Bk. A, p. 35...WIT: Wm. Young, W. W. Templeton, Jno. H. Dendy.

WALKER Keturah--Chn: Allen, Bones, Hogan, Azariah, Elizabeth Shaw, Debly Ann Wilcott, Emily Shaw, Emaline Madden, chn, of Patsy Milan dec'd viz: Wm, John. Debly Ann, Jane, Elizabeth...EXR: Son Hogan...9 Mch. 1843--5 May 1845...Bk. A, p. 50...WIT: John H. Coleman, Wm. Nelson, Azariah Walker.

WALKER Moses--Wife Elizabeth...Chn. mins...Bro. Jathrow..."Elizabeth & John Walker agree to abide by abv. writing"...1 June 1791...Bk. A, p. 36...WIT: Thos. East, Jas. Bell.

WATKINS Charles--EXR: wife Eli§abeth, James Abercromie...30 July 1810...Bk. D-1, p. 427...WIT: Charles Watkins, Mary, Nancy & John Cochran.

WATTS James--Son James.."my chn"...named are: Elihue C. Watts, Priscilla Griffin, Narcissa Goodman, Betsy Chapman...EXR: Elihue, William & John Watts...2 Oct. 1839-- 7 June 1842...Bk. A, p. 27...WIT: W. B. Meriwether, Hazel & Elizabeth H. Smith, Marcus Dendy, Martha Walker.

WATTS John--Wife Peggy...Sons: Richard, John Pollard, Braxton, Beaufort...Daus: Elena K., Louisa, Narcissa, Cornelia, Elmira, Peggy, Matilda Vaughan...EXR: Sons Beaufort, Braxton, Richard, Nathanl Day...14 Sept. 1812--26 Oct. 1812...Bk. D-1, p. 90...WIT: James Vaughan, Similion Deale, Mrs--Pollard.

WATTS Nancy C--2 y.daus: Sarah P. & Margaret E. "all my chn"...EXR: son James W. Watts...8 Mch. 1845--10 Mch. 1845...Bk. A, p. 49...WIT: J. E. Gray, John D. Williams, H. M. Phinny.

WELLS Aaron--Est. to mother Rebecca & sister Elizabeth Wells...Bro. Elisha...EXR: Bro. Moses Wells...pvd. 30 May 1806...Bk. C-1, p. 233.

WELLS Elisha--wife Elizabeth, EXR...1 Nov. 1813--27 Feb. 1820...Bk. E, p. 65...WIT: John Cook, Drury Sims Jr., John Hitt.

WESSON(?Wasson) John--Wife Elizabeth...Chn: Hicks, Sarah, Polly, Marhta...EXR: Father Henry Wesson, Jesse Jones...1 July 1805...Bk. C-1, p. 165...WIT: Absolom Harwell, Benj. Wesson.

White James--"chn"...EXR: Wife Elizabeth...19 July 1807--5 June 1817...Bk. D-1, p. 368...WIT: William Chiles, Rhoda & James Young.

WHITEHEAD William--Chn: William, John, Nancy, Benjamin, Thomas, Donel, Stephen, Sarah Strain, Jane Alberson, Linsa Adkins, ?Milla...EXR: Wife Margaret, Charters Nickels...22 Mch. 1805--8 Oct. 1805...Bk. C-1, p. 178...WIT: J. N. Johnson, Jas. Strain.

WHITMORE Joseph--Dau. Sarah Duncan...gr.son George Whitmore, min..."prop. div. bwt. all chn. & heirs of those dec'd"...EXR: Son George...27 May 1803--20 Nov. 1803... Bk. C-1, p. 131...WIT: Whitmore & Dred Jones, Reubin Flanagan.

WHITTEN John Sr.--Chn: Sidney, John Jr., Sally Henly, Ann Jacks, Fanny Ray, Susan Kennedy...EXR: Son Sidney, Claxton Ray...3 July 1828--2 Jan. 1832...Bk. F, p. 381... WIT: John F. Kern Jr., Alfred Kern.

WHITWORTH Cinthea(Cynthia)--Dau. Frances Elizabeth gets all...Trustees & EXR: Daniel Rudd of Newberry friend & relation, Henry Burton...14 May 1846...Bk. A, p. 98...WIT: Anthony F. Golding, John H. Goodman, A. G. Cook.

WILKS Whitehead--Wife Eliza...3 pts. one to dau. Eliza & her hus. Samuel Henderson... to chn. of dec'd son Cornelius...to son Joseph...to son Thomas all claim I have to my father's est...EXR: J. H. Irby, Dr. John Davis...8 Nov. 1847...Bk. A, p. 123...WIT: Saml Fleming, R. E. Todd, William J. Blakely.

WILLARD John--Wife Patty...Daus: Polly, Elizabeth, Sarah...EXR: Son Meager...29 June 1816--2 Nov. 1816...Bk. D-1, p. 342...WIT: J. L. Neely, Walter Burges, Elizabeth Davenport.

WILLIAMS David--Sons: Samuel M., Henrv R., Joseph H., Leonard, Robert, Ephraim, William A., Dr. James(sons all had col. educ.)...Daus: Elizabeth A. Miller; Frances Clary; Mary Metts...EXR: Sons Henry & Leonard...26 Mch. 1853--11 Oct. 1853... Bk. A, p. 163...WIT: W. J. Whitmire, R. C. Cannon, A. C. Garlington.

WILLIAMS James A.--Wife Mary...Sons: Daniel, John & 4 youngest, viz-James Alwood, Franklin, Washington, Elihu...Daus: Sarah Cooper, Elizabeth Ann Cooper...EXR: s.l. Charles & Reubin Cooper...6 Jan. 1816--20 Jan. 1816...Bk. D-1, p. 252...WIT: William Hudgens, R. H. Owins, W. Tinsley.

WILLIAMS Mary--Sons: Elihue Duke, Franklin, Washington W...Daus: Elizabeth w. of Reubin Cooper & her dau. Mary Amanda...EXR: Sons Elihu, Wash...12 Aug. 1826--15 Apr. 1828...Bk. F, p. 162...WIT: Anthony Golding, Saml Goodman, John W. Williams.

WILLIAMSON Agnes--Dec'd hus. James...Sons: Dr. Wm. Williamson, James McCollums... Dau. Jane w. of Hamon Miller...Trustees: Albert & Franklin Miller...9 Jan. 1845... Bk. A, p. 76...WIT: John Nickles, Willis Benham, James Davis.

WILLIAMSON Elisha--"If wife Elmina should not have a living child by me"...Dau. Essie Brown & her chn. John & Clarissa Lovelace...gr.chn: Elisha Williamson, Elizabeth L. Arnold...EXR: wife...7 Aug. 1851--23 May 1853...Bk. A, p. 156...WIT: R. L. Stephens, John K. ?Suson, Charles Murphy.

WILLIAMSON Jane--Dau. Mary Campbell...EXR: Son Sanders Williamson, Ira Gambrell... 29 Apr. 1840--8 Oct. 1842...Bk. A, p. 24...WIT: Benj. Arnold, Joel Stone, Stephen Stone.

WITSON(?Wilson) Benjamin--Sons: David S., John, Benjamin, James...Daus: Elizabeth

?Gray, Mary Burns, Isabella McConnel, Jane & hus. Abraham Gray, Larey w. of William Boyd, Martha, Margaret, Ann Scott a min...EXR: Wife Elizabeth, James & David S. Wilson...23 Apr. 1815--3 June 1815...Bk. D-1, p. 207...WIT: Wm. Neal, Enos

WILSON Charles--Dau. Mary...Sons: James, Charles, "six other chn"...EXR: Son Thomas, friend Elijah Watson...4 June 1820--13 June 1820...Bk. E, p. 82...WIT: Charles & James Crawford, Charles Wilson Jr.

WILSON John--Mother personal prop...land to William, James, Jeane Grant, William Ware or Mare...EXR: William Ware...11 Dec. 1800...Bk. A, p. 266...WIT: Edmond & M. Wood.

WILSON John--Wife Jean..."all my chn" mins...EXR: Turner Richardson, Robert Allison Sr...11 Aug. 1823--3 Apr. 1826...Bk. F, p. 14...WIT: James Todd, J. A. Lynch, C. Stone.

WOLF George--Son George...Dau. Nancy...EXR: Wife Nancy, Capt. Saml Henderson... 7 Jan. 1806--30 Jan. 1816...Bk. D-1, p. 258...WIT: Wm. Dunlap, Wm. Montgomery, John Swelevan(Sullivan).

WOLF John F.--Daus: Isabella Saxon, Elizabeth Milner...EXR: Wife Mary, son George, Samuel Davis...prop. left in trust of Hugh Saxon, George Wolf...3 Feb. 1820--5 Mch. 1820...Bk. E, p. 150...WIT: Saml Davis, Patillo Farrow, J. A. Mathews.

WOLFF Mary--Son George F. Wolf & his 5 chn. viz-John S., Melton Y., Charles S., James R., Mary...gr.sons: Lewis, Elizabeth & John Saxon...EXR: John F. W. Saxon... 26 Feb. 1842--4 Jan. 1845...Bk. A, p. 46...WIT: Christopher Burns, H. & R. C. Saxon.

WOOD Joseph--Son Zadock...EXR: Wife Elizabeth...13 Mch. 1817--3 Nov. 1817...Bk. D-1, p. 419...WIT: James H. Harden, Coleman Carlisle, James Bobbs.

WRIGHT Samuel--Sons: Eldest William G., minors James & Samuel...Daus: Elizabeth, Frances, Polly, Nancy, minors...Wife Patience, educ. chn. & at her death, div. bwt. all...EXR: Bro. William Wright...23 Sept. 1808--6 Jan. 1809.

YOUNG Abner--4 chn: Dorothy, Isabel, James, Emma Florella or Hosalla(confused)... EXR: Wife Rebecca...Dau. Lucinda dec'd...20 Mch. 1833--2 Sept. 1833...Bk. F, p. 497... WIT: John Mason, John & William Hunter. (The dau. Dorothy md. T. E. Herbert; Isabella md. Dr. Geo. Young)

YOUNG George Sr.--Chn: George, Elizabeth, Mary, Lettie Rowland, Jane Whitmore, Thomas' two chn: George & Thomas...EXR: A. McCreary, Bro. Christopher Young, son George...1 Feb. 1826--4 Nov. 1839...Bk. F, p. 497...WIT: Thos. Young Jr., Christ Young Jr., John Boyce.

YOUNG James--Sons: James & Robert youngest chn. & "should they move to western country, sell my lands...rest of chn. have had theirs"...25 May 1796...EXR: Wife, sons James & Robert, George Anderson...WIT: Andrw. Middleton, Abner Young...Bk. A.

YOUNG James Sr.--Sons: John, James...Daus: Betsy Carter, Polly Medley, Betty, Lucy, Sally...EXR: Zachariah Bailey, William Burnside...21 Nov. 1807--7 Dec. 1807...Bk. C-1, p. 283...WIT: James Holley, Thomas & Mary Powell.

YOUNG James--Wife Mary Ann..."my chn"...EXR: Sons Gallatin & Wm. Augustin, friend Turner Richardson Esq...25 June 1824--16 Oct. 1824...Bk. E, p. 429...WIT: William Moore, Hugh Saxon.

YOUNG Joseph--Chn: Robert, Joseph, John, Elizabeth Roland...EXR: James son of Wm.

NINETY-SIX.

Fort Ninety-Six.

stands near the scene of the first bloodshed in South Carolina during the Revolutionary War. Here the British built a star-shaped redoubt in 1780, which was besieged by General Greene in 1781. Later in the same year the fort fell to the Americans, and Ninety-Six was moved to the railroad a short distance from the original site. Greenwood State Park is near by.

Courthouse, Newberry

OLD COURTHOUSE (1826), CAMDEN; Designed by Robert Mills

first American architect,
  one of South Carolina's most
    gifted sons.

Winnsboro Courthouse, begun in 1820-

MISCELLANEOUS REFERENCE DATA

Most of the original claims for Revolutionary Service are filed at the State Historical Commission in Columbia, S. C. These were paid by "INDENTS" or script money and the majority were settled by the state with public lands or forfeited estates. Mr. A. S. Salley, as Secretary to the Historical Commission, has edited and printed for the Commission, nine volumes of STUB ENTRIES TO INDENTS, Three, of ACCOUNTS AUDITED (thru letter B) which are filed in approximately some 10,000 envelopes, two volumes of NAVY RECORDS, and other books. The Commission also has custody of the records that were filed in the Secretary of State, Comptroller General, Treasurer's and Surveyor General's offices. Mortgages, marriage settlements and miscellaneous books are indexed. There is a file of loose manuscripts, also photostatic copies from the War Department, Washington, of some companies of the Revolutionary War.

At the State Library in Columbia is available, what is known as the MORTALITY SCHEDULES-census records of 1860, 1870, 1880--which give such data as: names of persons dying the preceding year, date of death, residence, age; Caroliniana Library: Copies of the wills of the counties of the state formed before 1853, except these: Beaufort, Colleton, Chesterfield, Georgetown, Lexington, Lancaster, Orangeburg. The earliest records were filed in Charleston, but after the Revolution, in the various districts, until about 1785 when the separate counties were functioning. The Charleston Library Society, founded 1748, has an extensive collection of South Caroliniana. In each county, estates settled in Court of Equity, furnish much genealogical material and original manuscripts, while these Court-houses offer records that can be found nowhere else.

Among books furnishing proof for Revolutionary service for South Carolinians, we name: Gibbes Documentary History of S.C; Memoirs of American Revolution As Relating To State of S.C. by John Drayton; McCrady, History of S.C. in the Revolution 1780-1783; Mills Statistics & Handbook; Force's American Archives; Saffell's Revolutionary Record; South Carolina Histories by Ramsay, Chapman, Simms, White, Landrum, Wallace, Yates-Snowden; Historical Register of Continental Army by Heitman; History of The Old Cheraws by Greeg; O'Nealls Annals of Newberry; Historic Camden by Kirkland & Kennedy; History of Edgefield by Chapman; History of Spartanburg by Landrum etc; D.A.R. Lineage books and Magazine; S. C. Histl. & Geneal. Magazine; Transactions of Huguenot Soc. of S. C., and other books named within these pages.

AN AMERICAN RIFLEMAN.

179

Goose Creek, Episcopal Church in Berkeley County,
oldest church building standing in South Carolina. (1711-19), NEAR CHARLESTON

The Oldest American College Library Building,
University of South Carolina

WOODROW WILSON SHRINE

First Presbyterian Columbia for a time had as it's Stated Supply Pastor, Dr. Joseph Wilson, the father of Woodrow Wilson, and a few blocks is the former Wilson home designed by the mother of the President and built by his father; it is now a shrine, purchased by voluntary subscriptions and is in charge of the American Legion. The home contains many of the original pieces and relics of the former home. The parents and sister of Woodrow Wilson are buried in the First Presbyterian Church yard.

Ruins of Millwood ante-bellum home of General Wade Hampton

Calhoun Mansion. Members of this family were massacred by Indians in 1760. A descendant, John C. Calhoun, the great statesman, member of Congress, Secretary of War, Secretary of State, Vice-President of the United States.

From the massacre of the Anthony Hampton family, five sons were left. One son, Wade served in the Revolution. His son, Colonel Wade II, with Andrew Jackson. His son, General Wade III was governor of South Carolina 1876-1878.

181

THE GREAT SEAL OF THE STATE

From Drayton's Memoirs of the American Revolution (chapter 18,

" So soon as the government under the Constitution of March, 1776, were organized, the necessity of having a public seal became evident; and, on motion in the General Assembly, it was resolved, That his Excellency, the President and Commander-in-Chief, by and with the advice and consent of the Privy Council, may, and he is hereby, authorized to design and cause to be made a Great Seal of South Carolina, and until such a one can be made, to fix upon a temporary seal.*

" In pursuance of this resolution, William Henry Drayton, and some of the Privy Council, were charged with designing the Great Seal, and causing it to be made; and in the mean time, a temporary public seal was adopted by the President and Privy Council, for purposes of State. The first use of this temporary seal (which appears to have been the Seal-at-Arms of the President) was for commis sioning the civil officers of the government, and for a pardon is sued by Presi- dent Rutledge, dated 1st May, 1776, in favor of a person who had been convicted of manslaughter before Chief Justice William Henry Drayton, and his Associate Justices, at a court commenced at Charles Town on the 23d April, 1776.† In these commissions, it was called his (the president's) seal, but in pardons and other instruments, it was afterwards called '*the Temporary Seal of the said Colony*,' or '*the Temporary Public Seal*'; and, it was used from that time throughout the year 1776, until about the 22d May, 1777; as on that day, President Rutledge issued a pardon under '*the Seal of the said State*,' omitting the word *temporary*; whence there is reason for believing the Great Seal was then made; and from that time the temporary seal does not appear to have been used. ‡

[* See Journals of the General Assembly of South Carolina for 1776, in the office of the clerk of the House of Representatives, at Columbia.]

[† See Book of Miscellanies and Bills of Sale in the secretary's office, Charleston, S. S., pages 1, 2.]

[‡ The author remembers seeing the mould or *dye* of the Great Seal, brought by the artist who was engraving it, to his father, William Henry Drayton, at his residence in Charles Town, for his inspection; but he cannot fix what particular time it was. From some circumstances which occurred, he believes it was not in the winter.]

"The device for the armorial achievement and reverse of the Great Seal of the State of South Carolina, is as follows:

"ARMS.—A Palmetto tree growing on the sea-shore, erect; at its base, a torn-up Oak tree, its branches lopped off, prostrate; *both proper.* Just below the branches of the Palmetto, two shields, pendent; one of them, on the dexter side, is inscribed March 26th, the other, on the sinister side, July 4th.

"Twelve spears, *proper,* are bound crosswise to the stem of the Palmetto, their poitns raised; the band uniting them together bearing the inscription QVIS SEPARABIT. Under the prostrate Oak is inscribed *Meliorem Lapsa Locavit ;* below which appears in large figures 1776. At the summit of the Exergue are the words SOUTH CAROLINA; and at the bottom of the same, ANIMIS OPIBUSQUE PARATI.

"REVERSE. A woman walking on the sea-shore, over swords and daggers; she holds in her dexter hand a laurel branch—and in her sinister, the folds of her robe; she looks towards the sun, just rising above the sea; *all proper.* On the upper part is the sky, *azure.* At the summit of the Exergue are the words DUM SPIRO SPERO; and within the field below the figure is inscribed the word SPES. The Seal is in the form of a circle, four inches in diameter, and four-tenths of an inch thick.

"It was not designed until after the fort at Sullivan's Island had defeated the British fleet, as all its devices will prove. The fort was constructed of the stems of the Palmetto trees, (*Corypha Palmetto,*) which grow abundantly on our sea-islands—which grew on Sullivan's Island at the time the fort was made, when the battle was fought, and which grow there at this day.

"The ARMS were designed by William Henry Drayton, and the original executed by him with a pen, bearing a great similitude to what is represented on the Seal, is in the possession of his son. It, however, contains more devices, but this is easily reconciled, by supposing all he had designed was not deemed by the President and Privy Council necessary for the Great Seal. The explanation of this side of the Seal is the following: The Palmetto tree on the sea-shore represents the fort on Sullivan's Island; the shields, bearing March 26th and July 4th, allude to the Constitution of South Carolina, which was ratified on the first of those days; and to the Declaration of Independence, which was made by the Continental Congress on the last of them. The twelve Spears represent the twelve States which first acceded to the Union. The dead Oak tree alludes to the British fleet as being constructed of oak timbers—and it is prostrate under the Palmetto tree, because the fort, constructed of that tree, defeated the British fleet; hence the inscription, *Meliorem Lapsa Locavit,* is appropriately placed underneath it; under which 1776 is in large figures, alluding to the year the Constitution for South Carolina was passed; to the battle fought at Sullivan's Island; to the Declaration of Independence, and to the year when the Seal was ordered to be made.

16

"The REVERSE of the arms is said to have been designed by Arthur Middleton, often mentioned in these memoirs, and who was the father of Henry Middleton, at present ambassador from the United States of America to the Court of Russia. The Woman walking along the sea-shore strewn with swords and daggers, represents Hope overcoming dangers, which the sun, just rising, was about to disclose in the occurrences of the 28th of June, 1776; while the laurel she holds signifies the honors which Colonel Moultrie, his officers and men gained on that auspicious day. The Sun rising in great brilliancy above the sea, indicates that the 28th of June was a fine day; it also bespeaks good fortune."

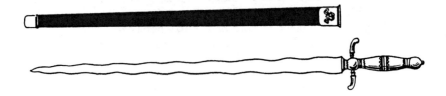

THE SWORD OF STATE

This sword hangs from the front of the Senate Rostrum during daily session of the Senate and is carried by the Sergeant-at-Arms on all State occasions. It was made in Charles Town (Charleston) and bought May 5, 1704, for £26 11s 3d ($129.00).

MACE

The mace is the emblem of authority of the House of Representatives. Whenever the House officially attends in the Senate Chamber, and upon state occasions, the mace is always borne at the head of the procession. It was made in London in 1756 and is solid silver with gold burnishing. It is possibly the only mace in use in the United States which antedates the Revolution. It was used by the Commons House of Assembly until the Revolution.

Mottoes

"Animis Opibusque Parati"
(Prepared with minds and resources);

"Dum Spiro, Spero"
(While I breathe, I hope.)

Chief Agricultural Products and Commercial Industries

Farming: cotton, tobacco and truck produce
Farming
Textile manufacturing
Lumbering
Hydro-electric power production
Fishing and marketing sea foods

Canning foodstuffs
Fertilizer manufacturing
Mining: gold, tin, kaolin, granite and quarrying
Poultry and pigeon raising
Hog raising
Fruit growing and marketing
Shrubbery and flower nurseries

Operation of tourist hostelries
Paper manufactur

185

The Palmetto State

MAP OF SOUTH CAROLINA

THE SULLIVAN FAMILY
IN IRELAND AND AMERICA

Archeology leads us to believe that the Gaelic Race conquered Ireland about the 4th century B.C. They came from some country east of Gaul by way of the North sea, which later became known as SCYTHIA. The ancient progenitor of the Sullivans about 1,000 B.C. was Milesius, king of the Gaels. His son, Heber, was ancestor of Aengus. There follows Owen Mor, King of Munster who married Beara, daughter of the King of Spain. His son, Oilioll Olum, was 237th monarch of Munster and died A.D. 234. Finghin was the 14th Christian King and grt-gr-father of King Aengus. There were seven generations before SUILDHUBHAIN who lived about A.D. 950 when surnames were first adopted. There were 101 generations from the beginning to SUILDHUBHAIN (O'SUILEABHANS, pron. Sooeeliavan, Sullivan).

The Sullivans were living along the river Suir in eastern Ireland when the over-whelming hordes of the Anglo-Norman invasion (about 1169) compelled them to migrate to the southwest (counties of Cork, Kerry, Limerick). The southern branch of Sullivans in America, descend from Sir Owen O'Sullivan, who sat in Parliament 1585 (reign of Queen Elizabeth). It is not to be assumed that everyone who bears the name SULLIVAN today, descends from this line. One must establish that his ancestor left Ireland during the Cromwellian period or the great upheaval of 1641-1654, when "all the nobility . . . were banished and their lands confiscated . . . any still there by 1 May 1654 would be put to death." Many fled to Spain and other countries. Reaching America was John Thomas Sullivan to Virginia 1655 (our line). Florence Sullivan was Master of a ship bringing first settlers to Charleston, S.C., and he was also Surveyor-General of the Province, and Sullivan's Island named for him. The ancestor of General John Sullivan of the American Revolution settled in Maine.

SULLIVAN FAMILY DESCENDED FROM

CHARLEMAGNE 742/814, EMPEROR OF THE KNOWN WORLD, married
   HILDERGARD 757/782 (can trace to Geoffrey Plantagenet 1113/1151) m.
   Matilda of England 1103/1167, grdau. of

WILLIAM THE CONQUEROR, whose grdau. Eleanor, married Alphonse, 9th King of
   Castile who died 1214)

CHARLEMAGNE, married Princess Hildegarde of Swabia . . . had-

LOUIS LE DeBONNAIRE, King of France born 778, d. 840, reigned 814/40, m.
   Judith, dau of Guelph, Count of Andech & Bavaria. They had—Giselda & Louis,
   King of Bavaria. (Latter had - CAROLMAN who had Arnould, who had
   HEDWIDGE.)

PRINCESS GISELA (Giselle) m. 867 Eberhard, Count of Burgundy, son of Henrock,
   Duke of Friuli. (Wurts, Magna Charta) had -

PRINCESS ADELHEID, Countess of Burgundy who m. Ludolph, Duke of Saxony (Burke
   Vol. I, Ped I) Had -

OTTO, DUKE OF Saxony d. 912, m. Princess Hedwige dau. of Arnolph, Emperor
   887/99 & wife, Otta of Bavaria. (Arnolph was son of CAROLMAN, son of
   Louis I, King of Bavaria, son of Louis Le Debonnaire) Otto had -

HENRY THE FOWLER, Emperor 919/36 (born 876, d. 936) m. 2n Matilda of
   Ringelheim, dau of the Saxon count, Thiederick. (For mother of Henry, see -
   Burke Royal Fam. Vol. 1 Ped. L; also Royal Fam. by Lavoisne). Henry &
   Matilda had -

HEDWIDGE d. 956, m. Hugh Capet, Duke of France (p 184 Wurtz Magna Charta, Vol. I & II) They had -

HUGH CAPET, KING OF FRANCE 938/996, m. Adele or Adelaide, who according to Burke, was dau..of Otto I. Had -

ROBERT THE PIOUS 971/1031, m. 2n - Constantia. She was called "Constance of Provence," & was dau of Berenger Count of Provence. Had -

HENRY I, King of France, b. 1005, d. 1060, reigned 1031/60, married Anne of Russia, grdau. of the 1st CZAR Vladimir (3rd wife & dau of Jaroslaud). Had -

PHILIP I, King of France 1052/1108, reigned 1060/1108, m. 1071 as 1st wife, Bertha, dau of Florient Count of Holland. Had -

LOUIS VI, King of France 1081/1137, m. Alice or Adelaide of Savoy in 1115, dau of Hubert II, Count of Piedmont. Had -

LOUIS VII (1119/1180), m. 3rd Adelaide or Adela, dau. of Theobold II, Count of Champagne. He went on 2nd Crusade. They had -

PRINCESS AGNES OF FRANCE, married Adelem de Burg, Steward to King Henry II of England, Governor of City of Wexford, Ire. He was son of Wm. de Burgh, Earl of Cornwell (oldest Duchy of England) son of Robert, son of Harlowen de Burgh who married Arlotta, mother of William the Conqueror. (De Burgh, one most powerful families of Ireland, governors under the Kings of England. They trace through Geoffrey, Duke of Lorraine, who led the Crusades 1097, refused to wear a crown in Jerusalem. After him, the family have the cross on their armorial bearings.) Princess Agnes had -

WILLIAM FITZ-ANDELEM de Burgh, Lord Gov. of Ireland 1177, died 1204, m. 1st Lady Isabel of England (widow of Llewlyn, Prince of Wales). Had -

RICHARD MOR de Burgh the Great, Lord of Connaught & Trym; Lord-Lieut. of Ireland 1227. He died 1243, m. Lady Hodierna de Gernon (grdau of King Odo O'Connor & dau. of Robt. de Gernon by Una O'Connor). Had -

WALTER de BURGH, Baron of Connaught, Earl of Ulster & Constable of Ireland, who d. 1271. He m. Maude de Lacie, d. 1303 (dau. of Hugh de Lacie, Earl of Ulster & Constable of Ire. Sir Hugh came to Ireland 1171, was Lord Palatine & a descendant of Charlemagne.) Had -

RICHARD de BURGH 1259/1326, was 2n Earl of Ulster, Lord Justice of Ireland in 1296, died 1326, married Lady Margaret de Burgh, (dau. of John de Burgh, Baron of Lanville.) Had -

LADY JOAN de Burgh who m. 1st - 1312 Thomas Fitzgerald, 2n Earl of Kildare, d. 1359 (her father was Richard, known as "the Red Earl"). (McMurrough King of Leinster, in a power Struggle with other Irish Princes, asked some English nobles to come over & help him. Among these were the Fitzgeralds. These newcomers merged with the Celtic mass, - intermarried, adopted Irish language & customs. Maurice Fitzgerald was Justice of Ireland 1229. His descendant, 5 generations removed, was crowned King of Ireland 1315 at Dundale.) Had -

MAURICE FITZGERALD, 4th Earl of Kildare, d. 1390, m. Lady Elizabeth Burghersh (dau. of Sir Batholomew, Burghersh, Knt; 3rd Baron of Verdon, Lord Justice of Ireland, by 1st wife, Lady Maude Mortimer, dau. of Sir Edmund Mortimer, Baron of Wigmore) Had -

GERALD FITZGERALD, 5th Earl of Kildare, Lord Justice of Ireland in 1405, died 1410 who m. Lady Margery Rocheford (dau. of Sir John de Rocheford, Knt;

Lord of Thistledown by his wife Lady Margery Bereford dau. of Lord of Kill, Leixlip & Casthewarren). Had -

JOHN-CAM FITZGERALD, 6th Earl of Kildare, d. 1427. (He built the castles of Maynooth & Kilkea. The former was the famed stronghold of the Geraldines. The Earls of Kildare ruled in "the Pale" and intermarried with the Irish for some 300 years, until it was said they "were more Irish than the Irish," and her most loyal supporters). He had by wife Margaret de la Herne

THOMAS FITZGERALD, 7th Earl of Kildare, Lord Duputy of the Kingdom in 1454 & 1463 & d. 1478. He m. Lady Joan Butler who d. 1486. (Dau of James Butler, 7th Earl of Desmond & of royal descent from Edward I of Eng.) The Earls of Desmond's great territories extended over Limerick, Kerry, Cork & Waterford, and included some 575,000 acres. This land was confiscated in Elizabeth's reign & parcelled out to English settlers.) Had -

GERALD FITZGERALD, 8th Earl of Kildare, Lord Duputy of Ire. & in effect, actual RULER. He married Lady Allison (dau. of Sir Rowland Eustace of Harristown by Lady Maude, dau. of Jenico d'Artois, widow of John Dondall of Newton). In 1534 the Kildares declared war on England, and later 6 of them were hung.) Gerald had -

LADY ELEANOR FITZGERALD (sister of Gerald oge, 9th Earl of Kildare). She married 1st Donnell Mac Fineere Mac Carthy-Reagh, Prince of Carberry in Ireland. His mother was dau. of Donnell, 9th Lord of Bearehaven who d. 1520. Had -

LADY JULIA MacCARTHY, married DERMOD O'SULLIVAN, the Powdered, 11th Lord of Beare & Bantry, of Dunboy Castle, who d. 1549. (Donnell Mor, 8th Lord in descent from the first who assumed the name O'SULLIVAN, & lineal descendant of Eogan Mor, was the 25th in descent from Olioll Olum, the 237th Monarch of Munster, Ire. thru his son, Owen. This Donnell Mor's grt-gr-son, Aura-ny-Lacken, Lord of Desmond, was the 1st Lord of Beare & Bantry in Munster, & direct ancestor of Dermod the 11th Lord, who m. Julia MacCarthy.) Issue: Owen, Donel, Philip, Dernod, Joan

SIR OWEN O'SULLIVAN (or Eoghan) sat in Parliament 1585, died 1594, m. Helena Barry (dau. of James, Lord Barry, Fitz Richard Barry Roe by wife Ellen, dau. of Cormac na hory MacCarthy Reagh) Issue: Owen, John, Donel, Julia

OWEN O'SULLIVAN, flourishing 1612 (Carew's Pacata Hiberna p. 293. He had a regrant of DUNBOY Anno 9 James I.) Died 31 Aug. 1616. Married Helena dau. of Pierce Butler of Gregolt. She d. after 1616. Issue: Owen Donel, Dermod, Philip, Connor, Helena, Julia

OWEN-DONEL, b. after 1599, joined Rebellion of 1641, was attainted & fled the country. His family scattered among relatives & friends, and some came to America. He married Jo-Ann Elizabeth dau. of Thos. Brown & grdau. of John Brown. Issue: John (or called John Thomas for two maternal ancestors); Derman to American 1656 & left will; Elizabeth, Anne

JOHN O' SULLIVAN b. 1637, came to America 24 Oct. 1655 (Patent Book 3, p. 392, Land Office, Richmond, Va.) He came as minor with relative Elizabeth Sullivan. He appears in "a list of Lower Norfolk People in 1673 as 36 yrs. old (Clerk's Office, Norfolk, Va.; Wm. & Mary Quart. Vol. 26). He married 1st - Mary dau. of Owen Hayes of Lynhaven Parish (see his will). He m. 2n Sara dau. of Thos. Gore. In the early Virginia records the name is variously spelled: Usehullevan, Usuliman, O'Swellivant, O'Sullivan, Sullivan. The will of John Sullivan is recorded in Princess Anne County, Va.: Lynhaven Parish, dated 12 May 1698, prv. 7 Sept. 1698, Bk. 1, p. 194; see also State Library, Richmond, Va. Lands owned by him are mentioned in the will of Matthew Brinson 12 June 1681 (Jour. Irish - Amer. Soc. 25/103. Abstract of will of Owen Hayes, 25, 99). Issue: Owen, Morris, Mary, Amie & John with wife Hester who died bef. Father & had son John, m. Catherine Bright.

OWEN O'SULLIVAN I, b. Lynhaven Parish, Prin. Anne Co., Va. abt. 1673/4, was granted 240 acres 7 Nov. 1700 at Dam Neck, near Owen Hayes at Fish Pond (Prin. Anne Co., Va., Bk. 4, fol. 126) also granted 862 acres in Lunenburg County 10 Sept. 1755 (Pat. Bk. 32,631) granted 225 A 15 July 1760 (Bell's Free State); granted 160 Acres 10 Sept. 1755. The tithable List of Wm. Caldwell, taken 1749 for Lunenburg shows Owen Sullivan (Wm. & Mary Quart. 11, 57). Owen's will dated 12 Oct. 1768, prv. 6 Feb. 1769 in Charlotte County (this county cut off from Lunenburg 1764). Family records state he married several times, once in 1693 to Elizabeth, born 1678/9 dau. of Lt. Col. Thos. Claiborne (1647/1685) who m. Sara Fenn. Owen Sullivan's last wife appears to have been Mary Ruth Pleasants b. 1671/4, dau. of John I (1644/98) who m. abt. 1666 the widow Jane Larcome Tucker. The names - Owen, Claiborne, John, Pleasant, Elizabeth, etc. come down thru generations to present. Issue: 13 - Owen II, Charles, William, John, Pleasant, Mary (Mullins), Temperance (Farmer), Esther (Hart), Madeline, Margaret, Frances, Patience, Elizabeth.

OWEN SULLIVAN II, b. in Lunenburg, Va. 1699, d. 1790, m. May 1721 Mary Margaret Hewlett (Hulit, Hughlett, etc.) b. 4 March 1707 (dau. of Wm. Hewlett & Mary Fearne who was dau. of John Fearne & Mary Lee). Owen II is named in father's will. By deed 1 Oct. 1781 Owen Sullivan conveys to Chas. Crenshaw 151 acres "including the late dwelling house of the late Owen Sullivan deceased, devised to said Owen Sullivan by Will of Owen Sullivan deceased" (Charlotte Co., Va. D BK 3, p. 571). There are records of other sales from Owen Sullivan to James Mullins, Stephen Farmer, etc. A History of Sullivan family was compiled 1882 and published by Wm. D. Sullivan 1913. In it he states that the above Owen and wife Margaret Hewlett had 5 children to move from Virginia to South Carolina. They were: 1-James, m. 1st Meta Bolling; 2n Sara Harrison Choice; 2-Owen III, grant in S.C. 1773, m. Sally O'Dell Nelson; 3-Margaret, m. Col. Samuel Wharton; 4-Pleasant, m. Milly Kelly; 5-Charles, next in line

CHARLES SULLIVAN, b. Charlotte Co., Va. 2 Apr. 1728 died in Greenville County, S.C. 3 Nov. 1808, buried Lebanon Meth. Church, grave marked as Revolutionary soldier. He married 15 June 1749 the widow, Mary Charlton (Johnson) She b. 1 June 1722, d. 20 Dec. 1837. Issue 5 viz: 1-Moses, m. Milly Chandler; 2-Sara, m. Joseph Dunklin; 3-Claiborne, m. Mary Harvey; 4-Stephen m. Martha Powell; 5-Hewlett

HEWLETT SULLIVAN b. in Va. 28 Dec. 1763, d. Greenville County, S.C. 11 July 1830 Revolutionary solider. (Organized Company of Scouts) Married 19 Dec. 1787 Mary dau. of Joseph Dunklin (Revo. Patriot) She rendered Revo. Service also. He was large land and slave owner, Senator, buried at Lebanon Church yard. Issue 12: 1-Judge Dunklin Sullivan, m. Mary Mayberry dau. of Rev. soldier, moved to Ala.; 2-Dr. John C. Sullivan, m. Anne Hendricks Arnold; 3-Geo. W. Sullivan, m. Jane Washington Brooks; 4-Joseph P. Sullivan, m. Temperance Hamilton Arnold; 5-Elizabeth, m. Rev. Marmaduke Pinson; 6-Frances, m. Squire Calhoun; 7-Jane m. Samuel L. Moore; 8-Mary, m. James M. Latimer; 9-Thos. Jefferson, m. Sara Cureton; 10-Chas. P., 1st-Sara Smith; 2nd-Zelene Boyd; 11-Hewlett, Bach.; 12-James M. married 1st-Sara Mimms; 2nd-Lizzie Vaughan.

THOMAS JEFFERSON SULLIVAN I, b. 28 Dec. 1807, d. 13 Jan. 1866, m. on 12 Sept. 1833 Sara Moon Cureton. He was extr. of his father's estate. Issue: 1-Henrietta (Parkins); 2-Frances (Goodgion); 3-Adelaide (Huff); 4-Sara (Mahaffey); 5-Claudia (Huff); 6-John S., m. 1st-Clinkscales; 2nd-Allen; 7-Charles, m. Arrah Watts; 8-Thos. J. II

THOMAS JEFFERSON II, b. 24 Dec. 1852, d. 5 Nov. 1923, m. 11 Nov. 1884 Felicia Arnold Sullivan b. 9/1/1865, d. 5/26/1927. Issue: Joseph Giroud and Capt. Claudius (WWI) unmarried; Rev. Humbert Sullivan, Capt. WWII, m. Grace Pitts; Dr. Charlton Sullivan, m. Evelyn Peele; Malinda C., m. Arthur Holley. Sara next in line.

SARA LUCILE SULLIVAN, m. 6 March 1907 Erasmus Powe Ervin (descendant of Col. John Ervin of Revolution) Children 2-Elizabeth Felicia, m. Albert Stephens of Laurens; Houston Sullivan Ervin, m. Sara Louise Graham.

INDEX

Bambridge Henry 85
Banbury Wm 115
Banister Thos 30
Banpfreed Wm 115
Barnard Noble 114
Barnet Thos 119..Jno 121..
    Jacob 81..Robt 80..
    Saml 81..Wm 68,81..
    Joel 95
Barnwell Edw 85..Robt 67, 85..
    John 55, 67, 85
Barns James 84
Barker William 95
Barkley John 95
Baroth Aaron 117
Barr Christpr 120..Wm 83..
    Martin 95
Barre Jacob 95
Barron Archb'ld 95..Jas 83
Barry Andrw 95, 121..Jno 25, 67
Bartlett Josiah 95..Wm 108
Baruch Rufus 95
Baskerville Wm 95
Baskin Andrw 95..Wm 85
Bassett Francis 81
Basquin William 68
Bates Dennis 82..Zealous 95
Baty Simon 83
Baxter Andrw 81, 95..Jno. 95..
    Daniel 95
Bayle Joseph 85
Baylis William 119
Bean Daniel 119
Bearden Jno 82..Rich 82..Wm 82
Beasley Leonard 42
Beaver Marhias 81
Beatty Thos 95..Jno 95
Beck Jeoffrey 46, 95
Bedford Thomas 95
Bedon John 115
Bee Jos. 85, 86..Thos 114, 115
Beekman Barnard 55..Saml 55
Beem Thomas 115
Bel Thomas 114
Beers Gresham 95
Belk John 95
Belcher Robert 26
Belin Allard 55
Bellamy David 85
Bell Benj 119..Jas 84..Sam 95..
    Timothy 119..Thomas 121, 124
Bellinger Edmund 95..Jno 95
Benbow Edward 121
Benan James 95
Bennett Chas 30..Reuben 108..
    Thomas 121
Benson Thomas 83, 121

Bentham James 67, 95
Benton Felix 95..Sam 67..Lem'l 95
Berand Matthew 67
Berdsall Benj. 95
Beresford Richard 85, 86
Berrian John 95
Beverly Ray 108
Berry Jno 95, 118..Wm. 19, 119..
    Ludford 28..Hudson 95
Berryhill Alex 120
Berwick Jno 85, 86..Simon 115
Bethea (3) Jno 125, 95..Wm 95
Beryhia Alex 82
Bessent John 120
Betsell John 15
Betterton Joshua 30
Bethel William 95
Billen Stephen 95
Bird Jno 27, 120..Nathan 82..
    Mark 95.
Bishop Jas 81..Jno 23..Wm 49
Bissell Ebeneezer 95
Black Jacob 52..Jas 14..Wm 82..
    Jos 31, 81, 95, 121..
    Jno 31, 52, 95
Blackwell Abram 33..Saml 95
Blackburn Ambrose 95
Blackensderfer Christian 95
Blackstock Wm 95, 125
Blaikley (Blakely) Wm 17, 42, 96..
    Thomas 42
Blair Jno 120..James 96
Blake Edw 85, 86..Wm 115..
    John 57, 85, 86
Blakney John 121
Blalock Jeremiah 52
Blameyer William 57
Bland Robert 108, 96
Blanding Wm. 108
Blassingame Jno 96..Julian 108
Bleakney John 67
Bledsoe Bartlett 96, 118..
    Berryman 118
Blount Chas 108
Blundel Nathan 85
Blythe Saml 96
Bobbitt Wm. 34
Bobo (2) Sampson 121
Bocquet Peter 115
Boevie Rhoda 96
Boddie Nathan 96
Boggan Patrick 96
Boggs Aaron 96
Bolling Saml 96, 125..
    Wm 96, 125
Boles Saml 119
Bolt Abram 42..Robt 125

Bolton Matt 96..Robt 96
Bonds Morris 80
Bone Jno 81..Wm 81
Boney Jacob 80
Bonham Absolone 96
Bonneau Anthony 114
Bonner Jas 121..Will 83
Bonniot John 85, 86
Boone Thos 115..Wm 115
Booth Jno 44, 96..Henry 108
Boozer Henry 108
Boquet Peter 86
Bordeau Danl 85..Nathl 86
Bordin Rich 84..Wm 84
Bostic John 120
Bostwick Littleberry 96
Boswell Jesse 29
Bothwell John 115
Botsford Rev. Edmund 96
Bouchellon Joseph 96
Bouequet Peter 86
Bounetheau Peter 67, 85, 96, 115
Bourdeaux Danl 86..Nathl 86
Bourk Jno 81..Robt 81
Bowders John 84
Bowell Thomas 83
Bowen Benj 30..Robt 96
Bowers David 96
Bowie John 57, 108
Bowman James 81
Boyce Jno 96..Alex 57..Wm 84
Boyd Ed 84..David 96..Jas 125..
    Jno 96, 111..Wm 34, 125..
    Saml 125..Thos 119
Boyer Jno 82
Boykin Burrell 96, 114..
    Sam 67..Francis 57, 83, 120
Boys Nathan 96
Bozeman Ralph 120
Bradley Francis 46..Jas 87
Bradwell Nathl 57
Bracey Sackfield 96
Bracket Saml 96
Bradford Jno 96..Jos 96
Brandon Chrstpr 51..Matt 84..
    Thomas 67, 115
Branford Wm 85
Brann Wm 119
Braswell Henry 44
Bratcher Saml 28
Bratton Wm 67, 96
Brazell Richard 84
Breese Timothy 119
Bremar Francis 57, 86, 118
Brent Jno 120..Jas 96
Brewster Hugh 81..Jno 81..Wm 30,96
Brewton Miles 114

Brian Matt 83..Jas 96
Bricken Jas 85, 86
Bridgeman Erasmus 108
Briges Jno 82
Brisbane Adam 120
Britt Richard 20
Britton Danl 67..Henry 67
Brock Reuben 30, 96..Uriah 119
Brockington John 40
Brockman Jno 96
Brooks Zach. S. 37
Brookshire Jno 39
Broom Jno 37..Thos 81
Brothers Jno 121
Brotherton Wm 81
Broughton Alex 115..Thos 119
Browne Henry 96..Alex 80, 81..
    Arch'd 14, 67, 96..Geo 84..
    Bart'lt 96, 120..Chas 57, 96..
    Benj. 57..Bernard 96..Dan 96..
    Dennis 87..Hamlton 119..
    Jno (4) 16, 57, 96, 120..Jos 14..
    Jas 25, 30, 79..Rich 57, 84..
    Matt 121..Nathan 119..Sims 121..
    Dennis 87..Pollard 31..Tim 119..
    Saml 81, 96..Wm 27, 57, 117
Brownfield Robt 57, 79
Brownson Nath 57
Bruce Donald 96, 115
Bruidson Jno 80
Bryan Barnaby 117..Jas 83, 121..
    Henry 82..Jno 68..Sim 96..
    Jonthn 120..Nathan 96
Brush John 108
Brumbaugh Jacon 108
Bryant Chas 19..Henry 84..Wm 17
Buchanan Benj. 120..Jno 57..Pete
    114
Buckhanan Wm 31
Buck Jon 96
Buckhalter Marion 120
Budd Jno S. 57, 79, 85, 86
Bubier Jno 96
Buddin Jas 96
Buford Wm 83, 96
Bugg Sherwood 96, 120
Bull Stephen 68, 115..Jno 96
Bullock Hawkins 96, 120, 121
Bumpass Jno 121
Bunch Huck 81..Jerem'h 35
Burbage Thos 35
Burke Adinus 86..Aedanus 57
Burkhalter David 96
Burks Saml 119
Burkholdt Abram 68, 120..
    Peter 68
Burn David 39..Jno 96

Burnley Henry 96
Burnett Jacob 68
Burns Jno 42..Laird 120..
  Peter 80, 81..Sam 53
Burnsides Andrew 42
Burress Sol 96..Wm 108
Burrows Wm 115
Burton Jno 114..Saml 68..
  Richard 17
Busby Nedham 43
Bush Jno 57..Danl 96
Bussey Edw 96..Zadoc 119
Butler Jas 68, 96, 118..
  Jno 22, 68, 118 120..
  Pete 115..Pierce 68, 86..
  Rich 22..Sam 117..
  Thos 96, 114..Wm 68,118,121,96
Butterick Jos 96
Byers Jas 49
Byrd Jonas 81..Geo 96

C ***** C

Cade Drewery B. 96
Cadner Jno 80
Cain Jno 121
Caldwell Jas 45, 96..
  Jno 34, 57, 96, 114..
  Robt 81..Sam 119..
  Wm. 49, 57, 96, 120
Calhoun David 83..Pat 96, 115..
  Jno 11, 85, 96, 115
Calk Jas 82..Wm 82
Callahan Joel 39
Calmes Wm 45, 96
Calloway Jon 96
Calvert Jon 96
Caltell Benj 57..Wm 57
Cameron Allen 57..Jno 81
Camil John 83
Cammick David 80
Camp Thos, Jno 96, 126
Campbell Abram 30..Jas 53..
  Danl 81..Geo 84, 119..
  Hugh 117..Jno 81, 120..
  Robt 68, 81..Wm 96, 121..
  David 96..Whittaker 96
Canady Wm 22
Cannon Danl 68, 96, 115..Jas 121..
  Ellis 26..Henry 39, 121..
  Isaac 96
Cantalou Louis 108
Cante James 120..Saml 96
Capers Chas 115..Wm 57, 68, 96
Cardock Geo 84
Cardoza David N 35

Carey Jas 96..Jno 96
Carick Adam 84
Carn Danl 46..Lewis 46..Jno 57
Carmichael Jno. Duncan 108
Carnes Jno 79..Patrick 79
Caroll Jos 81..Jas 96..Sam 121
Carothers Wm 80..Andrw 96
Carson Jas 115..Jon 83..Jas 96
Carswell Jno 96
Cart John 35
Carter Danl 81, 120..Churchwell 96..
  Dale 96..Giles 96..Isom 13..
  Jas 46..Jno 81, 84, 96..Sam
  96..Thos 96
Cartwright Robt 96
Carwile Zach 96
Caruth Alex 83..Robt 108
Caruthers Hugh 81..Wm 84
Carver Jas 46..Rich 46
Carvil Zach 31, 96
Casey Chrstpr 119..Wm 119..
  Levi 115..Randolph 121
Cason Cannon 38
Castlebury Paul 49
Cater Thos 68, 96
Cattell Benj. 87
Causey Jas. 118..Jno 118
Cave Jno 97
Cazza Henry 83
Chaison Jonas 119
Chalmers Lionel 79
Chambers Jno 97, 119..Jos 120
Chandler Jesse 82..Jno 119
  Mord'ci 51, 97..Matt 97
Chapell Wm 81..Hicks 48, 97..
  Robt 97..Jas 97..
  Thos 97..Laban 108
Chapin Benj 97
Chaplin Wm 97
Charity Chas 23
Charnock Wm 57
Chase Nathl L. 97
Chavis Lazarus 46
Cheek Ellis 42
Cherry Lamuel 121..Sam 97..
  Peter 29
Chestnut John 57, 87
Childers Jacob 82
Childs Abram 97
Chloe Michael 97
China John 48, 97
Chitwood Danl 82..Jas 82..Jno 84
Chivesman Saml 97
Choice Tully 121
Choloque Denis 118
Christmas Richard 37
Clannahan Robert 24

190

Clapp Earl 97
Clark Gideon 81..Timothy 97..
    Jas 80, 82, 83, 97..Jno 53..
    Thos 120..Wm 97
Clarke Jesse 82..Jno 82..Jonas 82..
    Jonathan 85
Clefford Chas 68
Cleiland John 57, 79
Clement Edmund 49..Thos 119
Clements Culiver 119
Clendening Matt 83
Cleveland Benj 97..Robt 97
Cline Michael 97
Clinton Jas 121
Clyf Samuel 114
Coachman James 68
Coalter Michael 97
Cobb Abrous 83..Jesse 97
Cochran Robt 37, 68, 85, 86..
    Thos 85, 86..Wm 81
Cockrell Wm 14
Coe Ebenezer 97
Coffin Wm. 97
Cogburn Henry 51
Cogdell George 57
Cohen Jacob 85
Cohorn Hugh 83
Colby John 118
Colburn James 97
Colcock John 114
Coldwell Wm 82
Cole Henry 26..Abram 108..
    Martin 26..Thos 25..Jno 97
Coleman Chas 83..Jas 121..Jno 97..
    Noah 6..Wm 97
Colhoun John 42
Collends John 82
Collier Joseph 97
Collins Jno 49, 97, 121..Thos 97..
    Joseph 83, 97
Colly Mainyard 81
Colson Jacob 68
Comins Harmen 30
Con William 83..Jno 34..Thos 68
Conley Robert 14
Connall Jesse 121
Conner Edw 117..Jas 31, 82, 97..
    John 118
Conrad Steven 97
Converse Amos 97
Conway Saml 119
Conyers Chas 111, 108..Danl 68..
    Clement 57..Jas 68, 111, 108..
    Jno 97, 111..Norwood 85, 86..
    Straughan 48
Cook Jno 13, 20, 87, 117, 120, 125..
    Lewis 20..Wilson 68..

Burrell 84, 97..Wilson 68
    Nath 82..Thos 85, 87..Wm 37
Cookley Benj 97
Cooner Jacob 97
Cooper Benj 119..Geo 97, 121..
    Leonard 57..Ezek'l 97..
    Jerem'h 126..Thos 24..
    James 97..S. 68
Cope Brian 115
Copeland Ripley 48..Jno 97..
    William 47
Cordes John 115
Corgill Magnus 114
Corley Abner 37, 118..Jno 68, 118..
    Caleb 108..Nath 118.
    Sherod 118..Zacheus 118
Cornyorck Lewis 118
Corn Danl 46..Lewis 46
Cornwall Benj 97..
Corrigan Wm 97
Corry Nicholas 97
Cosnahan Joseph 97, 108
Corson Linsey 81..Robt 81
Costeng John 86
Cougaler Fran 81
Council Henry 97, 114
Couterier John 57, 68
Covington Benj 97
Cowan Andrew 121..Ish'm 80..
    Henry 97
Cowley Robt 14
Cox Chas 117..Jas 85, 86..Wm 43
Cox Saml 43, 97..Henry 108
Craig Alex 81..Jno 97, 114..
    Jas 97..Isaac 97
Crain Stephen 34..Jno 79..
    Mayfield 82, 120..Wm 39, 82..
    Stephen 97
Craps John 120
Crawford Bellamy 86..Geo 80..
    Joel 120, 121..Jas 81, 97..
    Jno 27, 126..Robt 68, 108..
    Saml 84..Pat'k 97
Crawley Charles 86
Cray Joseph 85
Crayton Charles 83
Crenshaw Stephen 119
Cress Philip 83
Creswell James 97, 114
Crington Joseph 115
Cripps Jno S. 85..Splatt J. 86..
    William 86
Crittendon Nath 97
Crocker Anth'y 49..Sol 49
Croes Joseph 17
Croft John 84
Crooker Turner 4

191

Croom Maj. 108
Cropper Jno 97
Crosby Tim'y 115..Thos 108
Crosley Saml 81
Crossland Ed 97
Crouch Henry 85, 86
Crow Abram 49
Crownover Danl 51
Crowther Isaac 57
Cudworth Benj. 85, 86..Nat 15
Culbertson Jos'h 121..Rob 42, 97
Culp Benj. 97
Culpepper Benj. 81..Jos 80
Culler Benj. 97
Cummens Jno 81, 83..Rich 85
Cumpton Thomas 83
Cunningham Arth'r 68, 97..
    David 117..Miles 83..
    Jas 41, 120..Jno 7, 97..
    Robert 83
Cureton Jno 114, 126..Wm 97
Curry Robt 83
Curtiss James 81
Curweethus Wm 84
Cuttino Wm 114

D ***** D

Dabbs Joseph 68, 97
Dacosta Isaac 87
Dacus Nathl 39
Dalyrimple John 97
Darnall Jos 97
Dantzler Jacob 97
Danell Joseph 68
Daniel Aaron 68..Ezek'l 44..
    Jno 57, 97, 120..Jas 97
Darby Benj. 121..Asa 97
Darden Geo 119
Dark Jno S 57
Darrant Chas 97
Darrell Edw 85, 86
Dash John 84
David Jno 69..Peter 27..Wm 97
Davenport Jas M. 97..Wm 97
Davidson Jos 9..Jon 97..Wm 97
Davier B. 69
Davies Jno 83..Saml 97..Jos 83..
    Myrick 97
Davis Abslm 120..Amos 97..
    Andrw 97, 120..Geo 53, 97..
    David 69..Fred 120..Jos 97..
    Harman 57..Henry 69..Jas 72..
    Jno 45, 57, 97..Jon'thn 39..
    Ransom 69..Robt 118..Sam 120..
    Sneed 83..Surrey 121..

Thos 118..Wm 69, 97, 120..
    Zach 118..Jos 97..Wm R. 57.
Day Saml 82..Wm 12, 119
Dayton Jonth'n 79
Deal Michael 84
Dean Joel 97..Julius 17..Thos 17
Dearman Wm 81
DeGraffenried Techarner 97
DeLeon Jacob 97
Deepnest Wm 83
De La Horn 79
DeLaney Jno B 117
D'Ellient Andrw 57
DeLoach Saml 118..David 97
Dennis Isiah 81..Jno 97
Denny James 83
DePriest Wm 108
Dessaussure Danl 69, 85, 86, 97..
    Louis 57..Wm 85
Dehasser John 81
DeTreville Jno LaB. 57
Devlin James 12, 97
Dew Thomas 97
DeWar Robt 85, 86
DeWitt Charles 69..Wm. 97
Deyo James 108
Dial Jerem'h 120..Martin 98..
    Henry 127
Dick Chas 28..Wm 108
Dickenson Benj 57
Dickey David 39, 81..Geo 119..
    Jno. 111..Robt 120
Dickson David 120..Jas 82, 98..
    Matt 98..Will 84
Dill Joseph 115
Dillard Jas 42
Dispair Benj 39
Disto Jesse 84
Dobson Coilion 98
Dixon Henry 57
Dobbins David 80
Doby John 98
Dodd Abel 119..Jno 115, 121..
    Jesse 121..Wm 30
Dodge Oliver 98
Doggatt Joel 57
Doharty James 69
Dominick Henry 45, 98
Donaldson Jas 57..Jno 114..
    William 98
Donnom Wm 57
Dorn Geo 98
Dorland Garrab 108
Dorsey Basil 98
Dorsius Jno 85
Doty Silas 98
Dougherty Jno 14
Douglas John 118, 98

192

Douthit John 98
Dow Danl 119
Dowall Jno 83..Geo 83, 121
Dowling Robt 98..Wm 98
Downes Wm 57, 98, 120
Downs Arthur 115..Jno 117
    Jonth'n 114..Walter 114..
    William 82
D'Oyley Danl 57
Dozier John 69, 98
Drake Albrittan 98..Aberlain
    98..Aug. Matt 98..
    Oliver 98
Drayton Charles 57..Glen 57..
    Stephen 57..Thos 69..
    Wm.H. 98, 114, 115
Drewery Fletcher 121
Driver John 117
Dubois David 57
Dubose Andrw 69..Elias 69..
    Isaac 57..Saml 98..
    Peter 48
Duckett Jos 98
Dudley Ambrose 98
Duff Andrw 87..Jas 57
Duffie John 81
Duggin Leo 84
Dukes Wm 108
Dunbar Thos 57, 117..Jas 98
Duncan Jno 6, 120..Wm 19, 98..
    James 98
Dunklin Joseph 121, 127
Dunlap Jos 85, 87..Wm 11, 42..
    George 98
Dunn Andrw 82..Jerem'h 98
Dupriest John 83
DuPuy Jno 98
Durant Henry 98
Durham Charnel 38, 69, 86
Durkins John 98
Dusenburg Charles 98
Dutarque Louis 57
Dwight Nath 114
Dysert Corn 84

        E ***** E

Earle Bayliss 98..Jno 98..
    Samuel 57, 98
Earnwood Wm 80
Easterling Wm 98
Eberly John 85
Eddins Benj 98, 119
Eden field David 120
Ederington Francis 69
Edmaston John 84

Edmonds Jas 85, 86..
    David 57, 58
Edson Jas 118..Jno 118
Edwards Abel 114..Wm 120..
    Henry 120..Jno 69, 85..
    Rich 98..Thos 98..
    Warren 85
Egan John 85
Elam Wm 98
Elbert Sam 120
Eldridge Christpr 98
Eliott Chas 82..Jno 83..
    Thomas 69, 85
Elkins Jno 83..Johnson 20
Ellerbe Robt 111..Wm 98..
    Thos 69, 111, 114
Elliot Thos. 57, 69, 86..Sam 69..
    Benj 69, 79, 114..Barnard
    57..Jos 57, 85..
    Wm 80, 84, 85
Ellis John 23
Ellison Robt 98
Ellsworth Chas 98
Embry Joseph 119
Emerson Henry 49..Jno 98
England Wm 119
Enlow Deason 25
Ensign Jno 98
Epes Peter 98
Epting Adam 98
Epperson David 108
Ervin Hugh 111..John 69, 98, 111..
    Saml 111
Erwin James 69..Wm. 98
Eskridge Burdett 118
Esom John 57
Espey Saml 98
Estill Wm 98
Eubank John 69
Evance Jas 82..Jno 84..Thos 57, 98..
Evans Batte 17, 98..Chas 69..Enoch
    69..Ezek'l 98..Geo 57, 69..
    Jno 85, 121..Perry 28..
    Roland 98..Nathan 98..
    Philip 39..Wm 98
Eveleigh Gei 57..Michl 57..Nich 57..
    Thos 85, 86
Everett Thos 98
Evins Alex 121
Ewell Jas 98
Ezell Hartwell 120..John 84

        F ***** F

Fain William 98
Farquhar Robt 98

Fambrough Thos 108
Farley David 120
Farmer John 39..Shadrack 39
Farr Jno 58..Robt 24..Thos 69, 115..
 William 98
Farrabe Caleb 108
Farrar Field 58, 79..Thos 58, 120
Farrow Thos 50, 69..Rosan W. 98
Farson Jno 82
Fathern Benj 81
Faust Burrell 98
Fayssoux Peter 58, 79, 85, 98
Fearn Jno 98
Feaster Andrw 98
Felder Henry 98, 121..Jno H. 98
Fellows Nath 119
Fenner Rich 121..Robt 121
Fenwicke Thomas 69
Ferguson Moses 80..Saml 79, 98..
 Thos 86, 114, 115
Feris James 87
Field James 58
Few Wm. 98
Files Abner 119..Jerem'h 119
Findley Jno 121..Jas 98..
 Jno 31..Paul 42, 108
Finnell Charles 119
Fishburne Wm 58
Fisher Adam 98..Geo 46..Sam 98..
 Jas 26, 86
Fitten Isaiah 83
Fitts Jno 98
Fitzgerald Jno 69
Fitzpatrick Thos 120..Wm 58
Fitzsimmons Chris 115
Fladger Chas 98..Henry 98
Flagg Geo 85, 86..Henry 58, 79
Flanagan Jas 81
Fleming Jas 26, 111..Jno 111..
 Wm 111, 118..Sam 128
Fletcher Jno 120..Wm 117
Fleorl Jno 98
Flewellyn Abner 98
Flinn Jas 82..Wm 37, 98
Flint Jno 84
Flood Thos 98
Flornay Matt 98
Floyd Abram 121..Andrw 55..
 Chas 120..Jno 98
Fogartie Jas 69..Jos 69
Foissin Peter 58
Folger Fred 98..Reuben 98
Forney Peter 98
Forbes Jno 58, 84..Robt 84..
 Thos 81
Ford (Foard) Jno 98, 114..
 Benj 86..Geo 69..Jas 69..
 Tobias 58..Wm 121

Forden John 82
Forister Wm 80..Jno 80
Forsythe Robt 98
Fort Albert 36..Dunn 118
Fortinberg Jno 83
Foster Jno 81..Josh 28..
 Wm 121..Abiel 99..Jas 99
Foust Jno 80..Wm 80
Fowles Oliver 86
Fox Wm 99
Foy Peter 118
Francis Saml 27
Francum Francis 15
Franklin Jno 81..Thos 119
Franks Marshall 119, 120..
 Saml 42
Fraser (Frazer) Alex 58, 99..
 Jas 31..Sam 83..Thos 99
Freeman Michl 82..Sam 42
Freer Chas 69
Fridig(Friday)Gabl 99
Fripp Jno 99
French Jos 82
Frey Phil 25
Frierson Geo 111..Robt 111..
 Jno 58, 111, 115, 99..
 Phil 111..Wm 111, 120
Frizell Jno 82
Fuller Arthur 42..Jno 99..
 Meshac 25..Nath 69..
 Rich 58..Stephen 24..
 Wm 86, 128
Fullerton Jno 69, 99
Fullton Jasper 108..Jas B. 53
Fulmer Jacob 43
Furman Benj 83..Wood 99
Futhy Wm 69

G ***** G

Gabeau Anthony 99
Gadsden Ghristpr 58, 61, 85, 86, 99..
 Phil 85..Thos 58, 87
Gaillard Chas 99
Gains Thos 22..Jos 99..Rich 108
Gaither Burgess 99
Gale Matt 99
Gamble Robt 99..Jno 70, 121
Galliway Jas 69
Galtry David 30
Galvan Wm 58
Garden Alex 58, 79..Jno 70
Gardner Jno 84..Wm 84, 99
Garkey Michl 80
Garner Saml 17
Garrard Jacob 120

Garrett David 27..Thos 27, 119
Garretson Jno 121
Garrick Isaac 118..Wm 119
Garrison Isaac 83..Jed 120
Garry Jno 99..Thos 99, 119..
  Charles 128
Garven Thos 108
Gaskie Michl 85
Gassaway Jas 23
Gaston Jas 82..Jno 99..
  Jos 3, 35, 99..Wm 120..
  Robt 58, 121..Wm. Robt 121
Gause Wm 99..Jno 108
Gatam Jno 84
Gaudy Ephraim 36
Gault Robt 41
Gayle Josh 87, 114..Matt 99
Gay Jas 108
Gaylord Saml 80
Gaze Noel 86
Geer Christian 85
Geiger Jno 99
George Gotlieb 99
Gerret Wm 83
Gremmell Jno 117
Gervais Jno L 58, 99, 115
Gibbes Wm H. 35, 70, 85, 86, 115, 99
Gibbons Jno 85, 86
Gibhart Adam 27
Gibson Eras 46, 99..Jno Jas 120..
  Jno 51..Silas 117..Wm 121
Gigailliat Gabriel 115
Gilbraith Jos 84
Gilbert Amos Alling 99..Asabel 99
Gilchrist Jno 99
Gilder Reuben 99
Giles Jas 83, 99..Nath 81..
  Thos 58, 115..Noah 99..
  Wm 99
Gilham Jacob 81
Gilkey Wm 99
Gill Archbd 81..Geo 34, 81..
  Jas 119..Jno 84
  Thimas 120
Gillaspie Jas 83..Andrw 111..
  Francie 114..Geo 99
Gillett Abram 79
Gillham Ezekl 120
Gilliam Robt 121
Gillihan Isaac 120..Jas 99
Gillon Alex 70
Gilmore Danl 29
Girardeaux Jno 35
Giroud David 114
Girardeau Jno 99
Girraud Peter 85
Givens Saml 99

Gladney Saml 99
Glasgo Robt 82, 99
Glass Fred 80
Glazier Jno 99
Glenn Jas 53, 99..David 99..
  Wm. C. 99
Glossom Nich 118
Glover Jno 17..Jos 70, 85, 99..
  Wilson 58
Glyn David 82, 115
Godbold Zach 119..Stephen 99
Godbolt Jas 70
Godfrey Thos 114
Goforth Preston 99
Goggans Wm 121..David 99
Golding Reuben 42
Goldsmith Wm. 99
Goldwire Jas 99
Golson Lewis 108
Goodall Robt 117
Goode Wm 50
Gooding Jno 99
Goodlett Jno 39
Goodman Benj 87..Wm 108..
  Jos 70
Goodson Thos 36..Wm 119
Goodwyn Jno 58..Rich 58..Robt 58..
  Uriah 58..Wm 58
Gordin Isaac 50..Jas 111, 114..
  Jno 111, 114..Roger 70, 99..
  Wm. 111, 99..David 99
Gorgan Jno 117
Gosard Isaac 80
Gosling Geo 13, 83
Gough Jno 70..Rich 70, 115, 121,
  99, 108
Gowan Jno 121
Gracy Robt 81
Grady Jno Wm 99
Graham Alex 84..Geo 83..Jas 35..
  Jno 119..Michl 108..
  Staf'd 47..Wm 99
Grant Jas 99..Wm 99
Graves Lewis 120..Jos 70..
  Jno 85, 86..Wm 85, 86
Gray Fred'k 31..Geo 58..
  Henry 15, 58, 117..Jas 58..
  Jacob 81..Jno 47, 83, 108..
  Peter 58
Grayson Jno 58, 99..Thos 85
Green Geo 31..I 70, 81..Wm 83..
  Jacob 119..Thos 83..Jno 99..
  Isaac 99.Peter 99
Greer Thos 81
Gregg Jas 70..Jos 99
Gregory Isaac 19..Thos 84
Gresset Wm 99

Grier Thos 99
Gresham Jno 47
Gribble Thos 81
Griffin Gid'n 82..Jesse 14..Jno
  84, 120..Owen 117..Ralph 121..
  Rich 99..Chas 99..
  Jas 99..Jos 99
Griffis Thos 82
Griffith Jos 70
Grigsby E 108
Grimball Thos 70, 85, 86
Grimes Wm 82
Grimke Fred 115..Jno F. 58..
  John P 115
Grisham Moses 34
Grist Benj 47
Gross Francis 86
Grott Francis 85
Gruber Philip 41
Guerrard Benj 85, 86
Guerry Saml 58..Stephen 58
Guest Wm 47
Guillaud Jas 86
Gules Wm 83
Gumeas Elias 99
Guin Jno N. 99
Gunnungust Fred 108
Gunter Henry 20..Jno 26
Gunnell Henry 108
Guthery Jas 51
Guyton Aaron 30
Gwin Jno 129

H ***** H

Hager Cymon 83
Haigler Jacob 46
Haile Benj 121..Jos 21
Hailey Wm 99
Hains David 83
Halbert Wm 99, 108
Halcomb Jno 3
Hale Wm 120
Haley Jno 79
Halks Jas 26
Hall Geo Ab 70, 85, 86..
  Jesse 47, 99..Saml 83..
  Jno 58, 117..Sol 32..
  Thos 58, 85, 86, 121..
  Wm 85, 86, 115, 99, 121
Haltiwanger Jno 99
Hallam Jno 121
Hamilton Andrw 48, 70, 99..
  David 38, 47, 85, 86, 99..
  Jno 58, 99, 111..Jos 70..
  Jas F 81, 111..Thos 99, 119..

Paul 121..Wm 82, 111, 121, 100
  Ann K. 99
Hambright Fred 99
Hammond Geo 70..Job 121..
  Abner 100..Chas 100..
  Jno 70..Saml 37, 70, 100..
  LeRoy 70, 115, 100
Hampton Edw 70..Jno 58..
  Henry 59, 70, 81..Thos 100..
  Rich 58..Wade 58, 80
Hancock Clement 86, 87
Hand Jno 81
Hanna Robt 53, 119, 121..Thos 50
Hanson Walter 100
Harbison Geo 120..Jas 35
Hamett Thos 99
Harris Tucker 108
Harchfield Henry 100
Hardaway Joel 58
Hardee Wm 20
Harden (in,ing) Wm 70, 120..
  Henry 100..Geo 119..
  Lewis 14
Hardgrove Jno 84
Hardwick Wm 114, 120
Hardy Christpr 87..Jno 100..Tho 100
Hardyman Jos 70..Thos 70
Hargett Jno 81
Hargrave Robt 70..Saml 70
Hariot Robt 114
Harleston Isaac 58..Jno 70
Harlow Benj 70
Harnsberger Conrad 100
Harrell Jerm'h 121..Zack 121..
  Lewis 100
Harrington Drury 51, 119..
  Wm H 70, 114..Henry 100
Harris Aaron 117..Arthur 100..
  Drury 81, 84..Edw 81..
  Goodman 12..Griffin 84..
  Hugh 100..Jas 81..Wm 82..
  Jno 30, 80, 81, 82, 100, 129..
  Mason 84..Matt 100..
  Thos 85, 86..Tucker 79..
  Sherwood 100..Robt 100
Harriss Micajah 70
Harrison Reuben 121..Benj 100..
  Constan 84..Jas 100..
  Richard 100
Harry Charles 119
Hart Arthur 114..Jas 84..
  Derrill 70..Jacob 82..
  Jno 58..Jos 84..
  Oliver 58, 79, 86
Hartthorn Jos 58
Hartly Thos 115
Hartwell Ezell 120..Jas 120

Jno 120..Landson 100
Harwood Thos 100
Harvey Robt 115..Thos 70, 120..
  Wm H 85, 86..Arnold 100
Haselden Wm 100
Haselaw Wm 108
Haskew Jno 114
Hastin Absalom 50
Hastings Robt 17
Hatch Benj 100..Jos 100
Hatcher Benj 100..Jos'h 100
Hatfield Saml 84
Hatton Fran 120
Hawkins Jno 119..Joshua 26..
  Thos 120
Hawk Jno 81
Hawthorne Jos 121
Hay Ann H 100..Melchoir 100..
  Hayne Isaac 71..Alex 10..
  Barth 82..Jno 100
Hayes Adam 82..Andrw 83..
  David 80..Hugh 82..
  Jas 84, 108..Dan 87..
  Jno 81, 82, 100..Wm 82..
  Moses 82..Nath 82..
  Jos 87, 100
Haynesworth Henry 100
Hazel Thos 114..Henry 100
Hazelton Wm 81
Hazzard Wm 58, 100
Head Jas 121..Rich M 29
Headlee Elisha 119
Healtey Chas 58
Heard Jno 58
Hearn Drury 37
Hearst Jas 108
Hempstead Stephen 100
Hemphill Sam 83..Wm 80
Heath Jordan 100
Henderson Ezek 39..J.W. 119..
  Sam 53, 100..Thos 47, 100..
  Wm 58, 115
Hendricks Wm 71
Hennenton Jno 58
Hennery(ry) Saml 114..Thos 114..
  Futhy 114..Jac'b 85, 87..
  Malcolm 121
Henson Jesse 84
Heran Jno 84
Herbert Thos 129
Heriot Robt 100
Herndon Benj 100
Herrick Ebenez 100..Israel 100
Herrin Wm 82
Hester Abram 39
Hewet Hill 118..Jno 80
Hews Thos 85

Hext Wm 58
Heyward Dan 71..Jno 71..
  Jas 85, 86..Wm 58..
  Thos 71, 85, 86..
  Nathl 100
Hickman Sam 118..Wm 100
Hicks Geo 71, 100, 114..
  Jesse 36
Higgins Jno 100
Hill Abram 81, 119..Josh 100..
  Hiram 119..Lodwik 84, 100..
  Wm 71, 83, 100..Squire 100
Hillhouse Wm 120
Hilton Jas 108
Hilyard Peter 37
Hinds Patk 115..Bartlett 100
Hinman Elisha 100
Hiott Jno 34
Hird Jno 71
Hogan Jas 115..Wm 38
Hodge Alex 119..Benj 48..
  Jno 51..Wm 81
Hodges Benj 58..Jno 32..
  Josh 100..Wm 44, 108
Hogiss Saml 83
Hogg Thos 119
Hogshead Saml 121
Holbrook Nath 100
Holcombe Thil 121
Holder Dan 51..Jesse 7
Holding Matt 71
Holiday Wm 115..Dan 119
Holland Jacb 119..Matt 80..
  Moses 100..Thos 100
Holley Richard 114..Sion 2
Holliman Jas 41
Hollingsworth Enoch 100..
  Jeptha 100
Hollis Jas 51..Jno 38..
  Moses 71..Wm 120
Hollister D. Elijah 100
Holloway Taylor 81
Holman Conrad 100
Holmes B. Jno 85..Isaac 85, 86..
  Orsamus 100..Wm 85, 86
Holroy Turpin 86
Holston Chrstpr 115
Holt Claiborne 26
Holtzclaw Cath R. 100
Hood Andrw 30..Jno 84
Hook Martin 100
Hope Jas 108
Hopper Jas 117
Hopkins David 100
Hopkinson Fran 100
Horlbeck Jno 100
Hopton Wm 115..Henry 108

Horn Alex 115
Hornby Wm 85
Horry Alex 114..Dan 58..
   Hugh 71..Pete 58, 115
Horseley Richard 53
Horton Thos 121
Hough Jos 108
Houlditch Wm 82
Hourston Jas 58
Houser Andrw 46..Geo 100
Houseal Wm 100
Houston Geo 83..Hugh 12..
   Jas 79..Sam 100, 119..
   Jno 121
Howard Ezek 47..Jno 120..Jos 119..
   Wm 81..Seth 100..Groves 100
Howe Dan 100..Sam 100
Howerton Jas 22
Howl Wm 37
Howland Lewis 2
Howle Wm 121
Howser Andrw 84
Hoyle Jno 108
Hubbard Wm 47
Hudson Hall 120
Hudgens Ambrose 100
Huff Benj 81..Steph 39
Huffman Jno 17, 83
Huger Benj 58, 114..Fran 58..
   Isac 58..Jno 71, 114
Huggins Benj 71..Jno 71, 100
Hugh Chas 82
Hughes Geo 82..Henry 58..
   Jas 118..Jos 100, 119..
   Thos 71, 85, 86, 100..
   Saml 82
Hull Jos 117
Humberger Joshua 83
Hume Alex 58
Humphreys Ablm 81..Dav 47..
   Jno 117
Hunt 39..Jo 83..Sam 100
Hunter Dav 71..Edw 83..Jno 83..
   Andw 100..Jas 100..
   Henry 100..Sam 84..Tho 80
Huntington Jas 100
Husbands Loami 117
Huske Jno 108
Hutto Henry 108
Huston Jno 84
Hutchins Jos 115..Drury 100
Hutchinson Drury 50..Saml 53, 83..
   Steph 17
Hutson Drury 83..Rich 85, 86..
   Thos 100
Hyatt Jacob 82
Hyde Martin 80, Jedk 80

Hylie Jacob 80
Hyrne Edmd 58..Henry 71

I ***** I

Inabinet Jno 100
Ingram Edw 100..Jno 100
Imhoff Jno L.S. 59
Ingles Lloyd 115..Wm 100
Inis Martin 83..Wm 83
Inlo Thos 17..Jno 23
Inmas S. 71
Irby Edm 71..Greaf 87..
   Jos Jr-Sr 87, 100, 121
Irish Martin 84
Irvin Saml 121
Irvine Wm 79
Irwin Jno 83..Robt 82
Isaacs Elijah 85
Isbell Pendleton 24
Ivey Robt 117
Izard Ralph 100

J ***** J

Jack Jas 83
Jackson Ambs 81..Bazil 59..
   Benj 35..Dan 120..
   Jno 71, 80, 84..Sam 82..
   Josh J. 17..Thos 84..
   Steph 71..Wm 59, 82
Jacob(s) Shadk 80..Dan 85..
   Joshua 82
Jaggers Nathan 121
James Alex 71, 111..Benj 80, 100.
   Dav 100..Geo 111..Jas 33..
   Henry 84..Elias 100..
   Jno 71, 100, 111..Robt 111..
   Rollen 83..Wm 111
Jamieson Jas 35..Jos 53..
   Robt 119
Jarvis Elisha 47..Sol 108..
   Nath 101
Jasper Wm 117
Jaudon Jas 121
Jeffers Allen 48..Litleby 84
Jeffries Alln 82..Berry 82..
   Geo 82..Nath 100, 121..
   Wm 121
Jefft Saml 118
Jeneret Jacob 71
Jenkins Arthr 81..Benj 71..
   Jas 48, 101..Reuben 71..
   Jos 59, 71, 101..Jno 71..
   Shadk 84..Thos 71

Jenny Jas 82
Jernigan Jos 101
Jervey Thos 117
Jeter Jas 51..Henry 101..
   Levi 120
Jewey Thomas 59
Jiles Wm 83
Jinkins Jas 71..Jno 84
Johannes Peter 81
Johnson Elij 48..Ellis 50..
   Howell 50..Jas 101..
   Jos 117..Levi 82..
   Rich 71..Noble 101..
   Robt 59, 79..Thos 79..
   Rowland 50..Wm 44, 71, 85,
   86, 101, 119
Johnston Dav 80, 82..Jno 101..
   Matt 83..Nathan 101..
   Thos 80, 108..Chas 108
Joiner Jno 71
Jolly Jos 101
Jon Henry 81..Thos 101
Jones Adam C. 101, 71..Abram 101..
   Chas 101..Britton 84..
   Dan 118..Ed 71, 115..Geo 85..
   Jacb 47..Jas 120..Matt 118..
   Jeremh 46, 101..Jno 59, 81, 101..
   Jonth 82..Matt 118..Nathn 40..
   N.W. 85, 87..Pete 101..Wm 117..
   Sam 40, 101.. Rich 59
Joor Joseph 59
Jordan Jonthn 71..Henry E. 101..
   Jno 81
Joyner Wm 81

K ***** K

Kaigler Andrw 121
Kalb Benj 121
Kalteissen Michael 59, 71
Karr Wm 81
Karwon Thos 71
Kea(Kee) Chas 14..Thos 72
Kean Jno 85, 86
Keels Jno 101
Keeler Jeremh 101
Keer Hance 84
Keith Alex 59..Corn Jr 101, 121
Keller Debault 121
Kelly Abram 21..Dan 72..Jas 72..
   Gresham 119..Jno 81, 117..
   Lloyd 120, 121..Timothy 129
Kelson Saml 82
Kendrick Sam 101
Kennamer Geo 108
Kenmoure Jno 53

Kennady(edy) Alex 80..Jno 101..
   Jas 59, 87, 121..Sam 101..
   Wm 101..Thos 119..Wm 121-9
Kennon Henry 85, 86
Kennerly Jas 101
Kent Chas 85..Phineas 101
Keowin Thos 85
Kerr Andrw 53,.Dan 101..Jos 5, 84
Kershaw Eli 59..Jno 115..Jos 101..
   Jasper 108
Kesler Jno 81
Ketchen Jos 101
Kever Jas 121
Keys Malcolm 11
Kilgore Benj 86, 101, 114, 115, 121..
   Henry 114..Jas Wm 129
Kilpatrick Robt 38, 101, 119
Kimble Robt 26..Fred 72
Kimbrough Jno 72
Kinard Michael 101
Kincaid Jas 72, 82, 101..
   Jno B. 119..Wm J. 119
King Chas 114..Benj 101..
   Fran 81..Geo 72..
   Hugh 80..Jas 17..
   Jno 50, 101..Jos 5, 119
Kinlock Francis 115
Kinnill Joseph 72
Kirby Archd 44..Jas 101
Kirk Jno 87..Thos 82..
   Lewis 101
Kirkland Moses 59..Fran 108..
   Wm 119..Reuben 101
Kirkpatrick Jas 14..Jno 108..
   Spencer 15
Kitts Martin 84
Kline Michael 83
Knap John 59
Knight Jas 72, 108..Jno 81,
   114, 121, 101
Knotts Benj 101
Know Jas 83
Knowlton Grant 28
Knox Jas 101..Hugh 16, 111..
   Jno 121..Robt 111..
   Sam 83..Wm 14
Kobb Abel 72..Joshih 59
Koger Jos 72, 101..Jas 108
Kolb Jehu 36..Abel 101..
   Thos 27
Kytle Jacob 39

L ***** L

Lacy Edw 72..Jas 59
Ladson Abram 72..Jas 59..Thos 72

Laggett Josh 118
LaGroue Adam 121
Lake Thos 101
Lamar 120..Thos 101
Lambley Wm 119
Lamkin Stephen 108
Lancaster Saml 82
Land Lewis 39..Wm 101..Moses 120
Lane Jesse 101..Job 101
Landsder Robt 81
Langdon Thos 72
Langford Dan 59
Langston Sol 101..Laeodicia 101
Lanman Jas 121
Latner Nich 19
Lathrop M 108
Lanier Burwell 101
Larray Michael 101
Laurens Henry 114, 115, 129..Jno 59
Laval Wm 4
Lavender Hugh 119
Lawrence Isaac 121..Benj 101..
   Jas 50..Mich 81
Laws Matt 84
Layle Wm 86
Lazarus Marks 35, 101
Learmouth Alex 115
Lea Gabrielle 101..Jas 101
Leach Jas 101..Nehemh 101
Leary Corn 101
Lebby Nath 85, 86
Lecesne Chas Fred 101
LeCompte Jno 101
LeConte Jno E 101
Lee Jno 38..Andrw 101..Jos 101..
   Josh 101..Arthur 108..
   Stephen 86..Thos 121..
   Wm 72, 85, 86, 121
Leech David 101
Leeland Jno 101
Leeper Jno 119
Legaree Benj 72, 86..Jas 59, 115..
   Sam 72..Dan 115..Tho 85, 86..
   Sol 35, 115
Legran Oliver 81
Leirner Michael 115
Lemon Robt 119
Lennart Wm 108
Leonard Lock 87..Laughlen 101
Letcher Wm 101
Lequeare Jno 83
Lesene Jno 85
Lesesne Jno 86..Thos 59
Lessenee Peter 114
Lessonbury Reuben 83
Leston Thos 59
Lethgow R 72

Lett Jas 26
Levacher St. Marie 59
Lever Abram 85
Lewis Chas C 114..Jas 118..
   Jno 13, 85, 86, 101..Sam 119..
   Ann M 101..And 101..
   Mich 118..Wm 72, 101..
   Fielding 108
Lewellyn Abram 108
Libby Nath 101
Lide Robt 101..Thos 101
Liddell Geo 59..Wm 121..
   Andrw 101
Liddle Moses 72
Liddy Jno 83
Lide Robt 72, 129..Jno 129..
   Thos 72, 114, 129
Ligan Blackman 19
Lightwood Edw 115
Liles Jno 120
Limerick Patk 81
Linder Danl 72
Lindsay Jno 120, 72
Lindley Zeba 101
Lining Chas 59, 121
Linn Alex 83, Martin 119
Linton Saml 80
Lipham Fred 84
Lipperd Wm 121
Lipscomb Joel 119..Jas 108..
   Wm 101, 130
Lisle John 59
Lister 44
Liston Thos 85
Lisse Leonard 83
Little James 108
Littlejohn Chas 119..Jas 101
Liveston Abram 83, Henry 83
Livingston Henry 32, 101..
   Wm 72, 85, 86..Jno 101
Lloyd Benj 59..Ed 59..Jos 83..
   Martin 72
Loch Alex 81
Lochman Jno 59, 79, 86
Lock Rich 101
Lockwood Josh 101
Lockman Chas 79
Lockhardt Saml 86
Lofton Thos 119
Logan Andrw 32..Fran 72..Geo
   72..Hugh 83, 101..Jno 102..
   Wm 85, 86, 115, 102, 121
Lohner Jon 43
Long Jno 82..Felix 102..Robt 42..
   Henry 102..Jacob 102
Longmire Wm 121
Looney Jno 2, 30

Lott Wm 82
Love Alex 81, 101, 130..Dav 101..
  Hezk 121..Robt 101..Sam.41..
  Wm 59, 121
Loveday John 85, 86
Low(e) Jno 26..Jno P 108..
  Basil 108, 17..Dennis 17..
  Rob 108
Lovell Jas 102
Lowell James 102
Lowndes Rawlins 114, 115
Lucas Chas 117,.Jno 102, 121
Lucust Matt 81
Lumbley Matt 81
Lunsford Swanson 102
Lushington Rich 72, 85, 86
Lusk Jas 82, 120..Robt 82
Lybert Henry 86
Lyell Robt 59
Lyford Wm 115
Lyles Arramans 72..Jas 72..
  Jno 72
Lymme Jno 102
Lynch Thos Jr 59
Lyne(s) Wm 72, 102
Lynn Jas 119, 121..Dav 102..
  Jno 102
Lyon(s) Edw 12..Gathridge 72..
  Robt 81..Wm 81

M ***** M

McArthur Danl 103
McAbee Vardrey 121
McAbley Wm 108
McAdam John 32
McAllister Andrew 8
McBee Silas 120
McBride Jas 86..Wm 51
McCaferty Jno 81
McCaide Jno 117
McCain Hans 83..Hugh 83..Jos 83..
  Nathl 103
McCalla David 103
McCaleb Wm 120
MCall Dav 83..Hext 86..
  Geo 103..Hugh 73..Jas 73, 120..
  Jno 73, 83, 115..
  Sherrod 120
McCallaster Jno 83
McCammon Matt 82, 121..Jas 84..
  Jno 81
McCants Nathl 103
McCattry Robt 109
McCauley Jas 114
McCaw Jas 35

McClain James 10
McClary Robt 82
McClaud Donald 81
McClasky Joseph 121
McClean Jas 117
McCleary Saml 80
McCleeland Wm 73
McClendon Travis 103
McClerath Wm 84
McClery Saml 84
McClure Jas 82..Jno 73, 103..
  Rob 121..Sam 82..
  Wm 121
McClung Jno 103
McClurken Thos 35, 120
McColtry Wm 73
McCormick Rob 84..Jno 103
McCord Chas 103..Mark 103
McCoy Mech'd 83..Redden 49..
  Jno 103..Wm 103
McCracken Hugh 83..Jas 83..
  Wm 83
McCrady Edw 85, 86
McCravy Thos 103
McCree Wm 84, 103
McCreery Robt 73, Thos 103
McCreight Tobt 38
McCrery Arch'b 26
McCullough Geo 73
McCune John 15
McCurby Arch'd 82
McCurdy Jno 81, 103
McCutcheon Jno 119
McDaniel Arch'd 73..Ed 121..
  Wm 84
McDavid Jas 103..Jno M. 130
McDearmon Thos 121
McDill Jno 35..Thos H 121
McDonald Adam 59..Arch'd 117..
  Chas 86..Donald 45..Jas 51, 59
  Jno 49, 119..Pat 83
McDougal Alex 121
McDow Thos 41
McDowell Jno 117..Chas 103..
  Jas 103..Thos 82, 84..
  Margt 103..Jas 83
McElveen Wm 49
McElwee Wm 103
McEntire Robt 83
McFadden Isaac 82..Rob 103
McFalls Jno 83
McFarlin Geo 32
McFerring Arch'd 120
McGachy Jno 81
McGaughey Saml 119
McGarrough Jos 103
McGaw Wm 120
McGay Wm B. 120

McGee Mich 103..Jesse 130
McGibenay Hugh 83
McGilivray Robt 115
McGill Jno 111..Sam 111, 103
McGinnis Chas 59
McGlane Jno 83
McGoch Jno 84
McGowan Wm 121, 130
McGrew Wm 84, 103
McGregor Jno 103
McGuines Andrw 83
McGuire Elij 119..Merry 59
McGwigin Dan 82
McHaffey Oliver 21
McIntosh Alex 59, 73..Wm 30,
 49, 121
McIver Chas 118..Evander 103
McJunkin Jos 9, 73, 103..Sam
 103, 115
McKaskell Kenneth 40
McKenzey(ie) Will 83, 103..
 Wm 83..Alex 81
McKeown Alex 108
McKinney Jas 60..Jno 121
McIlahany Wm 87
McLeon Eph 103
McMaster Hugh 103..Jas 103
McMorris Wm 103
McMahon Peter 30..Jno 42..
 Arch'd 47
McManess Thos 73
McMichea David 83
McMillan Danl 35..Jas 33
McMillian Danl 120
McMullen(an) Alex 117..Jas 120..
 Jno 81, 109..Rowley 121
McMurry Jno 41..Wm 108
McNeely David 84
McNeese Jno 114
McNeill Dan 60, 79..Hectr 103
McQueen Alex 59..Jno 73
McRae(w) Duncan 73..Fran 103
McWaters Jno 84
McWherter Aaron 81..Jno 103, 119
 Alex 81..Geo 81..
 Jesse 81..Jas 52
Machen Henry 102
Mack Jno 102
Maafield Jno 81
Macauly Jno 72
Mackey Thos 41, 108..Jas 102
Magee Elisha 73
Magner Henry 12
Magruer Elijah 82
Mahaffey Martin 114
Maham Hezekiah 59

Majors Benj 119..Jno 119
Makentier Jno 82
Mallette Gideon 120
Malone Corn 119
Maloy Wm 118
Mangum John 119
Manning Lawr 102
Manson Fred 102
Marbury Thos 102
Marion Benj 72..Jos 121, 102..
 Fran 59, 115, 117..Gab'l
 102, 121..Pat'k 130
Markham Jas 87
Marley Jno 115
Marlow Jno 117
Marr Andrw 115
Marques Isaac 102
Marsh Rob 29..Wm 102
Marshall Thos 60..Jas 102
Martin Edw 115..Elij 120..
 Jas 53, 59, 79, 102, 130..
 Jno 2, 59, 73..Jos 117..
 Lewis 119..Matt 102, 121..
 Martin 26, 84..David 102..
 Gatlop 102..Isaac 102..
 Kitchen 102..Rich 102..
 N 72..Nath M 82..Peter 82..
 Salathiel 121..Sam 82, 83..
 Thos 53..Wm 17, 72, 120
Martindale Russell 121..Wm 121
Mashburn Jas 81
Mason Benj 119..Bledsoe 118..
 Dav 102..Geo 11, 102..
 Jno 47..Luke 59..Rich 59..
 Wm 59
Massey Henry 41, 108..Wm 59, 85, 86
Masters Thos 19..Dav 108..Ven 85
Mathews Benj 73..Brice 117..Ed
 115..Jno 115..Jno R 73..
 Matlock 102..Rowland 84..
 Sam 102..Tim'y 102..Wm 83
Matlock Tim'y 102
Mattison Jas 102
Mattock Wm 83
Maulden Bucker 102
Mauney Val 102
Maxwell Edw 102, 121..Wm 102
May Benj 73..Jno 102..Jos 120
Maybank Jos 73, 102
Mayes Saml 121
Mayrant Jno 49
Mayret Abram 86
Mayson Jas 59, 121
Mazyck Dan 59..Steph 59, 73
Meadows Jno 50
Means Wm 120..Jas 102

Moe Geo 84
Meek(s) Adam 121..Moses 80
Mellichamp St. Lo 102·
Meetze Jno Y 102
Mellog Andrw 12
Melson Sam 39
Melton Isham 17
Mengel Adam 102
Mercer Richard 86
Merchant Wm 102
Meredith Henry 42..Elisha 102..
    Sam 102
Merneal Jno 83
Merrett Jas 30
Merriwether Thos 102
Merrill Benj 102
Mershimer Sebastian 102
Messenger Dav 108
Mey Flo. Chas 86
Meyer Philip 86
Michael Jno 86
Michau Jacob 121
Middleton Arth 85, 114..Jno 59..
    Henry 114, 115..Thos 73..
    Hugh 59, 115, 120
Mikell Jno 73, 102
Milledge Jno 102
Miller Chas 102..Dav 102..
    Jac'b 102..Jas 102..
    Robt 102
Miles Jesse 44..Jno 87, 114
Milford Jno 30
Mill Thos 115
Milligan Geo 79..Moses 20
Millin(g) Jno 80..Hugh 59
Mills Jno 81, 82
Milner Jno 102, 120..Sol 86, 121
Milvern Jno 87
Milwee Wm 30
Mimms Drury 102
Minich Adam 86
Minot Abram 86..Jno Sr-Jr 86
Mitchell Ant'y 114..Eph 59..
    Geo 39..Jas 59, 83..
    Jno 80..Sol 121..
    Wm 51, 59, 82, 102
Moberly Edw 121..Sam 121..Jeremy
    102
Mode Jas 82
Monaghan David 59
Moncrief Jno 86
Moffatt 102
Monday Jeremiah 102
Monk George 86
Monroe Malcolm 102
Monterip Rich 60
Montague Jno 102,.Pete 102
    Thos 102

Montgomery Jas 120..Wild 115..
    Hugh 102..Jas 102
Moody Chas 73
Moon G 114
Moore Chas 114..Dav 81, 102..
    Fran 59, 83, 84..Gully 114..
    Alex 102..Eliab 102..
    Phil 102..Henry 59, 121..
    Jas 102, 115..Jeremh 114..
    Jno 53, 82, 114..Martin 117..
    Steph 86, 102..Thankful 86..
    Thos 32..Wm 30, 102, 121..
    Zach 119..Saml 82
Moorer Jno 102..Jas 108
Morehead Chas 102..Wm 102
Mordecai Saml 102
Morgan Jas 119..Benj 102..
    Dav 102..Geo 102..
    Jonthn 86..Spencer 102..
    Wm 73
Morrell Jno 85
Morris Jno 44, 102..Julien 108..
    Mark 115..Thos 120
Morrison Jno 82..Patk 82
Morrow Davis 119..Jno 82, 102..
    Jos 35..Sam 50, 102, 119..
    Wm 45
Morton Jno 120..Oliver 102..
    Wilkinson 85
Moseley Jos 32..Azarh 102..Benj
    102..Jas 51..Sam 102..Rob 130
Mosher Jno 108
Moses Geo 102..Myer 102
Moss Geo 86, 103..Jno 121..Jos 53
Most Geo 103
Motes Jas 23
Motette Lewis 79
Motlow Jno 82
Motte Chas 59..Isac 59, 117
Mouatt Jno 85, 86..Wm 59
Moultrie Alex 73, 85, 86, 115..
    Wm 59, 64..Thos 59
Mouzon Henry 73
Moye Geo 103
Muckenfuss Michl 103
Mullin Jas 103
Mulloy Edward 103
Munnanly John 103
Muller Albert A 73
Mullinax Mathea 83
Munnerlyn Jas 73
Murcer Jas 120
Murchey Wm 84
Murff Jno 103
Murphy(ee) Malachi 114..Jno 120..
    Jacob 117..Maurice 73..
    Wm, 82, 86

Murray Dav 84..Jno 115..Josh 84..
  Wm 103
Murrell Wm 84
Murrow Jno 118
Musick T.R. 119
Myers Jacob 103

N ***** N

Nance Sherwood 52
Nagel Phil 108
Nason Joshua 103
Natch Edw 103
Neal Jas 16, 82..Steph 52..Thos
  121, 130..Henry 103
Neavill Isac 73
Neel Jno 87..Wm 81..Thos 109
Neele Wm 84
Neely Sam 83, 120
Neighbors Benj 82
Neil Thos 74
Nelson Jas 38, 83..Jno 60, 74, 111..
  Rob 83, 111..Sam 103, 111..
  Thos 111..Wm 111
Nesbitt Jonthn 103
Nesmith Robt 103
Nettles Wm 40..Geo 103..
  Zach 103
Neufville Jno 85, 86..Ed 74..
  Wm 60, 79, 86
Neville Jesse 47, 103
Newberry Thos 47
Newcomb Danl 103
Newton Younger 103..Mose 120
Newell Dav 81
Newman Reuben 50
Newson Benj 60
Neyle Philip 60
Nichols Henry 74..Jos 81
Nicholson Dav 121..Wright 103,
  121..Gideon 118..Wm 119
Nicles Thos 83
Nicleson Jno 83
Nimmonds Wm 103
Nims Ariel 103
Nisbit Wm 121
Nixon Geo 60..Jno 74..Hugh 103
Noble Alex 74..Wm 13
Noblet Saml 50
Noland Shadrack 82
Nollen Geo 119..Steph 119
Nones Benj 86
Norris Patk 119..Jno 103..
  Wm 103
North Edw 75, 85, 86
Norton Ichd 103

Nuckolls Jno 103
Norwood Jno 74..Geo 103..
  Thos 32
Nunn Joseph 118

O ***** O

Oakes Danl 103
Odam Aaron 28
Oden Alex 119
Odill Thos 103
Odingsell Chas 115
Odom Dan 3..Levi 44..Sion 44
Off Isaac 82
Ogier Geo 60..Lewis 103
Ogletree Wm 103
Oldham Geo 30
O'Heak Jas 109
Oliphant David 60, 79, 87,
  114, 115..Rob 83..Wm 60
Oliver Jas 117, 120..Pete 46..
  Tilson 47..Alex 103
Olt Abram 74
O'Neall Saml 121..Wm 121
Orr James 103..G 109
Osborn Jno 50..Ephrm 103..
  Robt 83
Osheals Jno 50
Osmun Geo 81
Osteen Sol 120
Oswald Wm 74
Ottersen Saml 74
Otis Eph 103
Ott Abram 103
Ousby Thos 60
Outlaw Alex 119
Outson Jonthn 84
Outz Peter 103
Overall Nathl 103
Overly Henry 119
Owen Fredk 31..Jno 86, 119
Owens Jno 84..Jas 103..Thos
  28..Wm 41
Owings Richard 42, 130

P ***** P

Pace Newsome 103
Page Jno 103
Pagett Joel 118
Paine Thos 118..Dav 104
Palmer Danl 52..Job 35, 86..
  Josh 52..Jno 103, 121..
  Jon'thn 104
Parcival Benj 104

Parham Drury 50, 104
Parker Dan 81..Jno 74..Wm 86..
    Jos 85, 86..Dav 104..
    Moses 104
Parkinson Jno 104
Parks Abrm 114..Jas 119..Sam
    104
Parr Arthur 121
Parrott Thos 48, 74..Jno 104
Parsons Dav 117..Wm 109, 131..
    Jas 82, 114, 115
Partridge Wm 60
Patrick Cain 104..Henry 131
Pasley Robt 74
Pate Jno 104..Matt 104
Patterson Alex 32..Josh 104..
    Wm Jos 104
Patton Jacb 111, 114..Jno 121..
    Matt 52, 104, 111
Paul Jacob 118..Jno 119
Paulling Wm 104
Pawley Benj 114..Geo 114..Wm 114
Pawling Wm 84
Payne Jno 104..Josh 104
Payton Jno 104
Pearce Jno 26..Josh 104
Pearson Jno 74..Moses 74, 104
Pearman Wm 104
Pech Bela 104
Peers Valentine 74, 104, 114
Peeples Henry 104..Jno 81
Pegues Claud's 74, 104, 114..
    Wm 114
Pellam Wm 81
Pendergrass Darby 115
Pendleton Henry 115..Jno 83..
    Philip 131
Pennington Kinchin 84
Penrice Edmund 117
Perkins Dav 74..Geo 119..
    Thos 45
Peronneau Henry 60..Jas 60..Jno 60
Perse Silas 104
Perrin Theus 114
Perritt Needham 28
Perry Benj 79, 104
Peters Chris 85, 86..Jno 104
Peterson Jno 47
Pettigrew Jas 119..Alex 104
Petrie Alex 60..Peter 121
Pettitt Henry 82
Petty Theop 120..Ab 104
Phelps David 109..Elij 104
Philip Hugh 46..Levi 24..Wm 83..
    Jno 104..Jonas 104..Hugh 104..
    Mourning 104
Pickens Andw 74, 115, 104, 121..
    Jos 74..Wm 121

Pickering Wm 86
Pike Thos 115
Pilkington Drura 44
Pillans Robt 86
Pinckney Chas 60, 86, 114, 115,
    121, 131..Thos 60, 86..
    Hopson 104
Pinson Moses 114
Pittman Jas 104, 120..Jno 120..
    Phil 121
Pitts Henry 42..Wm 87
Plantt Wm 23
Platen Fred V 60
Pledger Jno 74..Jos 60..Phil 114
Plowder Edw 74
Pocher Saml 104
Pockron Jno 115
Poe Jas 119
Poinsette E 79
Pointer Thos 7..Jos 104
Polk Chas 82..Ezek 60, 74, 121..
    Thos 83..Wm 74, 82, 104.
Pollard Rich 60..Wm 50..Rob 104
Ponder Thos 39
Pone Dav 84
Pool Jas 42..Jno 119..Wm 104..
    Sherman 119
Pope Thos 26..Barnby 104..Sol
    104..Folgu 104
Porcher Peter 104
Porter Hancock 52..Hugh 81..Jno
    118..Rob 81..Sam 32
Portman Jno 120
Post Jno 74
Postell Benj 60, 85, 86, 104..Jas
    74, 104..Jno 74, 104
Poston Thos 81
Potter Jno 104
Potts Thos 60..Wm 81
Powe Thos 115
Powell Gabl G 74, 115..Jno 24..
    Abslm 104..Jas 104..
    Sevin 104
Powers Nich 36
Poyas Jas 86, 115..Jno E 60, 79, 85,
    86, 104..Jean E 104
Prescott Jas 79..Jno 60, 79
Presnoll Jacob 82
Pressley David 31
Preston Walter 104
Price Isac 84..Chas 104..Sam 37,
    119..Samson 119
Prince Fran 60..Henry 39..Jno 114..
    Nich 40, 118..Wm 121
Prioleau Hext 74..Phil 86..Sam 85,
    86, 115
Prior Luke 74..Seth 104

Pristly Chas 81
Pritchard Geo 104
Proctor Micajah 35
Prothro Evan 104, 120, 121
Proudlove Wm 82
Provaux Adrian 60
Prue Jno 115
Pruett Josh 12, 104..Saml 32
Pruitt Abram 82
Pugh Elij 109
Pullam Wm 84
Purcell Rev. Henry 60, 117
Purser Wm 104
Purvine Jas 81..Jno 81
Purvis Gilbert 120..Jno 60, 74..
    Geo 104
Putman Israel 104
Pyatt Jno 114
Pyron Wm C 109
Pyles Reuben 104

R ***** R

Raeford Jon 104
Rackley Fran 83..Jos 83..
    Parson 83
Ragsdale Peter 104..Jno 104
Rainey Saml 104
Rall Thos 104
Raley Chas 120
Ralston Jno 104
Ramsburgh Jas 104
Ramsey(ay) Dav 79, 85, 86..
    Henry 60..Jesse 79..Jno
    121..Wm 119..Jos 60, 79
Randall Robinson 120
Randolph Abram 119
Rankin Thos 104
Rasche Jno H 60, 79..Isac 79
Rass Gustavus 81
Rasor Christian 104, 131
Ravenel 104
Rawlins Richard 49
Rawls Wm 120
Rea Henry 53..Robt 83
Read Jacob 74, 85, 86..Wm 60, 79,
    118
Reading Geo 119
Reams Joshua 17
Redmund Jno 74
Reed Benj 104..Geo 74, 83..
    Jas 114..Jno 83..Sam
    104..Thos 83..Wm 79, 84
Reese Chas 83, 104..Geo 31, 119..
    Jos 104
Reeve Wm 32..Enos 104

Reid Geo 86..Jno 80, 82..Wm 83..
    Rich 31..Fran 104..Jos 104
Reizer Jno 21
Renick Jas 121
Renfro Mark 104
Rest Jno 82
Reynolds Jno 74..Rich 74..
    Saml 121
Rhinehardt Coonrad 83..Prunen 50
Rhodes Danl 86..Jacb 82..Tho 119
Rice Aaron 104
Richards Jno 84..Amos 104..Josh
    50..Rich 109
Richardson Amos 118, 104, 132..
    Ed 60..Wm 60, 74, 104..
    Rich 60, 74, 115, 117, 104
Richey Jno 47
Riddick Jos 104
Ridgeway Jno 43, 114, 132
Rife Conrad 82
Rightly Jno 81
Righton Jos 36, 86
Riley Jno 120
Ringo Corn 121
Rinker Jacob 105
Ripley Paul 87..Jeptha 105
Risher(ter) Benj 105, 109
Ritchie Jno 45
Rivers Saml 36, 105
Roberson Jas 60
Roberts Benj 82, 115, 116..
    Jesse 81..Jno 81, 117..
    Owen 60, 117..Robt 49..
    Rich B 60, 117, 118..
    Reubn 105..Wm 33, 117
Robertson Edw 119..Isrl 83..
    Jas 81, 83, 119..Jno 80..
    Jos 86..Wm 38, 105
Robineff Jesse 82
Robinson Geo 75..Jno 81, 86..
    Jos 86..Thos 105, 115..
    Wm 83, 105..Isac 105..
    Peter 105
Robuck Jno 120
Roche Dav 114..Patk 75
Rochester Nich 28
Rodgers Alex 60..Edw 114..
    Jno 75, 114..Jos 81..
    Nath 82..Robt 114
Roe Jas 118
Roebuck Benj 75..Geo 50
Rogers Achilles 119..Alex
    79, 83..Chrstpr 60..
    Dan 37..Ethelred 114..
    Nath 52..Seth 82..Wm
    81..Benj 105..Lot 105
Rolison Wm 119

Roney Maurice 84
Roof Geo 115
Rooker Jno 53
Rooks Wm 86
Rosa Petru 105
Roseboom Garret 105
Ross Geo 114..Dav 105..Jno 80..
  Isac 83, 84, 119
Rose Hugh 60, 79..Sam 10
Rothmaler Erasmus 60, 105..
  Job 75
Rouse Albert 75..Wm 105
Roux Albert 60, 117
Rowan Benj 15
Rowe Henry 75..Christ 105
Rowland Peter 24
Roy Jos 119..Beverly 105
Royal Wm 105
Royse Sol 109
Rozier Wm 23
Ruff David 105
Rumph Abram 105..Dav 105
Rusche Jno H 117
Rushin Jno 120, 75
Rush David 105
Russell Dan 87..Jas 12..Jno 82..
  Rob S 119..Thos J 83..
  Thos 60, 119, 105..
  Wm 105, 119, 121
Rutledge Andrw 60, 132..Edw 75,
  85, 86..Geo 105..Hugh 85, 86..
  Jas 81..Jno 114, 115, 132..
  Robt 105..Thos 75, 86
Rutherford Jas 105..Robt 105
Ryan Jas 75..Jno 86

S ***** S

Sadler David 31..Jno 83, 84
Sallers Jno 81
Salley Jno 105
Sallins Jas 83
Salmon Geo 121
Salter Edw 105
Sample Jesse 121..Jno 119..
  Thos 121..Wm 82
Sanders Henry 121..Peter 105..
  Jno 86..Roger P 60..Thos
  52..Wm 75
Sandford Saml 82
Sansum Jno 85, 86
Sardezaa David 15
Sass Jacob 36, 105
Sartor Wm 105
Satterwhite Jno 114
Saunders Jas 114..Nath 75, 105, 114

Savage Henry 83..Jno 75..Sam 114..
  Thos 85, 87, 114..Wm 115
Sawyer Jos 119
Saxon Jas 22..Lewis 121..Yancy 87
Saxton Atha 6..Jas 82..Chas 132
Saylor Michael 84
Scarrem Rich J 119
Schreiber Jacob 60
Scoggins Willis 32
Scot(t) Wm 83..Dav 40, 109..Rob 82..
  Dennis 14..Jas 29, 119..Jno 31,
  86, 115..Jos 75, 105..Josh 81..
  Joyce J 105..Nath 116..Sam 105..
  Rich 84..Walter 120..Wm 60, 121
Scovel Elisha 105
Screven Benj 60..T. 76
Scriven Benj 114
Scruggs Timothy 119
Seagler Wm 82
Seay Jas 50
See Jno 109
Seddall Stephen 105
Sell Philip 81
Sellers Jacob 84..Gordon 105
Selman Jeremiah 121
Senf Christian 60
Sessions Jno 117
Sergreave Jno 105
Sevier Jno 105
Sevington Hugh 105
Sewell Jas 119
Sexton Chap O. 109
Shackleford Jno 105
Shaddin David 81
Sharp Jas 75, 83, 116..Wm 105
  Col. Starkey 109
Shealor Jno 80..Wm 80
Shelbie Evan 80..Thos 82
  Moses 82
Sheldon Whiting 105
Spenard Chas 119..Jas 105
Shield Jno 84..Rob 83..
  Thos 83..Wm 84
Shingler Geo 105
Shirley Thos 121
Shiving Jas 105
Shope Peter 83
Shores Chrisitan 121
Short Abram 82
Shrewsberry Stephen 86
Shubrick Jacb 60..Rich 60..
  Thos 60, 75, 115
Shubirch Rich 105
Shuford Jno 105
Sibert David 121..Jno 121
Simmons Chas 17..Ishm 82..
  Maurice 75, 121..

Stubbs Chas 119..Lewis 44, 106..
    Wm 44, 106
Stubblefield Wm S 37
Stuflebeau Jno 119
Stutstill Jno 120
Suddoth Benj 121
Sudre Peter 86
Sullivan Chas 114, 132..Dan
    83, 114..Geo 114..
    Hulet 114, 106..Jno
    38, 114..Jonthn 114..
    Moses 114..Patk 114..
Summer Geo 43..Fran 106..Jno A 106
Sumner Dav 106
Summerford Wm 53
Sumter Thos 62, 79, 135
Sunn Fred 62, 79
Susack Adam 114
Suthmeyer Jacob 84
Sutton Jacb 119..Jno 76..
    Rob 76
Swearingen Van 106
Sweedy David 106
Swetman Stephen 84
Swink Jno Little 106
Swinton Hugh 106
Switzer Henry 106, 121
Swords Jno 24..Wm 82

T ***** T

Taggart Wm 62
Talbot Haile 119
Talbert Rich 106
Talbird Thos 106
Taliaferro Jno 79, 106..Jack 109
Tandy Archilles 121
Tanner Josiah 121
Tarrant Jas 119
Tate Robt 81..Wm 62, 115
Tatnall Jos 106
Tarver Absolom 106
Taylor Fran 106..Benj 119..
    Dan 119..Chas 47..Geo 106,
    121..Jas 76, 106..Jno 84,
    82..Eldad 106..Jonthn 17..
    Jeremh 38, 120..Merdth 38..
    Othnell 106..Paul 86..Sam
    62, 76, 84..Thos 62, 76, 106,
    116, 135..Wm 25, 120
Teague Wm 121
Team Adam 48, 81
Tebout Tunes 76, 115
Teer Wm 106
Templeman Aron 83
Tenell Wm 84

Tenhimen Jas 76
Tennant Wm 106, 121
Terrell Geo 106, 121..Jas 76..
    Sam 76
Terry Nathl 106
Thatcher Obediah 106
Tharp Vincent 120
Theus Jas 76..Jeremh 62, 79, 117..
    Perrin 76..Simeon 62, 116
Thiveatt Edward 45
Thomas Edw 76, 119..Jas 121, 135..
    Jonthn 76, 106..Jno 51, 76, 82,
    114, 115..Rob 76..Steph 106..
    Tresham 76..Wm 106
Thompson Flanders 22..Jas 76, 85,
    119..Jno 27..Thos 76..Mat 106..
    Wm 62, 120
Tompkins Stephen 106
Thomson Andw 87..Chas 82..H. Jas 86..
    Moses 84..Rich H 85..Wm 82,106
Threaderaft Bethel 86
Threewitz Jno 106
Thelkeld Jno 106
Thrift Jno 47
Tidyman Phil 116
Tillman Fred 106
Tillotson Dan 106
Tillingast Col. D. 109
Timmons Jno 76
Timothy Peter 85, 86
Tinincase Henry 76
Tinsley Golding 51..Jas 51
Tisdale Jno 121
Todd Jno 85, 86
Tomb David 119
Tomiton Jasper 9
Tomlinson Thos 81
Toney Abram 82
Toney Drury 82
Toomer Anthy 76, 79, 85, 86..Josh 76
Tousinger Jas 109
Toux Villepau 116
Townes Wm 106
Towles Oliver 62
Townsend Paul 62, 116..Wm 28
Tozer Julius 106
Tracey Jas 81..Nath 121..Jas 52
Tramell Samson 82, 121..Thos 121
Trapier Benj 114..Paul 76
Travis Barret 135
Treadwell Reuben 106
Trent Thos 106
Treutlin Jno A. 106
Trezevant Theo 106
Tribble Jas 119
Troop Jas 118
Trott Benj 106

Troussiger Jas 86
Truesdale Nathan 119
Truhitt Stephen 25
Trull Joseph 81
Trustler Wm 116
Tubb Jno 119
Tucker Harbert 106..Rich 87, 114..
   Thos Tudor 62, 79
Tufts Simon 86, 116
Turnbill Andrew 79
Turner Geo 17, 62..Jno 106..
   Jas 82..Lewis 119..
   Noel 120..Starlg 118..
   Sterlg 76..Thos 22, 82..
   Zadoc 106
Turpin Jo seph 86
Tutt Benj 62..Rich 62
Twitchall Isaiah 10
Twitty Wm 83, 109

U ***** U

Uhthoff Anthony 117
Ulmer Jno Jacob 106, 109
Underwood Joseph 106
Uptegrove Peter 117

V ***** V

VanAuken Jno 106
Vance Nathl 106, 135..David
   109..Saml 106
Varden Steven 106
Valandingham Wm 41
Valentine Wm 62
VanArsdale 121
Vanderhorst Arnoldus 76..
   Elias 116..Jas 62..Jno 62
Vandever Edw 106..Geo 47
VanLew Jno 52
VanMeter Abram 109
Vanzant Garratt 82
Vaughan Joel 82, 119..Jno 51,
   109..Thos 51..Wm 49
Vaught Matthais 106
Veale James Carr 121
Verner Jno 47, 106
Vernon Alex 135
Venable Nathl 106
Vestals James 87
Vickers Jos 79..Sam 62, 79
Vidian Saml 79
Videau Peter 76
Vince Jos 106
Vincent Jesse 9

Vlieland Corn Van 62
VanPlater Fredk 117

W ***** W

Waddell Jas 15..Ed 106
Wadle Robt 84..Wm 109
Wade Geo 106, 62
Wagner Jno 116
Waiht Abram 76
Wait Jno 43
Wakefield Jas 87..Jno 76, 85
Waker Jno 83
Waldo Sam 106
Waldrop Jno 39, 82
Walker Alex 106, 121..Dan 106..
   Esther 106..Geo 26..Jas 83..
   Jno 106..Jesse 119..Math 120..
   Nath 106..Phil 82..Rob 82..
   Thos 106..Saml 81, 107
Walkup John 121
Wall Rich 36..Wright 107, 76
Wallace Dav 82..Jas 36..Jno 62,
   79, 107..Levy 81..Thos 20
Waller Benj 85, 87, 114..Geo 107..
   Jno 107..Thos 107
Walles Lazarus 82
Wallis Matt 80
Walter Jno Allen 62
Walton Newell 32..Wm 119
Wannamaker Jacob 107
Wansley Jno 107
Ward Dixsey 38..Enoch 107..Jno
   116..Jno P 62, 121..Wm 39,
   62, 83, 107, 119
Warden Jno 114
Ware Fredk 119..Jas 81..Rob 119..
   Wm 25, 84
Warriner Jas 107
Warham Chas 76, 86..Dav 81, 87
Waring B 77..Marton 77..Rich 77..
   Thos 86, 87
Warley Felix 62..Geo 62..Jos 62..
   Melchoir 116..Paul 62
Warnock Joseph 107, 120
Warren Josih 107, 118..Sam 62,119..
   Simpsn 32..Isah 109
Wash Wm 37
Waters Philm 77, 82, 115..Philp 82..
   West 82..Broadwine 107
Waties Jno 86
Watson Dav 107, 114..Gavin 114..
   Hesekh 107, 118..Jas 114..
   Jno 81, 114, 120..Michl 77,
   107, 114..Rich 118..Rob 81,
   114..Sam 62, 109, 119..Willis
   118..Zakiah 114

210

Watt Robt 117
Watta George 81
Watts David 45..Thos 84..Jno 135..
  Jas 107
Way Robt 87..Moses 107
Weatherspoon J 79
Weaver Henry 18
Webb Fran 109..Handley 118..
  Jerry 82..Jno 81
Weed Reuben 107
Weedere Augustine 107
Weedman Peter 45
Weeks Levi 13, 120
Weems Henry 11
Welch Geo 86, 87..Thos 107..
  Jno 86, 87
Wells Andw 87..Benj 8..Edw 81..
  Jas 119..Sam 119..Wm 83..
  Robt 107..Rich 107
Welsh Patk 81
Wenkler Conrad 84
Wertz Geo 107..Jno 107
West Cato 62..Jos 49..Leonard
  84..Wm 26, 107
Westbrook Saml 107
Weston Robt 120
Weyman Edw 77, 85, 87, 121
Whaler Thos 107
Wharton Saml 107..Aaron 81
Wharry Robt 79
Wheeler Benj 86, 87..Jno 117
Whiley Robt 117
Whitaker Jno 84..Hudson 109
White Archd 82..Arth 114..Benj
  82..Dan 51..Dav 81..Jas 107..
  Anthy 107..Henry 77, 84..
  Hugh 84.. Isac 86, 87..
  Jerry 82..Jno 84, 107, 111..
  Rich 82..Sam 118..Sims 62,
  77, 86..Steph 81, 82..Vassel
  107..Wm 107, 35, 121
Whitfield Luke 77..Needham 107..
  Wm 107
Whitehead Geo 83
Whitely Jno 117
Whitner Jas 107..Jos 107
Whitney Jas R 107
Whittaker Thos 107
Whittington Eph 77..Grf 120
Whittle Burrows 118
Wickley Jno 13, 62
Wickom Jno 62, 117
Wideman Adam 107
Wier Geo 35..Wm 82
Wigg Wm 86, 115
Wigington Geo 120
Wil Philip 87

Wilcox Wm 86
Wilds Jesse 77..Jno 77
Wiley Jacob 119
Wilfong Geo 107
Wilhelm Peter 45
Wilkes Hardy 87..Thos 107, 43
Wilkie Wm 86, 87
Wilkins Benj 77..Jas 86,87..Wm 107
Wilkinson Jno 84..David 109..Thos
  84..Morton 87, 107..Wm 84
Willard Jonthn 107
Williams Benj 117, 107..Chas 77..
  Dan 77, 87..Henry 7..Isac 120,
  121..Jas 77, 107, 114, 136..Jno
  80, 81, 109, 114..Jos 87..Moses
  H 121..Sam 107, 118..Steph 107,
  119..Elij 107..Thos 83, 117,
  120..Wm 107
Williamson Andw 77..Calvin 43..Jno
  62..Rich 117..Shadrk 77, 117..
  Thos 77..Wm 31, 114, 120
Williford Rich 49
Willis Rich 109
Willson (1) Jno 83, 24, 31, 83, 84,
  111, 118, 121..Dave 121..Ezekl
  84..Henry 36..Hugh 111..Humpy
  81..Jas 83, 120, 121..Jos 83..
  Newman 51..Rob 53, 107..Rusl
  118..Sam 79..Thos 49..Wm 77,
  82, 83, 111
Windham Amos 77
Windley Thos 109
Wings Jno 109
Wingo Jno W 107, 121..Wm 51
Winingham Jas 84
Winn Gallenus 120..Jno 24, 120..
  Rich 62, 77, 121..Zack 36
Winningham Jos 46
Winslow Jno 107
Winston Peter 107
Witcher Wm 107
Winton Nathan 119
Wise J 118..Saml 62
Wiseman Thos 18
Wish Jno 116
Withers Enoch 84..E E 80..Jno 77,
  114..Val 83..Wm R 62..
  Elisha 107
Witherspoon Dave 11, 107, 111..
  Gavin 77, 107, 111..Jas 107,
  111..Jno 77, 79, 111..Jos 77..
  Rob 77, 111..Wm 82
Withrow Jas 107
Wittington Nathan 44
Wofford Jos 107
Wolliston Jos 82

Wood(s) Aaron 53..Benj 107..Jno
51, 120..Dempsey 120..Henry
107..Leighton 107..Thos 81..
Wm 82
Woodward Thos 62..Wm 107
Woody Jas 119..Jonth 119..
Wm 119
Woolfolk Jno 119
Wooten Shadrack 109
Word Thos 22
Wornoch Jno 31
Worsley Zach 81
Wragg S 114
Wright Asa 39..Bolling 38..
Danl 120..Geo 114..
Isaç 77..Thos 114..Jos
107..Nicholson 107
Wrighton Jos 86
Wyatt Jas 82..Thos 119..
Wm 86, 107, 136
Wylie Jas 82..Jno 82..Wm 120
Wyles Wm 107
Wynee Williamson 120

Y ***** Y

Yancy Thornton 109
Yates Thos 84
Yeadon Rich 86, 87
You Chas 116..Thos 86, 116
Young And 81..Ben 114..Jno
39..Jacb 81..Jas 13, 107,
120..Jart 121..Levi 47..
Thos 9, 77, 107..Wm
82, 109, 114
Youngblood Jacob 121

Z ***** Z

Zackary Jno 107
Zane Isaac 107
Zenn Jacob 107
Ziegler William 84
Zubers Jno 107

WOMEN OF SOUTH CAROLINA

A ***** A

Aberlay, Ann (2) 90
Abney, Martha 90
Adair, Elizabeth 90..
Mary 89, 94..Sarah 90
Adams, Mary 90..Sarah 90
Addison, Mary 90
Akin, Ann 90
Alcorn, Catherine (2) 90
Alexander, Mary 94
Allen, Agnes 90..Judith 89
Allison, Dorothy 90..Rachel
(2) 90..Sarah 90
Alston, Elizabeth 90..Rachel
90
Altman, Sarah (2) 90
Anderson, Ann (2) 90..Margaret
(2) 90..Rebecca 89, 90..Ruth
90..Sarah 90
Andrews, Jane (2) 90
Annas, Elizabeth 90
Arnett, Hannah White 89, 95
Arnold, Annie Hendrick 89..
Temp 89
Arnst, Maria 90
Atchison, Mary 90
Atkins, Mrs. Elisha 90

Attoy, Mary 90
Austin, Elizabeth 90
Ayer, Frances 90
Ayers, Margaret 90
Axson, Elizabeth 90

B ***** B

Babb, Mary 90
Babilitman, Zaba 90
Bacot, Mary (2) 90
Bagwell, Jane 90
Bails, Elizabeth (2) 90
Bair, Barbara (2) 90
Baird, Winifred 90
Baker, Charlotte B (2) 90..
Elizabeth 90..Mary 89
Ball, Elizabeth (2) 90
Bampfield, Rebecca (2) 90
Bancart, Mary 90
Barber, Mary (2) 90
Bare, Mrs. John C 90
Barron, Rebecca 90..Sarah
90
Barry, Kate 94..Margaret C.M.
89
Batchelor, Mary 90

212

Baxter, Mary 90
Bayley, Lucy 90
Baynard, Eliza 90
Beale, Unice (2) 90
Beard, Mary 90
Beekman, Mrs. John 94
Benbow, Martha 90
Beresford, Dorothy 90..Sarah 90
Berwick, Ann (2) 90
Bolton, Agnes 90
Bonneau, Ann 90
Boobe, Sarah 90
Booth, Mary 94..May 90
Bounetheau, Mary 90
Bower, Catherine 90
Bowers, Sylvana 90
Bowman, Sarah 90
Box, Margaret 90..Mary 90
Boyd, Elizabeth 90..Martha 90
Boyls, Martha 90
Bradley, Elizabeth 89..Margaret 90
Brandon, Mrs. Agnew 90
Bratton, Martha 89, 94, 120
Brazel, Hannah 90
Brazell, Hannah 90
Breed, Priscilla 90
Brewton, Mary 89
Brice, Margaret 90
Bridges, Mary 90
Broughton, Ann 90
Brown, Grizell 90..Sarah 90
Brumfield, Elizabeth 90
Bryant, Sarah 90
Budd, Susannah 90
Bugg, Elizabeth 90
Burke, Elizabeth 90
Burns, Mary 90
Burrington, Elizabeth 90
Butler, Behethland F 89, 90..
   Jane 90..Sarah 90
Buzzard, Elizabeth 90

C ***** C

Caesar, Hannah 91
Caldwell, Mary 91
Campbell, Elizabeth 91..
   Miss Robt 84,89..Lady Sarah I,91
Campble, Elizabeth 89
Cannon, Mary 91
Cardin, Judith 91
Cardy, Ann 91
Carr, Jane 91
Carroll, Mary 91
Cason, Rosey 91
Castellaw, Ann 91

Cattell, Sabina 91
Chalmers, Ann 91..Elizabeth 91..
   Martha 91
Clyatt, Hannah (2) 91
Cobb, Judith 91
Cockfield, Mary 91
Colleton, Margaret S 91
Collins, Mary 91
Concil, Elizabeth 91
Connell, Mary 91
Conturier, Martha 91
Cook, Margaret 91..Rebecca 91
Cooper, Elizabeth 91..Mary 91
Corben, Elizabeth 91
Cordes, Ann 91
Cottheen, Charity (2) 91
Covington, Susan 120
Cow, Rachel 91
Cowen, Jane 91
Craig, Eleanor 91
Creech, Ann 91
Creighington, Elizabeth 91
Crosby, Hannah 91
Crouch, Mary 91

D ***** D

Darby, Elizabeth 91
Darling, Mary 91
Darrell, Frances 91
Dart, Amelia 91
Daughtery, Mary 91
Davidson, Sarah 91
Davis, Agnes 91..Jane 91..
   Mary (2) 91
Dawkins, Chloe 91..Elizabeth (2) 91
Dawney, Sarah 91
Daws, Margaret 91
Delaney Elizabeth 91
DePre, Mary Elizabeth 91
DeSaussure, Jane (2) 91
DeWar, Elizabeth 91
Dewees, Sarah 89
Dick, Mary 91
Dickerson, Sarah 89
Dillard, Mary 89
Dobin, Elizabeth 91
Donnom, Susan 91
Doughty, Elizabeth 91..Mary 91
Droze, Mary 91
Dunklin, Mary 89, 111
Dunlap, Margaret 91
Durn, Elizabeth 91

213

E ***** E

Edwards, Elizabeth 91..Margaret 91..
   Mary 91..Rebecca 91..Sarah 91
Eikester, Mary 91
Eldsworth, Susannah 89
Elkins, Ann 91
Ellington,, Amerinthia 91
Elliot, Elizabeth Knox 119
Elliott, Ann 89, 94..Jane 89..
   Mary 91..Sabina 91, 94..
   Sarah 91..Susanna 89, 94
Ellis Elizabeth 91..Mary(2) 91
Ellison, Elizabeth 91
Entelwein, Martha 91
Ervin, Elizabeth E 89, 111..
   Elizabeth J 89,111..Jan W 89,111
Evans, Elizabeth 91

F ***** F

Farrow, Rosannah Waters 89, 120
Felder, Sarah 91
Ferguson, Elizabeth 91..Mary 91
Fisher, Sarah 91
Fogle, Barbara 91
Fonches, Catherine 91
Fox, Mary 91
Frashers, Ann 91
Frazer, Elizabeth 91
Freer, Ann 91
Frierson, Mary 91
Fripp, Elizabeth 91
Fuller, Judith 91

G ***** G

Gaddis, Christana 91
Gardiner, Lucy 91
Gardner, Lucy 91
Gaston, Esther 94
Gaunt, Hannah M 89
Geiger, Emily 89, 94
Gest, Sarah 91
Gibbes, Mary Ann 94..Sarah R 89,94
Gignilliat, Mary M 91..Susan 91
Gilliam Elizabeth C 89
Gillon, Mary 89, 91
Glaze, Ann 91
Gleadow, Mary 89
Gloster, Margaret 91
Gordon, Margaret 91..Margaret G
   89
Gore, Margaret 91..Rachel 91
Graham, Sarah 91

Gray, Mary 91
Greenwell, Mary 91
Griffin, Mary 91
Griffis, Barbara 91
Grimball, Sarah 91
Guerraud, Elizabeth 89
Gupbell, Elizabeth 91

H ***** H

Haddon, Jennett 92..Mary 91
Haddick, Sarah 92
Haddock, Sarah 92
Haley, Mary 91
Hall, Mary 91..Mary Ann 91..
   Susan 91..Susanna T 91
Hamilton, Rachel 91
Hanby, Mrs. Jeremiah 92..
   Susannah 92
Hardin, Elizabeth 92
Harleston, Ann 92
Hart, Ann 91..Martha 120
Hartzog, Catherine 91
Hay, Ann H 89
Hayne, Susan 92
Heap(s), Sarah 92
Heath, Ethel 91
Heyward, Elizabeth 92..Mrs
   Thomas 89, 94
Hicks, Jane 92
Hill, Hannah 91..Mary 91..Milly 92
Hilton, Amy 92
Hodges, Rebecca 92
Hodsden, Mary 91
Hoffman, Catherine 91
Holcomb, Lucy 92
Holtzclaw, Catherine R 89
Hopkins, Sarah 92
Hopton, Sarah & daus 89
Howe, Jane 91
Howell, Martha 91, (2) 92
Hoyland, Anna 91
Hubbard, Abigail 92..Manoah 92
Huger, Martha 91..Mary 91
Huggins, Mary 92
Huntington, Lady S.C. 91
Hutto, Ann 91
Hyrne, Mary 91..Sarah Ann 92

I ***** I

Inabinet, Margaret 92
Izard, Charlotte 92

J ***** J

Jackson, Amey 92..Elizabeth 89..
Nancy 94
James, America 92..Elizabeth Ann
92..Sarah 89, 92, 111
Jenkins, Phoebe 92
Johnson, Mrs. Grissett 92,.Martha
92..Sarah 92
Jolly, Mrs. John 94
Jones, Elizabeth 92

K ***** K

Keith, Margaret (2) 92
Kelley, Margaret 92
Kelly, Miss James 84, 89
Kelsal, Mary Elizabeth 92
Kennan, Mary Ann 92
Kennedy, Ann 89
Kennelley, Elizabeth 92
Kettle, Elizabeth 92
Kibler, Lucretia 92
Kinlock, Ann 92
Kirkland, Susannah 92
Knap, Mary 92
Knight, Catherine 92
Knox, Elizabeth 92..Sarah 92

L ***** L

Ladson, Elizabeth 92
Lance, Ann 92..Ann M 92
Lane, Catherine 92
Langston, Dicey 94..Laodicea 89
LaRoche, Elizabeth 92
LaTour, Susan 92
Lee, Nancy 89..Sarah 92
Leitner, Maria B 89
Lenud, Elizabeth 92
Leonard, Mary 89
Lesesne, Mary (3) 92
Lewis, Eleanor 92
Lind, Agnes 92
Lindley, Elizabeth Hall 89
Lining, Sarah 92
Linn, Mary 92
Lipton, Mary 92
Liston, Martha 92
Little, Mary 92
Logan, Elizabeth 92..Martha 92
Lootholts, Sarah 92
Lowry, Jane 92

Mc ***** Mc

McCalla, Sarah 120
McCartty, Martha 92
McClure, Mary 94, 120
McClwur, Mary 92
McCord, Sophianisba 92
McDonald, Rachel 92
McDowell, Margaret O'N 89
McElveen, Mary 92
McGill, Hannah 92
McIlveen, Mary 92
McInSmith, Catherine 92
McJunkin, Jane 94, 120
McKay, Mrs. Cabton 92
McKelveen, Mary 92
McKindrick, Catherine 92
McLean, Jane 86 (2)89
McPherson, Sarah 92
McWharter, Elizabeth 92

M ***** M

Magdalen, Mary 92
Maid, Ann 92
Main, Rachel 89
Mallard, Susan 92
Maltby, Elizabeth 89
Mann, Susannah 92
Marion, Catherine 92..Esther 94
Marr, Elizabeth 92
Marshall, Mary (2)92..Sarah 92
Martin, Elizabeth 94..Grace 94..
Mary 92..Rachel 94..Susanna 92
Mason, Eleanor 92..Martha 92
Maxwell, Sarah 92
Mazyck, Mary 92
Melvill, Jane 92
Melville, Jane 92
Melvin, Martha 89
Mercer, Grace 92
Miads, Sarah 92
Miller, Mary 92..Jane 92
Minnich, Rebecca 92
Mixon, Frances 92
Moore, Dolley 92..Sarah 92..
Thankful (2)89
Moorer, Mary 92. (Morreau ?)
Morgan, Elizabeth 92
Morris, Anne 89
Morrow, Jane 94
Motte, Rebecca 89, 94
Moultrie, Mrs. & daus 85, 89
Mucklewain, Mary 92
Murphy, Sarah 92
Musgrove, Mary 89, 94
Myers, Mary 92

N ***** N

Nance, Elizabeth 92
Newton, Jane 92
Nieley, Sarah 92
Noles, Mary 89
Noot, Angelen 89

O ***** O

O'Bannon, Abigail 92
Odom, Margaret 92
Oliphant, Catherine 92
Oswald, Margaret 92
Otterson, Mrs. Saml 89, 94
Overstreet, Sarah 94
Owen, Elizabeth 89

P ***** P

Pagan, Jennett 92
Paggett, Sarah 93
Parsons, Susan 92
Patton, Jane 92..Sarah 93
Pearson, Tabitha 93
Pelot, Frances 92..Mary 92
Pendarvis, Sarah 93
Penney, Ann 92
Petty, Elizabeth 92
Philips, Elizabeth 93..Mourning 89
Pickens, Rebecca 89, 94
Pinckney, Eliza L 94
Pitman, Priscilla 92
Pon, Elizabeth 92
Ponder, Violet 120
Potts, Eleanor 92
Powell, Elizabeth 92..Sarah 93
Pratt, Mary 93
Prescott, Esther 93
Priggs, Eliza 93
Printer, Margaret 92
Punch, Mary 93
Pyatt, Mary 93

R ***** R

Ravenal, Elizabeth (2)93..D Elizabeth
  (2)93
Reading, Hannah 93
Reeves, Ann 93
Reggs, Elizabeth 93
Reiley, Ann 93
Rhodes, Elizabeth 93
Richardson, Dorcas N 89, 94

Rickenbacker, Ann 93
Ritchie, Mary 89, 93
Roberts, Mary 93
Robinson, Ann 93..Nancy 93
Ross, Elizabeth 93
Roulain, Susan 93
Rouse, Deborah 93
Rowdus, Elizabeth 93
Rows, Deborah 93
Rushing, Sabrina 93

S ***** S

Saller, Elizabeth 93
Saltus, Mary 93
Sanders, Margaret 93
Saunders, Ann 93
Savage, Martha 93..Ruth 93
Saylor, Elizabeth 93
Scanlan, Deborah 93
Scott, Frances 93..Joyce C 89, 94
Screven, Rebecca 93
Seigler, Mary 93
Sheed, Eleanor 89
Shilley, Drewsella 93
Shoemaker, Elizabeth 93
Simmons, Mary 93
Simpson, Isabel 93..Mary 93..
  Sophia (2)93
Sims, Isabella 94
Singleton, Ann (2)93
Singley, Rachel 93
Skirving, Elizabeth 93..Sarah 93
Slappy, Isabella 93
Smith, Anna M 93..Catherine (2)93..
  Elizabeth (2)93..Janet 93..
  Mary (3)93..Mrs. Christopher
  93..Susan 93
Snellgrove, Sarah 93
Snider, Mary 93
Snow, Hannah 93
Spring, Dorothy 93
Springer, Margaret 89
Spurlock, Elizabeth 93
St. Julien, Susan 93
Stanyarne, Ann 93..Elizabeth 93
Steele, Elizabeth 89
Stoll, Phoebe 93..Rebecca 93
Stone, Ruth 93
Stuart, Isabel 93..Mary 93
Sucuck, Ursala 93
Sullivan, Mary C 89
Summerford, Sarah 93
Suss, Susan 93
Swan, Mary (2)93
Sweet, Keziah 93
Sy(u)frett, Rebecca 93

Note: Most oft the work on this Index
was done by Mrs Walter Scott Welch,
Vice-President General N.S.D.A.R.,
of Laurel, Mississippi, and copy presented to Mrs. Ervin.

The Laurens County wills are not included in the index.

The Powder Magazine in Charles Town, built in 1703, in which the
South Carolinians stored their ammunition for their many wars.

CPSIA information can be obtained
at www.ICGtesting.com
Printed in the USA
FFOW02n0230190917
40077FF